One-Hit Wonders

One-Hit Wonders

An Oblique History of Popular Music

Edited by
Sarah Hill

BLOOMSBURY ACADEMIC
NEW YORK • LONDON • OXFORD • NEW DELHI • SYDNEY

BLOOMSBURY ACADEMIC
Bloomsbury Publishing Inc
1385 Broadway, New York, NY 10018, USA
50 Bedford Square, London, WC1B 3DP, UK
29 Earlsfort Terrace, Dublin 2, Ireland

BLOOMSBURY, BLOOMSBURY ACADEMIC and the Diana logo are trademarks of Bloomsbury Publishing Plc

First published in the United States of America 2022

Copyright © Sarah Hill, 2022
Each chapter copyright © by the contributor, 2022

For legal purposes the Acknowledgments on p. x constitute an extension of this copyright page.

Cover design by Studio Auto

All rights reserved. No part of this publication may be reproduced or transmitted in any form or by any means, electronic or mechanical, including photocopying, recording, or any information storage or retrieval system, without prior permission in writing from the publishers.

Bloomsbury Publishing Inc does not have any control over, or responsibility for, any third-party websites referred to or in this book. All internet addresses given in this book were correct at the time of going to press. The author and publisher regret any inconvenience caused if addresses have changed or sites have ceased to exist, but can accept no responsibility for any such changes.

A catalog record for this book is available from the Library of Congress.

ISBN: HB: 978-1-5013-6840-0
PB: 978-1-5013-6841-7
ePDF: 978-1-5013-6843-1
eBook: 978-1-5013-6842-4

Typeset by Deanta Global Publishing Services, Chennai, India
Printed and bound in the United States of America

To find out more about our authors and books visit www.bloomsbury.com and sign up for our newsletters.

To the two human jukeboxes of my family:
Dorothy Gibson Roberts (1902–91)
Martha Roberts Hill (1934–2016)

Contents

List of Figures		ix
Acknowledgments		x
The Chart of the Book: *One-Hit Wonders'* Top Hits		xi
	Introduction *Sarah Hill*	1
1	Buchanan and Goodman, "The Flying Saucer" Parts 1 & 2 (1956) *Paul Carr*	5
2	The Kingsmen, "Louie Louie" (1963) *Samuel Murray*	15
3	? and the Mysterians, "96 Tears" (1966) *Adam Behr*	21
4	The Easybeats, "Friday on My Mind" (1966) *Dai Griffiths*	29
5	Norman Greenbaum, "Spirit in the Sky" (1969) *Philip Auslander*	37
6	The Archies, "Sugar Sugar" (1969) *Jon Stewart*	51
7	Serge Gainsbourg, "Je t'aime moi non plus" (1969) *Philippe Gonin, trans. Jackie Ortiz*	61
8	Blue Swede, "Hooked on a Feeling" (1974) *Sarah Hill, with Bengt Palmers*	69
9	Wild Cherry, "Play That Funky Music" (1976) *Robert Fink*	79
10	Althea and Donna, "Uptown Top Ranking" (1977) *Paul Long*	93
11	Plastic Bertrand, "Ça plane pour moi" (1977) *Patrick McGuinness*	103
12	Nick Gilder, "Hot Child in the City" (1978) *Richard John Parfitt*	111
13	The Vapors, "Turning Japanese" (1980) *Abigail Gardner*	119
14	Aneka, "Japanese Boy" (1981) *Richard Elliott*	129
15	Toni Basil, "Mickey" (1981) *Tim J. Anderson*	139
16	Trio, "Da Da Da" (1981) *Tim Quirk*	153
17	Nena, "99 Luftballons/99 Red Balloons" (1983) *Melanie Schiller*	159
18	The Grateful Dead, "Touch of Grey" (1987) *Thomas Irvine*	169
19	A View from the Ground: Latin Quarter, "Radio Africa" (1986) *Michael Jones*	177
20	A View from the Desk: Product Management *Sarah Hill*	185
21	Shakespear's Sister, "Stay" (1992) *Áine Mangaoang*	195
22	OMC, "How Bizarre" (1996) *Geoff Stahl*	205
23	The Butthole Surfers, "Pepper" (1996) *Gina Arnold*	215
24	Chumbawamba, "Tubthumping" (1997) *Matt Grimes*	221
25	Meredith Brooks, "Bitch" (1997) *Asya Draganova*	233

26 New Radicals, "You Get What You Give" (1998) *Jon Gower* 243
27 Las Ketchup, "Aserejé" (2002) *Eulàlia Febrer Coll* 251
28 Gotye ft. Kimbra, "Somebody That I Used To Know" (2011) *Ellis Jones* 259

Contributors 267
Index 272

Figures

4.1	"Friday on My Mind" outline form	31
4.2	Backing vocal figure: 0:26-0:28	33
4.3	Chord progression at 0:30-0:32	33
6.1	A virtual smash. 7-inch (RCA-Victor, 1969)	52
7.1	*Jane Birkin/Serge Gainsbourg* (Fontana, 1969)	66
8.1	Blue Swede accepting their gold records at the EMI Stockholm studio, 1974	74
8.2	Bengt Palmers and Björn Skifs, 1980s	77
10.1	Althea and Donna	101
11.1	"Ça plane pour moi" 7-inch (RKM, 1977)	105
11.2	"Pogo Pogo" 7-inch (Pinball Records, 1977)	109
12.1	Love's Baby Soft ad	113
13.1	"Turning Japanese" 7-inch (United Artists Records, 1980)	124
13.2	"Turning Japanese" 7-inch, back	125
14.1	"Japanese Boy" 7-inch (Hansa, 1981)	134
15.1	"Mickey" video cheer formation	140
15.2	*The Roberta Flack Special* ad	143
15.3	Toni Basil in *Breakaway* (1966)	144
15.4	"Mickey" alternative video still	146
19.1	Guest list for Latin Quarter's Marquee show (1984)	183
21.1(a)	Bedside Manner: "Stay" video (1992)	199
21.1(b)	Angel of Death: "Stay" video (1992)	199
21.2	First Reaction: "Stay" video (2021)	202
21.3	"All the Queen's Horses": still from video (2019)	203
22.1	*How Bizarre* (Huh Records, 1996)	207

Acknowledgments

My first and biggest thanks go to the authors included in this volume. From the first freewheeling discussion about one-hit wonders through to the final materials deadline, it has been an absolute pleasure to work with them. Under normal circumstances, this project probably would have grown out of after-hours socializing at a pop conference; under Covid circumstances, this project blossomed on social media. The first round will definitely be on me whenever we are allowed to be in the same pub at the same time.

Our Bloomsbury editor, Leah Babb-Rosenfeld, has been enthusiastic and supportive of this project from the beginning, and I know I speak for all the contributors when I thank her for her help and patience over the last year.

It was inevitable that putting together a collection on *One-Hit Wonders* would leave me with some earworms. Call it an occupational hazard. But out of all the cacophony, one line kept burrowing further into my brain. The Sundays aren't included in this collection, and this is the only reference in these pages to their hit, "Here's Where the Story Ends" (1990; *Billboard* no. 1), but throughout lockdown I kept imagining this collection as "that little souvenir of a terrible year": here's what we did when we couldn't go to gigs, or sing in choirs, or play in bands, or teach in person, or hang out at conferences.

My lockdown story ends somewhere else, however: I started a new job, virtually, at the University of Oxford, just as the chapters for this collection started coming in. And on the home front, of all the people in the world to be locked down with, my husband, Jon, and our daughters, Elena and Onwy—not to mention Ianto the dog—are the absolute best. I am a lucky popologist and a luckier woman.

The Chart of the Book: *One-Hit Wonders'* Top Hits

Year of release	Title Producer (Songwriter)	Top spot US	Top spot UK
1956	The Flying Saucer (Parts 1 & 2) B. Buchanan, D. Goodman (B. Buchanan, D. Goodman)	3	–
1963	Louie Louie K. Chase, J. Dennon (R. Berry)	2	26
1966	96 Tears R. Martinez (R. Martinez)	1	37
1966	Friday on My Mind S. Talmy (G. Young, H. Vanda)	16	6
1969	Spirit in the Sky E. Jakobsen (N. Greenbaum)	3	1
1969	Sugar Sugar J. Barry (A. Kim, J. Barry)	1	1
1969	Je t'aime (moi non plus) J. Baverstock (S. Gainsbourg)	58	1
1971	Hooked on a Feeling B. Palmers (M. James)	1	–
1976	Play That Funky Music R. Parissi (R. Parissi)	1	7
1977	Uptown Top Ranking J. Gibbs (Althea & Donna, E. Thompson)	–	1
1977	Ça Plane Pour Moi L. Deprijck (Y. Lacomblez)	47	8
1978	Hot Child in the City M. Chapman (J. McCulloch, N. Gilder)	1	–
1980	Turning Japanese V. Coppersmith-Heaven (D. Fenton)	36	3
1981	Japanese Boy N. Ross (B. Heatlie)	–	1
1981	Mickey G. Mathieson, T. Veitch (M. Chapman, N. Chinn)	1	2
1981	Da Da Da K. Voormann (Kralle, S. Remmler)	–	2
1983	99 Luftballons (99 Red Balloons) M. Praeker, R. Heil (C. Karges, J.U. Fahrenkrog-Peterson)	2 (in English)	1 (in English)
1985	Radio Africa N. Gray (M. Jones, R. Keefe, S. Skaith)	–	19
1987	Touch of Grey J. Garcia, J. Cutler (J. Garcia, R. Hunter)	9	–
1992	Stay A. Moulder (M. Guiot, M. Detroit, S. Fahey)	4	1
1996	How Bizarre A. Jansson (A. Jansson, P. Fuemana)	1	5
1996	Pepper S. Thompson (B. Surfers)	26	59
1997	Tubthumping Chumbawamba (Chumbawamba)	6	2
1997	Bitch Geza X. (M. Brooks, S. Peiken)	2	6
1998	You Get What You Give G. Alexander (G. Alexander)	36	5
2002	Asereje M.R. Queco (M.R. Queco)	54	1
2011	Somebody That I Used to Know W. De Backer (L. Bonfá, W. De Backer)	1	1

Introduction

Sarah Hill

The remit was simple: choose a song, any song, and write about it. The follow-up was a bit trickier: make sure it was the sole hit for that musician or band; now off you go. Among the group of scholars, critics, and writers who accepted the challenge, there was quite a bit of chatter: what do you mean by "hit"? A hit *where*?

Here is the first snag. When we talk about "one-hit wonders" and "chart hits"—the "hit" is the song; the "wonder" is the musician—our points of reference are usually the *Billboard* Hot 100 or the Official UK charts. Charts exist in other countries, of course, but the historical dominance of the multinational record companies—at one point a "big six" of EMI, BMG, PolyGram, Sony, Universal, Warner; now whittled down to a voracious three of Sony, Universal, Warner—and the vast reach of their global products led to the commercial dominance of particular styles and genres, and of songs sung in English. The charts offer a snapshot of which songs or albums sold the most copies in a given week or year, and since 1958 the Recording Industry Association of America (RIAA) has recognized units sold by the bestowal of commemorative discs in a range of expensive metals: gold for 500,000 units sold, platinum for 1 million (since 1976), multiplatinum for 2 million (since 1984), diamond for 10 million (not a metal; since 1999).[1] Does this mean that gold records are historically the most important, or most influential, or most memorable songs ever recorded? Of course not. But does it mean that they are popular? Yes.

A case in point: "Macarena," by Los Del Rio, released in August 1995, was certified gold by the RIAA in May 1996, platinum in July 1996, double platinum in August 1996, triple platinum in September 1996, and quadruple platinum in October 1996. A one-hit wonder? Absolutely. Included in this collection? Alas, no. But it is worth thinking a little bit more about Los Del Rio regardless. They had had a minor hit on the US Latin Pop album charts with *A mi me gusta* (1993), but for some reason "Macarena" was the right song at the right time, as judged by its top placement on the charts in Australia, Belgium, Denmark, Finland, France, Germany, Israel, the Netherlands, Sweden, Switzerland, and the United States. None of their subsequent releases even registered, apart from the occasional spin-off ("Macarena Christmas," anyone?), but do not pity Los Del Rio: theirs is the kind of success, or ubiquity, that many bands would kill for.

---

[1] Full details and an interactive timeline of the gold and platinum certification process can be found at https://www.riaa.com/goldandplatinum60/; the British Phonographic Industry (BPI) criteria can be found at https://www.bpi.co.uk/brit-certified/award-levels/.

Would "Macarena" have been a global hit if it had not been remixed with new English lyrics? Spanish songs have reached the top of the *Billboard* charts in the past—"La Bamba" most notably—as have songs in French, German, Korean, and, yes, Latin;[2] but "Macarena" had one more thing going for it: choreography. "Dance crazes" occupy a special place in the history of pop music, from the Charleston (1926) to the Twist (1960), and right up to the viral dances fighting for space on the virtual floor today. These are dances that we recognize, whether by the tune or the beat or the hook. To situate "Macarena" in this noble tradition: the guests at a wedding reception in Winnipeg might not be able to sing along to the verses, but they can shout the refrain ("hey, Macarena!"), hands on their booty, swaying left, right, left, turn to the right.

In other words, lyrics are not always the most important component of a hit song. To use another example not included in this collection: Van McCoy's "The Hustle" (1975) captured the feel, if not the authentic experience, of New York disco culture, in a song that boasted all of five words ("Do it—do the Hustle!"). Its enduring popularity—and the ease with which most people the world over can still join in the dance (step, step, step, clap)—should remind us how often underground cultures have been co-opted for financial reward.[3] When a song is "mainstreamed" and decontextualized from its original culture, whether New York or Spain or any other place, it can continue to have a new life of its own, generating revenue for the record label, songwriter(s), producer(s), and musician(s) in the process.

It would have been possible to start this collection with the dance crazes and novelty hits that littered parlor pianos and Victrola cabinets in the early years of the twentieth century. There is plenty to say about satire and politics, humor and changing social mores in that "pre-history" of pop, and it has been said elsewhere;[4] for the purpose of concision we begin this history in the late 1950s. And while the first chapter in this collection does focus on a novelty song, it also establishes a pre-history of the music industry that should be familiar to anyone who has ever heard a song built on pre-existing samples. What you get in the subsequent chapters is a snapshot of popular music song writing and marketing, of audiences and the vagaries of taste. Not every song in this collection came out of Anglo-America, and not every song was originally sung in English, but each one poses questions about cultural centers and peripheries, about timeliness and timelessness, in an oblique history of popular music.

---

[2] Enigma's "Sadeness (Part I)" (Virgin, 1990) was based on a sample of the antiphon *Procedamus in pace*, taken from a recording by the Capella Antique München, *Paschale Mysterium* (Seon, 1977), and reimagined as an ambient house chill-out track. It reached number 5 in the US charts and number 1 in the UK charts, thus begging the question: Is the Capella Antique München a one-hit wonder? For a complete list of non-English *Billboard* chart hits, see www.billboard.com/articles/business/chart-beat/9327176/all-20-non-english-language-songs-hit-hot-100s-top-10/.

[3] "The Hustle" (Avco, 1975) was a top ten hit in eleven countries, and has been included on over 400 compilation albums. The commercial peak of disco was undoubtedly marked by the soundtrack of *Saturday Night Fever* (RSO, 1977), followed by the enormous mainstream success of the Village People. For a brief, first-hand account of the significance of disco music to underground gay life in the 1970s, see Richard Dyer, "In defense of disco," *Gay Left* 8 (Summer 1979): 20–3.

[4] See for example Charles Hamm, *Yesterdays: Popular Song in America* (New York: WW Norton & Company, 1979).

In thinking about each song's time and place, most of the contributors to this collection also ruminate on their song's afterlife. Not every song included here has a dance attached to it, nor has every song been tied in to television advertisements or movie franchises, but each has a story that takes it beyond a sterile *Billboard* number. Often that story is just about how the song hit the charts in the first place. This is not to suggest snobbery or value judgment, but rather to note that it is worth thinking a little bit about why some songs gain universal traction without any warning or precedent, and about how those songs impact on the lives and careers of the musicians behind them. To take another example not included in this collection: if asked to name a Proclaimers song, most people outside of Scotland would say, "I'm Gonna Be (500 Miles)." It was certified gold by the RIAA in May 1993, and the album *Sunshine on Leith* (Chrysalis, 1988) was certified gold in New Zealand and the United States, platinum by the BPI, and double platinum in Australia and Canada.[5] The Proclaimers' career has spanned over thirty years, and that one song has made its way onto the singles charts at three different times and onto the soundtracks of nearly a dozen films and television series. What do we understand about the Proclaimers' popularity arc by the fact that they had one verifiable international Top 10 hit five years into their career, and yet maintained a fanbase and audience for another twenty-five, sans notice on *Billboard*? If nothing else, it shows that charts are no indication of lasting power or influence, and that worldwide popularity is a fickle beast.

All of this by way of introducing a collection of essays written by a group of scholars, critics, and writers during the Great Lockdown of 2020. Authors were given complete creative freedom to write about their chosen hit and their chosen wonder in whatever way they wanted. The chapters are ordered chronologically according to the songs' release dates, which affords an overview of changing musical styles and an occasional soft echo across the collection. The songs included here might not make your ideal mix tape, but our goal is to get you to go back and listen to them again with fresh ears.

---

[5] *Sunshine on Leith* has had its own afterlife, most notably as the title of a Proclaimers-based jukebox musical (2007) and film (2013).

1

Buchanan and Goodman, "The Flying Saucer" Parts 1 & 2 (1956)

Paul Carr

Although released over fifty years ago, Bill Buchanan (1930–96) and Dickie Goodman's (1934–89) double-A-sided novelty recording, "The Flying Saucer" (comprising "The Flying Saucer Parts 1 & 2," henceforth called "Flying Saucer"), provides an interesting early instance of two contesting phenomena that were destined to become pervasive competitors in the global music industry: sampling and industry litigation. After some regional success, the tracks, which are noted as the first example of a "mashup,"[1] climbed to Number 3 in both *The Billboard* and *Variety* top 100 by the end of August 1956. Both sides of the single tell a "fake news" story of the visitation of a flying saucer, featuring Buchanan as a disc jockey/newscaster reporting on how "spacemen" are visiting earth, with Goodman (aka John Cameron Cameron[2]) speaking to various members of the public as the flying saucer lands and flies away, on two occasions.[3] This kind of pastiche "fake news" broadcast is clearly influenced by Orson Wells' *War of the Worlds* radio drama (1938), which is also constructed as an otherwise "normal" reading, interspersed with a series of increasingly frantic news bulletins (initially during musical interludes), which report of explosions on the planet Mars, eventually resulting in an invasion of Earth, complemented by multiple interviews with "experts" and members of the public. Although disputed, the broadcast is often noted as causing concern among some members of the public, who when listening to it live believed it to be true. In this chapter I will outline how sampling, industry litigation, novelty recording, and mashup quotations combined in "Flying Saucer," resulting in the song's unique position in the history of popular music, despite the fact it was the only hit Buchanan and Goodman ever had.

It is important to note that pastiche novelty hits such as "Flying Saucer" were not uncommon prior to 1956, with artists such as Spike Jones ("Der Fuehrer's Face," 1942)

---

[1] See Kembrew McLeod, "Authorship, Ownership and Musical Appropriation," in *The SAGE Handbook of Popular Music*, ed. Andy Bennett and Steve Waksman (London: Sage, 2015), 598–612.
[2] A play on the broadcaster John Cameron Swayze.
[3] Side A features the initial appearance of the flying saucer and although it exits at the end of "The Flying Saucer Part 1," it returns—and leaves again on "The Flying Saucer Part 2."

and Victor Borge ("A Lesson in Composition," 1945) being indicative examples of artists who achieved notable success by parodying existing music.[4] Indeed, just a few years before Buchanan and Goodman's recordings, Patti Page's version of "(How Much is That) Doggie in the Window" was Number 1 for eight weeks in 1953. Novelty records like Page's though did not follow in the tradition of Jones and Borge, who targeted a certain *irreverence* toward their subject matter, be it the Nazi regime or the entire notion of "high art," an impertinence which, as we will see, also permeated the narrative of "Flying Saucer." Although it did not achieve mainstream success, Babs Gonzalez's "Cool Whalin'" (1952) is arguably the most interesting precursor to "Flying Saucer," as it is comprised of a succession of quotes from well-known songs, such as "How High the Moon," "Blue Moon," "Nobody Knows the Trouble I've Seen," and "It Don't Mean a Thing if It Ain't Got that Swing." Although Gonzalez's recording clearly drew on the tradition of jazz musicians' practice of quoting segments of other "standards,"[5] the contention surrounding "Flying Saucer" centered on the use of multiple *recorded* "samples" by artists such as Elvis Presley, Fats Domino, and the Platters, spliced up on tape and inserted into the narrative, with the "samples" distorting the meanings and connotations of the original recordings. Buchanan and Goodman were therefore accused of violating not only the copyright in a succession of songs (therefore seemingly infringing the performance copyright) but also the "mechanical" copyright in the recordings.

Unlike later use of sampled material in styles such as hip-hop--and in the aforementioned track by Babs Gonzalez--much of the sampled recordings on "Flying Saucer" were very current and, most importantly,[6] were used not as a "mark of respect," but as a means of ridicule, in a manner similar to Richard Middleton's notion of "destructive parody," a form of primary signification where the quoted text is taken out of its more "serious" context.[7] For example, the declaration "flying saucers are real" on "The Flying Saucer Part 1" is followed by an excerpt from "The Great Pretender" by The Platters (1956), while the statement "we're going to hear the words of the first spaceman ever to land on earth" is quickly followed by a segment of Little Richard's "Tutti Fruiti" (1955). As a final set of examples, when members of the public are asked on "The Flying Saucer Part 1," "what would you do if the saucer were to land," Buchanan and Goodman's innovative use of technology allows the listener to hear Little Richard state, "duck back in the alley" ("Long Tall Sally," 1956), Fats Domino

---

[4] "Der Fuehrer's Face" is a parody of what was the official anthem of the Nazi Party—"Horst-Wessel-Lied." Victor Borge's "A Lesson in Composition" parodies a number of "great" composers' "master works" such as Schubert's *Unfinished Symphony* (claiming, "I don't think we will ever get ready, he couldn't even finish it himself") and the 3rd movement of Chopin's Piano Sonata no. 2 in Bb Minor (claiming the death march is too "gay").

[5] See Daniel T. Oakland, "Remembering in Jazz: Collective Memory and Collective Improvisation," *Lambda Alpha Journal* 28 (1998): 16–27.

[6] In *The Billboard*'s end-of-year Top 50 for 1956, "The Flying Saucer" is placed at Number 30, but interestingly, no fewer than eight of the featured samples were also hits that year: The Platters' "The Great Pretender" (no. 12); Little Richard's "Long Tall Sally" (no. 45); Elvis Presley's "Heartbreak Hotel" (no. 1); Don Cherry's "Band of Gold" (no. 38); Bill Haley and the Comets' "See You Later Alligator" (no. 33); The Platters' "My Prayer" (no. 4); and Carl Perkins' "Blue Suede Shoes" (no. 18).

[7] Richard Middleton, *Studying Popular Music* (Milton Keynes: Open University Press, 1995), 221.

report that "what [he's] gonna do, is hard to tell" ("Poor Me," 1955) and Elvis Presley resort to "tak[ing] a walk down lonely street" ("Heartbreak Hotel," 1956). In addition to sampled segments of songs being used as a means of forging Buchanan and Goodman's transformative narrative, artists' names are also lampooned, with The Platters referred to as The Clatters, Smiley Lewis as Laughing Lewis, The Penguins as The Pelicans, Fats Domino as Skinny Dynamo, Carl Perkins as Pa Gherkins and Chuck Berry as Huckle Berry, all of which would arguably infringe trademark copyright in the current music industry.

According to Goodman's biography (written by his son), "the Music Publishers Protective Association claimed 'The Saucer' was guilty of at least nineteen instances of copyright infringement and unauthorised use of copyright material."[8] One such instance is outlined in the July 28, 1956, edition of *The Billboard*, which reports on the popularity of "Flying Saucer" in regions such as Cleveland, and how publishers, diskeries, and artists were plotting to "bring it back to earth."[9] In this article, it is worth noting the aggressive language of attorney Julian Abeles, who, acting on behalf of "various publishers," verified how his "first targets would be distributors and pressing plants," after which he would "go after anybody who touched the record—as contributory infringers."[10] The article also reports on the "scathing injunctions" that diskeries and publishers issued, quoting exclamations such as "if this is allowed to pass then anything goes," and "if we can't stop this nothing's safe in our business," statements which clearly depict the concern certain parts of the music industry were experiencing. This edition of *The Billboard* also reports how the plaintiffs had charged Buchanan and Goodman's record label Luniverse with "unfair competition" for alleged "dubbing of portions of the [their] recordings." Somewhat paradoxically, although causing the aforementioned stream of litigation, record publishers were also noted as being "upset that their hits were not included," with an unnamed music executive reporting in *The Billboard* that "If you're not on the 'Flying Saucer,' you're nowhere." These comments may have been due to "Flying Saucer" being credited a month later in *The Billboard* as reviving "sales interest in at least one of the old rock and roll disc hits excerpted on the record," with The Penguins' "Earth Angel" (a hit a year earlier) and Little Richard's "Long Tall Sally" "spurt[ing] ahead since the disc ["Flying Saucer"] hit the market."[11]

A later edition of *The Billboard* reported how Buchanan and Goodman "won" the first round, "when judge Henry Clay Greenberg denied [pending trial] the plaintiffs application for a temporary injunction," claiming "the defendants [had] cleverly

---

[8] Jon Goodman, *The King of Novelty: Dickie Goodman* (Indiana: Xlibris Corporation, 2000), 30. This figure makes sense, as side A includes eleven samples and side B eight. This includes one song which is used twice, "The Great Pretender" (1956). This number is indeed confirmed in the 28th July, 1956, edition of *The Billboard*.

[9] A term that is not in common use today, "Diskeries" were record manufacturers, who when looking through past editions of *The Billboard*, at some point in their history may also have been record companies/labels (For example RCA and Columbia). In the case of "Flying Saucer," Diskeries were suing due to what they saw as "unfair competition," believing that purchasing a record that contained so many "samples" would result in the public not buying the originals. This was later deemed not to be the case.

[10] Ables stated he would also include radio stations and disc jockeys in this category.

[11] See "'Earth Angel' Flies Again," *The Billboard*. August 18, 1956.

and artfully . . . devised interesting novelty records which make use of portions of records . . . under exclusive contract with the plaintiffs and others."[12] Despite four labels (Imperial, Aristocrat, Modern, and Chess) and two performers (Fats Domino and Smiley Lewis) filing for an injunction to prevent the future sales of all Buchanan and Goodman recordings, "Judge Henry Clay Greenberg sided with Buchanan and Goodman, denying the injunction because he believed that the single was clearly a parody and not a violation of anyone's copyright"—believing they had "created a new work, rather than simply copying someone else's music."[13]

Although there is no concrete evidence that "Flying Saucer" boosted record sales or indeed introduced rhythm and blues artists to white America, it is unquestionable that the recording tapped into the American zeitgeist, with the subject matter of "flying saucers" being pervasive at the time in the news and in popular culture. In 1956, for example, the 1947 "Roswell Incident" was still very much in the general public's memory, with the *Roswell Daily Record* famously having a front-page account entitled "RAAF Captures Flying Saucer On Ranch in Roswell Region."[14] Indeed, just a year prior to the release of "Flying Saucer," in 1955, the US Air Force acquired "Area 51" in the Nevada desert, and both America and Russia reported their intentions to launch satellites into space, which cumulated in Russia's launch of Sputnik 1 in 1957— which was effectively the start of the "space race." Media occurrences such as these and numerous other "public sightings" of flying saucers gave authors such as Isaac Asimov (e.g., *The Martian Way and Other Stories*, 1955), Arthur C. Clarke (*The Sentinel*, 1953), and in particular the Hollywood film industry the context to produce movies such as *The Flying Saucer* (1950), *Devil Girl from Mars* (1954) and *Earth Vs. The Flying Saucers* (1956), which was released just weeks prior to Buchanan and Goodman's record. Indeed, McLeod points out how rock 'n' roll developed "roughly contemporaneously with the era of space exploration," with the genre's "first hit," "Rocket 88" (Jackie Brenston and His Delta Cats, 1951), not to mention bands such as Bill Haley and his Comets having names linked to the phenomena.[15]

When one considers "Flying Saucer" retrospectively, it is apparent that Buchanan and Goodman's record label used radio, independent release, and independent record distribution alongside the innovative use of technology and the popular theme of space invasion, to showcase their product. In doing so, they challenged existing music industry hegemonies, in particular via their use of what was later to be known as "sampling," with a number of authors citing "Flying Saucer" as the first time this musical phenomenal was used: McLeod calls it "the earliest example of sound collage in mainstream musical styles" and "the first lawsuit involving what would later be

---

[12] See "Modern Joins in Luniverse Suit; Quick Action Skedded," *The Billboard*, November 17, 1957. By this point "Flying Saucer" was already off the charts.
[13] Kembrew McLeod, "Confessions of an Intellectual (Property): Danger Mouse, Micky Mouse, Sonny Bono and my Long and Winding Path as a Copyright Activist-Academic," *Popular Music and Society* 28, no. 1 (2005): 79–93 (p. 82).
[14] See *Roswell Daily Record*, July 8, 1947.
[15] Ken McLeod, "Space Oddities: Aliens, Futurism and Meaning in Popular Music," *Popular Music* 22, no. 33 (2003): 337–55 (p. 340).

known as sampling," while Demers calls Goodman "the first pop artist to create a commercially successful audio collage."[16]

It is also important to point out that "Flying Saucer" was actually only the start of what Cooper describes as a "UFO comedy series," with "Flying Saucer the 2nd" (1957), "The Flying Saucer Goes West" (1958) and "Flying Saucer the 3rd" (1959) the recordings that followed.[17] Cooper did not mention the first recording the duo released post "Flying Saucer": "Buchanan and Goodman on Trial" (1956), another "break in" record, which again used samples of 1956 hits such as "Rip it Up" (Little Richard), "I'm in Love Again" (Fats Domino), and "Hound Dog" (Elvis Presley). All of these artists were of course included on the original recording, but it is the incorporation of Little Richard's "Tutti Fruiti" and Nappy Brown's "Open Up That Door" (1956), actual tracks which were also included on "Flying Saucer," which seemed to invoke more specific acts of defiance. "Buchanan and Goodman on Trial" depicts a narrative where Buchanan and Goodman are "on the run," eventually taken to court for their "crimes," trialed, and set free. When asked if they "have anything to say," the piece cuts to "you ain't nothing but a hound dog," a sarcastic jibe at the music industry, which is in nature similar to Frank Zappa's "Porn Wars" (1985), which features actual footage from the Parents Music Resource Centre hearings he was involved in during the 1980s.[18] Zappa was of course a known champion of not only the "novelty song," but also the cut and paste techniques that were pioneered by Buchanan and Goodman. It is also interesting to note that "Flying Saucer" was covered immediately by Dewey, George & Jack and the Belltones ("Flying Saucers have Landed" Part 1 and Part 2 (1956)), Sid Noel and his Outer Spaceman ("Flying Saucer," 1956), Alan Freed, and Al "Jazzbo" Collins and Steve Allen ("The Space Man," 1956). Although attempting to exploit the popularity of the original, none of these records were hits—and most importantly, although using a very similar narrative, these versions used (sometimes embarrassingly bad) re-recorded versions of the songs, which reduced the humour, defiance, originality and industry litigation.[19]

In the year 2021, science-fiction themes are still pervasive in popular culture, with the *Star Wars* franchise recently purchased by Disney, movies such as *Men in Black* (1997) and *Independence Day* (1996) and TV series such as *X Files* and *Star Trek* still pervading popular culture. In music, science-fiction themes continued through the 1960s with bands such as Pink Floyd ("Interstellar Overdrive," 1967) and David Bowie ("Space Oddity," 1969), the 1970s with bands such as Yes ("Astral Traveller," 1970) and

---

[16] See McLeod, "Authorship, Ownership and Musical Appropriation," p. 601 and Joanna Demers, *Steal that Music: How Intellectual Property Law Affects Creativity* (Georgia: The University of Georgia Press, 2000), 76.

[17] Lee Cooper, "Greatest Hits From Outer Space," *Rock Music Studies* 2 (2013): 203–5 (p. 203).

[18] See Claude Chastagner, "The Parents' Music Resource Centre: From Information to Censorship," *Popular Music* 18, no. 2 (1999): 179–92. The PMRC features in Gina Arnold's chapter for this volume, on the Butthole Surfers' "Pepper."

[19] The "Compulsory Right" to remake a work has been in place since the copyright act of 1909. If one wishes to reuse a recording, however, it requires permission. An interesting UK version of the track was also released by Syd Laurence and Friends in 1956, entitled "The Answer to the Flying Saucer U.F.O (Men From Mars)," which actually samples the Buchanan and Goodman original—although they did not litigate.

Emerson Lake and Palmer (*Brain Salad Surgery*, 1973), the 1980s with bands such as Hawkwind ("Sonic Attack," 1981), and the 1990s–2000s, with artists such as Radiohead ("Paranoid Android," 1997), Coheed, and Cambria (*Good Apollo, I'm Burning Star IV, Volume One: From Fear Through the Eyes of Madness*, 2005), Muse (*Black Holes and Revelations*, 2006), and Iced Earth (*Dystopia*, 2011) all continuing the tradition. According to McCleod, themes such as these take us outside of the everyday, to a future world while "simultaneously reminding us of our location and what it means to live there."[20]

To conclude, when we ask why "Flying Saucer" happened when it did, there are a number of potential answers. Aside from what has already been discussed, the reason for the unprecedented litigation was possibly because the record came out as rock 'n' roll was just starting to break, so publishers and record companies would have been understandably concerned that the sampling of their product would have taken away what could have been very lucrative financial returns. It is also important to note that the record came out during the era of McCarthyism in North America, where many Americans were accused of being communist sympathizers. "The Saucer," in addition to some science-fiction texts such as *Invaders from Mars* (Alperson, 1953) and *Forbidden Planet* (Wilcox, 1956), arguably served as political allegories, whereas in the case of "The Saucer," the fears of the nation could be filtered through a humorous lens—representing the much-needed relief in paranoid troubled times. Finally, "Flying Saucer" has to be considered technologically as well as socially. Like Buchanan and Goodman, composers such as Pierre Schaeffer (*Orphée 53*, 1953), Pierre Boulez (*Études 1 Sur un Son*, 1951), and Karlheinz Stockhausen (*Konkrete Etüde*, 1952) also began using tape manipulation in the early 1950s when working in the genre of musique concrète. This provides a broader context for "Flying Saucer," all of which points to the future. To quote Attali in 1985:

> Music is prophecy: its styles and economic organization are ahead of the rest of society because it explores, much faster than material reality can, the entire range of possibilities in a given code. It makes audible the new world that will gradually become visible.[21]

Buchanan and Goodman's 1956 novelty hit in many ways paved the way for artists such as Public Enemy, Freelance Hellraiser, Negativland, and Danger Mouse, to name but a few. Like Buchanan and Goodman, all of these artists were litigated against by the record industry and are indicative examples of the "new world" that Attali was referring to. Unfortunately, as opposed to favoring recording artists, the litigation of powerful entertainment corporations is continuing to stifle creativity, not support it. Just as industry litigation facilitated sub-standard versions of "The Saucer" in the mid-1950s, it also forced Public Enemy in the 1990s to drastically alter their sound, so that "transformative appropriation . . . [was] rendered all but impossible because of

---

[20] McCleod, "Space Oddities," 338.
[21] Jacques Attali, *Noise: The Political Economy of Music* (Minnesota: University of Minnesota Press, 1985), 11.

licencing fees."[22] Reports that Ariana Grande had to pay 90 percent of her royalties to Rodgers and Hart in 2019 to incorporate fragments of "My Favourite Things" (1959) in her song "7 Rings" (2019) indicate the situation has not changed—indeed it has arguably gotten worse. In an alternative universe far away from here, where recording corporations learned their lessons from this "one hit wonder," and then granted without question all transformative use of their catalogues, one can only dream of the music we could be listening to today. With an EU directive extending the period of copyright in recordings from fifty to seventy years in 2011,[23] one has to say that Buchanan and Goodman's Flying Saucer may have landed, but freely available transformative use of recordings may never take off.

References

Ahlgrim, Callie (2019), "Ariana Grande Gets Less Than 10% of Royalties From '7 Rings,' Her Most Popular Single Ever—Here's Why," *Insider*. Available online: https://www.insider.com/ariana-grande-7-rings-royalties-rodgers-and-hammerstein-my-favourite-things-sample-2019-3 (accessed September 02, 2021).

Anonymous (1956), "'Flying Saucer Takes Off'; Pubbers, Diskers Do a Flip." *The Billboard*, July 28, 1956. Available online: https://books.google.co.uk/books?id=fUUEAAAAMBAJ&pg=PA17&lpg=PA17&dq=Flying+Saucer+Takes+Off;+Publishers,+Diskers+Do+a+Flip."&source=bl&ots=ns3mPP1bj6&sig=ACfU3U3rRi5f2yP3t6sjSNyJbQFFab_ZLA&hl=en&sa=X&ved=2ahUKEwiw99Gqu-DyAhWHhf0HHdrpBZkQ6AF6BAgCEAM#v=onepage&q=Flying%20Saucer%20Takes%20Off%3B%20Publishers%2C%20Diskers%20Do%20a%20Flip."&f=false (accessed September 02, 2021).

Anonymous 2 (1956), "'Earth Angel' Flics Again." *The Billboard*, August 18, 1956. Available online: https://books.google.co.uk/books?id=iwoEAAAAMBAJ&pg=PA39&dq=Earth+Angel+flies+again&hl=en&sa=X&ved=2ahUKEwjzyrOgv-DyAhWKYMAKHdlmD1oQ6AEwAHoECAsQAg#v=onepage&q=Earth%20Angel%20flies%20again&f=false (accessed September 02, 2021).

Anonymous 3 (1957), "Modern Joins in Luniverse Suit; Quick Action Skedded," *The Billboard*. November 17, 1957. Available online: https://books.google.co.uk/books?id=fgoEAAAAMBAJ&pg=PA16&dq=Modern+Joins+in+Luniverse+Suit;+Quick+Action+Skedded&hl=en&sa=X&ved=2ahUKEwiMvPqAwODyAhVWQUEAHQooAwwQ6AEwAHoECAIQAg#v=onepage&q=Modern%20Joins%20in%20Luniverse%20Suit%3B%20Quick%20Action%20Skedded&f=false (accessed September 02, 2021).

Anonymous 4 (1947), "RAAF Captures Flying Saucer on Ranch in Roswell Region," *Roswell Daily Record*, July 8, 1947. Available online: https://airandspace.si.edu/multimedia-gallery/roswell-daily-record-newspaper-ufo (accessed September 02, 2021).

Asimov, Isaac (1955), *The Martian Way and Other Stories*, New York: Doubleday.

---

[22] Demers, *Steal That Music*, 119.
[23] See "A Post Implementation Review (PIR) for EU Directive 2011/77/EU, Which Increased the Term for Sound Recordings From 50 to 70 Years," https://www.gov.uk/government/publications/copyright-term-extension-for-sound-recordings.

Attali, Jacques (1985), *Noise: The Political Economy of Music*, Minnesota: University of Minnesota Press.
Carr, Paul, ed. (2013), *Frank Zappa and the And*, Abingdon: Ashgate.
Chastagner, Claude (1999), "The Parents' Music Resource Centre: From Information to Censorship," *Popular Music*, 18 (2): 179–92.
Clarke, Arthur C. (1953), "The Sentinel," in *Expedition to Earth*, New York: Ballantine Books.
Cooper, Lee (2003), "Greatest Hits From Outer Space," *Rock Music Studies*, 2: 203–5.
Demers, Joanna (2006), *Steal that Music: How Intellectual Property Law Affects Creativity*, Georgia: The University of Georgia Press.
Gehman, Nev (1953), "The Hottest Pop Label During the First Third of the Year Has Been Mercury!: Accent on Quality Seems to Pay Off," *The Billboard*, May 16, 1953, 29. Available at: https://books.google.co.uk/books?id=LA0EAAAAMBAJ&pg=PA29&dq=The+Hottest+Pop+Label+During+the+First+Third+of+the+Year+Has+Been+Mercury!:+Accent+on+Quality+Seems+to+Pay+Off&hl=en&sa=X&ved=2ahUKEwilhPLbxeDyAhWLRkEAHfe1BEUQ6AEwAHoECAkQAg#v=onepage&q=The%20Hottest%20Pop%20Label%20During%20the%20First%20Third%20of%20the%20Year%20Has%20Been%20Mercury!%3A%20Accent%20on%20Quality%20Seems%20to%20Pay%20Off&f=false (accessed September 02, 2021).
Goodman, Jon (2000), *The King of Novelty: Dickie Goodman*, Indiana: Xlibris Corporation.
Herman, Arthur (2000), *Joseph McCarthy: Re-examing the Life and Legacy of America's Most Hated Senator*, New York: Simon and Schuster.
Lule, Jack (1991), "Roots of the Space Race: Sputnik and the Language of US News in 1957," *Journalism and Mass Communication Quarterly*, 69 (1–2): 76–86.
McLeod, Kembrew (2015), "Authorship, Ownership and Musical Appropriation," in Bennett and Waksman (eds.), *The SAGE Handbook of Popular Music*, 598–612, London: Sage.
McLeod, Kembrew (2005), "Confessions of An Intellectual (Property): Danger Mouse, Micky Mouse, Sonny Bono and my Long and Winding Path as a Copyright Activist-Academic." *Popular Music and Society*, 28 (1): 79–93.
McLeod, Kembrew and Peter DiCola (2011), *Creative Licence: The Law and Culture of Digital Sampling*, Durham and London: Duke University Press.
McLeod, Ken (2003), "Space Oddities: Aliens, Futurism and Meaning in Popular Music," *Popular Music*, 22 (33): 337–55.
Middleton, Richard (1990), *Studying Popular Music*, Milton Keynes: Open University Press.
Oakland, Daniel, T. (1998), "Remembering in Jazz: Collective Memory and Collective Improvisation," *Lambda Alpha Journal*, 28: 16–27.
UK Government (2018), "A Post Implementation Review (PIR) for EU Directive 2011/77/EU Which Increased the Term for Sound Recordings From 50 to 70 Years." Available online: https://www.gov.uk/government/publications/copyright-term-extension-for-sound-recordings (accessed June 23, 2020).
Vizzini, Bryan, E. (2009), "Cold War Fears, Cold War Passions: Conservatives and Liberals Square Off in 1950s Science Fiction," *Quarterly Review of Film and Video*, 26: 28–39.

Recordings

Alperson, Eduard, L. (1953), *Invaders from Mars*, Edward L. Alperson Productions.
Borge, Victor (1945), "A Lesson in Composition," Philips, 429 693 BE.

Bowie, David (1969), "Space Oddity," Philips, BF1801, 304 201 BF.
Brenston, Jackie and his Delta Cats (1951), "Rocket 88," (1951) Chess, 1458.
Brown, Nappy (1956), "Open Up That Door," Savoy Records, 451187.
Buchanan and Goodman (1956a), "The Flying Saucer Part 1," Luniverse, 101.
Buchanan and Goodman (1956b), "The Flying Saucer Part 2," Luniverse, 101.
Buchanan and Goodman (1956c), "Buchanan and Goodman on Trail," Luniverse, 102.
Buchanan and Goodman (1957), "Flying Saucer the 2nd," Luniverse, 105.
Buchanan and Goodman (1958), "The Flying Saucer Goes West," Luniverse, L 108.
Buchanan and Goodman (1959), "Flying Saucer the 3rd," Comic Records, CR 500.
Conrad, Mikl (1950), *The Flying Saucer*, Colonial Productions Inc.
Coheed and Cambria (2005), *Good Apollo, I'm Burning Star IV, Volume One: From Fear Through the Eyes of Madness*, Columbia, 520471 2, COL.
Danziger, Edward J., and Harry Lee Danziger (1954), *Devil Girl From Mars*, Danziger Productions.
Devlin, Dean (1996), *Independence Day*. Centropolis Entertainment.
Dewey, George and Jack and the Belltones (1956), "Flying Saucers have Landed Part 1 and Part 2," Raven Records, 700.
Domino, Fats (1956), "I'm in Love Again," Speciality, SP-579-45.
Emerson, Lake and Palmer (1973), *Brain Salad Surgery*, Manticore, MC 66669, K53501.
Floyd, Pink (1967), "Interstellar Overdrive," *The Piper at the Gates of Dawn*, Columbia Records, SCX 6157.
Freed, Alan, Al "Jazzbo" Collins and Steve Allen (1956), "The Space Man," Coral, 61693.
Gonzalez, Babs (1952), "Cool Whalin," Babs Records, 6402.
Grande, Ariana (2019), "7 Rings," Republic Records, B0029782–21.
Iced Earth (2011), *Dystopia*, Century Media.
Hawkwind (1981), "Sonic Attack," Sonic Attack, RCA, RCALP 6004, PL 25380.
Jones, Spike (1942), "Der Fuehrer's Face," Bluebird, B-11586.
Laurence, Sid and Friends (1956). "The Answer to the Flying Saucer" U.F.O (Men From Mars), Cosmic Records, 1002.
Muse (2006), *Black Holes and Revelations*, Warner Bros. Records, 1-44284.
Noel, Sid and his Outer Spaceman (1956), "Flying Saucer," Luniverse, 45-3331.
Page, Patti (1953), "(How Much Is that) Doggie in the Window," Oriele, CB 1156.
Parkes, Walter, F. and Laurie MacDonald (1997), *Men in Black*, Columbia Pictures.
Platters, The (1956), "The Great Pretender," Mercury, B 45–689.
Presley, Elvis (1956a), "Heartbreak Hotel," RCA Victor, 20-6420.
Presley, Elvis (1956b), "Hound Dog," RCA Victor, 20-6604.
Radiohead (1997), "Paranoid Android," *Ok Computer*, Parlophone, NODATA 02, 7243 8 55229 1 8.
Richard, Little (1955), "Tutti Fruiti," Speciality, 561.
Richard, Little (1956a), "Long Tall Sally," Speciality.
Richard, Little (1956b), "Rip it Up," Speciality, SP-579-45.
Schneer, Charles, H. (1956), *Earth Vs. The Flying Saucers*, Clover Productions.
Wilcox, Fred, M. (1956), *Forbidden Planet*, Metro-Goldwyn-Mayer.
Yes (1970), "Astral Traveller," *Time and A Word*, Atlantic, 2400 006, 2400006.
Zappa, Frank (1985), "Porn Wars," *Frank Zappa Meets the Mothers of Prevention*, Barking Pumpkin Records. ST-74203, ST 74203.

2

The Kingsmen, "Louie Louie" (1963)

Samuel Murray

At the top of SW 13th Street in Portland, Oregon, just before the intersection with Burnside, is a small row of shops next to a parking lot. There doesn't appear to be anything particularly special about this place, but this was a site of great provenance for the Portland music scene. A small plaque commemorates April 6, 1963, when the Kingsmen recorded their version of "Louie Louie." This was a cover version that would not only bring Richard Berry's iconic rhythm and blues hit to international attention, but also become the spark that lit the fuse of the Portland Music Scene and ultimately made it one of the most prominent music cities in the Pacific Northwest.

"Louie Louie" has gained its place in rock legend by being one of the most covered songs in history: *Mojo* magazine proclaimed in 2015 that "there are over 2000 (and counting) versions of 'Louie Louie,' with ever more still being released and performed."[1] The Kingsmen's version deserves particular attention, not only for being the band's sole hit but for the mythology surrounding its dramatic impact on American youth culture, resulting in perhaps one of the most bizarre FBI investigations in the Bureau's history.

"Louie Louie"'s connection to youth culture began when The Kingsmen, who were fans of the Tacoma, WA band The Wailers,[2] decided to add the song to their cover sets in clubs and dances across Oregon. In his book *Louie Louie*, Dave Marsh gives a detailed account of how the group encountered the song between sets while playing The Pypo Club in Seaside, Oregon:

> On their break, the Kingsmen watched as kids pumped dimes and quarters into the Pypo Club's jukebox. But the kids weren't playing a variety of records. They punched the same button over and over—the one that spat out the Wailers' "Louie Louie." As *duh duh duh, duh duh* filled the room the crowd danced avidly, shingalinging themselves into a frenzied sweat.[3]

---

[1] My first encounter with the song was The Three Amigos cover in 1999. For information on other cover versions of "Louie Louie" see Paul Stokes, "10 Great Versions of Louie Louie," Available online: https://www.mojo4music.com/articles/stories/10-great-versions-of-louie-louie/ (accessed 25 September 2021).
[2] Not to be confused with Bob Marley and The Wailers, this band are often referred to as The Fabulous Wailers.
[3] Dave Marsh, *Louie Louie* (New York: Hyperion, 1993), 81.

The band knew they were onto something and took the cover into their sets, performing it to audiences who were probably already fans of The Wailers' song, which was then heard on jukeboxes across the Pacific Northwest. Marsh describes how the Kingsmen really understood the power of the song: "One Friday night in April 1963 at the Chase, the Kingsmen decided to try an experiment. They would play, one time only, a double-length set—an hour and a half—consisting of nothing but one song."[4] The audience were enthralled and just kept dancing: it was raw innovation and soon gained widespread popularity. The Kingsmen used the song's popularity to their advantage, growing a following through their dedication to it.

"Louie Louie" had also attracted the attention of the rival group, Paul Revere and the Raiders, who also incorporated it into their live performances. Both bands soon rushed into the studios to record it on wax—as Marsh remarks, "into the very same recording studio, Portland's Northwest Recorders, to make their separate 'Louies' the very same week."[5] Marsh has also pointed to a long debate between the bands and scholars alike, about who recorded the track first. Portland radio DJ Craig Walker announced on air that he had researched and discovered that the Raiders had recorded the song on April 11, 1963, and The Kingsmen on April 13, but Marsh's own research in the CBS records archives suggests The Kingsmen recorded the record first; their records show that the Raiders didn't record their version until April 25.[6] It was widely expected that the Raiders, a more popular band across the Pacific Northwest, would have had the bigger success with "Louie Louie," but the charts tell a different story. The Kingsmen peaked at Number 2 on the *Billboard* Hot 100 chart on December 14, 1963, held off the Number 1 spot by another definitive one-hit wonder, The Singing Nun, singing "Dominique." The previous week's chart showed The Kingsmen's version at Number 4, with Paul Revere and the Raiders' version bubbling under the hot 100 at 103. In this battle The Kingsmen had beaten Paul Revere, a historical irony not lost on most.

One of the joys of listening to "Louie Louie" is not really being able to understand the lyrics.[7] The audio levels of the song, true to garage rock conventions, make the lead vocals barely audible, a feature the band would replicate live, which also led to a lot of mystery and intrigue. While Richard Berry's original recordings of the song are clear, over time only the hook line, "Louie Louie, Oh no!," is commonly known. This loss of lyrical meaning has allowed fans to project their own interpretations onto the song, but it was this common lack of understanding that propelled The Kingsmen's version into infamy.

In February 1964 "Louie Louie" ended up on the desk of the FBI laboratory, having been submitted for investigation after a member of staff of Sarasota High School raised the alarm that the Kingsmen's version was obscene and corrupting young minds. The FBI's "Louie Louie" file includes a letter written to then attorney general

---

[4] Ibid., 88.
[5] Ibid., 95.
[6] Ibid., 95.
[7] Comments on YouTube bear this out: "A time when you have no idea what he's saying yet still groove to the music"; "Proves you don't need lyrics to have a good song to sing along to," (https://www.youtube.com/watch?v=1RZJ4ESU52U).

Robert F. Kennedy by a parent concerned that their daughter had bought a copy of this obscene record:

> The lyrics are so filthy that I cannot enclose them in this letter. . . . These morons have gone too far. . . . This land of ours is headed for an extreme state of moral degradation what with this record, the biggest hit movies and sex and violence exploited on TV. How can we stamp out this menace????[8]

An interpretation of the lyrics was enclosed with the letter, and although it is not clear if it was transcribed by the concerned parent or by someone in the FBI, the report stresses that the lyrics read as follows:

> Oh no, grab her way down low
> There is a fine little girl waiting for me
> She is just a girl across the way
> Then I take her all alone
> She's never the girl I lay at home
> Tonight at ten I'll lay her again
> We'll fuck your girl and by the way
> And . . .on that chair I'll lay her there
> I felt my bone . . . sh . . . in her hair
> She had a rag on. I moved above.
> It won't be long she'll slip it off
> I held her in my arms and then
> And I told her I'd rather lay her again[9]

Needless to say, when these lyrics are compared with the original, it is easy to conclude that whoever transcribed these lines had themselves an obscene mind and had probably expected to find obscenities.[10] Having checked for subversion by listening to the song at a variety of speeds, the FBI subsequently concluded that "because the lyrics of the song on the record could not be definitely determined in the laboratory examination, it could not be determined whether it is an obscene record."[11] There is, however, a mild obscenity hidden in the recording. If you listen very carefully at 0:54, drummer Lyn Easton can be heard shouting "fuck," due to his dropping a stick. Oddly enough, the FBI didn't pick up on this delightful hidden surprise. Thus, even with its vast expertise in counterintelligence and cryptography, the FBI just could not work out what on earth The Kingsmen were singing.

This misunderstanding of the lyrics drew on a wider historical context of youth culture being seen as subversive, with music often analyzed for signs of corrupting

---

[8] See FBI, "Louie Louie (The 60s Song)," FBI Vault, p. 12. Available online: https://vault.fbi.gov/louie-louie-the-song/louie-louie-the-song/view (accessed December 30, 2020).
[9] Ibid., 13.
[10] Due to copyright restrictions the original lyrics could not be printed in this chapter, but they can be found for reference through a quick internet search.
[11] FBI, "Louie Louie," 23.

influence. It seems unfortunately fitting that this "subversive" recording should have come from Portland: due to draconian alcohol laws—established during prohibition and yet to be repealed—most Portlanders cannot go to gigs until they reach the age of twenty-one. Accessing live music across the state has often meant taking risks and sticking it to the authorities with fake IDs, or finding the kindly bouncers who might open the back door to a venue. Take those acts of rebellion and add the opening strains of "Louie Louie" and it would not matter what the lyrics were; it was just raw, exciting music. If the adults didn't want them to access it, it must have been good!

Despite the furor of the FBI investigation shining a national spotlight on the Kingsmen, the band would never again reach the dizzy heights of a Number 2 single. Though "The Jolly Green Giant" did chart at Number 4 in 1965, it is certainly not as ingrained in the collective memory of music fans in the same way that "Louie Louie" is, and did not have the same level of international success. Therefore, it could be argued that the Kingsmen were indeed a one-hit wonder. A one-hit wonder is often a pejorative, an accusation of a lack of talent:

> It does imply that a performer was a one-trick pony. It triggers perceptions about limited musical talent, limited song production skills, and even limited energy as a professional artist. Issuing a single hit recording, but never duplicating that feat again, amounts to failure by omission.[12]

But it is rather simplistic to suggest that failure to repeat high chart success indicates a lack of musical ability, when it is more often a failure of marketing and promotion. Many formative works failed to chart but still maintain their position in the pop canon: Dolly Parton's "Jolene," Elton John's "Tiny Dancer," and AC/DC's "Highway to Hell." Lee Cooper even concedes that "the world of one-hit wonder recordings is much too diverse and complex to be blanketed by the simple fiction of personal artistic laxity."[13]

There is, however, an inherent value added to songs that combine commercial success with a major contextual impact that enables the songs to last the test of time. "Louie Louie" is such a song. Though it has had repeated success and longevity with countless cover versions, The Kingsmen's recording is arguably the most successful version, and the one heard as definitive by a wide cross-section of music fans. And while it is certainly the band's most successful recording, it earned its place in rock mythology through the FBI's investigation of the beguiling power of its indecipherable lyrics: a combination of context, musical innovation, and rebellious spirit makes this song a unique offering and an incomparable hit.

It is not derogatory or critical to label The Kingsmen a one-hit wonder. The band's talents have endured, and the surviving members of the group still play to large audiences. "Louie Louie" has simply become almost disembodied from the rest of the band's catalog, defining the band by a moment in time and a music scene yet to come—because thanks to the FBI and national record sales, America's musical interest started to focus around Portland, Oregon. Portland already had a strong network of venues and

---

[12] B. Lee Cooper, "Audio Reviews," *Popular Music and Society* 44, no. 1 (2021): 113–18.
[13] Ibid.

performing groups, but none had managed to capture the national imagination in the way The Kingsmen did, and "Louie Louie" was the first in a string of one-hit wonders that helped progress the music scene in the city: "Harden my Heart" by Quarterflash (1981) and Nu Shooz's "I can't wait" (1985) led to Portland's role in the 1990s grunge movement, and on to more recent success of indie-folk groups like The Decemberists, Y La Bamba, and Blitzentrapper, jazz musicians such as Esperanza Spalding,[14] and more recent hip-hop success from rappers such as Aminé.

The Kingmen's recording of "Louie Louie" has such a strong connection to Portland that it is almost as if the song was written in the city and for it. While the words don't speak of the city, or even tell a story of it, the sound the Kingsmen created still resonates within the scene today. It is such a strong part of the city's history that April 11, Richard Berry's birthday, was duly declared "Louie Louie" day, and during its annual celebrations, musicians from across the city unite to perform the song together. Portland's famous Voodoo Doughnuts even created a doughnut in honor of "Louie Louie." By embracing the history of the song, local authorities have found innovative, new ways of etching it into the city's cultural heritage, creating opportunities for cultural pilgrimage and tourism. The plaque that sits on the wall of the building at the top of SW 13th Street has allowed fans to come and feel a bit of music history, to make the journey to see where the definitive version of "Louie Louie" was recorded.

In 2018, the Kingsmen's lead singer, Jack Ely, passed away, leaving behind an indecipherable legacy. But do the lyrics really matter? Who needs words? When you can sing that riff: "duh-duh duh, duh duh, duh-duh duh, duh duh." Oh no!

References

Billboard (2020), "Chart History: The Kingsmen." Available online: https://www.billboard.com/music/the-kingsmen/chart-history/HSI/song/574833 (accessed December 30, 2020).

Cooper, B. Lee, (2021), "Audio Reviews," *Popular Music and Society*, 44 (1): 113–18.

Dietsche, Robert (2005), *Jumptown: The Golden Years of Portland Jazz, 1942–1957*, Corvallis: Oregon State University Press.

FBI (1964), "Louie Louie (The 60s Song)," FBI Vault. Available online: https://vault.fbi.gov/louie-louie-the-song/louie-louie-the-song/view (accessed December 30, 2020).

MarshDave (1993), *Louie Louie*, New York: Hyperion.

Stokes, Paul (2015), "10 Great Versions Of Louie Louie." Available online: https://www.mojo4music.com/articles/20118/10-great-versions-louie-louie (accessed December 30, 2020)

---

[14] "Louie Louie" was the city's first national and international hit, but it must be said that Portland's musical roots were firmly driven by the jazz at the center of the African American community. See Dietscher's *Jumptown: The Golden Years of Portland Jazz, 1942–1957* (Corvallis: Oregon State University Press, 2005) for a full history. The lack of attention paid to the Portland jazz scene was due in part to the racist attitudes towards black musicians in the city—and in the state of Oregon at large, which until 1926 had laws preventing black citizens from owning property, living, or working in the state. This is a good moment to reiterate that "Louie Louie," written by a black musician, was only brought to international attention by a white band.

3

? and the Mysterians, "96 Tears" (1966)

Adam Behr

"96 Tears," recorded and released by Question Mark and the Mysterians in 1966,[1] is one of a number of contenders—several of which could be described as "one hit wonders"—for the title of "first punk song," or at least as the primary standout in a range of proto-punk works. It's a crowded field. Candidates for progenitor of punk range back from just before the mid-1970s through the rough-and-ready singles from The Kinks and The Who (before their evolution into concept albums) to the "ur-text" of the Kingsmen's 1963 version of Richard Berry's "Louie Louie."[2] The case for "96 Tears" is strong, in terms of critical uptake at least, as well as its musical components. The first use of "punk" in the specific context of music is often ascribed to Dave Marsh in his review of a Question Mark and the Mysterians gig for *Creem* in May 1971.[3] Lester Bangs—another early champion of the punk aesthetic, however defined—also waxed enthusiastic, calling it "one of the greatest rock and roll songs of all time and the real beginning of my story."[4] Alternatively, or additionally, Question Mark and the Mysterians have been cited as a seminal or "quintessential" "garage rock" act,[5] an acknowledgment of the earlier roots of a stripped-back approach to popular music production celebrated in punk.

Nomenclature aside, the simplicity and rawness of "96 Tears" place it squarely in the trajectory from early rock and roll to punk as a plausible stepping stone. Repetitive and bleak lyrics, vocal delivery a couple of notches above a monotone, noisy and raw

---

[1] Styled variously as "Question Mark" and as "?".
[2] Bill Osgerby, "'Chewing out a rhythm on my bubble-gum': The Teenage Aesthetic and Genealogies of American Punk," in *Punk Rock: So What? The Cultural Legacy of Punk*, ed. Roger Sabin (London: Routledge, 1999), 159.
[3] The lineage is, as ever, complex. Nick Tosches, also of *Creem*, had used punk more generally in reference to youth culture in 1970, but Marsh's coinage is most commonly associated with punk *rock* in particular. Lars J. Kristiansen, Joseph R. Blaney, Philip J. Chidester and Brent K. Simonds, *Screaming for Change: Articulating a Unifying Philosophy of Punk Rock* (Lanham: Lexington Books, 2012), 6.
[4] Lester Bangs, *Psychotic Reactions and Carburetor Dung: The Work of a Legendary Critic: Rock'N'Roll as Literature and Literature as Rock 'N'Roll*, ed. Greil Marcus (New York: Alfred A.Knopf, 1987), 40.
[5] Roberto Avant-Mier, "Latinos in the Garage: A Genealogical Examination of the Latino/a Presence and Influence in Garage Rock (and Rock and Pop Music)," *Popular Music and Society* 31, no. 5 (2008): 564

guitars, yet danceable and infused with tinges of pop through its signature electric organ lick (that still manages a degree of emotional chill through its shrillness),[6] the song's "numb nihilism,"[7] as Jon Savage puts it, straddles the teen heartbreak of the pop that preceded it and the alienation of the punk that would follow. While its punk credentials have been burnished by a UK Top 20 cover by The Stranglers in 1990, the distinctive core features of "96 Tears" in combination with its dynamic flatness have served as a template for a range of interpretations across the popular musical spectrum, from soulful and funky run-outs by Jimmy Ruffin (recorded in 1966) and Aretha Franklin (in 1967) to a gamut of stylistic inflections from the Modern Lovers, Inspiral Carpets, Primal Scream, Eddie and the Hot Rods, and Suicide.

But interesting as it is to trace the lineage and influence of "96 Tears," there is as much to be gleaned from a view of the Mysterians and their hit in their own right, and for what their own story reveals of popular music's processes and history. While "96 Tears" unquestionably dominates their legacy, as with many "one hit wonders," Question Mark and the Mysterians enjoyed additional, if minor, successes over the course of their career. And as with many "one hit wonders" the song that was the epicenter of that career can be examined for what it typified of its time, as well as what it foreshadowed. "96 Tears" topped the US charts at a moment when rock was starting to flex its muscles within the mainstream of popular culture and the Mysterians' moment in the spotlight on their journey from the margins, and back again, saw them intersect with trends that demonstrate key aspects of popular music's evolution and context in the latter half of the twentieth century.

Migration and Mixtures

Prevailing constraints and affordances deriving from industry and legal structures have a bearing on what music reaches public prominence. In his study of the early explosion of rock and roll, Richard Peterson uses the "production of culture" model to answer the chronological question, "why 1955?"[8] While Peterson's account gives the context for foundational stars like Elvis, Chuck Berry, and Jerry Lee Lewis, the social tides and industrial currents alike prevailed upon the lesser storied participants in popular culture—one-hit wonders included. While a comprehensive "production of culture" account of "96 Tears" is beyond the scope of this discussion, it is worth considering the surrounding contexts to see how—as much as it prefigured the grit and snarl of punk—Question Mark and the Mysterians' defining hit can illuminate the contours of its own historical moment in popular musical history.

In a number of ways we can view "96 Tears" as a kind of exemplar, synecdoche even, of the cultural and industrial trends that shaped rock culture in the mid-1960s. First,

---

[6] Accounts differ as to whether this was a Farfisa, a Vox Continental, or a Lowery organ.
[7] Jon Savage, *England's Dreaming: Anarchy, Sex Pistols, Punk Rock and Beyond* (London: Faber and Faber, 2011), 82.
[8] Richard A. Peterson, "Why 1955? Explaining the Advent of Rock Music," *Popular Music* 9, no. 1 (1990): 97–116.

it shows the omnivorousness of popular culture in appealing to and incorporating a range of communities across the USA, alongside the important intersection of local record labels and radio stations with the national picture.

The band members, leading up to and during their spell in the charts, were all Mexican Americans who grew up around Saginaw, Michigan, amid a migrant community that had traveled there for work on farms and in the General Motors factory established in the 1950s. Originally a trio consisting of drummer Robert Martinez with guitarists, and cousins, Larry Borjas and Bobby Balderrama, the group played surf-guitar-style instrumentals. With the younger members still at school, opportunities for playing were initially limited but in the peer-driven, almost ad hoc nature of band formation, and with British influences percolating through, Martinez's brother Rudy (Question Mark) was recruited. Balderrama recalls:

> No one in the band was really a singer. We wanted to find a singer, and we knew Question Mark and he said he could sing. Actually, my sisters knew him because he had a reputation as one of the best dancers around the area, you know? And my sisters used to go watch him dance, so they recommended Question Mark, and we tried him out and he sounded real good. He covered Mick Jagger, and we thought, "Well, we could do a lot of Rolling Stones cover songs . . ." So we started doing that.[9]

The melange of influences, traceable both into and out from the band's sound, crystallized with the addition of thirteen-year-old Frank Rodriguez on organ. Ed Morales highlights the significance of the organ as a constituent of the "Tex Mex" sound, driven by a combination of economic necessity and a reach for modernity by the "conjunto" ensembles; comparatively cheap organs like the Farfisa and Vox Continental were used to supplement the traditional accordion.[10] Balderrama cites the Moody Blues as an example of the organ sound in popular bands that helped to push the Mysterians in that direction, along with other British bands like the Beatles and Rolling Stones, via the *Ed Sullivan Show*.[11]

Another piece of the puzzle was the band's image—sunglasses, anonymity, and an air of otherworldly detachment. Here, there was a combination of popular cultural consumption and the natural eccentricity of Rudy Martinez. The band name derived from an otherwise obscure Japanese science-fiction movie and its titular aliens—*The Mysterians*. Their singer took on the name "Question Mark," claiming to have eventually done so legally, and initially attempting to go by just the symbol "?" but being prevented from this by officials who said that their computers would not be able to process the

---

[9] Legs McNeil, "Question Mark & the Mysterians: The Making of '96 Tears,'" *Vice* February 26, 2014, Available online: https://www.vice.com/en/article/jmbpdd/question-mark--the-mysterians---the-making-of-96-tears (accessed June 30, 2021).
[10] Ed Morales, *The Latin Beat: The Rhythms and Roots Of Latin Music from Bossa Nova to Salsa And Beyond* (Cambridge: Da Capo Press, 2003), 290
[11] McNeil "The Making of 96 Tears."

symbol alone.[12] He has also, variously, claimed to have been born on Mars and to have lived on Earth since the time of the dinosaurs.[13]

With the core of the band's aesthetic in place, the shadow of the Vietnam War precipitated a final line-up change as Larry Borjas and Robert Martinez found themselves in line for conscription and, according to Balderrama, decided to enlist in the armed forces to give themselves the option of being posted to Germany rather than Vietnam. With Eddie Serrato replacing Martinez on drums and Frank Lugo joining on bass, the band stabilized and began writing. "96 Tears" itself emerged from a Rodriguez organ riff, taking shape via Question Mark's lyrics and the repeated refrain of "too many teardrops," which, the singer claims, he had written before joining the group— "It just had to be brought back to the surface again."[14] An initial title of "69 Tears" was rejected as catchy, but at risk of censorship for sexual connotations before Serrato proposed switching the numbers around to "96." "All of a sudden," says Balderrama, "there were light bulbs and stuff . . . YEAH. THAT'S IT!"[15]

The American rock and roll foundations for Question Mark and the Mysterians' sound, then, were refracted through a lens of migration—of music and people. The "overlaps between Texas conjunto music, the British invasion and garage rock,"[16] as Morales puts it, drew on and synthesized their musical forbears, the commercial music of the day, and pulp science fiction.

> *96 Tears* used the organ as a percussive instrument the way Afro-Cuban music does, building to an other-wordly, moody apotheosis, especially when combined with Martinez's eerie vocals. The Mysterians' music seemed to announce that as Mexican-Americans, they felt like aliens.[17]

Up against the Industry

Like many "one hit wonders," Question Mark and the Mysterians had a measure of success beyond the song for which they are remembered, though with rapidly diminishing commercial returns. The 1966 follow-up to "96 Tears," "I Need Somebody" reached Number 22 on the *Billboard* charts, with 1967's "I Can't Get Enough of You Baby" making it to Number 56. Album success was more limited still, with 1966's *96 Tears* reaching Number 66 and its successor—*Action*—failing to reach the charts.

---

[12] Mark Wedel, "Mysterians' Frontman Faces Some Questions from His Past," *MLive - Kalamazoo Gazette*, April 5, 2007, Available online: https://www.mlive.com/kalamazoo_gazette_extra/2007/05/mysterians_frontman_faces_some.html (accessed June 30, 2021).
[13] William Tsitsos, "Racial Transparency Theory Applied to Musicians Who Claim to Be Aliens," *Popular Music and Society* 37, no. 1 (2014): 27.
[14] Gary James, "Gary James' Interview with Rudy Martinez of Question Mark and the Mysterians," *ClassicBands.Com* (nd), Available online: http://www.classicbands.com/QuestionMarkInterview.html (accessed, June 30, 2021).
[15] McNeil "The Making of 96 Tears."
[16] Morales, *The Latin Beat*, 290.
[17] Ibid.

But their story, characteristically, pivots around their signature song, industrially as well as aesthetically. Their moment in the sunshine illustrates the significance of local labels and radio stations, as well as the communities they served, and the trajectories and patterns of commercial activity and exploitation of the mid-1960s.

The band returned to local label owner Lilly Gonzales, who had told them the year before that they were not ready yet but to come back later. Gonzales, with her husband Joe "Pato" Gonzales, ran a Mexican store in Saginaw, and a label—Bego Records—which released Mexican music in Texas. She took the band to a studio in Bay City, Michigan, to record "96 Tears" and "Midnight Hour" in April 1966 and, deciding to market the band as a rock and roll act, launched and put them out on her Pa-Go-Go Label in Michigan, pressing 500 copies for the band to take to local radio stations. This was pivotal, recalls Balderrama:

> I hate to say this, but back in the 60s there was a lot of prejudice. I think if we had gone to a white record company, they would have just laughed at us. I think they would've turned us down, because we were so young. We were only in high school, you know? Miss Gonzales gave us a shot.[18]

Here, the network of local radio stations was key. The band took copies of the song to stations in Saginaw, and then Flint, playing promotional gigs for the stations, and featuring on "Battle of the Songs" shows that increasingly demonstrated the song's popular appeal, which motivated them to push it to stations in Detroit. The song made Number 1 in Flint, which drove radio interest, and consequently sales, in Detroit until it topped the charts in the state, also attracting the attention of regional stations in Canada.

Record store autograph sessions followed and then, as their commercial appeal waxed, national interest and the familiar story of moving to a larger label for a flash of national notoriety and subsequent decline. For Question Mark and the Mysterians were also pivotal to the career of record label mogul Neil Bogart, who would later found Casablanca records, signing Kiss and being instrumental in the rise of disco with acts like Donna Summer and the Village People. "96 Tears" had attracted the attention of a label—Cameo Parkway—with national reach and a strong relationship with the TV show *American Bandstand*.[19] Bogart, a sales manager at Cameo, bought the rights to "96 Tears," precipitating television appearances, a re-release on Cameo for national distribution, a Number 1 single in the USA and Canada that also charted in the UK and France, as well as tours with the Beach Boys.[20]

The journey from Saginaw to *American Bandstand*, though, was also characteristic of a degree of naivety on the part of young musicians, and a rapidly integrating record industry. Following the initial impact of "96 Tears," the band's relationship with Cameo-Parkway cooled and, according to Question Mark, Bogart's insistence that they

---

[18] McNeil, "The Making of 96 Tears."
[19] Fredric Dannen, *Hit Men: Power Brokers and Fast Money Inside the Music Business* (New York: Vintage Press, 1991), 164.
[20] McNeil "The Making of 96 Tears."

record covers, their own material to be relegated to B-sides, triggered the departure of Serrato and Rodriguez and then a reluctant approach to promotion from the record company.

> So we recorded the singles and were recording the album and things were not happening for us any more—we got ripped off for a bunch of money but we still had an album to finish. . . . Its [sic] not that we couldn't record or write good songs any more—if you had no promotion by a major label you weren't going to go anywhere. If they just recorded you because you had a contract but they did nothing to promote or distribute the records, without any push every record was going to chart lower and lower.[21]

Meanwhile, Cameo Parkway had troubles of its own. Its founders having departed, the label struggled to maintain its commercial profile into the late 1960s and an acquisition by ABCKO, owned by the notoriously hard-nosed Allen Klein—who would soon become embroiled in the Beatles' acrimonious endgame—led to tensions with Bogart, who would soon jump ship himself.[22] Question Mark and the Mysterians recorded briefly, and unsuccessfully, for a string of other labels before, adrift commercially, the group came apart—Balderrama took other work away from music before drifting back to it in the 1980s while Question Mark plowed on with a rotating line-up of replacements.

The story of a young band, ascending from a local circuit via an independent label before being propelled to fame by a major player, and then cast aside amid a tortuous round of internecine business squabbles, is a familiar one—almost archetypal. Question Mark and the Mysterians' rapid ascent and decline is a marker of how the American record industry worked in the mid-1960s, at the moment when singles were starting to give way to albums as the central commercial unit, and the industry started moving towards the concentration that characterized the 1970s.[23]

Coda

Their tenure at the top may have been brief but the impact of Question Mark and the Mysterians was not easily dampened. It was a show *after* their initial salad days, during their commercial fade-out, that prompted Dave Marsh's fulsome review. And Question Mark's persistence has paid dividends, of a sort, in light of popular culture's propensity for recycling and nostalgia. As for many bands, the re-union trail beckoned. The original line-up reformed briefly in the mid-1980s with more substantive activity

---

[21] Question Mark and Susie Martin, "AS SEEN THROUGH THE SHADES OF QUESTION MARK of ? and the Mysterians," *It's Psychedelic Baby, Magazine*, January 24, 2015, Available online: https://www.psychedelicbabymag.com/2015/01/as-seen-through-shades-of-question-mark.html (accessed June 30, 2021).

[22] Dannen, *Hit Men*.

[23] Paul D. Lopes, "Innovation and Diversity in the Popular Music Industry, 1969 to 1990," *American Sociological Review* 57, no. 1 (1992): 57

in the 1990s, re-recording their original album in 1996, since Klein still owned the rights to the original recording, and releasing a moderately successful new album *More Action* in 1999. Their fortunes since have been variable. Serrato died of a heart attack in 2011 and Balderrama fought prostate cancer in 2017; he still records, and in 2019 self-released a book about his guitar influences. While Question Mark lost his possessions in a 2007 house fire, the affection in which the band was held became evident through benefit concerts to help him out, and he tours still. In 2014, Bay City's Mayor declared "96 Tears" the "Official Rock and Roll Song of the City,"[24] at once a small-scale honor compared to the international and historical reach of the song and an appropriate marker of the band's origins as Michigan youngsters—a line from the melting pot of influences in the early 1960s to the global reach of their song.

Question Mark and the Mysterians did not become rich, and are not icons as individual musicians. But their career stands as an indicator of popular music's capacity to revitalize and recombine a diverse set of inputs—from Mexican migrant workers and their cheap instruments, through American-influenced British bands via popular television and cinema—into an explosive three minutes that resonates far beyond their local roots. The vicissitudes of a shifting industry may have only granted them one hit. Sometimes one hit is all it takes.

References

Avant-Mier, Roberto (2008), "Latinos in the Garage: A Genealogical Examination of the Latino/a Presence and Influence in Garage Rock (and Rock and Pop Music)," *Popular Music and Society*, 31 (5): 555–74

Bangs, Lester (2003), *Psychotic Reactions and Carburetor Dung: The Work of a Legendary Critic: Rock'N'Roll as Literature and Literature as Rock'N'Roll*, Greil Marcus (ed.), New York: Alfred A. Knopf.

Dannen, Fredric (1991), *Hit Men: Power Brokers and Fast Money Inside the Music Business*, New York: Vintage Press.

James, Gary, (nd), "Gary James' Interview With Rudy Martinez of Question Mark and the Mysterians," *ClassicBands.Com*. Available online: http://www.classicbands.com/QuestionMarkInterview.html (accessed June 30, 2021)

Kristiansen, Lars J., Joseph R. Blaney, Philip J. Chidester and Brent K. Simonds (2012), *Screaming for Change: Articulating a Unifying Philosophy of Punk Rock*, Lanham: Lexington Books

Lopes, Paul D. (1992), "Innovation and Diversity in the Popular Music Industry, 1969 to 1990," *American Sociological Review*, 57 (1): 56–71.

Martinez, R. and Susie Martin (2015), "Question Mark and Susie Martin, 'AS SEEN THROUGH THE SHADES OF QUESTION MARK of ? and the Mysterians,'" *It's Psychedelic Baby, Magazine*, January 24, 2015. Available online: https://www.psychedelicbabymag.com/2015/01/as-seen-through-shades-of-question-mark.html (accessed June 30, 2021).

---

[24] Cole Waterman, "Mayor to Dedicate '96 Tears' as Bay City's Official Rock and Roll Song," *MLive*, July 27, 2014, Available online: https://www.mlive.com/news/bay-city/2014/07/mayor_to_dedicate_96_tears_as.html (accessed June 30, 2021).

McNeil, Legs (2014), "Question Mark & the Mysterians: The Making of '96 Tears,'" *Vice* February 26, 2014. Available online: https://www.vice.com/en/article/jmbpdd/question-mark--the-mysterians---the-making-of-96-tears (accessed June 30, 2021).

Ed Morales, (2003), *The Latin Beat: The Rhythms and Roots of Latin Music From Bossa Nova To Salsa And Beyond*, Cambridge: Da Capo Press.

Osgerby, Bill (1999), "'Chewing Out a Rhythm on My Bubble-gum': The Teenage Aesthetic and Genealogies of American Punk," in Roger Sabin (ed.), *Punk Rock: So What? The Cultural Legacy of Punk*, 154–69, London: Routledge.

Peterson, Richard A. (1990), "Why 1955? Explaining the Advent of Rock Music," *Popular Music*, 9 (1): 97–116.

Savage, Jon (2011), *England's Dreaming: Anarchy, Sex Pistols, Punk Rock and Beyond*, London: Faber and Faber.

Tsitsos, William (2014), "Racial Transparency Theory Applied to Musicians Who Claim to Be Aliens," *Popular Music and Society*, 37 (1): 22–32.

Waterman, Cole, (2014), "Mayor to Dedicate '96 Tears' as Bay City's Official Rock and Roll Song," *MLive*, July 27, 2014. Available online: https://www.mlive.com/news/bay-city/2014/07/mayor_to_dedicate_96_tears_as.html (accessed June 30, 2021).

Wedel, Mark (2007), "Mysterians' Frontman Faces Some Questions from His Past," *MLive Kalamazoo Gazette*, April 5, 2007. Available online: https://www.mlive.com/kalamazoo_gazette_extra/2007/05/mysterians_frontman_faces_some.html (accessed June 30, 2021).

4

The Easybeats, "Friday on My Mind" (1966)

Dai Griffiths

In this chapter, I intend to consider the phenomenon of the one-hit wonder from an analytical perspective close to the musical text. I aim to look inward, to suggest reasons that this specific track works as a one-hit wonder, rather than to look outward, to its historical status as a lone hit for this particular band. My presentational approach builds on Walter Everett's 2008 *Foundations of Rock*, in that detailed musical analysis is supported by frequent reference to the track.

My textual orientation notwithstanding, however, the claim can readily be made both for The Easybeats as a one-hit-wonder and for "Friday on My Mind" as their one hit. The Easybeats formed in Australia in 1964 and disbanded there in 1969. "Friday on My Mind" was recorded and released in the UK in 1966, and became an international hit soon thereafter, as represented by singles charts: Australia and the Netherlands Number 1, New Zealand Number 2, UK Number 6, Germany Number 10, USA Number 16.

It is immediately important to note that in Australia the band were not one-hit wonders: five singles reached the Australian top ten before "Friday on My Mind" was released in late 1966 (in 1965: "She's So Fine" Number 3, "Wedding Ring" Number 7; in 1966: "Women (make you feel alright)" Number 4, "Come and see her" Number 3, and "Sorry" Number 1), with one after "Friday on My Mind" ("Heaven and Hell," Number 8 in 1967). Even in claiming "Friday on My Mind" as a one-hit wonder, I have to make too much of the track's success in countries other than Australia. Be that as it may, "Friday on My Mind" is The Easybeats' enduring track, and it is unlikely that even the pop aficionado will know those other, localized hits. The Easybeats' career can be interpreted as an arch of rapid ascent, the peak of "Friday on My Mind," then gradual descent. Summed up, their career starts with celebrity and hits in Australia; they relocate to London, where a decisive role is played by producer Shel Talmy; the hit arrives followed by attempts to consolidate its achievement and momentum; and finally they return to localized activity, and the group's eventual demise.[1]

"Friday on My Mind" is less the isolated foray into the record industry and more a phenomenon that saddles the band's subsequent career. Perhaps the "one-hit"

---

[1] Chris Welch, liner notes, *The Easybeats: The Definitive Anthology* (Repertoire Records, 1996).

point to focus upon—though space won't allow proper consideration—is the period immediately after "Friday on My Mind," and the decision over how to follow and build upon its success. Among several possible alternatives, the track ultimately chosen was "Who'll Be the One?," released in 1967. By this point, The Easybeats were based in London: although formed in Australia, all five band members were born in Europe: two in Holland (Harry Vanda, lead guitar, and Dick Diamande, bass), two in England (Stevie Wright, singer, and Gordon Fleet, drums), and one in Scotland (George Young, rhythm guitar, the older brother of Malcolm and Angus Young of AC/DC). A BBC radio session for Saturday Club includes a conversation with disc jockey Brian Matthew, in which the issue is spelled out: "we didn't want to follow 'Friday on my Mind' with another 'Friday on my Mind.'" For The Easybeats at that crucial point, "Friday on My Mind" was the issue.

What makes "Friday on My Mind" work? And, by implication, why is it so good? I hear the words to the song as put together for the song's purpose by young musical amateurs: that is to say, musical rather than literary amateurs. Typical of their time, a group of musical autodidacts lands upon song as their creative focus, and so have to generate words as well as music, but they're in it, so to speak, for the music.[2] The words for "Friday on My Mind" take the working week as their starting point: the five days from Monday to Friday are mentioned in the first verse and compressed in the chorus's last line: "Monday I'll have Friday on my mind." The poetic conceit is familiar: "Monday's child is fair of face." Or an example in song: "Blue Monday," written by Dave Bartholomew, first recorded by Smiley Lewis (Imperial, 1953) and famous in the version by Fats Domino (Imperial, 1956), although here the week extends to Saturday morning rather than The Easybeats' Friday night. By comparison, however, The Easybeats' track—fast (190 beats per minute) and filled with musical detail—requires considerable labor in performance, replicating in music the "grind" of repetitive work. At the start of the second verse, the line "do the five-day grind once more" corresponds in song to "do the verse and chorus once more." Set next to the sweating Easybeats, the musicians on "Blue Monday" sound like they might at any time "pull a sickie." Covering "Friday on My Mind" in Sydney, Bruce Springsteen and the E Street Band bestow their imprimatur of blue-collar hard work, which Simon Frith long ago identified as theatrical invention.[3] "Friday on My Mind" is a song concerned with labor, then, with its narrator working in its second verse for an unspecified "rich man," but whose worker is a solitary man, considering only his inner life, the emotional ascent of his working week as Friday approaches and quickly disappears. Fellow workers are absent, and perhaps the rich man dissuades Union membership. Is there a pension scheme? The singer possesses a girlfriend as "my girl," but all we learn is that "she's so pretty": not much.

---

[2] Dai Griffiths, "Function and Construction of Rock Lyrics," in *The Bloomsbury Handbook of Rock Music Research*, ed. Allan Moore and Paul Carr (London and New York: Bloomsbury Academic, 2020), 165–78.

[3] See Simon Frith, "The Real Thing: Bruce Springsteen," in *Music for Pleasure: Essays in the Sociology of Music* (Cambridge: Polity, 1988), 94–101.

0'00	First Verse	('Monday morning feel so bad')
0'22	Transition	('Wednesday just won't go')
0'32	Chorus	('Gonna have fun in the city')
1'03	Retransition	('Monday I'll have Friday on my mind')
1'08	Second verse	('Do the five day grind once more')

Figure 4.1 "Friday on My Mind" outline form.

To be blunt, the words to this track go only so far, in my view, thrown together for the purpose of the song: this is not at all unusual. That said, some technical details of the words are noteworthy. The song contains in its second verse a notable enjambment: "I know of nothing else that bugs me . . .," musical gap, next line, ". . . more than working for the rich man." The words also bear two traces of its time: in the second verse, "Hey, I'll change that scene one day" and, in the chorus, "She is out of sight to me." "Scene" corresponds to the OED's noun, 8 (e) ("a social environment or milieu characterized by a particular activity, pursuit, way of life, etc., especially when considered fashionable"), while "out of sight" is in the OED a lengthy entry (including "slang, originally U.S.: excellent, incomparable, wonderful, extraordinary") which, as "outasight" (adjective) has an entry from *Surf International* in Australia for 1968: "we check them [girls] out at lunch time—outasight!" "Bread" for money in the chorus is OED noun 4 (c) with a first entry of 1935, USA.

Moving now to the music, I want chiefly to draw attention to the remarkable compressed form of the song, its rich musical detail presented in so short a time (Figure 4.1). My "transition" refers to the "pre-chorus" although, in this case, one could also evoke Sheila Davis's term "climb," which "functions as aural foreplay, to extend and increase the song's emotional tension by delaying the arrival of its climactic section."[4] My "retransition" functions both as a coda to the chorus and a link from chorus back to the verse.

The song then repeats the formal plan a second time—different words for verse, same words for chorus—before a coda reaches the recorded fade by two iterations of material from the chorus opening (0'32-0'42). The track as a whole lasts 2'38: first verse (0'00), second verse (1'08), coda: (2'18), end of fade (2'38). To be bluntly critical, the end is disappointing if typical, a "useless" coda to fade. Another record of the same period, "Don't sleep in the subway"—written by Tony Hatch and Jackie Trent and a single for Petula Clark in 1967—followed its harmonically daring material with a disappointing and "useless" coda to fade. Fades on record always require dead-ends in concert, and subsequent cover versions of "Friday on My Mind," of which there are many, also face that challenge or decision. The version by Earth Quake from 1973, for

---

[4] Sheila Davis, *The Craft of Lyric Writing* (Cincinnati: Writer's Digest Books, 1985), 55.

example, includes (at 3'13–3'36) a brief musical invention to end on a Beatles "added sixth" chord.

The essential musical content of "Friday on My Mind" occupies one minute eight seconds, and what sixty-eight seconds! Broadly, the song is a verse in E minor and a chorus in A major. The David Bowie who covered the track for Pinups in 1973 had followed the same broad shift (in this case E major to A major) in "Life on Mars," on his album *Hunky Dory* in 1971. One immediate way into the music is the song's vocal line, which ascends from the first note E (0'03) by an octave and a fourth to A for "I'll spend my bread" (0'52): hear and see Springsteen's characteristic strain at that point of his concert performance. Along the ladder the melodic rungs are: low E ("Monday morning"), B ("coming Tuesday"), high E ("gonna have fun in the city"), high A-F sharp ("I'll spend my bread"), finally B as midway resting point ("mind," 1'02 and "mind" 1'04). The transition itself (0'22–0'32) traverses an octave by step, A to A flat and ending on high G. The vocal line with its words imparts the song its drive and broad energy.

The true "wonder" of this hit record, however, resides in its detailed musical content. The following analysis treats each section in turn.

0'00-0'20: verse

The verse starts on the chord of E minor (0'00) but ends on A minor (0'21), a basic motion from chord i to chord iv. The very first phrase has E minor moving to D major via an implied A chord as dominant of D: Gary Moore's cover version misses out the intervening A (to its detriment, I think). The D chord (at "bad," 0'07) introduces in the guitar a marching figure (D-A-D-A), which proves a significant musical motive.

The second phrase (0'13) brings in an important detail: an additional, secondary melody, in this case a guitar solo but which role or function, as melodic counterpoint, is then passed over to backing vocals, wordless then wordy. The progression in the second phrase is a shift from E minor (0'13) to A minor (0'20) via connecting chords V/E (B7, 0'15) and V/A (E7, 0'18): the melodic figure is found in guitar (0'15–0'18) and divides in two, thrice an upper neighbor note (C-B, E-D sharp, G sharp-F sharp) then descending by step between the F sharp of B7 and the D of the following E7 (0'17). The guitar solo includes a most unusual G sharp, before descending as G natural: the G sharp may be a daring melodic adventure, or there might also be issues of intonation in the performance, with the G sharp-a "too sharp" G natural. (My thanks to Huw Thomas for help on this point.)

0'20-0'32: transition

At 0'20, the verse has settled on A minor, commencing the passage that leads to the chorus. Spanning the transition is an underlying shift from A minor to its relative major, C major at 0'30 ("mind"), but the arrival at C major is brief indeed, the music immediately whisked to A major for the chorus (0'32). The short transition thus employs both A major as the parallel major of A minor and C major as its relative major. A major at 0'23 commences the transition, leading as temporary dominant to D minor (0'25), before arriving at C major (0'30). At the melody's peak, the singer

A	-	-	-	-	-	-	-	F
A	B flat	A	G	A	G	F	E	F
CUN			LN		PN		LN	

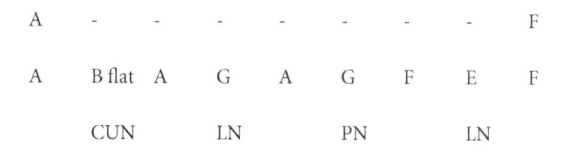

Figure 4.2 Backing vocal figure: 0:26-0:28.

reaches (0'29) an expressive, chromatic A flat before settling on the high G. Finally, two times melodic counterpoints are added, now wordless backing vocals, a melodic figure that carries into the chorus. The figure traverses a third within the chord, decorating the interval with neighbor and passing notes. Thus, at 0'26-8, A and F, as notes of D minor, generate this figure, with CUN and LN as chromatic upper and lower neighbor notes and PN as passing note (Figure 4.2).

When first heard at 0'21-3, due to the mixture chord at 0'23, the voice ends the figure with C sharp rather than C natural, the *tierce de Picardie*. It is during the transition that the bass guitar becomes more prominent and develops the marching (1-5-1) figure from 0'06, for example, at 0'28.

Just before the chorus (0'30-2), the song inserts one of its most dramatic moments, three chords that generate high harmonic zest, but which effectively pad out the A major to come. Simply executed as barre chords on the guitar, the progression is a series of dominants (Figure 4.3).

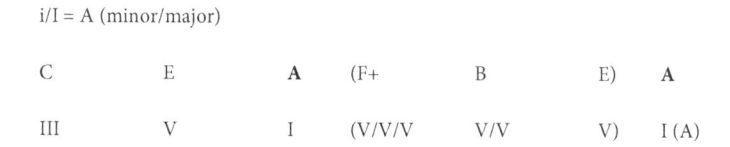

i/I = A (minor/major)

C	E	A	(F+	B	E)	A
III	V	I	(V/V/V	V/V	V)	I (A)

Figure 4.3 Chord progression at 0:30-0:32.

0'32–1'03: chorus
The chorus is a passage in A major, ending with a strong and standard cadence: V 6/4-V7, but landing instead by mixture on A minor for the retransition (1'03). The chorus divides in two, the first ending with a brief tonicization of B minor, chord ii (0'48). Thereafter ("I'll spend my bread"), D major (IV, 0'50) leads downward to B7 (II7, 0'53) then back to D (0'55) as predominant before the cadential chords (0'58–1'02).

The first part of the chorus (0'32) adopts the character of call and response, as the vocalist declaims the melodic line to a response from backing vocals adapting the third-filling figure from the transition (as at 0'37-8): it is tempting for listeners themselves to supply the backing vocals. The chords supporting the chorus' opening juxtapose A major with C sharp minor, chord iii, first as a neighbor relation (0'35), then as a progression (0'40) leading to D major, IV (compare D minor in the transition, 0'24). D then leads to a briefly tonicized B minor (0'48) via an intervening F sharp chord as V/ii in A major (0'46). Over this latter progression, the backing vocals emit short, repeated, wordless notes: F sharp-A sharp-B, presumably a reference to the vocal style of the Swingle Singers, which members of the band mentioned in interviews.[5]

The chorus' second part starts at 0'50, and is now not only a two-voiced call and response but also with separate words, rather than words in lead vocal and vocal effect in the backing vocals. Also, where the chorus' first part has lead vocal answered by backing vocals, the order is now reversed: "Tonight," say the backing vocals, "I'll spend my bread," says the lead singer. In his solo version of this song, Glenn Tilbrook sings both parts, as though to say as one, "Tonight I'll spend my bread." Alongside the lead vocal's high point, the three-times repetition of "tonight" over those particular chords generates considerable energy at this point of the chorus. The shift from D to B7 and back again (0'50-58), an expansion from and contraction back to D, brings out a chromatic semitonal element (D-D sharp-D) which is a feature that develops across the song: for example, A minor to A major (C natural-C sharp, 0'21-3), G-B7-E7-A (D-D sharp, G sharp-A, 0'13-20), D-F sharp-B (A-A sharp-B, 0'43-50). The cadential chords (0'58-1'01) bring welcome if brief reduction of momentum after the song has driven forward and upward so consistently. At this stage of the song, the bass guitar is playing the rapid, repeated notes that were heard in the Swingle Singers' vocal part at 0'43-50. It's all go.

1'03–1'08: retransition

A most important section, this expressive passage leads the music into a kind of "no-man's land" so that the verse can pick up again in E minor (1'08). The voice's melody attends back to stepwise motion traversing a fifth as a reminder of the opening melody that follows in verse two. Minor chords return: A minor rather than major. The chords progress: A minor (1'03)—D major (1'05, D minor in some versions, Squeeze's for example)—G (1'06, VII of A minor), landing on E major (1'08), so that a final mixture (E major to E minor) is needed to lead to the verse's return. In the retransition, the bass guitar plays the marching I-V-I figure that has emerged across the song, with pedal notes (A-E-A) under the chords above (again, this is varied in some of the cover versions). The retransition is thus an impressive gathering together of elements of the song as a link from chorus to second verse.

By way of summary, and to turn to energetics as metaphor, "Friday on My Mind" is a rapid and intense build-up of energy and tension, achieved in the short time of verse and chorus. All that can happen, as the track exists, is to go through the motions again as the second verse, and end in the lame fade. Thus it is that cover versions do little with "Friday on My Mind" other than render it faithfully with regard to the original, partly because it's so fast and requires considerable musical skill, but mainly because its musical information is so packed and necessary. The British songwriter Glenn Tilbrook, who covered "Friday on My Mind" both alone and in his band Squeeze, once described an imaginary Squeeze compilation as *A Fistful of Chords*,[6] and the same title could apply to The Easybeats classic; it's no surprise that so fine a musician as Tilbrook

---

[5] See liner notes for *The Definitive Anthology*.
[6] Chris Difford, Glenn Tilbrook and Jim Drury, *Squeeze Song by Song* (London: Sanctuary Publishing, 2004), 83, 93.

admires the song. Richard Thompson too, who, in his 2003 project *1000 Years of Popular Music*, happily followed "Friday on My Mind" with Glenn Tilbrook's "Tempted."

The recording of "Friday on My Mind" was produced by Shel Talmy, who played a significant role in developing a distinctive sound for the emergent British rock music of the mid-1960s. If the ear pricks up at tracks by the Creation, the Kinks, and the Who on *Making Time: A Shel Talmy Production* (2017), the Easybeats are represented by 1967's "Lisa"—it's partly because their proto-rock sound appears alongside diverse pop music and folk-rock (the latter by Pentangle and Roy Harper). In the helpful interview with Alec Palao, Talmy describes working with Keith Grant and Glyn Johns as engineers: "I knew of course that being a producer and being an engineer are two entirely different jobs and it's very difficult to do both."[7] It was Glyn Johns who engineered "Friday on My Mind" at IBC Studios, 35 Portland Place, London. Talmy describes his production principles:

> I went for thickness and I went for volume. I wanted my records to be the loudest thing out there. I liked creating edgy product that pushed the envelope, keeping in mind that rock was relatively new with no preconceived notions, so those of us there at the beginning had the great good fortune of setting the standards.[8]

One imagines The Easybeats for three long years facing audiences that think the one thing of one-hit wonders: when will they play their one hit? My analysis suggests that "Friday on My Mind" is even less: not only a one-hit wonder, it's also a one-minute wonder. "Friday on My Mind" has the same relation to The Easybeats as one-hit wonders have to musical output in broader terms. As the one-hit wonder is the one transcendent track in a career, however short, the first minute (and a bit) is the transcendent material of "Friday On My Mind." One-hit wonders remind us that musical pieces or works or songs or tracks also turn upon magic moments within. "Friday on My Mind" is in its entirety a magic moment and eight seconds, a one-minute wonder.

References

Davis, Sheila (1985), *The Craft of Lyric Writing*, Cincinnati: Writer's Digest Books.
Difford, Chris and Glenn Tilbrook and Jim Drury (2004), *Squeeze Song by Song*, London: Sanctuary Publishing.
Everett, Walter (2008), *Foundations of Rock: from "Blue Suede Shoes" to "Suite: Judy Blue Eyes,"* New York: Oxford University Press
Frith, Simon (1988), "The Real Thing: Bruce Springsteen," in *Music for Pleasure: Essays in the Sociology of Music*, 94–101, Cambridge: Polity.
Griffiths, Dai (2020), "Function and Construction of Rock Lyrics," in Allan Moore and Paul Carr (eds.), *The Bloomsbury Handbook of Rock Music Research*, 165–78, London and New York: Bloomsbury Academic.

---

[7] Alec Palao, liner notes, *Making Time: A Shel Talmy Production* (Ace Records, 2017).
[8] Ibid., 7.

Discography

Bowie, David (1973), *Pinups*, RCA.
Earth Quake (1975), *Rocking the World*, Beserkley.
The Easybeats (1996), *The Easybeats: The Definitive Anthology*, Repertoire Records.
Moore, Gary (1987), *Wild Frontier*, 10/Virgin.
Palao, Alec (2017), *Making Time: A Shel Talmy Production*, Ace Records.
Thompson, Richard (2003), *1000 Years of Popular Music*, Beeswing.
Various artists (2017), *Making Time: A Shel Talmy Production*, Ace Records.
Welch, Chris (1996), *The Easybeats: The Definitive Anthology*, Repertoire Records.

Concert Recordings

Springsteen, Bruce (Sydney, September 2, 2014). Available online: https://www.youtube.com/watch?v=iMMpSiG57Zo (accessed January 19, 2021).
Squeeze (Port Chester, NY, October 15, 2016). Available online: https://www.youtube.com/watch?v=tCkjuwixCdE (accessed January 19, 2021).
Tilbrook, Glenn (Windelsham, Surrey, December 10, 2016). Available online: https://www.youtube.com/watch?v=0_8lxFH3WpU (accessed January 19, 2021).

Radio Session

The Easybeats, recorded March 21, 1967, broadcast April 1, 1967. Available online: https://www.youtube.com/watch?v=Fr0UJrEVW2w (accessed January 19, 2021).

5

Norman Greenbaum, "Spirit in the Sky" (1969)

Philip Auslander

Even as Norman Greenbaum's "Spirit in the Sky," released at the end of 1969, slowly climbed the charts during the first half of 1970, peaking at Number 1 in the UK in March,[1] at Number 3 on the *Billboard* Hot 100 in April, and at Number 1 on the *Cashbox* Top 100 in May, no one predicted that it would become one of the best known and most loved songs in American popular music. Yet, fifty years after its initial release, it is ubiquitous: even those unfamiliar with "Spirit in the Sky" as a radio hit probably have heard it in one of the more than 100 movies, television shows, and advertisements in whose soundtracks it has been included. "Spirit in the Sky" is a staple in the repertoire of hard rocking bar bands, and numerous artists, ranging from pop choral group The Mike Curb Congregation to British rockers Blue Mink to German New Wave singer Nina Hagen, have covered it. It is also said to be one of the most popular song selections for funerals.

Greenbaum is a cultural hero of mine. When I was a young Jewish rock fan coming of age in New England in the 1960s and 1970s, he was one of the few identifiably Jewish rock musicians of the time. He was also local, born and raised in an Orthodox Jewish family in Malden, Massachusetts, just a few miles northeast of my hometown of Newton Centre. I heard "Spirit in the Sky" on the radio and loved it, but I was confused. Why would a clearly Jewish musician write and record a song steeped in Christian theology? Was he a Jew for Jesus, a popular term for Messianic Jews in the 1960s? I hoped not.

Greenbaum (b. 1942) attended Boston University for two years beginning in 1960, ostensibly studying liberal arts but actually spending most of his time on the music scene, hanging out with legendary Boston disc jockey Arnie "Woo Woo" Ginsberg and playing what he describes as "folky kind of music."[2] "From the start," he has said, "my love was for the country-blues and old timey stuff that I heard the folkie types

---

[1] "Spirit in the Sky" reached Number 1 on the UK charts three times: Greenbaum's version in 1970, by Doctor and the Medics in 1986, and Gareth Gates's version in 2003.

[2] Jason M. Rubin, "'Going to the Place That's the Best'—Norman Greenbaum Returns Home to Malden," *The Arts Fuse*, October 27, 2019. Available online: https://artsfuse.org/189372/music-feature-going-to-the-place-thats-the-best-norman-greenbaum-returns-home-to-malden/ (accessed November 12, 2020).

playing in the coffeehouses in the Boston area."[3] This was the period of the fabled Boston/Cambridge folk music scene that rivaled the parallel scene in New York City's Greenwich Village in talent and importance. Greenbaum describes himself as hanging "around clubs in Boston featuring folk artists like Joan Baez, The Jim Kweskin Jug Band,[4] Eric Von Schmidt, Dave Van Ronk, The Holy Modal Rounders, The Fugs, Tom Paxton, Tom Rush, Taj Mahal, and very early appearances by Bob Dylan,"[5] most of whom performed at the epicenter of the scene, Club 47 (later Passim) in Harvard Square, as well as other area venues. Greenbaum's list includes locals like Baez, who lived with her family in Newton and also attended Boston University very briefly, Von Schmidt, the Kweskin band, Taj Mahal, and Tom Rush, who was enrolled in Harvard University. The others named were denizens of Greenwich Village. Greenbaum himself performed in Boston-area coffee houses, including Café Yana, a significant venue on the folk circuit whose roster included Kweskin, the Holy Modal Rounders, and Dylan. In 1965, following a friend's suggestion, he decamped for Southern California.

Jug Band Music: Dr. West's Medicine Show and Junk Band

Once settled in Los Angeles, Greenbaum joined with friends to create Dr. West's Medicine Show and Junk Band, which he has described as a psychedelic jug band. Historically, jug band was "an instrumental ensemble style developed by African Americans from the urban South in the 1920s and 30s as a popular novelty entertainment" that featured energetic, informal musicianship employing a range of home-made instruments such as the jug and washtub bass alongside kazoos, guitars, and banjos.[6] The folk movement of the 1960s saw the revival of the jug band, of which Jim Kweskin's group was the most successful and influential. Greenwich Village-based jug bands included Dave Van Ronk and the Ragtime Jug Stompers and the Even Dozen Jug Band—John Sebastian, later of the Lovin' Spoonful, and Maria D'Amato (later Maria Muldaur), who also played with Kweskin, were among its twelve members.[7]

Given Greenbaum's background as a folk musician and his love of old-time music, it is not surprising that he took the jug band as a model for his new group, but whereas the jug bands on the folk circuit garnered most of their repertoire from the jazz and blues of the 1920s and 1930s, Dr. West's Medicine Show was a vehicle for Greenbaum's own

---

[3] Wayne Jancik, "Norman Greenbaum," *One Hit Wonders: A Musical Revue*, 1997. Available online: http://www.onehitwondersthebook.com/?page_id=12981 (accessed November 9, 2020).
[4] According to an urban legend, Greenbaum performed with The Jim Kweskin Jug Band under the name Bruno Wolf, a rumor that is sometimes presented as fact. Wolf, a founding member of the Kweskin group, is an elusive figure also known as David Simon but apparently is not Greenbaum.
[5] A. J. Wachtel, "Norman Greenbaum," *Music Museum of New England*. Available online: https://www.mmone.org/norman-greenbaum/ (accessed November 13, 2020).
[6] Paul Oliver, "Jug Band," *Grove Music Online*, July 25, 2013. Available online: https://doi.org/10.1093/gmo/9781561592630.article.A2241933 (accessed November 10, 2020).
[7] Danny Kalb, who studied guitar with Van Ronk, and Steve Katz, also a guitarist, were members of the Village Stompers and the Even Dozen Jug Band, respectively. Both would go on to be founding members of the Blues Project in 1965 and both are in the pantheon of Jewish rock musicians.

songwriting, in which he evoked earlier genres and styles.[8] Greenbaum acknowledges the influence of The Jim Kweskin Jug Band, which is described as offering a "mix of folk-blues, old time camp and gonzo humor [that] was easily weird enough for the hippies."[9] Greenbaum aimed for a similar tone, updated for the lysergic era:

> I was Dr. West and I wanted it to be something more than just a band, I wanted to do a show with jokes and stories. I wrote most of the material. We painted our faces and had light shows.[10] We got signed after one audition. You know, it was the start of the flower power generation. Everything was psychedelic.[11]

The word *junk* in the band's name was a pun, but it also referred to the group's propensity to "rub, whack, or blow on such objects as a washtub, whiskey jug, Taiwan finger piano, Tibetan temple block, and their favorite, a 1949 Buick bumper bracket."[12] No less a luminary than Frank Zappa, who had demonstrated the use of a bicycle as a musical instrument on *The Steve Allen Show* in 1963, reportedly enjoyed their jokey theatricality.[13]

Presented with an opportunity to record, Dr. West's Medicine Show issued a single, "The Eggplant that Ate Chicago," in 1966, which reached Number 52 on the *Billboard* Hot 100, following it up with an album of the same title released the next year.[14] Like many of the songs on the album, which opens with "Patent Medicine" to emulate the medicine show theme of their live performances, "The Eggplant That Ate Chicago" is light and humorous, an intentionally goofy take on the familiar monster movie trope of a giant mutant creature devouring a city. Featuring washboard, kazoo, harmonica, and a solo on junk percussion along with "wah wahs" and "wack-a-doos" from Greenbaum and second vocalist Bonnie Zee Wallach, the song evokes an old-fashioned "good timey" feeling similar to Sopwith Camel's "Hello Hello," with which it shared the Hot 100 in December of 1966, though it is more laconic and less camp. In 1968, the group performed two songs in the film *Jigsaw*, including the titular theme, written by

---

[8] Greenbaum wrote all of the songs on the group's album save one, "How Lew Sin Ate," a humorous take on recreational drug use, written by Bonnie Zee Wallach, the group's second singer and kazoo player.
[9] Brett Milano, *The Sound of Our Town: A History of Boston Rock and Roll* (Beverly: Commonwealth Editions, 2007), 37.
[10] Greenbaum has claimed that Dr. West's Medicine Show was one of the first bands in Los Angeles to employ a light show.
[11] Rubin, "'Going to the Place That's the Best.'"
[12] Jancik, "Norman Greenbaum."
[13] Richie Unterberger, "Biography: Dr. West's Medicine Show and Junk Band," *allmusic.com*. Available online: https://www.allmusic.com/artist/dr-wests-medicine-show-junk-band-mn0001589033/biography (accessed November 10, 2020).
[14] The album *The Eggplant that Ate Chicago* was rereleased in 1969 in the United Kingdom and in 1970 in the United States as *Norman Greenbaum with Dr. West's Medicine Show and Junk Band*, presumably to capitalize on the success of "Spirit in the Sky." Whereas the UK rerelease consisted of the entire original album, the US version was missing two songs, including the song after which the earlier album was named. Dr. West made an inexplicable reappearance in 1974 when Greenbaum issued a single, "Nancy Whiskey," which was credited to "Norman Greenbaum (Dr. West's Medicine Show and Junk Band)."

Greenbaum and another former folkie, Barry Kane.[15] Now billed as Dr. West's Medicine Band, the version of the group seen in the film had metamorphosed into a four-man (Bonnie Zee Wallach was not in evidence) psychedelic rock group. The song "Jigsaw," which was released as a single, has the requisite elements to make it a respectable entry for any psych-rock anthology—echo effects, fuzz guitar, portentous lyrics about altered states of mind, and a relatively unusual violin solo—but at this stage, the group was otherwise indistinguishable from the multitudes of minor psychedelic rock bands populating the clubs on the Sunset Strip.

The Genesis of "Spirit in the Sky"

Instability in the membership of Dr. West's Medicine Show, coupled with a desire to play electric music, led Greenbaum to form a rock band to play clubs in Los Angeles, including the storied Troubadour in West Hollywood, where he was approached by the producer Erik Jacobsen, with whom the Lovin' Spoonful had achieved an impressive string of hits in 1965–6 and who also had worked with Sopwith Camel and singer-songwriter Tim Hardin, among others.[16] Jacobsen induced Greenbaum to leave his band and embark on a solo career, signing him to a three-album production deal with Warner/Reprise. Over the course of three months in 1969, they worked on the *Spirit in the Sky* album at Coast Recorders Studios in San Francisco. Joining them were guitarist Russell DaShiell and bassist Doug Killmer, both of whom were associated with the band Crowfoot, drummer Norman Mayell, a fixture on the San Francisco music scene who played with such local groups as Sopwith Camel and Blue Cheer, and the Stovall Sisters, a gospel vocal group from Oakland.

Listening to Greenbaum's acoustic demo for "Spirit in the Sky" enhances one's appreciation of the instrumental and vocal arrangements and studio magic that make the finished product so compelling.[17] Although the demo is at the same medium-fast tempo as the final product (129 bpm) and the song's famous boogie riff is already in place, this performance has the feeling of a country blues being sung on a front porch. The addition of the electric bass guitar playing the riff in unison with the guitar and, especially, Mayell's drumming lock down the song's meter (as against Greenbaum's somewhat freer approach in the demo) and turn it into an irresistible blues shuffle. The addition of handclaps, tambourine, and the Stovall Sisters' call-and-response vocal parts bring distinctive elements of gospel into the song not anticipated in the demo.

---

[15] In 1961 and 1962, Barry Kane was part of a folk duo with Barry McGuire called Barry and Barry. In 1962, both joined The New Christy Minstrels, a large commercially-oriented folk vocal ensemble.

[16] Robert Christgau, in a *New York Times* article titled "Who Makes Singers Great?" (January 18, 1970, D32) singles out Jacobsen's production of Greenbaum's album for praise. Describing Greenbaum as a "wryly talented but somewhat insubstantial songwriter-vocalist," Christgau opines that "Jacobsen has managed to set each song [on the album] individually . . . in the context of an overall sound that embodies Greenbaum's vantage." He concludes: "It is the music which makes the album work, and it is as much Jacobsen's as Greenbaum's."

[17] Norman Greenbaum, "Spirit in the Sky (Demo)," recorded 1969, track 16 on *Spirit in the Sky*, Varèse Sarabande, 2001, compact disc.

Greenbaum played the song's signature fuzz-tone guitar riff on a Fender Telecaster customized with a built-in electronic distortion device created by one of his former Dr. West band mates, rather than a pedal. As Greenbaum recalls, "it was a unique thing. It was a nine-volt battery, a couple of wires, and a switch. The Fender Telecaster played like a regular guitar, but when I wanted to do that, I switched it on."[18] This guitar and its one-of-a-kind device were later lost or stolen and never recovered. The riff itself is a conventional but catchy boogie blues riff similar to the one Canned Heat had used for "On the Road Again," their 1967 hit, which in turn was inspired by John Lee Hooker's "Boogie Chillen" (1948). Greenbaum acknowledges the similarity to Canned Heat and other boogie rock riffs, saying, "I think we all just ripped off the old guys from the 1920s who laid down this beat."[19] He attributes the distinctiveness of his sound to finger-picking, rather than playing with a plectrum. DaShiell developed the lead guitar parts that many subsequent guitarists have sought to emulate when playing the song. "Regarding the 'beep beeps' as I call them, when the producer asked me to play some fills in between the verses, as a joke I said how about something spacey like this. . .. I saw him stand up in the control booth and he said 'that's it! let's record that!' so we did."[20]

According to Greenbaum, "There was resistance to releasing 'Spirit in the Sky' as a single. First of all, it was too long. It's about four minutes.[21] Plus it was so weird.

---

[18] Angie Martoccio, "Norman Greenbaum on 'Spirit in the Sky' at 50: 'The Interest in It Just Doesn't Wane,'" *Rolling Stone*, January 17, 2020. Available online: https://www.rollingstone.com/music/music-features/norman-greenbaum-interview-spirit-in-the-sky-934508/?fbclid=IwAR04Yj1wyF5kEgR6_ZliY-aucJiWI_fXj_CwVlyNiKW6LkiKiIVENKmNRv8 (accessed November 14, 2020).

[19] Ray Shasho, "Exclusive Interview: Norman Greenbaum Reveals the True Origin of "Spirit in the Sky,'" *Classic Rock Here and Now*, December 23, 2011. Available online: http://www.classicrockhereandnow.com/2011/12/exclusive-interview-norman-greenbaum.html (accessed November 11, 2020).

[20] Richard Metzger, "Spirit in the Sky," *Dangerous Minds*, June 27, 2012. Available online: https://dangerousminds.net/comments/spirit_in_the_sky_youve_know_the_song_you_entire_life_here_is_the_music_vid (accessed November 13, 2020).
Here is DaShiell's full explanation of how he achieved his sound on the record from the same source:

> Using a 2-pickup Gibson, set the neck pickup volume to zero, bridge pickup volume to max, with the pickup switch in the middle position (with Gibson wiring this gives you silence in the middle position). Do a string bend, picking the B & E strings together with one hit, just ahead of the beat, then use the pickup switch to kick in the bridge pickup in triplets (6 per bar) as you let the B string bend down two frets.
>
> I mainly used two positions on Spirit, which is in the key of A. For the low position, fret a stationary C note (8th fret) on the E string while bending the B string up to an A note for your starting-position, then pick the two strings together once while the guitar is silent and work the pickup switch as you let the A note bend downwards to a G. For the high position, do the same thing at the 15th fret holding a stationary high G note on the E string while bending down from E to D on the B string.

[21] By 1969, a great many "underground" or "freeform" FM rock stations were happy to play songs longer than four minutes or entire album sides. AM Top 40 stations still wanted songs to be two to three minutes long to fit their formats, however. Many artists catered to this need by issuing two versions of their songs: a longer one that would appear on their album and a shorter radio edit or single version. Canned Heat's "On the Road Again" is a case in point: whereas the album version is nearly five minutes long, the single version is three and a half minutes. Writing in *The New York Times* in 1968, John S. Wilson identifies Richard Harris' rendition of "MacArthur Park" as a

Here's a Jew singing about Jesus with this fuzz box going 'brrrrrr.'"[22] The song was released as a single only after two others failed to chart, but it had been designed from the start as radio fodder. As Greenbaum recalls, "We specifically mixed it on small speakers so it would sound good in a car."[23] Although the song was destined for the Top 40, Greenbaum had a hippie affect that might have played well to the audience for progressive rock radio, and Warner/Reprise split the difference in terms of marketing the song. A radio advertisement in the countercultural style of the time features a stereotyped South Asian male voice backed by classical Indian music inviting the listener to "come with me to Spirit in the Sky and see Norman 'Cosmic' Greenbaum."[24] The "key" to this adventure proves to be the opening riff of the song. An advertisement directed to the trade that appeared in *Billboard* in the issue for February 21, 1970, shares the jokey tone of the radio spot by introducing a singer "formerly known as Blood, Sweat & Greenbaum," but clearly positions the song in the context of Top 40 radio by stating that Bill Gavin, an important radio consultant and programmer, had chosen it as a Hot Tip and mentioning regional radio stations that had programmed it.

The Gospel according to Norman Greenbaum

Greenbaum has cited three sources of inspiration for the lyrics and themes of "Spirit in the Sky." The incident that prompted him to put pen to paper was seeing the country artist Porter Wagoner perform "Pastor's Absent on Vacation" on his television program in 1968. Additionally, he "had come across a greeting card that said 'Spirit in the Sky.' And it was American Indians sitting in front of a tipi, with the fire going and being spiritual towards what they had deemed God, which was a spirit in the sky. I think it was the Hopi." The third source was the television Westerns he had watched as a child.[25]

> Then I started thinking about the Hopi Indians, the pastor's on vacation, and as a kid watching cowboy shows and hearing that the bad guys—when they were dying from a shootout—always wanted to be buried with their shoes on. All this is starting to connect. I said to myself, "Well, I've never written a religious song. I've

---

watershed: a seven-minute song regularly played in its entirety on Top 40 radio ("A 7-Minute Song Is Climbing Fast," *The New York Times*, May 24, 1968, 38). The record label's concern over the length of "Spirit in the Sky" indicates that the song was seen as destined for Top 40 radio rather than the more counter-culturally oriented FM rock radio.

[22] Tom McNichol, "A 'Spirit' from the '60s That Won't Die," *The New York Times*, December 24, 2006. Available online: https://www.nytimes.com/2006/12/24/fashion/24norman.html/ (accessed November 5, 2020).

[23] Shasho, "Exclusive Interview."

[24] "Norman Greenbaum Radio Promo," track 17 on *Spirit in the Sky*, Varèse Sarabande, 2001, compact disc. The use of a South Asian sounding voice in the radio advertisement anticipates one of the stranger turns in the history of "Spirit in the Sky." Gareth Gates's 2003 version features the main cast of *The Kumars at #42*, a very popular BBC television situation comedy about an Indian family living in London. In the video, the song receives a full Bollywood dance treatment.

[25] Greenbaum's reference to Westerns, which unexpectedly makes his song a cousin to Bob Dylan's "Knocking on Heaven's Door," also accounts for the otherwise inexplicable use of a deserted western town as the setting for a 1969 promotional film for "Spirit in the Sky."

written some oddball songs, but some serious songs, I can do that." I just sat down, and it all came together.[26]

Wagoner's "Pastor's Absent on Vacation" is not precisely a song—it is a recitation, essentially a poem or story spoken against background music. Recitations, historically a staple of country music, are usually sentimental, inspirational, or homiletic narratives. Wagoner's recitation is particularly akin to a homily. In rhyming couplets, he tells the story of an old man who goes to his church but discovers it is closed; a sign explains that the pastor has left on vacation. What follows are the old man's reflections on this dereliction of duty that culminate as he imagines arriving at Heaven's gate upon his death only to find a sign explaining that since Jesus is on vacation, Heaven is closed. Greenbaum's song is a direct response to this scenario: "That guy wanted salvation, and the preacher was on vacation! So without thinking about it, I made up for what didn't exist in Wagoner's song: In 'Spirit in the Sky,' the preacher isn't on vacation,"[27] enabling the protagonist to ensure his ultimate standing with the Spirit in the Sky by "having a friend in Jesus."

That Greenbaum wrote and recorded a religiously themed song in 1969 shows he had his finger on the cultural pulse. The late 1960s saw the emergence of the Jesus People movement, sometimes referred to as Jesus Freaks, which Larry Eskridge describes as a "collision between old-time evangelical religion and 1960s American counterculture."[28] He goes on to note that "the Jesus People movement marked the first time that American evangelical youth received a go-ahead to replicate the larger youth culture" rather than being expected to emulate the parent culture.[29] Greenbaum clearly understood the appeal of his song in these terms: "they don't see it as a heavy religious trip being pounded on them by an elder."[30] This movement, whose origins can be traced to the 1967 Human Be-In in San Francisco and subsequent hippie-oriented missions in the Haight-Ashbury district, became by the early 1970s a "widespread evangelical youth culture" that extended across the United States and gained considerable cultural presence and attention in the press.[31] Contemporary Messianic Judaism arose from the same context, as young people whose sense of Jewish identity had been renewed by the events of the Arab-Israeli War in 1967 sought to express this identity in ways that reflected their alignment with radical movements: "The countercultural ethos of authenticity . . . encouraged some to reject the 'gray-flannel-suit Judaism' of their parents."[32] Inspired by the Jesus People, Messianic Judaism adopted charismatic and evangelical strategies to attract this contingent.

---

[26] Martoccio, "Norman Greenbaum on 'Spirit in the Sky' at 50."
[27] Jonathan Cott, "A Space Oddity," *Rolling Stone*, March 20, 1997, 32.
[28] Larry Eskridge, *God's Forever Family: The Jesus People Movement in America* (Oxford: Oxford University Press, 2013), 5.
[29] Ibid., 7.
[30] Quoted in "New Rock Discovers Old-Time Religion and Sends Hymns into the Top 40," *The New York Times*, March 28, 1970, 34.
[31] Eskridge, *God's Forever Family*, 145.
[32] Carol Harris-Shapiro, *Messianic Judaism: A Rabbi's Journey through Religious Change in America* (Boston: Beacon Press, 1999), 26.

These intersections between the youth counterculture of the 1960s and charismatic forms of evangelical Christianity created the setting for an efflorescence of religiously themed rock and pop music in the early 1970s noticeable enough for some to propose the new genre categories of Jesus Rock and God Pop. The evolution of Christian rock and folk music made by and intended for young Evangelicals, and of radio programs to promote this music, was an important development of this period, but religious themes also started to appear in mainstream pop music and on Top 40 radio.[33] Prior to "Spirit in the Sky," the most notable entry into this category was the gospel crossover hit "Oh Happy Day" by the Northern California State Youth Choir, later known as the Edwin Hawkins Singers, which reached Number 2 in June of 1969. Much less successful in terms of US chart placement but still significant was Billy Preston's "That's the Way God Planned It," which reached Number 62 on the Hot 100 in 1969 but received further attention through Preston's performance in the 1972 film of *The Concert for Bangladesh*. Also in 1969, Janis Joplin recorded "Work Me Lord"; "Presence of the Lord" appeared on Blind Faith's album; and the Byrds released "Jesus Is Just Alright," their version of a song first recorded by gospel group the Art Reynolds Singers in 1966 that barely scraped the bottom of the Hot 100 late in the year. The Doobie Brothers experienced greater success with their rendition of the song in 1972. The Byrds had also recorded a version of the Louvin Brothers' "The Christian Life" for their 1968 album *Sweetheart of the Rodeo*.

"Spirit in the Sky" was the harbinger of a spate of radio songs with religious themes in the early 1970s that included, among others, Pacific Gas & Electric Company's "Are You Ready?," the Beatles' "Let It Be," and George Harrison's "My Sweet Lord," all in 1970; two singles from the concept album *Jesus Christ Superstar* in 1970 and 1971; "Put Your Hand in the Hand" by Ocean, a Canadian rock group (1971); "Day by Day" from the original cast album of the musical *Godspell* (1972); and Steeleye Span's "Gaudete," an unexpected hit in the United Kingdom in 1973.[34] Harrison's song, with its refrains of "Hare Krishna" and "Hare Rama," is the only one of these to draw on a religious tradition other than Christianity.

Greenbaum's haphazard combination of Christian theology and Native American religion, both derived from popular cultural sources rather than from direct familiarity, proved to be provocative to some Christians. Curiously, they did not object to his calling the deity the Spirit in the Sky rather than Lord or Father, but they did take exception to his perspective on sin: "Never been a sinner/I never sinned/I got a friend in Jesus." This flies in the face of general Christian belief. As Linda Woodhead suggests, "Christianity across the ages tended to accept the main thrust of an Augustinian interpretation" of the Fall that led to Adam and Eve's expulsion from the Garden of Eden that holds "their actions were utterly sinful . . . their action has corrupted their very nature, and this corruption has been inherited by every member of the human

---

[33] Randall J. Stephens, *The Devil's Music: How Christians Inspired, Condemned, and Embraced Rock 'n' Roll* (Cambridge: Harvard University Press, 2018), 146–89.
[34] A 1971 album titled *Jesus Christ Greatest Hits* on the Rare Earth imprint of Motown Records by songwriter and session pianist Leonard Caston under the name the God Squad included versions of many of the songs mentioned here and others.

race."[35] From this perspective, there is no one who has never sinned, and sinners have no recourse other than to seek salvation through Christ. Greenbaum seems to propose the opposite: that he has a friend in Jesus because he is not a sinner. Greenbaum's Jewishness, which might explain his unorthodox Christian theology, and which was so obvious and important to me, was either lost on his exegetes or led them to suspect he was mocking their beliefs. For his part, Greenbaum insists he was not making fun of Christian tenets, but acknowledges his theological error and attributes it to his orientation toward a different faith. "I did flub it I guess, cause if I was a Christian and was writing from that mindset, I would have said, 'I've been a sinner.' But since I didn't have that upbringing, it never occurred to me that it was wrong."[36]

Many Christian or gospel artists have covered "Spirit in the Sky"; some have chosen to alter the offending lyric. The Christian rock group DC Talk changed it to "You know I'm a sinner/We've all sinned," and such others as Southern rockers The Kentucky Headhunters, Christian artist Jamie Slocum, and the gospel group Five Blind Boys of Alabama made similar changes in their versions. But a great many Christian and gospel artists have not found it necessary to alter the lyrics. These include Dorothy Morrison, the lead singer for the Edwin Hawkins Singers, who recorded a soul version in 1970, and gospel artists like the Stovall Sisters, who had sung backup on Greenbaum's session then released their own version, and the Lee Patterson Singers. A version by Melvin Couch, a Georgia-based gospel music entrepreneur and performer, includes a change in the lyrics that does not alter Greenbaum's original meaning: "I never knew a sinner/Cause I've never sinned." Greenbaum's questionable grasp of theology clearly has not kept his song from being embraced by Christian musicians and their audiences.

Larry Norman, one of the originators of Christian rock, whose biographer has called him "the pied piper of the Jesus Movement,"[37] also chose not to change the song's words, but for a different reason. He recorded the song in 1974 for an album intended as a critique of "the commercial exploitation of Jesus Christ" in popular music in which he included versions of many of the songs mentioned here as well as others by Leon Russell, Jackson Browne, Paul Simon, and Randy Newman.[38] Norman presumably left the lyrics intact to mock the song. His upbeat acoustic version of "Spirit in the Sky," however, is notably humorous, as a singer imitates DaShiell's famous guitar parts vocally. Although Norman intended his version as satire, if one is not aware of his agenda, it can come across primarily as a group of friends enjoying themselves while performing a raucous version of the song.

---

[35] Linda Woodhead, *Christianity: A Very Short Introduction* (Oxford: Oxford University Press, 2004), 27.
[36] Grant Britt, "Norman Greenbaum, 'Spirit in the Sky,'" *American Songwriter*, 2013. Available online: https://americansongwriter.com/behind-song-norman-greenbaum-spirit-sky/ (accessed November 11, 2020).
[37] Rebecca Au-Mullaney, "Larry Norman, the Pied Piper of the Jesus Movement," *The King's College*, April 2, 2018. Available online: https://www.tkc.edu/stories/larry-norman-pied-piper-jesus-movement/ (accessed November 22, 2020).
[38] Larry Norman, Liner Notes, *Streams of White Light into Darkened Corners* (AB Records, vinyl LP, 1977).

Aftermath

Touring in support of his hit record, Greenbaum opened for the Doors, the Moody Blues, Grand Funk Railroad, Delaney and Bonnie, John Mayall, and Commander Cody and His Lost Planet Airmen, and headlined at the Matrix in San Francisco. Flush with success, Greenbaum installed his young family on a ranch in Petaluma, California, where he raised goats. "People wanted another 'Spirit in the Sky' from me, and it couldn't be," he has said. "That song was too special."[39] His follow-up single, the boisterous "Canned Ham," which reached Number 46 on the *Billboard* Hot 100, is in a very different vein, closer in its whimsy and its celebration of the simple things to his songs for Dr. West's Medicine Show than to "Spirit in the Sky." To me, it seemed just the right waggish gesture that the Jewish musician who put out a song about Jesus would next produce a joyful tribute to a distinctly non-kosher food product. Greenbaum's subsequent single, "California Earthquake," opens with a heavy fuzz guitar, but did not replicate his earlier accomplishment, charting at only Number 93 in 1971. His three-album deal with Warner/Reprise yielded *Back Home Again* in 1970 and *Petaluma* in 1972, both employing the same musicians with whom he had worked on *Spirit in the Sky*. *Petaluma*, a charming paean to small-town, rural life, saw Greenbaum return to his musical roots in acoustic folk and old-time music with the help of Ry Cooder on mandolin and slide guitar and, on washtub and jug, Fritz Richmond, who had been a founding member of The Jim Kweskin Jug Band.

By 1973, Greenbaum's career in music was effectively over, as was his life as a goat rancher. He withdrew from the public eye, found employment as a short-order cook, and worked his way up to sous chef positions in restaurants in the San Francisco area. In 1987, "Spirit in the Sky" appeared on the soundtrack of the film *Maid to Order*, the beginning of the song's second life. After the song was used prominently in *Apollo 13* in 1995, the record label Varèse-Sarabande released a compilation of Greenbaum's music from Dr. West on, and went on to reissue the *Spirit in the Sky* album on compact disc in 2001. The song has appeared regularly in films, television programs, and advertisements, providing Greenbaum with a modest living.

"Spirit in the Sky" is often used as "a sort of signpost for a particular period in American popular culture,"[40] as, for example, when Wayne and Garth begin their training with a veteran roadie in *Wayne's World 2* (1993). It is also often used to augment peak experiences with quasi-spiritual dimensions, such as the ascent of Apollo 13. Nike used the song both in this way and for its religious resonance in its 2006 commercial "Briscoe High Game Day," one in a series of narrative advertisements about a fictional high school football team. "Spirit in the Sky" underscores the entire commercial, which begins in a classroom on game day and ends on the football field. The action is timed to the song such that when Greenbaum is first heard invoking Jesus, the scene shows the team kneeling in prayer prior to the game. The chorus corresponds with the team's winning of the game.

---

[39] Cott, "Space Oddity."
[40] Ibid.

Whether or not Norman Greenbaum should be considered a "one-hit wonder" is an open question that hinges partly on how one defines a hit. Arguably, he was a one-hit wonder twice, since both he and Dr. West's Medicine Show and Junk Band are often described this way. Although "Spirit in the Sky" was his only Top 10 hit, he reached the charts both earlier with Dr. West's Medicine Show and Junk Band's "The Eggplant That Ate Chicago" and later with "Canned Ham" and "California Earthquake." He also achieved regional airplay with "Jubilee" and "I. J. Foxx," and had three albums on a major label as a solo artist. Although he distanced himself from the hit record that "made my life and destroyed my life at the same moment,"[41] declaring in the song "Grade A Barn" on *Petaluma* that his life on the farm is "such a long way from 'Spirit in the Sky,'" Greenbaum subsequently embraced his identity as "the guy who did 'Spirit in the Sky.'" He has sat agreeably for interviews about the song many times over the years after refusing to do so in the early 1970s. His website is called spiritinthesky.com; his Facebook handle is "Norman Spirit Greenbaum." Through the website, he sells CDs that reflect his entire musical career, while the other merchandise he offers—hats, bags, and shirts—all display "Spirit in the Sky" logos.

In 2019, the City of Malden commissioned Jesse Melanson, an artist based in Austin, Texas, to make a mural commemorating the fiftieth anniversary of "Spirit in the Sky." At the ribbon-cutting ceremony, Greenbaum, then seventy-seven years old, led the crowd in a singalong. *Jewish Boston* reported on his remarks at the podium:

"As a musician and young kid, we dream of writing songs," he mused at the mic. "We hope that someone will like them. We have aspirations for getting a band together, hopefully a gig or two, getting someone to manage us, getting us a record contract. And when all that happened for me, I thought that was the greatest thing ever."

He paused. "This," he said to the room, "might have topped it."[42]

References

Au-Mullaney, Rebecca (2018), "Larry Norman, the Pied Piper of the Jesus Movement," *The King's College*, April 2, 2018. Available online: https://www.tkc.edu/stories/larry-norman-pied-piper-jesus-movement/ (accessed November 22, 2020).

Britt, Grant (2013), "Norman Greenbaum, 'Spirit in the Sky.'" *American Songwriter*. Available online: https://americansongwriter.com/behind-song-norman-greenbaum-spirit-sky/ (accessed November 11, 2020).

Christgau, Robert (1970), "Who Makes Singers Great?" *The New York Times*, January 18, 1970. Available online: https://www.nytimes.com/1970/01/18/archives/who-makes-singers-great.html. (accessed November 16, 2020).

---

[41] Ibid.
[42] Rick Tenorio, "The Gospel According to Greenbaum," *Jewish Journal*, October 25, 2019. Available online: https://jewishjournal.org/2019/10/24/the-gospel-according-to-greenbaum/ (accessed November 10, 2020).

Cott, Jonathan (1997), "A Space Oddity," *Rolling Stone*, March 20, 1997.
Eskridge, Larry (2013), *God's Forever Family: The Jesus People Movement in America*, Oxford: Oxford University Press.
Greenbaum, Norman (1969), *Spirit in the Sky*. Recorded 1969. Varèse Sarabande, compact disc, 2001.
Harris-Shapiro, Carol (1999), *Messianic Judaism: A Rabbi's Journey Through Religious Change in America*. Boston: Beacon Press.
Jancik, Wayne (1997), "Norman Greenbaum," *One Hit Wonders: A Musical Revue*. Available online: http://www.onehitwondersthebook.com/?page_id=12981 (accessed November 8, 2020).
Martoccio, Angie, (2020), "Norman Greenbaum on 'Spirit in the Sky' at 50: 'The Interest in It Just Doesn't Wane.'" *Rolling Stone*, January 17, 2020. Available online: https://www.rollingstone.com/music/music-features/norman-greenbaum-interview-spirit-in-the-sky-934508/?fbclid=IwAR04Yj1wyF5kEgR6_ZliY-aucJiWI_fXj_CwVlyNiKW6LkiKiIVENKmNRv8 (accessed November 14, 2020).
McNichol, Tom (2006), "A 'Spirit' From the '60s That Won't Die." *The New York Times*, December 24, 2006 (accessed November 5, 2020).
Metzger, Richard (2012), "Spirit in the Sky," *Dangerous Minds*, June 27, 2012. Available online: https://dangerousminds.net/comments/spirit_in_the_sky_youve_know_the_song_you_entire_life_here_is_the_music_vid (accessed September 25, 2021).
Milano, Brett (2007), *The Sound of Our Town: A History of Boston Rock and Roll*. Beverly: Commonwealth Editions.
"New Rock Discovers Old-Time Religion and Sends Hymns Into the Top 40." *The New York Times*, March 28, 1970. Available online: https://www.nytimes.com/1970/03/28/archives/new-rock-discovers-oldtime-religion-and-sends-hymns-into-the-top-40.html (accessed November 19, 2020).
Norman, Larry. *Streams of White Light into Darkened Corners*. Released 1977. AB Records, vinyl LP.
Oliver, Paul (2013), "Jug Band," *Grove Music Online*, July 25, 2013. Available online: https://doi.org/10.1093/gmo/9781561592630.article.A2241933 (accessed November 10, 2020).
Rubin, Jason M. (2019), "'Going to the Place That's the Best' — Norman Greenbaum Returns Home to Malden," *The Arts Fuse*, October 27, 2019. Available online: https://artsfuse.org/189372/music-feature-going-to-the-place-thats-the-best-norman-greenbaum-returns-home-to-malden/ (November 12, 2020).
Shasho, Ray (2011), "Exclusive Interview: Norman Greenbaum Reveals the True Origin of "Spirit in the Sky."" *Classic Rock Here and Now*, December 23, 2011. http://www.classicrockhereandnow.com/2011/12/exclusive-interview-norman-greenbaum.html (November 10, 2020).
Stephens, Randall J. (2018), *The Devil's Music: How Christians Inspired, Condemned, and Embraced Rock 'n' Roll*, Cambridge, MA: Harvard University Press.
Tenorio, Rick (2019), "The Gospel According to Greenbaum," *Jewish Journal*, October 25, 2019. Available online: https://jewishjournal.org/2019/10/24/the-gospel-according-to-greenbaum/ (November 11, 2020).
Unterberger, Richie, "Biography: Dr. West's Medicine Show and Junk Band," *allmusic.com*. Available online: https://www.allmusic.com/artist/dr-wests-medicine-show-junk-band-mn0001589033/biography (accessed November 10, 2020).

Wachtel, A. J. (2020), "Norman Greenbaum," *Music Museum of New England*. Available online: https://www.mmone.org/norman-greenbaum/ (accessed November 13, 2020).
Wilson, John S. (1968), "A 7-Minute Song is Climbing Fast," *The New York Times*, May 24, 1968. https://www.nytimes.com/1968/05/24/archives/a-7minute-song-is-climbing-fast-macarthur-park-is-played-on-radio.html. Accessed November 17, 2020.
Woodhead, Linda (2004), *Christianity: A Very Short Introduction*. Oxford: Oxford University Press.

6

The Archies, "Sugar Sugar" (1969)

Jon Stewart

> . . . the fact is that "Sugar Sugar" is great Rock 'n' Roll, and there's nothing rebellious about that at all. I mean that's right from the belly and heart of capitalism.[1]

It is perhaps unfair to label The Archies as one-hit wonders, yet "Sugar Sugar" remains their best-known release by a huge margin. In late 1969 it spent four weeks at number one on the United States's *Billboard* Hot 100 and eight weeks at Number 1 in the British singles chart, before topping the end-of-year rundowns in both countries, where it eclipsed major releases by The Beatles ("Get Back"), the Rolling Stones ("Honky Tonk Women"), and Frank Sinatra ("My Way"). "Sugar Sugar" eventually became a hit in around twenty other territories worldwide. What follows examines the song from two perspectives. The first explains how a group of session musicians on a Saturday morning children's television show shattered the creative restraints of Bubblegum Pop. The second presents "Sugar Sugar" as a case study in evolutionary psychology, in which the lyric's central theme (sweetness as a metaphor for romantic love) articulates a universal human desire with profound existential implications.

The Archies: From Artifice to Art

Theodor Adorno's famous derogation of the culture industry centered on his critique of repetition, standardization, and interchangeability in mass-market products.[2] In that context The Archies were a conspicuously superficial group. Their creator, legendary talent manager Don Kirschner, was first hired by the producers of NBC TV's musical situation comedy show *The Monkees*. As the publisher for important songwriters

---

[1] Lester Bangs, "Lester Bangs Interview with Sue Mathews (May-13-1980) PART 1/Side 1," *cousincreep blog*. Available online: https://soundcloud.com/cousincreep/lester-bangs-interview-with (accessed July 1, 2021).
[2] Theodor Adorno, "On Popular Music," *Studies in Philosophy and Social Science* 9 (1941): 17–48.

from the Brill Building scene such as Carole King, Gerry Goffin, Neil Diamond, and Phil Spector, he was well-positioned to source a string of potential hit singles for the production. The show's instant success helped establish the kind of commercial collaboration between media companies and the popular music industry familiar in contemporary talent competitions and reality TV series such as *American Idol* and *The X-Factor*, where the process of manufacturing artists is now so transparent it has become the entire purpose of the program. Yet *The Monkees* still maintained a patina of authenticity, which became apparent when Kirschner was dismissed before the show's second season after the band insisted on performing their own compositions. This incident provided the impetus for Kirschner's involvement in a CBS TV cartoon show, in which the animated performers eliminated any conceivable challenges posed by troublesome human actors, principally because they didn't need paying and they couldn't rebel. As such The Archies became the ultimate manufactured cultural commodity: a group conceptualized and realized entirely as artifice—one that never appeared on stage together, never toured or conducted a single media interview, yet somehow achieved an international smash hit (Figure 6.1).

The Saturday morning children's cartoon that hosted the band, *The Archie Show*, was itself an entirely formulaic product—the final link in a chain of productions that recycled familiar characters in idealized locations. It starred Archie Andrews as a typical all-American teenager who founded a pop group with his high school friends in the fictional small-town of Riverdale. The show was drawn from the well-known *Archie Comics*, a publication that told the wider story of Andrews and his pals. The *Archie*

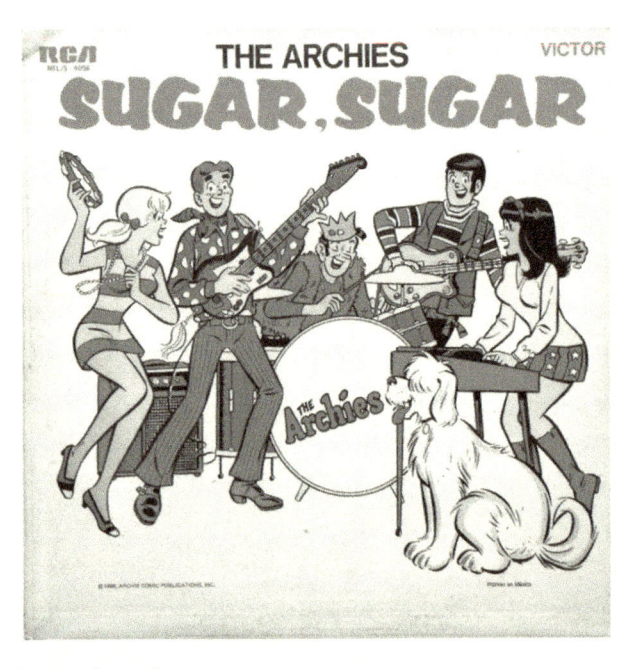

Figure 6.1 A virtual smash.

Comics was, in turn, inspired by a pre-existing "everyman" narrative: the extraordinarily popular Andy Hardy movies, which presented nostalgic portrayals of family life in the late 1930s and early 1940s and made Mickey Rooney the biggest Hollywood star of his generation. Like many standardized television sitcoms, every episode of *The Archie Show* was structured around a familiar routine: a self-contained story featuring Archie was followed by a weekly dance segment, then a musical performance from the band. Each closed with a skit from The Archies' drummer Jughead Jones and a second self-contained Archie story. *The Archie Show* also became known for its prolific use of a popular contrivance in the commercial television industry: canned laughter. This was inspired by primetime series such as *The Flintstones* and *The Jetsons*, which had no possibility of audience feedback because they were filmed in stop-motion animation, so added a laugh track to imitate the atmosphere of a live production. As the first Saturday morning cartoon to employ this device, *The Archie Show* established a tradition in children's television that continued for the next two decades in programs such as *Scooby-Doo, Where Are You!*—which, incidentally, derived its name from The Archies' single "Feelin' So Good (S.K.O.O.B.Y.-D.O.O.)."

As *The Archie Show*'s most enduring cultural artifact, "Sugar Sugar" itself provides a microcosm of the producers' strategy of artful repetition. This occurs in the words of the title and the alternating "honey honey" phrase in the first line of the chorus. It also defines the song's arrangement via alternating A sections and B sections where a short four-bar verse is followed by two eight-bar choruses, one eight-bar verse, two eight-bar choruses, one eight-bar verse, then four eight-bar choruses. As a result, the song's catchy refrain repeats a total of eight times and constitutes sixty-four of the song's eighty-four bars. Despite the obvious duplication, this is still an economical composition. No section is wasted or underdeveloped, and by the time it progresses into the final run of choruses, the song is already in a playout mode, where each of the final four sections features a different improvised vocal line. The chord sequence in the chorus also models this creative repetitiveness. The four bars of alternating tonic and sub-dominant chords I-IV-I-IV (for those who wish to strum along, this is counted as "D234 / G234 / D234 / G234") are followed by an injection of energy as the same pattern runs once more in double time for a single bar of I-IV chords with just two beats each (which is counted as "D2G4"). Finally, under a ringing high note, an octave vocal leap from D to D during the last two syllables of the "candy girl" hook, the accompaniment shifts from sub-dominant to dominant (the V chord, for a count of "A234") before ending on a classic I-IV-V turnaround phrase ("D234 / G2A4"). With the exception of two passing notes that fall on the fourth degree (G) for the words "oh" and "you," the chorus melody is drawn entirely from the major pentatonic scale (D, E, F#, A, B), a familiar strategy in the simplest and catchiest of pop tunes.

The straightforward arrangement of "Sugar Sugar" allows plenty of space for an extraordinarily upbeat interpretation. The result is a recording so infectious it effectively transforms contrivance into art form. The vocalists' delivery aligns so completely with the intent of the songwriters their objective could not be more palpable: this is a song that celebrates the exhilaration of teenage romance. It is important to note, however, that the lyrics do not exhibit a lustful desire. That would not be appropriate given the age of the television audience. In keeping with the idealized all-American family setting, the protagonists declare their love for each other, sing about kissing rather than sex, express their wonderment, and imply they are embarking on a lifelong relationship not a short-lived encounter. (The original *Archie Comics* are more overtly suggestive, yet even here Archie still went on to marry his childhood sweetheart.) What is often taken for the song's most erotic image, a lyric appropriated by Def Leppard for the title of their hit single "Pour Some Sugar on Me," was intended only as an innocent metaphor. Brill Building songwriter Toni Wine, who sang the line, recalls it signified nothing other than "people kissing each other . . . dogs licking you . . . sugar is just a form of love."[3]

The song's unashamed positivity is reinforced by the impeccable musicianship of top session players whose performance is snappy and very much "in the pocket," making "Sugar Sugar" extremely danceable as a result. The emphasis on the first syllable of the title word "Sugar" on the downbeat of each chorus, and the prominent James Jamerson-style bass groove that syncopates around the noticeably straightforward drums, punctuated by only the briefest Motown "pick up" fills, imbue it with the subtle funk of classic library music recordings from the same era. After establishing the overall feel and perfecting Chuck Rainey's bassline, the musicians were encouraged to enjoy themselves: "It just was a very easy session . . . a fun session . . . a blast. We just knew that something huge was going to happen," confirmed Wine—adding that a friend who came to meet her for lunch that day, songwriter Ray Stevens, ended up contributing to the hand claps.[4] This and other percussion parts, such as the loud shaker throughout, and the tambourine that lifts each repeat chorus section, contribute significantly to the lively atmosphere. This child-friendly palette is enhanced by an unusually soft acoustic guitar, strummed by a cardboard matchbook after Andy Kim broke his only plectrum, and the complete absence of the trebly electric guitar that usually defined the band's sound.[5] The classic Bubblegum Pop keyboard riff in the chorus, commonly thought to be a Vox Continental transistor organ with the drawbars set to imitate a bassoon or English horn, was doubled with the bright woody attack of a xylophone to compliment the song's bouncy infectiousness.

It is, of course, easy to criticize the naïve optimism of Bubblegum Pop. As sometimes happens with music genres, its name was coined in affection but repeated as slur.[6] "Sugar Sugar"'s composers, Jeff Barry and Andy Kim, recalled their frustration at the reluctance of radio station programmers to air the track, which ran defiantly against the spirit of the times: "It was 1969—the year of Woodstock. The year of underground music. Really the birth of FM."[7] Over the years since then, Adorno's famous critique of

---

[3] Quoted in "Toni Wine," *Songfacts Interview* (2007: https://www.songfacts.com/blog/interviews/toni-wine).

[4] Ibid.

[5] Laura Pinto, "'Sugar, Sugar' by The Archies: Still Sweet after 45 Years," *Laura's Oldies Room* (2014). Available online: https://oldiesconnection.wordpress.com/2014/09/20/sugar-sugar-by-the-archies-still-sweet-after-45-years/ (accessed July 1, 2021).

[6] David Smay and Kim Cooper, *Bubblegum Music Is the Naked Truth* (Los Angeles: Feral House, 2001), 5.

[7] Prato, "Andy Kim," *Songfacts Interview* (2017). Available online: https://www.songfacts.com/blog/interviews/andy-kim (accessed July 1, 2021).

assembly line production houses, such as the Brill Building where Barry and Kim first met, morphed into a "rockism versus poptimism" debate in the broadsheets and the blogosphere during the early 2000s. Clearly the innocent joy of "Sugar Sugar" chafes against the entrenched cynicism of more "authentic" forms of music whose primary purpose is confronting established power structures. From this perspective the idealized vision of youthful courtship portrayed by The Archies is not just unrealistic; it is also morally vacuous. Then again, perhaps the great achievement of "Sugar Sugar" was to demonstrate that even manufactured artists can have value if their output is well crafted and skillfully executed. The "rockism versus poptimism" dispute seems trite when compared to the bitter culture war now raging across social and mainstream media, which has become a battleground between the two irreconcilable paradigms of biological essentialism and social justice. Intriguingly, "Sugar Sugar" also raises questions pertinent to this discourse, too.

"Sugar Sugar" and Evolutionary Psychology

Natural selection was once a controversial thesis but Charles Darwin's "dangerous idea" is now widely accepted as the explanation for all life on earth. Today there is effectively no meaningful biology other than evolutionary biology.[8] Darwin closed *On the Origin of Species* with the prediction that his revolutionary proposal would also influence other subject areas, anticipating what we now know as evolutionary psychology: "In the distant future I see open fields for far more important researches. Psychology will be based on a new foundation, that of the necessary acquirement of each mental power and capacity by gradation."[9] Yet this branch of his theory has struggled to gain widespread approval, in part because it has never shaken off an unfortunate association with reactionary ideology.

In the 1970s, Pulitzer Prize–winning biologist E. O. Wilson attempted to synthesize evolution and sociology from the perspective of progressive secular humanism,[10] but his work met with such resistance that it was almost thirty years before evolutionary psychology finally coalesced into a coherent field. The claim that modern behaviors are molded by long-standing evolutionary pressures remained vigorously contested throughout that period. Interestingly, some of this debate revolved around the central metaphor of "Sugar Sugar": the origins of the human "sweet tooth." Stephen Jay Gould suggested there was no real neurological or paleontological evidence for such phenomena, dismissing the entire field of evolutionary psychology with the memorable phrase "just-so stories."[11] Nonetheless, over the decades that followed researchers in

---

[8] See Daniel C. Dennett, *Darwin's Dangerous Idea: Evolution and the Meanings of Life* (New York: Simon & Schuster, 1995) and Theodosius Dobzhansky, "Nothing in Biology Makes Sense Except in the Light of Evolution," *The American Biology Teacher* 35, no. 3 (1973): 125–9.
[9] Charles Darwin, *On the Origin of Species by Means of Natural Selection, or, The Preservation of Favoured Races in the Struggle For Life* (London: J. Murray, 1859), 488.
[10] E. O. Wilson, *Sociobiology: The New Synthesis* (Cambridge, MA: Harvard University Press, 1975).
[11] See his Stephen Jay Gould, "Sociobiology: The Art of Storytelling," *New Scientist* 80, no. 1129 (1978): 530–3 and "Evolution: The Pleasures of Pluralism," *New York Review of Books*, June 26, 1997: 47–52.

bioarchaeology and biocultural anthropology established solid connections between prehistoric diets and current food consumption. The "mismatch hypothesis," which posits that modern humans carry maladapted behavioral traits from ancient environments, is now our most credible explanation for the contemporary obesity and diabetes epidemic.[12]

That culture is a sociobiological phenomenon found in hunter gatherer communities, that it conferred group survival advantages in early hominins, and that it can even be detected among other species of primate, is a far less contentious assertion today. A plethora of research demonstrates the evolutionary roots of universal human characteristics such as homicidal urges, disgust responses, incest taboos, and sexual preferences.[13] There is even a growing body of evidence for common practices in cultural forms such as music.[14] Evolutionary psychology is now a robust and expanding field with a raft of well-established journals, handbooks, and anthologies. Some corners of the discipline remain sequestered by conservative voices, yet others have inspired scholarship in more liberal subfields such as literary Darwinism and feminist evolutionary psychology.[15] Of course the suggestion of a causal relationship between evolution and culture brings an unwelcome challenge to orthodox constructivism in cultural and social studies, not least because this paradigm has done so much to expose structural inequities and empower marginalized communities. Yet if evolutionary psychology cannot be dismantled or ignored, can it be accommodated in a progressive manner? Every new theoretical approach to popular music brings its own rewards, and interdisciplinarity in science and the arts has already inspired useful research clusters in psychoacoustics, transhumanism, music technology, and the digital dissemination of music. Pop songs explore so many visceral experiences there must be some overlap with universal human preferences. "Sugar Sugar" is particularly interesting here because it synthesizes two basic existential necessities: food and procreation.

An evolutionary understanding of any cultural phenomenon, including the lyrics of "Sugar Sugar," begins with the distinction between *proximate* and *ultimate* explanations. *Proximate* explanations are those concerned with the appeal of an individual artifact, in this instance the superficial analogy of sweetness-as-reward that forms the central

---

[12] For more see G. J. Armelagos, "The Omnivore's Dilemma. The Evolution of the Brain and the Determinants of Food Choice," *Journal of Anthropological Research* 66, no. 2 (2010): 161–86; Anthony J. Basile, David B. Schwartz, Joseph Rigdon, and Hamilton Stapell, "Status of Evolutionary Medicine within the Field of Nutrition and Dietetics: A Survey of Professionals and Students," *Evolution, Medicine, and Public Health* 1 (2018): 201–10; Daniel Lieberman, *The Story of the Human Body: Evolution, Health, and Disease* (New York: Pantheon Books, 2013); and Staffan Lindeberg, "Paleolithic Diets as a Model for Prevention and Treatment of Western Disease," *American Journal of Human Biology* 24, no. 2 (2012): 110–15.

[13] For example, David Buss, *Evolutionary Psychology: The New Science of the Mind* (London: Routledge, 2016).

[14] For example, Samuel A. Mehr, Manvir Singh, Dean Knox, Daniel M. Ketter, Daniel Pickens-Jones, S. Atwood, Christopher Lucas, Nori Jacoby, Alena A. Egner, Erin J. Hopkins, Rhea M. Howard, Joshua K. Hartshorne, Mariela V. Jennings, Jan Simson, Constance M. Bainbridge, Steven Pinker, Timothy J. O'Donnell, Max M. Krasnow, and Luke Glowacki, "Universality and Diversity in Human Song," *Science* 366, no. 6468 (2019): eaax0868.

[15] See for example Anne Campbell, *A Mind of Her Own: The Evolutionary Psychology of Women* (Oxford: Oxford University Press, 2013).

metaphor in the song. In the proximate explanation, The Archies use "sugar" and "honey" as terms of endearment because sweet foods induce overwhelming feelings comparable to that of romantic love. *Ultimate* explanations look for underlying motivations and preferences at a holistic level, those that might be shared by an entire population. Why things happen, rather than what happens. The underlying reason why the taste of sugar or honey is comparable to the prospect of a romantic encounter is because both trigger our internal reward systems. This is the *ultimate* explanation, emotional responses that evolved over millions of years under the existential pressures of natural selection. The love expressed in "Sugar Sugar" encourages pair-bonding just as lust facilitates the replication of our genes. None of us would be here had our ancestors not been driven to procreate and, bizarrely, every human being alive today is the end result of an unbroken chain of reproduction dating back to a single-celled bacterium that emerged over three billion years ago. The food cravings expressed in the song encourage nutrition just as their antithesis, disgust, protects us against pathogens. This heightened sensitivity toward energy-rich nourishment conferred a significant survival advantage in an evolutionary landscape where such foods were scarce and unimaginably difficult to obtain, and where famine was a seasonal threat. By increasing the prospect of survival into adulthood these dietary preferences also increased the prospect of successful procreation, and this cycle—enacted across hundreds of thousands of generations—is precisely why courtship and carbohydrates remain unshakeable human desires.

Humanities scholars often overlook the fact that the whole basis of their subject area, the last five millennia of recorded human activity, is immaterial in the evolutionary timescale. Yet it is no coincidence that gathering honey, the earliest form of sugar, is clearly depicted in one of our oldest artifacts—the 9,000-year-old cave paintings in the *Cuevas de la Araña* near Valencia, Spain. Indeed, the sentiments expressed in "Sugar Sugar" have a long cultural and economic heritage. Honey and bees were associated with money, medicine, royalty, and deities in ancient Greece, Rome, and Egypt, while Yahweh led the Israelites to the land of "milk and honey" in the Old Testament book of Exodus. References abound in premodern and early modern English literature, too. Geoffrey Chaucer's *Miller's Tale* contained such erotic similes as "her mouth was sweet as ale and honey" while Shakespeare's plays and sonnets displayed a keen familiarity with bee-keeping lore.[16] Sugar first came to Europe as an expensive import from Caribbean slave plantations, a commodity equal in value to the Asian spice trade. Cheap domestic supplies only became available after the cultivation of beet, at which point sugar became universally popular as a complement to the bitter taste of coffee, tea, and chocolate—fashionable hot beverages also imported from the New World. As food production industrialized during the twentieth century, sugar became the prime ingredient in cold sodas such as coca-cola and lemonade, products often marketed toward children alongside the breakfast cereal and confectionary commercials that punctuated *The Archie Show* on Saturday mornings. This had consequences beyond

---

[16] See Richard Grinnell, "Shakespeare's Keeping of Bees," *ISLE: Interdisciplinary Studies in Literature and Environment* 23, no. 4 (2016): 835–54.

the near ruination of human dentition, and two centuries after the abolition of the transatlantic slave trade, cane plantations now contribute to deforestation and ecological crises across the global south. Modern commercial sugar production offers a striking comparison with petroleum: one provides humans with energy while the other fuels machines, and both remain among the most heavily traded commodities in the globalized capitalist economy.

The Archie Show segment for the performance of "Sugar Sugar" begins at Riverdale Carnival's kissing booth, where Veronica and Betty from the band are selling "sugar candy kisses . . . and real ones too" for $1 at an impressive-looking sweet stand heavily laden with confectionary. This vignette establishes the link between sugar and romantic desire before the song begins, and it continues as a recurring comedic device when different band members return to the booth for smooches during The Archies' rendition. Sugar metaphors are multi-layered throughout the lyric. Kisses from the "candy girl" are "sweet" like the "summer sunshine." That same summer sun, of course, also nourishes the flowers visited by bees to make the "honey honey" that alternates as a term of endearment with the song's "Sugar Sugar" title phrase. The instant hit and empty calories offered by processed carbohydrates are also indicated in the style of music The Archies play, Bubblegum Pop, where several associated artists employed similar metaphors. The song "Yummy Yummy Yummy," for example, was recorded by both Ohio Express and the 1910 Fruitgum Company. Sweetness remains a surprisingly common metaphor for the rewarding experience of a loving relationship in classic compositions from almost every pop genre. Notable examples include James Taylor's "How Sweet It Is (To Be Loved by You)" or Anita Baker's "Sweet Love." It has also been used to convey overt sexual desire (Nina Simone's "I Want a Little Sugar in My Bowl," The Runaways "Cherry Bomb"), narcotics (The Jesus and Mary Chain's "Just Like Honey" or "Psychocandy"), and the irresistible lure of transgressive acts (Chuck Berry's "Sweet Little Sixteen," Little Richard's "Tutti Frutti," or the Rolling Stones' "Brown Sugar"). Sometimes, although only very occasionally, artists even write about confectionary (such as The Beatles' "Savoy Truffle").

"Sugar Sugar" is a repetitious children's song performed by the most conspicuously manufactured band of the 1960s and, at the same time, a genuinely creative artwork that transcends the limitations of its genre. Its central metaphor synthesizes two elemental human appetites found in all cultures that reach back far beyond our known history. Evolutionary psychologists regard written and recorded artifacts as an archive of the psyche, a repository for our deep-seated motivations, and song lyrics are no exception to this rule. Might the throwaway candor of Bubblegum Pop constitute a new set of research data here? As every archaeologist knows, the waste material disposed of in an ancient midden can be just as informative as any hoard of precious metal. For these reasons and more, the spontaneous abandon captured in this simple composition is pure pop gold. As Lou Reed famously conceded: "I wish I'd written it."[17]

---

[17] Lester Bangs, "Lou Reed: A Deaf Mute in a Telephone Booth," *Let It Rock*, November 1973. Available online: https://www.rocksbackpages.com/Library/Article/lou-reed-a-deaf-mute-in-a-telephone-booth (accessed July 1, 2021).

References

Adorno, T. W. (1941), "On Popular Music, " *Studies in Philosophy and Social Science*, 9: 17–48.

Armelagos, G. J. (2010), "The Omnivore's Dilemma. The Evolution of the Brain and the Determinants of Food Choice," *Journal of Anthropological Research*, 66 (2): 161–86.

Bangs, L. (1973), "Lou Reed: A Deaf Mute in a Telephone Booth," *Let It Rock*, November 1973. Available online: https://www.rocksbackpages.com/Library/Article/lou-reed-a-deaf-mute-in-a-telephone-booth (accessed July 1, 2021).

Bangs, L. (1980), "Lester Bangs Interview with Sue Mathews (May-13-1980) PART 1/Side 1," *cousincreep blog*. Available online: https://soundcloud.com/cousincreep/lester-bangs-interview-with (accessed July 1, 2021).

Basile, A. J., D. B. Schwartz, J. Rigdon and H. Stapell (2018), "Status of Evolutionary Medicine within the Field of Nutrition and Dietetics: A Survey of Professionals and Students," *Evolution, Medicine, and Public Health*, 1: 201–10.

Buss, D. (2016), *Evolutionary Psychology: The New Science of the Mind*, London: Routledge.

Campbell, A. (2013), *A Mind of Her Own: The Evolutionary Psychology of Women*, Oxford: Oxford University Press.

Cooper, C. and K. Smay (2001), *Bubblegum Music is the Naked Truth*, Los Angeles: Feral House.

Darwin, C. (1859), *On the Origin of Species by Means of Natural Selection, or, The Preservation of Favoured Races in the Struggle For Life*, London: J. Murray.

Dennett, D. C. (1995), *Darwin's Dangerous Idea: Evolution and the Meanings of Life*, New York: Simon & Schuster.

Dobzhansky, T. (1973), "Nothing in Biology Makes Sense Except in the Light of Evolution," *The American Biology Teacher*, 35 (3): 125–9.

Gould, S. J. (1978), "Sociobiology: The Art of Storytelling," *New Scientist*, 80 (1129): 530–33.

Gould, S. J. (1997), "Evolution: The Pleasures of Pluralism," *New York Review of Books*, June 26. 47–52. https://www.nybooks.com/articles/1997/06/26/evolution-the-pleasures-of-pluralism/ (accessed September 5, 2021).

Grinnell, R. (2016), "Shakespeare's Keeping of Bees," *ISLE: Interdisciplinary Studies in Literature and Environment*, 23 (4): 835–54.

Lieberman, D. (2013), *The Story of the Human Body: Evolution, Health, and Disease*, New York: Pantheon Books.

Lindeberg, S. (2012), "Paleolithic Diets as a Model for Prevention and Treatment of Western Disease," *American Journal of Human Biology*, 24 (2): 110–15.

Mehr, S. A., M. Singh, D. Knox, D. M. Ketter, D. Pickens-Jones, S. Atwood, C. Lucas, N. Jacoby, A. A. Egner, E. J. Hopkins, R. M. Howard, J. K. Hartshorne, M. V. Jennings, J. Simson, C. M. Bainbridge, S. Pinker, T. J. O'Donnell, M. M. Krasnow and L. Glowacki (2019), "Universality and Diversity in Human Song," *Science*, 366 (6468): eaax0868.

Pinker, S. (2002), *The Blank Slate: The Modern Denial of Human Nature*, New York: Viking.

Pinto, L. (2014), "'Sugar, Sugar' by The Archies: Still Sweet After 45 Years," *Laura's Oldies Room*. Available online: https://oldiesconnection.wordpress.com/2014/09/20/sugar-sugar-by-the-archies-still-sweet-after-45-years/ (accessed July 1, 2021).

Prato, G. (2017), "Andy Kim." Available online: *Songfacts Interview*. https://www.songfacts.com/blog/interviews/andy-kim (accessed July 1, 2021).

Wilson, E. O. (1975), *Sociobiology: The New Synthesis*, Cambridge, MA: Harvard University Press.

Wiser, C. (2007), "Toni Wine," *Songfacts Interview*. Available online: https://www.songfacts.com/blog/interviews/toni-wine (accessed July 1, 2021).

7

Serge Gainsbourg, "Je t'aime moi non plus" (1969)

Philippe Gonin, trans. Jackie Ortiz

While Gainsbourg was living an all-consuming relationship with Brigitte Bardot, the story has it that one day she whispered in his ear, "Write me the most beautiful love song that you ever wrote." Dubious words perhaps, but it doesn't matter. In one night, Gainsbourg composed one of the torrid songs only *he* knew how to write, for his muse. In one night? Not really, because as he would, Gainsbourg recycled a soundtrack he had just composed for a movie, *Les Coeurs Verts* (*The Naked Hearts*, dir. Edouard Luntz, 1966). The movie, like its director (who passed away in 2009), is today forgotten, but the music, written for a dancing scene (probably recorded in May 1966), was destined to another future. It would become an international hit. Its title, "Je t'aime moi non plus" (I love you me neither), is said to have been inspired by a quote by Salvador Dalí: when asked what the differences were between Picasso and him, Dalí reportedly said, "Picasso is Spanish, me too. Picasso is a genius, me too. Picasso is a communist, me neither."[1]

Gainsbourg Goes Pop

Once coined a "Rive Gauche" composer,[2] Gainsbourg realized in the mid-1960s that the pop music phenomenon (called *Yéyé* in France) was inescapable.[3] "An international

---

[1] This affirmation by Jane Birkin was asserted by Gainsbourg, who, in an earlier interview, already confessed to Michel Lancelot that he had discovered Dalí's joke afterward. See Gilles Verlant, *Gainsbourg* (Paris: Albin Michel, 1992), p. 196 and Michel Lancelot, "Gainsbourg Psychosé," *Rock & Folk* 32 (1969): 47–50 & 67.
[2] Rive Gauche, the Left Bank of the Seine. A bohemian, avant-garde neighborhood in the early to mid-twentieth century. Translator's note.
[3] "Yéyé" is a term coined by Edgar Morin in 1963 in *Le Monde*. That article was recently translated and published as E. Morin, P. W. Hawkins, and B. Lebrun, "The *Salut les copains* generation," *Popular Music* 39, no. 3–4 (2020): 393–400.

musical genre was born in Liverpool and we cannot deny it anymore, plain and simple! We cannot stand still," he once explained to Denise Glaser.[4]

Mostly influenced by jazz, until then Gainsbourg had said that "rock brings a very interesting rhythm." While writing songs for the young generation at the time (France Gall, Claude François, Petula Clark, and Brigitte Bardot, already), he also published pop-sounding singles under his own name that he recorded in London with English musicians: "Docteur Jekyll et Mister Hyde," "Qui est 'in'? Qui est 'out'?," "Torrey Canyon," "Ford Mustang," which were soon to be compiled in the album, *Initials B.B.* At the time, he also recorded a television musical called *Anna*, directed by Pierre Koralnik and broadcast on French television on January 13, 1967. Starring along with Gainsbourg were Anna Karina and Jean-Claude Brialy.

The Initials of B.B

Toward the end of October 1967, Gainsbourg recorded with Brigitte Bardot again. Two tracks for the *Show Bardot* were scheduled to air on television around Christmas. "I was recording 'Harley Davidson,' late one night at the Barclay studios on Friedland Avenue.... After the recording session, at the dinner table, I grabbed Serge's hand under the table."[5] Gainsbourg became the lover of the woman who was then—and still is—no less than a myth. The B-side to "Harley Davidson" was "Contact"; the disc came out on December 11, 1967.

The romance between Bardot and Gainsbourg only lasted a few weeks. Bardot described it as "a crazy love–the love you only find in dreams—a love that will stay in our memories and in history. He would spend his nights writing marvelous songs on my old Pleyel piano. One morning, he played me his gift of love: 'Je t'aime moi non plus.'"[6]

"Je t'aime moi non plus" was recorded in two sessions: the backing tracks on November 23 and the lead vocals on December 10, with arrangements by Michel Colombier. Bardot recalls:

When we recorded "Je t'aime moi non plus" late at night at the Barclay studios, we each had a microphone. We were standing next to each other, holding hands. I was a little ashamed to mimic the sounds of making love to him, sighing and moaning with pleasure in front of the technicians. But after all I was only acting a situation like I did in the movies. And Serge would reassure me by pressing my hand, winking at me, smiling, kissing me. It was good, it was beautiful, it was pure, it was us.[7]

---

[4] See *Discorama* (13 avril 1966).
[5] Brigitte Bardot, *Initiales B.B.* (Paris: Grasset, 1996), 431.
[6] Ibid.
[7] Ibid., 432.

The song was supposed to appear on the B-side of the couple's next single, "Bonnie and Clyde," an adaptation of "The Trail's End," a poem written by the real Bonnie Parker and recited by Faye Dunaway in the movie that Arthur Penn had just directed. But Bardot was married to Gunther Sachs at the time and her husband, although perfectly aware of the relationship between Gainsbourg and his wife, was not going to have it this way:

> [Gunther Sachs] vehemently reproached me of my affair with this horrible guy, this Quasimodo-like troubadour with whom I exposed myself to ridicule him. If only I had been discreet, he would have turned a blind eye but he had to react, he couldn't afford to accept it anymore, and so on.[8]

Hence and with deep regrets, Bardot asked Gainsbourg and Philips Recordings not to publish the song. On December 21, 1967, she wrote a letter to the company in which she asked "for deep, private and serious reasons to not release 'Je t'aime moi non plus' in any case."[9] With a heavy heart, Gainsbourg accepted and wrote to Louis Hazan, the manager of Philips Recordings, asking him not to release the song. A few days later, Gainsbourg explained to Jean-Pierre Elkabbach on radio France Inter the reasons that led him to this decision:

> No way I create a scandal with this song, it's too beautiful. It's an erotic single that would have been rated adults-only but the music is very pure. I have always written cynical songs and they were accepted, for the first time in my life I write a love song and it's denied. So be it.[10]

The single released at the time replaced "Je t'aime moi non plus" with two songs: "Comic Strip" and "Bubble Gum." The affair with Bardot turned out to be a fling. And while leaving for Almeria, Spain, Bardot broke up with Gainsbourg. Broken and despondent, Gainsbourg wrote his parting gift: "Initials B.B." (drawing inspiration from Anton Dvorak's Symphony No. 9, "From the New World"). It was only in 1986, once divorced from Gunther Sachs, that the actress authorized the release of her version of the song, under one condition: that the profits would go to her animal rights foundation. Twenty years too late, the scandal had dwindled out and this release had a much less powerful effect than the version Gainsbourg and Jane Birkin released in 1969.

Jane B.

If the story of this song—rated in 2005 by Neil Spencer at the top of the "Ten most x-rated records"[11]—began with Bardot, it is another female singer who would carry

---

[8] Ibid., 432–3
[9] Sébastien Merlet, ed., *Le Gainsbook. En studio avec Serge Gainsbourg* (Paris: Seghers, 2019), 216.
[10] Ibid.
[11] See https://www.theguardian.com/observer/omm/the10/story/0,1487369,00.html.

it onto the top of the charts. Despite his disappointment, Gainsbourg cared about his love song and set out to find another voice for it. Bardot didn't want it? Bardot wasn't his mistress anymore, so another woman would sing it.

It all started on a movie set in 1968: *Slogan* (dir. Pierre Grimblat). Gainsbourg, at first and with an attitude, ignored the one who was supposed to be his female partner in the film: a young woman, whose only feat at the time was her role in Antonioni's *Blow Up* (1966)—a movie with which she had already started a small scandal by appearing completely naked. Jane Birkin had also played in another movie, still rather obscure to this day: *Wonderwall* (dir. Joe Massot, 1968), whose soundtrack had been composed by George Harrison. Freshly arrived in Paris in 1968 and speaking next to no French at all, Jane Birkin didn't know anything yet about the man who would soon become her mentor.

> I even thought his name was Serge *Bourguignon*, it was the only French dish I had remembered the name of. Vexed, he had given me, in front of my mother, a little red book called *Cruel Songs*. With these words written inside the cover: *To Jane, here's a few cruel songs amongst which Je t'aime . . . moi non plus . . . .*[12]

The idea to record the song with Mireille Darc, another actress, was then finally abandoned. It was going to be Jane. Gainsbourg, who had preciously kept an acetate pressing of Bardot's version, played it to Birkin. At first she hesitated, but Gainsbourg managed to convince her and even gifted her other songs, among them "Jane B," an actual portrait of the young singer, duplicating Nabokov's words (written in French) from *Lolita*.

An entirely fresh version of "Je t'aime moi non plus" was recorded in 1968 in London, at the Philips and Chappell studios. With Michel Colombier then off to other projects, Arthur Greensdale was to compose the new arrangements (notably the string parts) in keeping with the spirit of Colombier. The organ that replaced the guitars in the version recorded for *The Naked Hearts* was reused. It immediately evoked another 1967 hit: Procol Harum's "A Whiter Shade of Pale", whose melody was freely inspired by Johann Sebastian Bach, reached the top position in the British charts in June 1967.

Two themes, two patterns, one for the verse, one for the chorus, constituted the track: a common practice in Gainsbourg's work. The verses were spoken; the melody was never sung, only in the chorus. And this was where the difference between Bardot and Birkin lay: "She did not dare sing, she was so intimidated. So, one day, she started the note, with fright, one octave too high. Amazing, what a discovery it was!" Gainsbourg later explained.[13] Jane recalled that Gainsbourg loved the high-pitched singing: "He found it more perverse." Gainsbourg chose to bring the vocal frailness of his new muse to the fore, very different from the warm and very erotic connotation of Bardot's voice. He was going to take advantage of this child-like, crystal sound that

---

[12] https://www.lemonde.fr/culture/article/2013/08/26/jane-birkin-serge-gainsbourg-etait-un-provocateur-avec-une-ame-follement-romantique_3465660_3246.html.

[13] Quoted in Merlet, *Le Gainsbook*, 233.

Birkin offered him. The almost liturgical organ added an erotic weight to this mix that was to become explosive.

"Je t'aime moi non plus," the Sweet Smell of Scandal

At Philips, the smell of scandal that was brooding in the song was a little scary to the managers. But they wouldn't ban the disc. The head of Philips in France, who knew the Bardot version, was said to have declared: "Listen kids, I'm ready to go to jail, but for an LP, not a 45rpm. Go back to London and record a long-playing disc. We'll release it under cellophane."[14] The two lovers then embarked on a London-bound ferryboat to record four new tracks that would form—with the three others recorded in London in the winter of 1968—the *Jane Birkin Serge Gainsbourg* album (June 1969).[15] To avoid the censorship heat, the disc was released in France as an adult-only album.

Back in France, Jane and Serge checked back into their hotel (l'Hôtel des Beaux-Arts in Paris).

> The basement had been converted into a dining hall with niches where sophisticated people would dine late at night. There was a record player and a DJ and one night, Serge slipped "Je t'aime moi non plus" under the needle. The fancy customers suddenly stopped eating, forks and knives in the air and Serge whispered to me, in excitement: I think we got a hit record![16]

The single was released in France in 1969. Jane Birkin appeared alone on the original cover; the name of Serge Gainsbourg appeared only in small print. She also starred alone on the LP's sleeve, despite the title *Jane Birkin Serge Gainsbourg*. According to Jane it was "a deliberate choice. He wanted me to be associated with this success" (Figure 7.1).[17]

In 1971, Gainsbourg revealed to Carmen Tessier in *France-Soir* that "it was the Queen of Holland who first asked for the censorship of 'Je t'aime moi non plus'. You didn't know she had shares in Philips? I owe her my wealth."[18] In turn, the Vatican unleashed its anger. The Italian daily *Osservatore Romano*, published by the information bureau of the Vatican, classified the song obscene. One could read in the *Giornale d'italia*: "Within three or four minutes, Gainsbourg and Jane Birkin utter more sighs,

---

[14] Jane Birkin, *Munkey Diaries* (Paris: Fayard, 2018), 135.
[15] The four new tracks were "Orang Outan," "Sous le Soleil Exactement" (a cover of the song sung by Anna Karina in the 1967 musical *Anna*), "18–39," and "Le Canari est sur le Balcon." The latter adds lyrics to the second theme composed for *The Naked Hearts* by Gainsbourg and entitled "My Green Heart" or "Scène de Bal 2." The three others were "L'Anamour" (the cover of a song interpreted by Françoise Hardy in November 68) b/w "69 Année Érotique" (released in December 1968); "Élisa" (a cover with lyrics based on a theme composed by Michel Colombier for the soundtrack of *L'Horizon*) b/w "Les Sucettes" (released in January 1969); "Manon," recorded for the soundtrack of Jean Aurel's *Manon 70* (a track rejected by Aurel, unlike *New Délire*).
[16] Birkin, *Munkey Diaries*, 135.
[17] Quoted in Perrin, *Le Monde* (2013).
[18] *France-Soir*, May 5, 1971.

Figure 7.1 Cover of the *Jane Birkin Serge Gainsbourg* LP (1969), copyright Jean D'Hugues / Universal Music France.

moans and groans than a herd of copulating elephants."[19] "We were banned by the Pope," Birkin explained,[20] His Holiness becoming their "best press agent," according to Gainsbourg. This public outcry had Gainsbourg declare: "The Catholics and the Protestants, what a double win!"[21]

On August 25, 1969, six months after the release of the single, Italian radio stations banned the track from their waves. Jane Birkin even affirmed that "the executive manager of Phonogram in Italy was sent to prison and excommunicated,"[22] which is not entirely false since he was sentenced to two conditional months in prison and had the company fined. The Italian radio stations were soon to be followed by the Swedish (September 10) and the Spanish (September 13). France made the LP an adult-only disc. Then the British radio censored it. In South America, "People would bring it home hidden in Maria Callas sleeves!"[23]

In France, while Serge and Jane made the front page of *Rock & Folk*,[24] *L'Express* magazine coined the song, in the issue of September 22, 1969, "a duo in minor moans." Everywhere else "Je t'aime moi non plus" was censored yet remained high in the charts, except in the United States, where it struggled to stay in the Top 100. One would

---

[19] Quoted in Verlant, *Gainsbourg*, 209.
[20] Birkin, *Munkey Diaries*, 135.
[21] *France-Soir*, May 5, 1971.
[22] Sylvie Simmons, *Serge Gainsbourg. Pour une poignée de Gitanes*, trans. Léna Le Roux (Rosières-en-Hayes: Camion Blanc, 2004), 116.
[23] Birkin, *Munkey Diaries*, 135.
[24] Issue no. 32, September 1969.

have liked to believe Sylvie Simmons when she said the song would barely reach the symbolic 69th position ("Je t'aime moi non plus" actually reached the 58th position on March 14, 1970).[25] Under pressure from the Queen of the Netherlands, Philips ended up suspending the pressing of the single, locking up the stocks, and forbidding the sales. The track, however, managed to reach the second position in the British charts on July 30, 1969. Serge Gainsbourg put an end to his contract with Philips-Fontana and negotiated with Major Minor Records,[26] an independent company, for the distribution of the song in the UK, which soon happened.[27]

The single made its way back into the British charts in the week of October 4, 1969, and this time reached the top position. "Je t'aime moi non plus" then obtained the achievement to be not only the first censored single to become number one but also the first number one sung in French in the UK charts. It would stay at the top for thirty-one consecutive weeks. Forced to follow the rule of the charts, the BBC systematically played a version replacing Jane's "moans and groans" with an instrumental version played by the Sounds Nice, entitled "Love at First Sight." This instrumental version also seduced the listeners and reached the top of the charts. In France, according to Sébastien Merlet,[28] Gainsbourg gave the operating broadcasting permit of the song to Lucien Morisse,[29] one of the founders of the Europe 1 radio station and executive manager of the Disc'AZ record company. Morisse did not stop there: he negotiated on an individual basis, country by country, from Europe to Latin America, from Australia to South Africa, so the banned single could come out again.

By association, the *Jane Birkin Serge Gainsbourg* LP had already suffered censorship. Already the case for the Norwegian version of the LP (replaced by *La Chanson de Slogan*),[30] the song was entirely wiped out of the second French pressing and replaced by "La Chanson de Slogan" like it had been on the Norwegian version of the LP.[31] The song was not even reintegrated in the 1972 re-edition, nor in the following ones, simply because Philips did not hold the rights to it anymore. It was only in 2001, in the first edition of the French CD, that "Je t'aime moi non plus" would permanently reintegrate the album's track-listing.[32]

Despite the censorships and bans, the disc was a huge success. In 1971, interviewed by Denise Glaser, Gainsbourg confessed: "I thought I would sell 25,000 copies and I must have sold 3.5 or 4 million of it! I would have been happy with 25,000." He added,

---

[25] https://www.billboard.com/music/serge-gainsbourg/chart-history/hot-100/song/580321.
[26] Label created in 1969 by Philip Solomon and the founder of the pirate radio station Radio Caroline, Ronan O'Rahilly.
[27] https://www.discogs.com/fr/Jane-Birkin-Serge-Gainsbourg-Je-TaimeMoi-Non-Plus/release/1687183.
[28] Merlet, *Gainsbook*, 245.
[29] https://www.discogs.com/Jane-Birkin-Avec-Serge-Gainsbourg-Je-Taime-Moi-Non-Plus/release/2559134.
[30] https://www.discogs.com/fr/Serge-Gainsbourg-Jane-Birkin-Jane-Birkin-Serge-Gainsbourg/release/5712774.
[31] https://www.discogs.com/fr/Serge-Gainsbourg-Jane-Birkin-Jane-Birkin-Serge-Gainsbourg/release/5766913.
[32] https://www.discogs.com/fr/Jane-Birkin-Serge-Gainsbourg-Jane-Birkin-Serge-Gainsbourg/release/394237.

"this song made my fortune but I didn't wish for it. I wrote this song because I found it beautiful and as erotic as can be."[33] In 1975, Serge Gainsbourg decided to turn his main song into a film. New arrangements of the same theme (recorded by Jean-Pierre Sabar) are heard all along the movie that portrays the story of Johnny-Jane, a short-haired, breastless, androgynous young lady (played by Jane Birkin).

In 1979, while in Jamaica to record his reggae album with the specialists of the genre, Gainsbourg had to face the carelessness of musicians, being a Frenchie. Jane Birkin relates that Sly Dunbar once told Robbie Shakespeare that "there was only one French song that he respected, the one with the moaning girl. Serge then shouted: 'Hey that's my song!' The Jamaicans couldn't believe it. 'You wrote that?!' They then proceeded to record their parts in one day."[34] With the magic of one song, the Frenchie had managed to permanently win the trust of his musicians. To this day, "Je t'aime moi non plus" is still one of the most scandalous songs to ever have been written.

References

Bardot, B. (1996), *Initiales B.B.*, Paris: Grasset.
Birkin, J. (2018), *Munkey Diaries*, Paris: Fayard.
Gonin, Ph. (2021), *Serge Gainsbourg, Histoire de Melody Nelson*, Rouen: Densité, coll. Discogonie.
Lancelot, M. (1969), "Gainsbourg Psychosé," *Rock & Folk*, 32.
Merlet, S., ed., (2019), *Le Gainsbook. En studio avec Serge Gainsbourg*, Paris: Seghers.
Perrin, L. (2013), "Jane Birkin : 'Serge Gainsbourg était un provocateur avec une âme follement romantique." Available online: https://www.lemonde.fr/culture/article/2013/08/26/jane-birkin-serge-gainsbourg-etait-un-provocateur-avec-une-ame-follement-romantique_3465660_3246.html (accessed September 5, 2021).
Simmons, S. (2004), *Serge Gainsbourg. Pour une poignée de Gitanes*, trans. Léna Le Roux, Rosières-en-Hayes: Camion Blanc (French translation).
Verlant, G. (1985 [1992]), *Gainsbourg*, Paris: Albin Michel (Le Livre de Poche).

DVD

Desnos, Y. and Y. Grasland (2000), *Serge Gainsbourg: Intégrale de Serge Gainsbourg à Gainsbarre de 1958 à 199*, DVD, Universal Pictures France.
Reviron, F., ed., (2005), *Serge Gainsbourg: d'autres nouvelles des étoiles*, DVD, Universal Music.

---

[33] https://www.dailymotion.com/video/xq5ug3.
[34] Perrin, *Le Monde*.

8

Blue Swede, "Hooked on a Feeling" (1974)

Sarah Hill, with Bengt Palmers

Unlike the other songs included in this collection, "Hooked on a Feeling" was already a hit for two artists before Blue Swede recorded it: BJ Thomas (1969; No. 5 on Billboard's Hot 100) *and Jonathan King (1971; No. 23 on the UK singles chart). It is safe to say that the Blue Swede version is the one that has crept into the ears of most people around the world, whether as an oft-anthologized single or as temporal color in* Guardians of the Galaxy.[1] *Producer Bengt Palmers kindly agreed to a virtual chat with me about his career and the trajectory of "Hooked on a Feeling."*

Bengt Palmers: So maybe we should start with my giving a brief idea of who I am and what I've done?

Sarah Hill: Yes, please.

BP: Great. I was born in 1948. At an extremely early age I became a record producer. So when I was a producer and arranger and had simultaneously the Number 1 and Number 2 in the Swedish Top 10, I was only twenty years old. Or young. Which I fortunately didn't understand at that time. And I have produced more than sixty singles in the Swedish top charts during the years; how many albums I've produced, I've lost numbers of. So I've been very, very productive, if that's the proper word for it. And toward the end of the 1970s it was a very traumatic time for me, because my father passed away. He actually committed suicide, because he was the victim of a very banal accident that left him with constant pain, 24-7, and he couldn't live with the pain. And I realized then that I had been so focused on being a good boy to impress my father, that when he chose to leave in that fashion, it changed my life very much. I understood then that I couldn't spend 25 hours a day in the recording studio, which I did, and if I wasn't in the recording studio, I was at home

---

[1] *Guardians of the Galaxy* (dir. James Gunn, 2014) is the tenth film in the Marvel Cinematic Universe. "Hooked on a Feeling" is heard initially via character Peter Quill's Walkman, and then underscores the scene where Quill and other protagonists are taken to The Kyln, an interstellar prison. It is also a key sonic ingredient in the film's trailers, and the opening track of the soundtrack album, *Guardians of the Galaxy: Awesome Mix Vol. 1* (Hollywood, 2014), which was a Top 10 hit in eight countries and certified platinum or multiplatinum in six.

writing arrangements, orchestral arrangements, or writing songs—because I've written over 400 songs, of which many have been popular and fortunate to reach the charts. So I branched into other areas of the entertainment business, and I've written the music score for eleven Swedish feature films—that is, cinematic movies—and I have also written four scripts for very successful films, and I have been the cowriter of two very successful stage musicals. And the script that I have just finished is for my fourth book, so I have three published books behind me, so to speak. That's a very brief idea of what I've been doing.

SH: You're talking about fifty-four years of activity. That's very impressive—not only that you've maintained a pace and success for that long but that you were able to work through personal anguish the way that you did. You said you were twenty when you started producing?

BP: When I went to school I studied hard because I wanted my parents to be proud of me. I was the only child. My mother had born a child prior to my birth, but it was stillborn. So I guess when I was born my parents didn't take another chance, so I never got a sibling, a sister or brother. But that was ok with me, and I studied very hard, and I was totally focused on becoming a civil engineer. But I took up the guitar when I was around ten years of age, and so in school we had what we called—how should I translate it?—morning gatherings in school, and I performed a number of songs there, prior to the start of the school day. So the guys at school knew I was writing my own songs, and one guy recommended me one day when I was seventeen, I guess, to join a songwriters' competition, which was arranged by the Stockholm gymnasiums, the schools, and the Swedish Broadcasting Corporation. And I won, and the next year, when I was supposedly going to engineering school, I got a call from the Swedish Broadcasting Corporation, and they said, "Would you like to get a job here, where you write songs that reflect current events?" So I couldn't say no to that. Of course not. And pretty soon, a year and a half, maybe two, I got an offer to become a record producer, and so it all started.

SH: Those songs that you wrote for the Swedish Broadcasting Corporation: did you sing them yourself?

BP: Yes, I did. And I've never sung since then, if you know what I mean. Having worked so much with Björn Skifs, the singer in Blue Swede, of course, he's still my biggest idol as a singer, and we sing at parties together, but I mean, he's a singer and I'm not.

SH: It's interesting that you mention the songs that you wrote, because that's very similar to something that happened in Wales back in the mid-1960s. When Dafydd Iwan was still a university student, studying architecture, he was given a spot on weekly television to sing a topical song. He tended to take melodies that already existed—American folk tunes or Pete Seeger songs, or something by Bob Dylan—and set new Welsh lyrics to them, and he basically grew Welsh popular music from that point onward. That was the thing that prevented

English-language popular music from infiltrating Welsh youth culture. So at the time when you were writing those songs, what was Swedish pop culture like? Was English the main language of popular music, or was Swedish?

BP: Sweden is a comparatively small country by population compared to Germany or Spain or Italy or France, so when Hollywood movies came to Europe, in those bigger countries they overdubbed them with local actors. However, Sweden, as with I guess Norway and Finland and Denmark—Scandihoovia, as I call it—they made subtitles. And in combination with the English music or American music influx, Swedes in general became very familiar with the English/American languages. Swedes are very, very good at the English language—except me, when I'm sitting here talking to you!

SH: You're doing fine; don't worry!

BP: Ok. So what happened, if we go back to when I started writing those songs for the Swedish Broadcasting Corporation, I of course as a young guy with a guitar, was very influenced by American folk music—we're talking about Kingston Trio, Peter, Paul & Mary, Pete Seeger you just mentioned—but then again, in '63, something happened which starts with a "B" and continues with "eatles," which had an enormous impact on everybody, me included. So from being just a troubadour with a guitar, I got involved with other musicians and other instruments, of course. I'm pretty good at electric bass, and I can cheat a lot on keyboards. I'm not a keyboard player, but I can fake it.

SH: So there was never any worry then, that Swedish was not going to be a pop language? That English was going to take over?

BP: No, no, no. Of course, then as well as today, in Sweden, songs are recorded in both English and Swedish. But you may know that with Max Martin and a horde of other guys—mostly guys, but also girls—they are the most prolific songwriters and producers in the *Billboard* charts.

SH: I wondered about the Beatles, because I know in Finland there were Finnish versions of Beatles songs, which are absolutely note-perfect. I mean, not perfectly played, but they are absolute replicas. So I wondered if the same thing happened in Sweden as well, where the four-piece from Lund decided to give it a try.

BP: If you look at the British Invasion, so-called, during the 60s, with the whole list—the Beatles, the Stones, blah blah blah—their songs were never covered in Swedish. They were holy.

SH: So on the radio you would have heard English pop as well as Swedish pop?

BP: Yes, but mostly the English pop was *it*. It was so much better than Swedish pop.

SH: And then around the same time did you have pop magazines?

BP: Of course. We had a weekly pop bible called *The Picture Journal*, if I translate it roughly.

SH: What is it in Swedish?

BP: *Bildjournalen*.

SH: And also girl singers as well?

BP: Yes—I mentioned when I had Number one and two simultaneously in the charts, one of them was a girl. But it was predominantly a male thing. Pop groups were mostly guys.

SH: Yes, this is a common problem around the world. So then in the mid-60s, late 60s, was psychedelia a thing? Were you getting the expanded consciousness kind of music as well?

BP: Yeah. Actually, during my time at the Swedish Broadcasting Corporation, they sent me away with Nagra tape recorders, if you're familiar with those clumsy old things. And so I interviewed Frank Zappa; I interviewed Graham Nash; I interviewed the Bee Gees when they came to visit Sweden. And looking back at it, I mean I can't for the life of me understand that I really did it. I mean, I was eighteen, nineteen years of age.

SH: Have you looked back on any of those interviews to see what you asked?

BP: No, no, no. It's under the bridge, as they say.

SH: The reason I ask about psychedelia is that I went back and listened to the other versions of "Hooked on a Feeling," and I found the BJ Thomas version so interesting, because I hadn't expected it to be so firmly 60s-sounding. I mean, it's got the sitar intro, and then it's got the lush violin arrangement; but between the BJ Thomas and Blue Swede, there were the two other versions: Jonathan King and the Twinkle Brothers.[2]

BP: The what? The Twinkle Brothers?

SH: The Twinkle Brothers, the reggae version.

BP: Never heard! What?

SH: The Twinkle Brothers, from 1971.

BP: So is that where Jonathan King got the reggae feel from?

SH: I'm not sure which one came first. But there's an obvious similarity between the Jonathan King and the Twinkle Brothers versions, because they both use the "ooga chucka." What interests me about the BJ Thomas, just to start from the beginning, is that vocally, he's the most similar to Björn Skifs. They have the same timbre, I think; they have the same vocal quality.

BP: I agree.

SH: They've got perfect intonation and just a beautiful projection of the words. But the vocal line in the Jonathan King version is closer to the melody that Björn Skifs sings. So from the BJ Thomas version to the Blue Swede version, there's this gradual addition of all the stylistic attributes of each of the recordings. The Blue Swede version seems like an interesting conversation with all the versions that came before it. But about the "ooga chucka": wherever it came from, in the Jonathan King version he doesn't pronounce every syllable.

---

[2] B. J. Thomas (Scepter Records, 1968); Jonathan King (Decca, 1971); The Twinkle Brothers (FRM, 1971).

BP: When it comes to the "ooga chucka" thing, I know that Johnny Preston had a hit in 1959 with "Running Bear."³ And "Running Bear," if I'm not totally wrong, is the name of a Native American guy. And all through Johnny Preston's song, or at least during the choruses, there is a "ooh-ooh-nnh-nnh...." I think the idea was that it should sound like a Native American rhythmic chant. Do you follow?

SH: Yeah. I mean, we probably wouldn't try to do that today, but...

BP: No! No, but I think that Johnny Preston's "Running Bear" from 1959 inspired the "ooga chucka" thing. I'm pretty convinced of that. What I should like to point out specifically now we're talking about Blue Swede's recording of the song is that usually when you go into a recording studio with a group, or session musicians for that matter, usually that is the first time that you attack the song. It can either be that you're making a cover version of some earlier song or it's a totally brand new song. But usually that is the first time you attack the song—you find out what kind of beat, what kind of mood, what kind of sound, what kind of blah blah blah is this going to be. But with me and Blue Swede and "Hooked," the thing was that Björn and the guys had started playing it in different venues on stage. And Björn came back and said that the audiences are there going wild, so I suggest we should try to record it. That was a very unique situation for me, because when the guys came into the studio, we never talked about what are we going to do about it, because they knew what they were going to play. There was never a written chord progression, or for that matter for the two horn guys, whatever notes they should play, because they had played it so much live. So my job—this is rather interesting, or I find it very important in what you're going to write—my job as a producer was probably one of the simplest jobs I've ever done. Because the guys already knew how to play the song, right? But my *real* job with the recording, when it was finished, was how on earth, or how the fuck am I going to get this released in territories outside of Sweden, which was a very, very long process. In those days it was—I mean, if you got a Swedish recording released in other Scandinavian countries like Norway or Denmark, that was a big thing. But to have it released in the United States? I mean, this was really pre-ABBA.

But let me stay for a while on this, because of course I first approached the sister company to EMI Svenska in the States, which was Capitol Records, and they said they didn't find it suitable for their territory. And then I bombarded every American record company in those days, and there were many independents, like A&M Records, Casablanca Records, blah blah blah, Capricorn Records, and so forth—and finally CBS Records, later Sony Records, CBS came back. And I still remember the name of the guy who was the international A&R guy at CBS Records: Sol Rabinowitz. And he of course became my hero, because he heard what I heard in the recording,

---

³ Johnny Preston's recording of "Running Bear" (J. P. Richardson) was released as a single (Mercury 1959) and reached the top of the *Billboard* chart in January 1960. It was also the lead track on *Running Bear* (Mercury 1960).

and as head honcho at CBS Records, he wanted to release it in the States. And then I had to go back to Capitol Records to say hey, I need what was called a general rejection, which meant that Capitol would say that it was ok that Blue Swede could record for three years for CBS Records. And then Capitol came back with the most astounding answer, saying, "No, we want to release it!" They had already said no to it, but I think they were basically afraid that CBS were going to get a hit with it, and they changed their mind. And then it exploded.

Now, a very important thing, because I mentioned ABBA a few minutes ago--"Hooked" became No. 1 on the *Billboard* charts on the 6th of April, 1974. And that very day, ABBA won the Eurovision Song Contest in Brighton, with "Waterloo." So that was on the very same day as the Swedish group Blue Swede became Number 1 in the States, ABBA won the Eurovision Song Contest with "Waterloo," which was their stepping-stone onto the international market. And boy, did they have a success.

SH: I've heard of them, yeah.
BP: You have? Oh really?
SH: They've had a few hit singles. So was there any talk at the time of a Swedish Invasion?
BP: No. I mean, the British Invasion had numerous pop groups; we had two.

Figure 8.1 Blue Swede in EMI Studios in Stockholm (1974), being presented with gold singles by two Capitol Records employees (Bengt Palmers center-left, kneeling in front of Björn Skifs).

SH: Ok, two things. First: Blue Swede is one of the great band names in history. It's an absolutely brilliant band name. Second: I maintain that "Hooked on a Feeling" influenced ABBA, because if you listen to "Take a Chance on Me," it starts exactly the same. It's not "ooga chucka" but it's "take a chance, take a chance": it's using the voice as a rhythmic instrument. So I don't know if you've ever claimed copyright. . ..

BP: No, I think that's purely accidental.

SH: But it's a nice little echo. I can't think of many other songs that start that way.

BP: It's ear-catching, definitely.

SH: Because of that "ooga-chucka," did Jonathan King ever come back and ask for a piece of the royalties?

BP: No, but he took out a full-page ad in *Billboard* magazine, sounding very, very sore, and unfortunately—I mean, if he had been a good singer, I could have sympathized with it, but the thing is, he's not a singer. He was a very good entrepreneur, but when you compare his version to Björn and the boys' version, it's clear which of them has the highest hit potential, which also has been noted and certified. I think that Jonathan King's version of "Hooked" reached the 23rd position on the UK singles chart, which says a lot.

SH: It almost sounds like he's doing it as a novelty song, though. He doesn't seem to be taking it seriously.

BP: No, I agree.

SH: So for that reason, you can't really hear Jonathan King's "ooga chucka" as an interesting musical event, because the rest of it sounds like, what are you trying to do here. But I think because Blue Swede use it in a tightly arranged performance, which as you say was clearly polished for however long by performing it live before the band put it on vinyl, it could be a successful single rather than just a one-off novelty hit. I'm not really sure why the BJ Thomas version didn't do better than it did, but it really hasn't aged well.

BP: I think it reached Number 5 in the *Billboard* charts, so that's pretty good.

SH: It is, but it hasn't survived as well. It's very dated. It's a weird combination, the sitar and the violins; it's so stuck in its time.

BP: Absolutely. The sitar thing—you're correct, absolutely.

SH: Saying that, the Blue Swede version speaks to the 70s in a very particular way, too. In the *Guardians of the Galaxy* movie, for example, we recognize it as a mid-70s sound; but it's also music that's still very present somehow. Most people will have heard it, whether or not they can remember where or why. But if you played them the BJ Thomas version, it wouldn't mean a long echo from the 60s; it would mean "stuck in the 60s." But you weren't necessarily aiming for the American market when you recorded the song?

BP: No, no. Like I said, in those days, to have a Swedish recording released in the UK or the US, that was a pipe dream. But when we had done the recording, it dawned upon me that, Jesus, if ever there was a Swedish recording that *could* become a hit in the United States, this was it. And that was why I was so eager, and why I spent so much time trying to get it released in the States. And as we know, it paid off.

SH: It sure did. I know the first time I heard it was on a 45 that my sister had bought back in 1974. So imagine my surprise, sitting down to watch the Marvel movie with my daughter, and sort of reliving the sounds of my youth—it was a wonderful moment. Do you imagine a future life for the song, or do you have any idea about how you want it to live on?

BP: The *Guardians of the Galaxy* soundtrack was a rebirth of the recording, a huge rebirth. And it was also interesting that on that soundtrack there are Marvin Gaye and God knows how many big artists, and still Hollywood Records, the Disney label, they chose to put "Hooked on a Feeling" as track number 1. That says a lot.

SH: It does. And that soundtrack works really well on its own as a mix tape. There is a story—I don't know if it's apocryphal or true—that you had first heard the song because you saw Jonathan King on *Top of the Pops*? Am I remembering this right?

BP: Yes, I visited London in 1971, and since in Sweden we didn't have any good pop programs on television, I wanted to see *Top of the Pops*, of course. And that's when I heard Jonathan King's version, and I liked it so much that I bought it the next day in HMV on Oxford Street. And then when Björn started his band, he wanted me to come up with ideas for songs that they could perform live, so I gave him a bundle of singles, one of them being "Hooked." And the rest is history.

SH: How did you meet Björn initially?

BP: Björn was singer and keyboard player in a group called Slam Creepers. It's a very, very strange name, but it would take twenty minutes to explain why. And to my ears he was the only Swedish guy in a Swedish pop band who could sing. I mean, in those days, every teenage boy wanted to be a pop singer, and very few of them were. But Björn was. He was a very good singer. He's still a very good singer. So when he was that keyboard player and singer in that band, I thought of him as the only good pop singer in Sweden, and so then it happened that when I came to EMI Records, Björn's then-manager said, "I think you should try to talk to Bengt," so I was the lucky one to have my favorite singer wanting me to record him and produce him.

SH: And it's turned into a fantastic partnership as well.

BP: Yes.

SH: I know that Blue Swede had the follow-up hit after "Hooked on a Feeling." Did they try to maintain a career in the States?

BP: When "Hooked" became a hit here in Sweden, what I immediately had to do was come up with an album. I came up with an idea—there was a 70s song by a California group called The Association. They had a ballad called "Never My Love," and I had an idea of making an up-tempo version of it. That was the follow-up to "Hooked" in the States, and it reached Number 7, which wasn't that bad, either.

SH: So I know I can't call you a one-hit wonder. I don't mean to offend . . .

BP: No, and you have probably never heard it, have you?

Figure 8.2 Bengt Palmers and Björn Skifs, 1980s.

SH: Well I did listen to it, after you reminded me. Just doing my research. But I also wanted to say that one of the things that Björn's voice and Blue Swede's "Hooked on a Feeling" particularly remind me of is a song called "Sing Me a Rainbow" by the Sons of Champlin. It's one of those songs that I can't figure out why it wasn't a bigger hit. But I think Bill Champlin's voice and Björn's voice have a real similarity.

BP: Yeah, I agree.

SH: I don't know if it was a stylistic thing, that a lot of men in the late 60s, early 70s adopted, or just happened to sing like—

BP: Probably. Bill Champlin was a very good singer—and he's still a very good singer.

SH: There's a strength to both of their voices. Because there's a live version of Blue Swede on YouTube singing "Hooked on a Feeling"—not a lip-sync; it's live, and it's extraordinary how note-perfect it is compared to the recording. But then, if it started off as a live song first, it makes sense that there would be such a seamless relationship between them. I guess what I'm trying to say is that it makes sense that Blue Swede was able to succeed in the US market at the time that it did, because there was something very familiar about Björn's voice. And he doesn't sing with an obvious or weird accent, to American ears, anyway. So it wouldn't have been strange in any way. Thinking about the 70s market in general, it makes a lot of sense to me. But also, it's just a great song.

BP: Yep.

9

Wild Cherry, "Play That Funky Music" (1976)

Robert Fink

The problem of the twentieth century is the problem of the color line.
—W.E.B. Du Bois, 1903

Admit it—you've danced to it, maybe at a wedding, or a bat-mitzvah, or even a *quinceañera*; and I'll bet you've actually, at least once, made that obligatory half-turn on the dance floor and shouted out its irresistible hook; and even if you've never lowered yourself that far, you'd certainly recognize those eight lightly syncopated syllables anywhere, as one of the most stinging memes in American pop music, journalistic shorthand for anyone, from white rappers and reggae musicians to Republican presidential candidates, who try to act more Black than they have a right to.

Play that funky music, white boy.

Ouch. PTFM/WB, as we'll henceforth abbreviate it, is ubiquitous as a catchphrase because the phenomenon it indexes is so problematic, and yet so ubiquitous as to be completely unremarkable. It denotes the societal privilege inherent in *reverse crossover:* the tendency of non-Black members of the dominant culture to assume that they can just go ahead and do things like play the distinctive music of Black people and take on the Black cultural style they admire without somehow paying for it. Reverse crossover has been the morally dubious engine of popular music since the first white boy strummed a banjo and started dancing in a style picked up from the Black men who labored alongside him; it shadowed the birth of ragtime, jazz, swing, and (oh my god yes) rock 'n' roll; it will undoubtedly still be a pop music reality on the day you read this chapter.[1]

---

[1] On the roots of minstrel "crossover," see Dale Cockrell, *Demons of Disorder: Early Blackface Minstrels and their World* (Cambridge, 1997). PTFM/WB is often used to index instances of white performance that remind those reporting on them of minstrelsy, up to and including the revival of the original blackface practice itself; see, as an example, Darren Keast, "Play That Funky Music? Across the Country, Historical Minstrelsy is Re-emerging to the Shock of Many," *The [St. Louis] Riverfront Times*, November 19, 2003. https://www.riverfronttimes.com/stlouis/play-that-funky-music/Content?oid=2464344 (accessed September 07, 2021).

But what separates PTFM/WB from run-of-the-mill appropriation, what makes it interesting, is its *autological* character. Autology happens when a text itself is an instance of the thing it describes or narrates. Autologies in pop music can be trivial (new dance records tell you about the new dance craze) or unsettling (Leonard Cohen can let you in on the harmonic sleight-of-hand behind "Hallelujah" even as he breaks your heart with it). "Play That Funky Music" is autological on a mass-cultural scale: thanks to its huge success—it was one of the first singles to sell 2 million copies and be certified "platinum," the Wild Cherry album it was on did the same, the song, performance, and the record were all recognized with major awards, and the band were declared the most promising new artists of 1976 in *Billboard*—it became *the* paradigmatic example of the reverse crossover move its autobiographical narrative celebrates, and thus uniquely implicates anyone caught dancing, singing, or moving to the grooving in its shady, self-reflexive logic. Wild Cherry thus almost *had* to be a one-hit wonder. You only get away with this particular autology once, white boy.

I am, accordingly, going to follow Du Bois by making the color line the dividing line of my two-part story. This was the line in the American musical sand across which the four white boys of Wild Cherry sauntered so optimistically in the Bicentennial summer of 1976, the dividing line of my story. No false integration here: let's accept that the story of PTFM/WB adds to dubious cultural appropriation the even more dubious claim that those stolen from were "asking for it." To repurpose two terms that critics often link in this context, the song wants to be *loved* for its *theft*, and, of course, that kind of demand will resonate differently either side of the color line. The white perspective on PTFM/WB we already know from the record itself and its industry reception, although some details of time and place can add shading and local (yes) color. But understanding what PTFM/WB could mean to Black folk requires actually listening to their voices, not just ventriloquizing them. It will be necessary to look at complex traces left in both the Black press and the white racial imagination by the song's runaway success. Some of the darker content we find will turn out to have been there all along, a dark autology that, when it hits you, may demand that you lay down more than just the boogie.

Changing Rock 'n' Roll and Minds

Self-identified "boogie singer" Robert Parissi was born on December 29, 1950, in Mingo Junction, Ohio, a small steel town on the western side of the metropolitan region that begins in Pittsburgh, Pennsylvania, and sprawls across the northern West Virginia panhandle to end at Stuebenville, Ohio, home of Franciscan University and the birthplace of another successful Italian American entertainer, Dino Paul Coletti (*aka* Dean Martin). Parissi put together a group called Wild Cherry in Steubenville sometime around 1970. They had little trouble burning up the one-night stands over the next four years, building a following up and down the Ohio Valley. Gigging around the southern and eastern reaches of the state, Wild Cherry was navigating a racial landscape shaped by the Great Migration, barnstorming in and out of gritty factory cities like Pittsburgh, Canton, Akron, and Dayton, where working-class Blacks had sought jobs during the postwar boom. This was the demographic responsible for the explosive crossover of rock 'n' roll in 1950s Cleveland, and Wild Cherry was following in the footsteps of white blues-and-boogie bands with multiracial audiences like The Jaggerz, out of Pittsburgh, or the James Gang, with whom they later shared a Cleveland-based manager and promoter, Mike Belkin. There are no recordings of Wild Cherry from the early 1970s, but I imagine their original material sounded something like the James Gang's 1971 chart hit "Funk #49," which fully lives up to its name, with barely decipherable lyrics riding over Joe Walsh's churning guitar-based funk, all punctuated by a descending unison riff obviously copped from Sly and the Family Stone's "Sing A Simple Song."

White boys in the Ohio Valley kept on playing that partially funky music for years, influenced, no doubt, by the waves of Black musical innovation that were changing rock 'n' roll and minds in the upper Midwest, one record at a time. Draw a loose triangle connecting Pittsburgh and Detroit to Cincinnati and you capture most of Wild Cherry's natural touring habitat; you will also circumscribe an extraordinary flowering of Midwestern funk. The Pittsburgh-Cleveland-Detroit axis passes north of Steubenville to run through Canton, home to the O'Jays before they decamped to Philadelphia; the Detroit-Dayton-Cincinnati axis transects the Ohio Players and their mercurial keyboardist Junie Morrison (Dayton), who left in 1974 to record solo for Westbound Records and later joined George Clinton's Parliament/Funkadelic collective in Detroit, along with William "Bootsy" Collins (Cincinnati) and Michael "Kid Funkadelic" Hampton (Cleveland). All these musicians were influenced by some combination of Jimi Hendrix, James Brown, and Sly Stone, and together they created a market for riff-heavy, guitar-driven instrumental funk rock with strong psychedelic overtones that appealed to both Black and white audiences.

Thus the narrative laid out in the verses of PTFM/WB rings true, *if* you take it as the lightly fictionalized story of a local rock band facing a stylistic choice while touring the Pittsburgh-Detroit-Cincinnati triangle in the funk-crazy middle years of the 1970s. By then, Joe Walsh, who'd left the James Gang in 1972, was out in California country with the Eagles, and things had gotten so low for guys like Parissi that he gave up the band to manage a steakhouse in western Pennsylvania. But when he went to sell his last guitar, he hit it off with the dude who showed up to buy it and decided to rebuild Wild Cherry with him. In late 1975 Parissi and his new lead guitarist Bryan Bassett were playing a mix of hard rock and Led Zeppelin covers at a new futuristic dance club called 2001 on the north side of Pittsburgh, when somebody cornered their tall blonde drummer, Ron Beitle, between sets, asking, "Are you going to play some funky music, white boys?"[2] Everybody involved now remembers the 2001 Club as a "disco," because its owner, Tom Jayson, later franchised the concept across western Pennsylvania and upstate New York at the height of the white disco boom, turning it into what cultural historian and rock critic Alice Echols analogized to a minor-league "McDonald's of the glitter-ball

---

[2] Scott Mervis, "Obituary: Ron Beitle; Played that Funky Music for Wild Cherry," *Pittsburgh Post-Gazette*, December 13, 2017. Available online: https://www.post-gazette.com/ae/music/2017/12/13/Ron-Beitle-Played-that-funky-music-for-Wild-Cherry/stories/201712130135. (accessed September 07, 2021).

world."[3] But at the time, nobody would have gone to suburban Pittsburgh for what we would now recognize as New York-style disco music, with its glossy surfaces and four on the floor beat; the mostly Black clientele that night would have expected hometown funk, some Ohio Players or Isley Brothers, or even just above-average imitators like the Jaggerz or the James Gang, local white boys who could still rock a dance floor every once in a while, if you asked them nicely.

Just When It Hit Me

I'll wager the workaday transaction just discussed is not how you pictured the pivotal moments of PTFM/WB going down. To be fair, that's because the song, whose verses tell the story of a gigging band just trying to satisfy their customers, suddenly switches genre and perspective for the chorus. When Parissi, who's been telling us about his life as a rock 'n' roll performer, decides to "disco down and check out the show" at some fictionalized version of Club 2001, he does so as an enthralled spectator. Evidently another band is playing there, and the patrons, singing, dancing, moving to the grooving, are just *digging* their music. Swept up in the mostly Black crowd, so does he; the funk hits him, hard.

Thanks to the musical craftmanship of Parissi and his bandmates, it hits the listener hard as well. PTFM/WB, like most funk-soul chart hits, overlays its nonstop cyclic repetition with a basic teleological structure familiar to generations of popular songwriters. During the verses, the dancing groove stays close to home, with little or no harmonic motion; in the words of a pioneering formal taxonomist of funk, listeners are suspended in one long moment of "presence and pleasure."[4] But as the chorus approaches, a paradoxical constriction of the groove—dropping the bass out, additional layers of beat, more unison riffs, increased circling around the tonic pitch—signals that a change is going to come. Songwriters sometimes call this type of pre-chorus section the "channel," because it channels all the song's energy into the hook, which in this case arrives with platinum-record-selling force: at the words "somebody turned around," the bass re-enters and the track turns itself around and surges upward, so that the entire pentatonic groove can reconstitute itself a disorienting (because non-diatonic) minor third higher. In retrospect, this will turn out to have been a completely logical thing to do: the bassline of the chorus moves through the flat third, then the flatted fifth degree of the prevailing blues scale, composing out as chord roots (Em^7-Gm^7-$B^{\flat}m^7$, for the musos) the altered scale degrees used in the verses for melodic inflection. But in the

---

[3] Alice Echols, *Hot Stuff: Disco and the Remaking of American Culture* (Norton, 2010), 198. The plans for Jayson's fast-food disco empire were laid out in Jesse Kornbluth's bemused report on "Merchandising Disco for the Masses," *New York Times Magazine*, February 18, 1979, 5–9. Available online: https://www.nytimes.com/1979/02/18/archives/merchandizing-disco-for-the-masses-the-franchiser.html (accessed September 07, 2021).
[4] Anne Danielsen, *Presence and Pleasure: The Funk Grooves of James Brown and Parliament* (Wesleyan University Press, 2006).

moment, when it hits you, the sudden, disorienting harmonic shift *up*—and then up *again*—is quite dizzying.

The experience of musical vertigo on the dance floor is exhilarating, the drop in the pit of the stomach as the chorus winds its way back down to the tonic a visceral example of musical autology. Putting us in the audience with him, rather than on stage, the song's narrator abandons us up to the power of the Black music he is copying; when that power hits *you*, you may feel that you've been given permission by the song (and the imaginary Black voices in it) to do as he did, and let its embrace carry you across the color line in a self-abandoning act of racial impersonation.[5] (You do *not* have that permission; keep reading.) Apprehended this way, the song is a testimony, with the cry of PTFM/WB as its narrative pivot: the descent of the spirit, the breaking open of the heart, the moment of conversion. I was blind, but now, in a crowd of dancing witnesses, I see. Once I was a boogie singer, but now I'm funkin' out in every way!

The historian and cultural critic Raymond Williams coined the term *structures of feeling* to analyze the inchoate political patterns traced out by countless individual moments of affective reaction to everyday life (food, landscape, clothing, sound) which leave a trace in the collective cultural record through representation in literature, film, and music.[6] Let's counterpoise to PTFM/WB another highly charged moment close to the musical color line, to get an inkling of the complex structures that tend to lurk behind that groovy feeling.

John Fahey, the pioneering "American Primitive" guitarist and blues revivalist, described his first encounter with country blues, on a record by Blind Willie Johnson, as "a hysterical conversion experience where in fact I had liked that kind of music all the time, but didn't want to." The funky sounds coming off the old shellac hit the suburban white boy hard: "We played it and I had this visceral reaction. I almost threw up. I said, 'Please put on some Bill Monroe records so I can get back to normal.' But here's the trick: by the end of the Bill Monroe record the Blind Willie Johnson thing was still going through my head, and I had to hear it again." George Henderson, in the critical study of Fahey from which these interview snippets are taken, notes that this kind of emotional conversion narrative is a well-worn trope with white aficionados of the blues, signifying that a complex game of authenticity is underway. Claiming that *I am the sort of person stopped in their tracks, felled by music*, as Henderson sums up this structure of feeling, gives one license to appropriate, even to cross back over the color line in blackface. (Fahey's first solo LP devoted one side to what he pretended were lost 78 rpm recordings of an old bluesman named "Blind Joe Death," going so far as to concoct a fake discography and liner notes to back up his racial impersonation.)[7]

---

[5] The reference gives proper respect to a key text in the Black interpretation of Black music, Samuel A. Floyd's *The Power of Black Music: Interpreting Its History from Africa to the United States* (Oxford, 1996).

[6] Raymond Williams, "Structures of Feeling" (Chapter 6) in *Marxism in Literature* (Oxford: Oxford University Press, 1977), 128–35.

[7] George Henderson, *Blind Joe Death's America: John Fahey, the Blues and Writing White Discontent* (University of North Carolina Press, 2021), 166–68. Henderson references the discussion of blues authenticity in Kimberly Mack, *Fictional Blues: Narrative Self-Invention from Bessie Smith to Jack White* (University of Massachusetts Press, 2020).

This *felled by (black) music* trope provides the basic through-line for Wild Cherry's eponymous 1976 album. None of the other tracks lives up to the promise of their hit single, but the band burns through Wilson Pickett's gospel-inflected "99 ½ (Won't Do)," and lays down an almost note-for-note copy of the Commodores' "I Feel Sanctified." In both cases the religious roots of the material harmonize with the title track's feeling structure, as does the rather lamer cover of the Motown classic "Nowhere to Run." The album's closing track, "What in the Funk Do You See," is an emotional bookend for the opener, returning to the same alternating-note riff and minor pentatonic feel. After a series of leading rhetorical questions about the funk ("Is it the beat that makes you wanna dance? / Is it the message that makes you take a chance?"), the title phrase acknowledges that while these white guys might not look like they should know what funk is, sonic blackness has "really got a hold on" them, haunting their dreams, driving them if not to distraction, then at least to the other side of the color line, leaving the whole countercultural project of "rock" in the dustbin of music history:

> Woke up one night and feeling so strange
> This reggae music was playing in my brain
> The mass confusion is driving me insane
> The hell with Woodstock, I'm going on Soul Train!

After you stop laughing, you have to admit it's a breathtaking change of allegiance for a white rock band to pledge. And, as with Dr. Hook's plaintive ode to being on "The Cover of Rolling Stone," it actually worked: after the huge success of their first album and despite the dispiriting flop of their second, Wild Cherry went on *Soul Train* on April 15, 1978, to promote yet another crossover funk-rock album and play their one big hit. They were only the second all-white American act to do so.[8]

Losing Every Step of the Way

For Black journalists covering the racial politics of the music industry, the appearance of a white act like Wild Cherry on the premier Black-controlled television music program was not a cause for celebration. That same week, an acerbic report appeared in *Jet* magazine under the no-nonsense headline "White Stars Cross Over and Get Rich on Black Music." *Jet*'s new West-Coast bureau chief, twenty-eight-year-old Ronald Kisner, did not mince words:

> No the Bee Gees, Elton John, Billy Joel, Samantha Sang and Steely Dan aren't Black, but you might think so, if you've been tuning in Black radio stations since

---

[8] Dennis Coffey, the Motown session player and fuzz-tone guitarist who played on the Temptations' "Cloud Nine" and "Ball of Confusion," was the first, playing his own hit, "Scorpio," on January 8, 1972. All the other white acts that played *Soul Train* between his appearance and Wild Cherry's were foreign nationals: Gino Vanelli (Canada), Elton John (UK), David Bowie (UK), and the Average White Band (UK/Scotland).

the post-civil rights struggle days. These singing stars and a spattering of more like the Average White Band and Wild Cherry have managed to make mega hits by draining purses from white and Black communities equally dry. Like updated Al Jolsons, these performers have Black-voiced-and-tracked their cuts masterfully to win Black listeners for the most part without ever having to play before any substantial Black audiences. They can, like the latter-day Northern carpetbaggers who ravished the South, take the money and run.[9]

Kisner's reporting shows that a lack of reciprocity, not lack of authenticity, was the major complaint from Black industry professionals. Unlike Top 40 stations, which retained the power to draw the color line around their majority white audiences, Black-identified stations felt pressured to enable whites crossing over. (The program director of Atlanta's WAOK concedes that, in the aftermath of *Saturday Night Fever*, "It's hard sometimes not to play white artists.") Kisner went back to his Midwestern roots and interviewed Eddie Levert, a veteran of the Ohio funk scene, who, as lead singer for the O'Jays, had toured with Wild Cherry as a supporting act the previous year. Levert's experience was that "if a white act is good enough Blacks will accept them," but that the color line didn't flex the other way: "Why not put the Bee Gees and the O'Jays together in concert? What I get from both white and Black promoters is that whites and Black will not mingle well together in concerts. My position is that you've got to try it."

Still, there had always been an undertone of skepticism in the Black press about the popularity of crossover acts like Wild Cherry with the Black audience that made up their readership. Kisner claims that mainstream record labels deliberately tried to efface the whiteness of popular crossover artists like Tom Jones and the Bee Gees, to the point that many Black radio listeners only became aware that a group like the Average White Band or Wild Cherry was made up of white musicians when they finally appeared on *Soul Train*. He had a point: not a single image of the all-white band appears anywhere on Wild Cherry's first two album covers, which take their cue instead from the soft-focus sepia eroticism of the Ohio Players. (The objectified females draped across *Electrified Funk*, Wild Cherry's sophomore LP, are racially ambiguous to an exquisite degree, their snow-white outfits setting off café-au-lait skin tones that could pass for either light-skinned "black" or aggressively bronzed "white," depending on who's looking.)

But even if you didn't trust the official charts put out by *Billboard*, *Cashbox*, and *Record World*—and many Black deejays did not—it was hard to argue with the evidence in the Black press itself: a correspondent from the *New York Amsterdam News* saw Wild Cherry rocking the capacity Madison Square Garden crowd assembled to hear the Isley Brothers; later in that tour, the *Oakland Post*'s gossip columnist relayed a report from the Coliseum in which they played better than the Isleys' other supporting act, Black Smoke, to the degree that their cover of "I Feel Sanctified" brought "wild cheers and 'bravo' from the Coliseum audience." Most tellingly, the in-house R&B record charts curated by most African American newspapers and magazines consistently highlighted

[9] Ronald E. Kisner, "White Stars Cross Over and Get Rich on Black Music," *Jet*, April 13, 1978, 16ff. Available online: https://books.google.com/books?id=c0IDAAAAMBAJ&pg=PA14 (accessed September 07, 2021).

both "Play That Funky Music" and the Wild Cherry LP. Kisner's own employer, *Jet*, tracked both records for months in its "Soul Brother Top 20," a chart determined directly by polling the readership with no industry input. Wild Cherry must have had a following among Black concertgoers: How else did they end up headlining the first night of the 1977 Atlanta Kool Jazz Festival, next to the Mighty Clouds of Joy, jazz legend Roy Ayers, Natalie Cole, the Temptations, and Lou Rawls?[10]

The Honkey's Got Soul?

So we have to assume that a lot of Black folks listened to PTFM/WB and genuinely enjoyed it. But where did that enjoyment come from, socially, and what did it mean, politically? Searching for an underlying structure of feeling that, given the discursive policing of the color line on both sides, will be even more fugitive than normal, we'll need to cast our net wide, sweeping up suggestive bits of memoir, criticism, and fiction, both Black and white, looking for fleeting traces of how it felt to "listen while Black" to white boys crowing about playing your funky music.

Bob Parissi took the huge success of "Play That Funky Music" on the R&B charts as validation from Black fans who he was proud to claim didn't know, and didn't care, if he and his bandmates were white. The designated follow-up to PTFM/WB on *Electrified Funk* was originally titled "The Honkey's Got Soul" (cooler heads prevailed) and depicts Wild Cherry successfully taking it to the stage in Detroit in the midst of a full-blown race riot:

I heard the brothers and the sisters
Shout something in a rage
They were screaming to me

Black now, white right, oh what a sight
I really didn't know the suckers was white
Baby don't you know (x3)
That the honkey's got soul!

---

[10] Marie Moore, "Fiery Concerts: Black & White Smoke," *New York Amsterdam News (1962-1993)*, October 9, 1976. Available from: https://www.proquest.com/historical-newspapers/fiery-concerts-black-white-smoke/docview/226546490/se-2?accountid=14512 (accessed September 07, 2021); Berry Weekes, "I Didn't Say That [Weekly Column]," *Oakland Post (1968-1981)*, October 17, 1976. Available from: https://www.proquest.com/newspapers/i-didnt-say-that/docview/371715990/se-2?accountid=14512 (accessed September 07, 2021). For the lineup of the 1977 Atlanta Kool Jazz Festival, see the *Atlanta Constitution*, June 11, 1977. Available from: https://www.proquest.com/historical-newspapers/lineup/docview/1617561401/se-2?accountid=14512 (accessed September 07, 2021). In addition to the *Jet* Soul Brother Top 20, singles and album charts appeared weekly in most Black newspapers of the period, including some digitized and indexed online, like the *Amsterdam News* and the Baltimore *Afro-American*.

(In the final chorus, "I really didn't know" becomes "It really doesn't *matter*"—but, of course, that was a delusion. As we'll see, it matters a lot.)

Some Black teens appear to have used Wild Cherry as a transitional object to move away from the "bubble gum soul" purveyed by Motown groups like the Jackson 5. Reminiscing for *Ebony* in 2016, African American pop critic Michael A. Gonzales recaptures the feeling of this cultural shift with writerly precision. The scene is set in the rec room of his older cousin's house in Pittsburgh, Pennsylvania, some forty years earlier:

> In the bicentennial summer of 1976, my cousin Denise suddenly announced to me, "Michael Jackson is played out"—and she wasn't the only one who believed that to be true. We were sitting in the gaudy basement of her parent's Pittsburgh home, the same Tiki-lit/wood paneled wall cellar where, a few years before, we played the Jackson 5's debut Motown single "I Want You Back" over and over and over. Throwing those memories aside, she spread out her new 45s on top of the bar: the mid-tempo balladry of the Brothers Johnson's "Good to You" (she loved her some bass playin' Louis); the grown-folks' soul of the O'Jays jam "Livin' for the Weekend"; and the White-boy funk of Wild Cherry's bugged out "Play That Funky Music."[11]

For Gonzales, the path through Wild Cherry led first to Zeppelin, then back across the color line to Jimi Hendrix, hip-hop, and an omnivorous career as a music critic. But white rock critics of the time were uniformly harsh about Wild Cherry; they had a sneaking suspicion that Blacks viewed the band's provincial white funk like they did, as an embarrassment: "Maybe the notion of a white man's imploring a black audience to 'get funky and crazy' strikes a black audience as amusing."[12] Black conservative cultural commentator (and linguist) James McWhorter also assumed, in 2004, that a self-deprecating, shuck-and-jive White Negritude was the not-so-subtle message of the song, since no self-respecting white person could *ever* hear its title phrase as anything other than a taunt:

> *White*—the nut is that we are game to watch him venture to produce and touch us with this music even though he's not of the race we associate the music with, and that we're all aware of the looming assumption that whites are at a disadvantage in channeling the spirit that makes the music live. Then *boy*—a kind of diminishment, getting on the record that we see the fellow as operating at a disadvantage because he wasn't born with it, getting him back for the eons during which black men were called "boy" by white bigots; now it's okay to tap *you* on the back of the head, White

---

[11] Michael A. Gonzales, "How *Off the Wall* Launched Michael Jackson into Orbit," *Ebony*, January 27, 2016. Available online: https://www.ebony.com/entertainment/off-the-wall-put-michael-jackson-into-the-stratosphere/ (accessed September 07, 2021).

[12] John Rockwell, "Pop: Jacksons Run into Interference at Coliseum," *New York Times*, April 12, 1977. Available online: https://www.nytimes.com/1977/04/12/archives/pop-jacksons-run-into-interference-at-coliseum-crowd-and-sound.html (accessed September 07, 2021).

Boy, because the times have changed and now we're where it's at, so prove yourself, White Boy—but you know that we're only calling you "boy" in the same vein of affectionate diminishment that we call each other "nigger."[13]

Jonathan Lethem's finely wrought novel of the same year, *The Fortress of Solitude*—a personal fable of late 1970s Brooklyn, doomed interracial solidarity, and the bifurcation of American musical culture—deploys PTFM/WB like a weapon against its white teenage protagonist, whose Black tormentors were not "affectionate" in their diminishment; they were relentless and without remorse:

> Every time your sneakers met the street, the end of that summer, somebody was hurling it at your head, that song. [It] was the soundtrack to your destruction, the theme. Your days reduced to a montage cut to its cowbell beat, inexorable doubled bass line and raunch vocal, a sort of chanted sneer, surrounded by groans of pleasure. The stutter and blurt of what—a tuba? French horn? Rhythm guitar and trumpet, pitched to mockery.[14]

Given the autobiographical precision of the narrative—almost everything in the book that doesn't involve comic book superheroes actually happened to Lethem—we can treat this passage like a primary source from the summer of 1976, preserving a particularly abrasive structure of feeling circulating just on the other side of the color line. Of course middle schoolers can be cruel; but Lethem, the narrator, wants us to feel the existential hatred behind the raillery, a structure of feeling stamped by slavery on America from the very beginning that, when looked at squarely, turns out to be a matter of life and death.

"Sing it through gritted teeth: WHITE BOY! Lay down the boogie and play that funky music 'til you die."

'Til You Die?

No surprises: I'm working my way around to the proposition that Robert Parissi had *no idea what he was messing with* when he scribbled down the words "play that funky music, white boy" on an empty server's pad during a set break at Club 2001 in 1976.

Or maybe he did. What *I* remember puzzling over in 1976, as a fifteen-year-old white boy, was the cadence at the end of the chorus, the precise moment Lethem evokes in the description above: after everybody piles onto the inexorable bass riff and rides it

---

[13] James McWhorter, *Doing Our Own Thing: The Degradation of Language and Music and Why We Should, Like, Care* (New York: Penguin, 2004), 188. I have retained McWhorter's explicit, racially charged use of the N-word, partially for the implied symmetry with "white boy," and partially because, as a Black conservative intellectual who is also a professional scholar of language, McWhorter has the right to deploy language as he chooses without "politically correct" editing or expurgation from a white academic.

[14] Jonathan Lethem, *The Fortress of Solitude* (Vintage, 2004), 109.

on down, Parissi's raunchy (*read:* Black) vocal picks up the last three words and repeats them twice, first as what Lethem heard as a sneer, and I thought was an incredulous question ('til you *die?*), then as what both Lethem and I agree was probably a groan of self-abasing pleasure (*aww,* 'til you *di-ie*).

In this reading, the white subject of the song vocally enacts his own destruction—a minor-league, disco version of the Wagnerian love-death—every time the chorus rumbles down to the tonic. *Oh, come on,* I hear you mutter—but consider this: the album version of the track, and early live versions, too, eventually leave this moment behind. The last time around, the tonic return at the end of the chorus is followed by *another* repeat that does not resolve. As Parissi ad-libs, autologically, "got to *keep on* playing funky music," the song freezes into place a third higher—and then, with a nod to Sly Stone, takes us *another* step higher, fading out into disco immortality a perfect fourth above its original pitch.

Autology becomes privilege here: if you're white, you can just keep on playing that funky music, and you might think that you can take what you want from Black culture and just walk away, scot-free. For obvious reasons, cover versions of "Play That Funky Music" by Black musicians are vanishingly scarce, but the one or two I've been able to find don't end this way. They play through the chorus twice, and, the second time, slow down the final riff until it comes to rest at the tonic with three stony downbeats for those three last words. It's a logical way to end the song in concert. (Or an episode of *The Voice* where the white contestant sings it as an interracial duet with his coach Cee Lo Green, accompanied by a miniature Cee Lo clone popping and locking.)[15]

But maybe it also means exactly what it says. Maybe that's what Parissi heard in the tone that night in Pittsburgh, maybe he just sensed it, maybe he laughed it off, but maybe, just *maybe*, Black folk are deadly serious about this. Go ahead and mess with our music, white boy, but there will be a price to pay. Maybe this time, it is *you* who will be forced to work until you die.

'Til. You. Die.
('til you DIE, motherfucker!)

How I Learned My Lesson

Does this seem melodramatic? Not if you actually listen to the stories circulating in Black culture. Interviewed in *Jet*, Los Angeles DJ Don Mack perceived guys like Parissi as an existential threat: "Whites are singing and talking like us. Pretty soon there won't be any need for us." It had long been taken for granted within the small cadre of Black media professionals that segregation of the airwaves and appropriation of Black

---

[15] Yes, that happened, on December 12, 2012. See https://www.youtube.com/watch?v=1HitcRQwgxM (accessed July 3, 2021).

musical creativity caused race hatred: "Blacks go around mad at whites, and say, 'White people are no good.' Many whites are being hated and they don't know why."[16]

Music historian Matthew Morrison has coined the term *blacksound* (the sonic equivalent of blackface) to name the profound cultural violations—stereotyping, appropriation, exploitation, erasure—that planted and nurtured an American music industry built on Black creativity but economically dominated by whites.[17] Reverse crossover, blacksound by another name, is thus a primal wound for African Americans, engendering persistent fantasies in which attempts to possess Black music by outsiders, even well-meaning ones, are punishable by death. Those familiar with the Black Arts Movement will remember Henry Dumas's speculative fiction, "Will the Circle Be Unbroken," in which the unearthly sonic power of a vibrating "afro-horn" instantly kills three white sensation-seekers who have forced their way inside Harlem's Sound Barrier Club during an experimental collective improvisation. It's worth noting that two of the three were also skilled and passionate mimics of Black music—until they died.

One of the most gothic versions of this fantasy was channeled by a racial outsider. The writer Hari Kunzru, of Kashmiri descent on his father's side, grew up in a Britain where he would have been classified as "Black," and his 2017 novel, *White Tears*, puts the *death* back into the legend of Blind Joe Death. Like John Fahey, its callow white protagonists trifle with the identity of a long-lost bluesman, in this case using the skills they developed wrangling drum breaks from old Black records for the benefit of white hipsters and hip-hoppers; unlike Fahey, they pay for their appropriation with their lives and the lives of everyone they love. (I told you it was gothic.) Kunzru did his research: his characters repeatedly echo the conversion narratives that blues record collectors like Fahey used to describe how they felt while listening to Black music on rare old 78s. But in this retelling, haunted by the wrongness of blacksound, the messages they hear coming off the grooves are vengeful, overtly menacing, distorted by historical guilt:

> I had listened to that record many times, but it was as if it had never broken my skin. The air was rent open by the sound; darkness poured in. *Babe I'll never die*, he sang. I'd always heard the line as frightened, the alcoholic singer afraid of the death he is swallowing: Sterno brand camping fuel strained through a cloth. But now I heard something else. A veiled threat. If what I've already swallowed doesn't kill me, nothing can. You will never be able to stop me, babe. I'll just keep on coming.[18]

---

[16] Media activist Donald Warden as quoted in Chester Higgins, "Fight Bias in Radio against Famous Blacks," *Jet*, June 24, 1971. Available online: https://books.google.com/books?id=rzcDAAAAMBAJ&pg=PA57&dq=Chester+Higgins,+"Fight+Bias+in+Radio+against+Famous+Blacks,"&hl=en&sa=X&ved=2ahUKEwi3sLS09uvyAhUSNn0KHXB7AfoQ6AF6BAgCEAI#v=onepage&q&f=false (accessed September 07, 2021).

[17] Matthew Morrison, "Race, Blacksound, and the (Re)Making of Musicological Discourse," *The Journal of the American Musicological Society* 72, no. 3 (2019): 781–823.

[18] Hari Kunzru, *White Tears: A novel* (Knopf, 2017), 87. The 78 rpm record being played is identified by the author as Victor 38535-A, Tommy Johnson's "Canned Heat Blues," from 1928.

Kunzru's novel is, in fact, an elaborate narrative labyrinth of white guilt, and it ends, as promised, in a torrent of white tears (and blood). But the real sin in the novel, as in the story of PTFM/WB, is pride. It's one thing to know and love Black music. It's quite another thing to believe you can impersonate it, and by virtue of that impersonation, efface responsibility for your own cultural privilege:

> —What do you mean? It's the best idea! These fuckers think this music was made in 1928, but actually we made it. We made it, fools! We made that shit last week! So who's the expert now? Who knows the tradition? We do! We own that shit!

Play that funky music, white boy.

Play that funky music 'til you die.

10

Althea and Donna, "Uptown Top Ranking" (1977)

Paul Long

I'm so in love, you know what I mean
I'm in love with Anthea and Donna
All that shit that goes
Uptown top ranking[1]

In January 1978, Vivien Goldman reported from Kingston for the UK music paper *Sounds* on her encounter with Althia and Donna.[2] The reporter anticipated that an album planned by the duo would fulfill the promise of their debut single "Uptown Top Ranking" (UTR). An established hit in Jamaica,[3] the record was about to end the nine-week-long run of Wings' "Mull of Kintyre" at the top of the UK chart. Goldman mused that the duo, while surprised by their sudden success, were perceptive and talented enough to use their profile in order to establish a music career: "People that hope to brush them aside as strictly joke business may find the joke's on them."[4]

The duo did make further singles (and Althea had already cut five discs for producer and singer Derrick Harriott), albeit all received with a lack of enthusiasm by record buyers. They delivered the album, its promise unrealized, and have thus far proven to be one-hit wonders. The point here is not to suggest that the joke is instead on Goldman: while the durability of an artist and their recordings are not available to even the most prescient of contemporaries, when success is registered with a Number 1 chart placing, who would bet against its reproduction? Of course, as evidenced across this volume, whatever the currency of the term, the categorization of one-hit wonder

---

[1] The Psychedelic Furs, "We Love You" (Epic, 1979).
[2] The original label and a later picture sleeve for UTR give the spelling as Althia. Later releases and coverage record her as Althea.
[3] Claudia Gardner, "Althea And Donna's 'Uptown Top Ranking' Digital Release Certified Silver By British Phonographic Industry," *Dancehall Mag*, November 12, 2020 (accessed January 01, 2021).
[4] Vivien Goldman, "Althia & Donna: Nah Pop No Style, A Strictly Roots...," *Sounds* (1978). Available online: http://www.rocksbackpages.com.ezproxy.lib.monash.edu.au/Library/Article/althia--donna-nah-pop-no-style- a-strictly-roots (accessed March 9, 2020).

can be moot, dependent upon the context in which the artist is framed and the position in time from which their achievement is delimited. Likewise, not all hits, whether a one-off or those heralding more durable careers, burn equally brightly. Indeed, while the one-hit wonder might appear to be the acme of pop's ephemerality, the appearance, elevation, and resonance of some records and artists are undiminished by an ascription of fleeting novelty.

The moment of Althea Forrest and Donna Reid is a suggestive one in the exchange economy of Jamaican and UK music culture, for thinking of how their record was heard and received. The specific context in focus here relates to the expanding Black presence in post-war Britain, of migrant expression and settlement in a largely hostile environment.[5] Echoing Paul Gilroy's notion of the public sphere function of Black music and its importance in this context, Caspar Melville describes how reggae (and soul) has provided a site for the circulation of ideas and sensibilities embodied in the networks of the "black Atlantic." The function of music, "carried on records and through the licensed and unlicensed airwaves, could be annexed to [...] identity work."[6] While Meville has in mind Black and white Londoners specifically, the sentiment can be expanded to capture a wider milieu in which the population of the UK was, and is, "engaged in exploring the formation, and the limits, of multiculture."[7]

An initial way of thinking of the role of UTR in this context of exploration is in terms of its mediation, translation, and transformation of various practices and representations in and around Jamaican music and culture. For instance, the attention afforded to a Jamaican hit record transposed to the UK generated questions regarding authenticity, a quality in which some commentators have been particularly interested. Katz, for instance, describes the song as a "novelty groove," repeating information recorded across reviews concerning Althea and Donna's status at the time of release as "two upper-class schoolgirls."[8] Whether the last of these is pertinent or otherwise, one of the song's refrains and themes can be heard as an insistence of legitimacy: "Nah pop no style, a strictly roots." Certainly, for many UK listeners, while UTR would have been heard as novel, this quality was allied to a sound and sentiment signifying reggae of contemporary and innovative stamp. As Walker notes, UTR's success in the UK can be understood as the moment in which "Jamaican deejay style breached the mainstream for the first time."[9] Goldman commented at the time of her interview that she was conscious of the dearth of female DJs in the Jamaican scene in which the particularly performative qualities of that role had emerged, namely creative intercessions into the sound of another's record. Althea and Donna thus appeared as genuine innovators

---

[5] See Huon Wardle and Laura Obermuller, "'Windrush Generation' and 'Hostile Environment': Symbols and Lived Experiences in Caribbean Migration to the UK," *Migration and Society* 2, no. 1 (2019): 81–9.

[6] Caspar Melville, *It's a London Thing: How Rare Groove, Acid House and Jungle Remapped the City* (Manchester: Manchester University Press, 2019), 78.

[7] Ibid.

[8] David Katz, *Solid Foundation: An Oral History of Reggae* (London: Bloomsbury, 2012), 860.

[9] Klive Walker, *Dubwise: Reasoning from the Reggae Underground* (Toronto: Insomniac Press, 2005), 238.

and were so recognized: "they're the first, and are billed as such on every poster round Kingston."[10]

Ultimately, any sense of UTR's originality is conditioned by its status as an "answer record," a response to "Three Piece Suit" (1975), a Jamaican hit by DJ Trinity (Wade Brammer) under the direction of producer Joe Gibbs. Trinity has spoken about the origins of his record, that inspiration came from his amusement in observing a man pursuing a much larger woman at a dance. One infers that the narrator of the song is a sharp-dressed Romeo—wearer of the title's three-piece suit, as well as stylish diamond socks ("and t'ing"). Trinity conveys a bawdy scenario of being seen with "the big fat thing" in Kingston's Constant Spring area, one involving a "rub up on the big bed springs." The encounter reveals the woman's voracious appetite as she "broke down me door and . . . asked me for more," advancing on the bed and furthermore demanding and drinking the narrator's beer. The excess of the scenario is underlined by the B-side "version" ("Big Fat Thing") and cartoon illustrations accompanying a full-length album also entitled *Three Piece Suit*, in which a man is dwarfed and collapsed into the bodily folds of a female figure.

Trinity's recording is an example of the DJ's intercession, a "talkover" or "toast" built upon Marcia Aitken's version of Alton Ellis's "I'm Still in Love with You" (as "I'm Still in Love with You Boy"). Trinity's vocal winds in and out of Aitken's avowals, creating a rather curious contrast of sentiment, between his farce and her yearning heartache. In turn, UTR takes the same rhythm track as its base: in this case, Aitken's vocal is removed, a mode of reworking and quotation which offers a conceptual complication to the idea of the "one-hit wonder." For instance, as Dick Hebdige notes, in 1976 there were at least twenty-five versions of "I'm Still in Love With You" at large.[11] Many of these were founded on the same material base as Aitken's, Trinity's, and Althea and Donna's records, a rhythm recorded by producer Gibbs and his in-house band The Professionals. In fact, UTR borrows much more from Trinity's record in sound, lyric, and sentiment. It quotes from it liberally: notably in terms of the repeated line "Love is all I bring" and a foregrounding of the detail of the singers' stylish dress and regular exclamation-punctuations of "ow!" The last is not in itself an innovative feature of "Three Piece Suit" in the context of reggae and deejay stylings, and Althea and Donna's pacing and placing is a direct copy.

Answer songs have a well-established lineage in popular music culture.[12] James Curtis, for instance, in his analysis of such records from the 1960s, suggests that the form tends to ride on the back of the popularity of the progenitor, resembling a parody on the basis that its meaning is dependent on familiarity with that original. The answer songs he cites were often themselves sole hits "by unknown singers whose lack of identity did not detract from the success of the record since only the song, and not

---

[10] Goldman, "Nah Pop No Style."
[11] Dick Hebdige, *Cut 'n' mix: Culture, identity and Caribbean music* (London: Routledge, 2003), 87.
[12] See B. Lee Cooper, "Response Recordings as Creative Repetition: Answer Songs and Pop Parodies in Contemporary American Music," *OneTwoThreeFour: A Rock 'N' Roll Quarterly* 4 (1987): 79–87.

the performer, mattered."[13] Given its success, this relationship was upended in the case of UTR.

The upending occurs too in terms of the gender politics of UTR. Althea and Donna's answer is a bold one, their lyric a confident riposte to Trinity and others for whom female independence and sexuality is a threat to be constrained. UTR's lyrics make an unapologetic point of the singers' pursuit of a good time: "Watch how we chuck it and t'ing." They celebrate their hipness and flaunt their peacocking up and down Constant Spring: lauding their fashionable khaki suits, pants (worn instead of modest skirts), as well as shocking halter back top "Say me give ya heart attack." The context for such reactions is a policing of a patriarchal and misogynistic society, evidenced in both Trinity's lyric and expectations associated with Rastafarian mores.[14] The latter is referenced in the figure of the "ranking dread" referenced in the song, albeit one who in this case appears to have been won over given "how we jamming and t'ing." For Goldman, the appeal of the song thus lies in the very fact that the artists are women: "the really important thing is that their voices are teasing without being coquettish, they're cheekily assertive—to re-phrase in punk parlance, Althia and Donna don't care." On this note, UTR's indebtedness to Aitken's sound also echoes the sentiment of that singer's "Narrow Minded Man," "a direct militant response" and challenge to the misogyny of a recording by the Meditations' "Woman Is Like a Shadow."[15]

Goldman expressed concern for Althea and Donna's fortunes in light of often nefarious dealings and contract arrangements in the Jamaican industry—particularly the nature of gendered imbalance and exploitation. Whatever the power of UTR, the confidence of Althea and Donna, and whatever happened to the fortune to which they were no doubt entitled, it is interesting to note the glossing of their achievement by a range of intermediaries. In the Jamaican context, and as reported by David Katz, Mikey Dread has laid claim to giving Althea and Donna a helping hand, having discovered the recording at Joe Gibbs' studio while in search of backing material for his own DJ performance: "Me ask them why them don't release it, and them never like the tune. From me start rinse it [air it on his own show], that blow up the place."[16] In the UK, Mike Hawkes, a producer for BBC DJs Kid Jensen and Paul Gambaccini, humbly recalled how "I predicted it would be a hit as soon as I heard it," observing, "it's jolly nice to be proven right."[17] The record suggests, however, that the key figure in giving a record national exposure in the UK was BBC DJ John Peel. His recollections offer insight into the lines of exchange between the Jamaica and UK music economies, and

---

[13] James Curtis, *Rock Eras: Interpretations of Music and Society, 1954–1984* (Bowling Green: Bowling Green State University Popular Press, 1987), 88.

[14] See Kieran Connell, *Black Handsworth: Race in 1980s Britain* (Oakland: University of California Press, 2019), 105; and Kadean Muschette Nichola Francis, Daniel Smith, Tatyana Johnson, Kimone Taylor, and Shereka Badchkam, "Sexual Agency in Contemporary Jamaica: The Case of the Nyhabinghi Empress," *Educational Research* (IJMCER) 2, no. 6 (2020): 21–4.

[15] Walker, *Dubwise*, 93.

[16] Quoted in Katz, *Solid Foundation*, 860.

[17] Quoted in Robin Katz, "Althea And Donna: Why It's A Hit Beyond Words," *Daily Mail*, January 2, 1978. Available online: http://www.rocksbackpages.com.ezproxy.lib.monash.edu.au/Library/Article/althea-and-donna-why-its-a-hit-beyond-words (accessed March 8, 2020).

the conventions of how BBC broadcasting worked in its treatment of music of the Black Atlantic. Having received a pre-release sample of the record and been impressed:

> [I] bought other copies of the import and took 'em round to other DJs and tried to persuade them to play it. . . . They all agreed it was a great record but wouldn't play it because it was like an import and so forth, so it was then picked up by Lightning . . . and then I think it went on to be picked up by Virgin and became a huge hit record.[18]

Prime among the claims of these mediators of the meanings of UTR are those of Trinity, who has discussed the extent to which the originality of his own record—possibly "the first dancehall tune"—was overshadowed by its imitator: "It's the first deejay song the people versioned. . . . My song was the only song who they did it over and it went into the British charts." Even more galling, he complains, "I didn't get any money but it's my melody and my words."[19]

Even allowing for the fact that it is unlikely that a *majority* of listeners to UTR would have encountered its direct antecedents,[20] and while there was something undoubtedly original about UTR in how it was heard, it did not arrive entirely unannounced. Aside from the rich import market serving black communities, in particular,[21] music of the Caribbean was not wholly unfamiliar to the UK charts, national radio, or outlets like the BBC's flagship television music program *Top of the Pops*. The singles chart had registered regular hits by Jamaican artists: Millie Small's "My Boy Lollipop," Number 2 in 1964, announced the sound of ska, and the artists and records following in this wake tracked the development of a variety of musical styles and genres. However, when viewed through the prism of chart success, like Althea and Donna and indeed Small, many of these would be remembered also as one-hit wonders, whatever their durability and importance as innovators. The richness of this variety and its presence includes The Upsetters with "Return of Django" (No. 5 in 1969); Bob and Marcia's version of "Young Gifted and Black" (No. 5 in 1970); Dave and Ansell Collins' "Double Barrel" (No. 1 in 1970); Ken Booth's version of "Everything I Own" (No. 1 in 1974); John Holt's cover of "Help Me Make It Through the Night" (No. 6 in 1974); and Susan Cadogan's "Hurt So Good" (1975, No. 4). In addition, by the mid-1970s a UK variant of reggae in the form of "Lovers Rock" had emerged,[22] while bands comprising

---

[18] Quoted at peel.fandom.com/wiki/Althea_%26_Donna.
[19] Quoted in Angus Taylor, "Interview with Trinity—Natural Chanter," *Reggaeville*, October 2, 2020. Available at www.reggaeville.com/artist-details/trinity/news/view/interview-with-trinity-natural-chanter/ (accessed January 1, 2021).
[20] Charts of specifically reggae music were compiled by magazines such as *Black Music*, founded in 1973 (later *Black Music & Jazz Review* later absorbed by *Blues and Soul*). Sales were evaluated with the help of specialized stores usually located in or patronized by the Caribbean community in particular, e.g., Black Wax and Don Christie in Birmingham, Intone, Record Corner, and Black Wax in London. Trinity and Aitken had both registered in specialist charts.
[21] See Michael de Koningh and Marc Griffiths, *Tighten Up!: the History of Reggae in the UK* (London: Sanctuary Pub Limited, 2003).
[22] See Lisa Palmer, "'LADIES A YOUR TIME NOW!' Erotic Politics, Lovers' Rock and Resistance in the UK," *African and Black Diaspora: An International Journal* 4, no. 2 (2011): 177–92

Black Britons such as Aswad, Steel Pulse, Misty In Roots, and Beshara had become established. With interest from labels like Island and Virgin, by the late 1970s roots reggae in particular was subject to what one marketing executive described as "the 'hard sell' treatment," with promotional materials circulated "just like we do with the pop artists—posters, streamers, special displays . . . we send our pluggers into the BBC."[23]

By way of comparison with the sizable if transient hits listed earlier, as well as the wider market for reggae music in the UK, I would argue that UTR received a reception around which a wider set of tropes were magnified. Fascinating to a range of observers was the record's argot, which merited explanation to a variety of audiences, thus framing the world of Althea and Donna as "Other." A literal translation of the lyrics was offered to the youthful readers of the specialized *Sounds*, by Goldman, and to those of the *Daily Mail* tabloid newspaper. For the latter, the record's success was a newsworthy event in spite of—or perhaps *because* of—the fact that it was supposed to be "virtually incomprehensible to British fans."[24]

Lacking an interest in the recording's musical origin, debt, and innovations, the presumption of the *Daily Mail*'s address to its readers was to correct a number of perceived misconceptions produced by the patois dialect of UTR. First, the song was *not* concerned with the UK's Top Rank chain of venues, rather, "[a]ccording to 17-year-old Althea Forrest, the title is a slang term for posing."[25] Second, the refrain "Nah pop no style, a strictly roots" was *not* a dedication to "earthy, roots reggae music" but instead another kind of claim to authenticity: in spite of appearances, the duo are not themselves posing but are, in fact, "down to earth." Finally, as if to disarm any sense of threat in the songs' otherness is the idea that it was conceived as a joke. Certainly, this is a narrative about the song that the duo themselves propagated—as repeated by Goldman and others—albeit one emphasizing its joyful and improvised qualities, accentuating a sense that they were intuitively innovative. Nonetheless, a joke may be taken up to excuse a host of issues.

The fascination with Althea and Donna's delivery connects here with the treatment of migrant speech as a curiosity to be scrutinized and policed, as were the broader sounds associated with Black migrant lives.[26] As Connell relates, the use of patois dialect by children was viewed by educators as evidence of an intellectual and cultural deficiency.[27] Patois was by no means universally smiled upon in Black culture and households, but its use could also provide an important communicative and bonding resource, particularly among generations born to migrants in the UK.[28] This resource was particularly associated with the positive Afro-centrism of Rastafarianism and accessed via the circulation of roots reggae records. Heard in this context, as a major

---

[23] Quoted in Hebdige, *Cut 'n' Mix*, 97.
[24] Katz, "Why It's a Hit."
[25] Ibid.
[26] See Jason McGraw, "Sonic Settlements: Jamaican Music, Dancing, and Black Migrant Communities in Postwar Britain," *Journal of Social History* 52, no. 2 (2018): 353–82.
[27] Connell, *Black Handsworth*, 45.
[28] Ibid., 106.

hit, UTR was the highly audible sound of authentic Jamaican inflections. It was heard in a wider cultural sphere in which the power of self-representation was limited and where Commonwealth migrants were the subjects of a host of racist slanders limiting opportunities for a respectful hearing.[29] Caribbean speech, for instance, was regularly lampooned in the UK media, denying any attention to what might be said in favor of the idea that how it was said was intrinsically ridiculous and at odds with an implied normality. This is evidenced in the form of the character "Chalky White," part of the act of popular entertainer Jim Davidson, for decades a fixture of UK TV. It was a performance that melded an egregious imitation of patois with an excess of bodily gestures deployed to connote "West Indianness" in order to deliver material that confirmed intellectual deficiency.[30]

Neil Spencer has commented that in spite of their popularity with record buyers, "The series of reggae hits that had made the UK's pop charts in the late 60s and early 70s seemed only to harden prejudice; Tony Blackburn, in his pomp as Radio 1's premier DJ, declared them 'rubbish.'"[31] It is instructive to note too that an introduction of the sounds of contemporary Jamaican and African music into John Peel's BBC playlist in 1969 was met with resistance from a considerable portion of his audience, expressed in hate mail and indeed threats to him and his family. As Peel's partner reports, the response of the DJ and his producer was simply to program more reggae records, and certainly from the early 1970s onward his BBC shows featured a wealth of such music.[32]

Such contexts prompt questions qualifying how, why, and with whom a song like UTR was popular and how it was understood. The moment of UTR was one in which the avowedly racist political party the National Front (NF) expanded its base and visibility. As Melville relates, the aim of the National Front was not only to oppose the development of a multiracial society but to destroy it.[33] In music, an on-stage racist tirade by Eric Clapton was punctuated by his use of the NF slogan to "Keep Britain White." The absurdity of a figure who had made his fortune as a disciple of Black music-making such pronouncements was on the one hand an instance of the ambivalent relationship some listeners might have with popular music, while on the other hand, it galvanized a progressive and unifying movement of protest in the form of Rock Against Racism.[34] Whatever the joking intent that originated UTR, its celebration of the *joie de vivre* of young women and crystallization of a particular set of sounds and styles at a particular moment offer an answer to both the gender imbalance of

---

[29] See Darrell Newton, *Paving the Empire Road: BBC Television and Black Britons* (Manchester: Manchester University Press, 2013) and Gavin Schaffer, *The Vision of a Nation* (Houndmills, Basingstoke: Palgrave Macmillan, 2014).

[30] Examples can be viewed on YouTube where comments veer from vilification to those asserting the harmlessness of the joke (see https://www.youtube.com/watch?v=4njiljpDIEg).

[31] Neil Spencer, "Reggae: The Sound that Revolutionised Britain," *Guardian*, January 30, 2011. Available online: https://www.theguardian.com/music/2011/jan/30/reggae-revolutionary-bob-marley-britain (accessed January 1, 2021).

[32] See John Peel and Sheila Ravenscroft, *Margrave of the Marshes* (London: Bantam, 2005), 258–9.

[33] Melville, *It's a London Thing*, 79, n. 6.

[34] This is covered in Ian Goodyer, "Rock Against Racism: Multiculturalism and Political Mobilization, 1976–81," *Immigrants & Minorities* 22, no. 1 (2003): 44–62.

music business and culture and also the hostility of British society. Thus, we should not neglect that in discussion of this febrile context the very audibility and visibility of acts like Althea and Donna in the public sphere were important affirmations of value, however fleeting. The fact of their success and elevation provided resources of hope for many, particularly those migrants struggling to make dignified lives. As "lost world" comments on YouTube, recalling being sixteen years old at the time of UTR's chart run: "trust me this song at the top of the charts was a big thing for carribbean kids at school. Like me."[35]

One problem with the ascription to records and artists as one-hit wonders is that it has the tendency to produce a sense of each as *sui generis*. This has the effect of removing them from contexts and connections to patterns of popular cultural tastes and in which their significance can be gauged. Even as UTR proved to be an exceptional kind of hit, its connectedness, impact, and durability can be affirmed: as they responded to Trinity, so in turn Big Youth's "Spanking Ranking" answered Althea and Donna. In this author's memory, the duo appeared across British light entertainment television programs, in performance and referenced as novelty, the song's lyrics taken up by a variety of artists—apparently affectionately, while also evincing the malign power of mocking imitation. On the duo's sole appearance on *Top of the Pops*, the BBC's in-house orchestra struggled to emulate the qualities of Joe Gibbs' house band The Professionals, whose personnel included Robbie Shakespeare on bass, drummer Sly Dunbar, and Earl "Chinna" Smith on guitar. Althea and Donna's wry looks in this performance suggest that the joke is definitely on someone else.

Subsequent to its chart run, the durability of the record and its popularity are suggestive for thinking of the afterlife of a one-hit wonder. The record has been widely sampled and reworked, the memory of UTR vying perhaps for the echoes and recognition of Aitken's and Trinity's precursors. The affective resonance of UTR is felt by those who encountered it upon arrival and who have discovered it since. As expressed in comments left at YouTube by "Tojazzer": "If this song doesn't make you happy, there is something wrong with you. I still have the 45 record I bought in Belfast when I was 10 years old"; c'rusty crooton' laments "Fk sake. I know nothing of this genre (for my sins). . . happened to catch this in the car on the [radio] Point me where to go with this!!"[36] As the UK DJ David Rodigan has said of UTR's endurance, "It was a massive song, still is. I can play that record at festivals for rock fans and 80,000 people will sing it."[37] The nature of UK nationalism and hostility to well-established as well as new migrants in the era of Brexit suggests, however, that some things remain unchanged in the location of UTR's greatest success.[38] Nonetheless, there continues to be optimistic power in the enduring joy and sentiment of Althea and Donna's promise that "Love is all I bring" (Figure 10.1).

[35] www.youtube.com/watch?v=joh37lrvf-s.
[36] https://www.youtube.com/watch?v=joh37lrvf-s.
[37] Quoted in Howard Campbell, "T'was the Year of Uptown Top Rankings," *Jamaica Observer*, June 8, 2017. Available online: http://www.jamaicaobserver.com/entertainment/t-8217-was-the-year-of-uptown-top-rankings_100189?profile=1116&template=MobileArticle (accessed January 01, 2021).
[38] See Wardle and Obermuller, "Windrush Generation."

Figure 10.1 Photograph by kind permission of Althea and Donna, courtesy of Tyrone Downie Jr.

References

Campbell, H. (2017), "T'was the Year of Uptown Top Rankings," *Jamaica Observer*, June 8. Available online: http://www.jamaicaobserver.com/entertainment/t-8217-was-the-year-of-uptown-top-rankings_100189?profile=1116&template=MobileArticle (accessed January 1, 2021).

Connell, K. (2019), *Black Handsworth: Race in 1980s Britain*, Oakland: University of California Press.

Cooper, B. L. (1987), "Response Recordings as Creative Repetition: Answer Songs and Pop Parodies in Contemporary American Music," *OneTwoThreeFour: A Rock'N'Roll Quarterly*, 4: 79–87.

Curtis, J. M. (1987), *Rock Eras: Interpretations of Music and Society, 1954–1984*, Bowling Green: Bowling Green State University Popular Press.

De Koningh, M. and M. Griffiths (2003), *Tighten Up!: The History of Reggae in the UK*, London: Sanctuary Pub Limited.

Gardner, C. (2020), "Althea And Donna's 'Uptown Top Ranking' Digital Release Certified Silver By British Phonographic Industry," *Dancehall Mag*, November 12. Available online: https://www.dancehallmag.com/2020/11/12/news/althea-and-donnas-uptown-top-ranking-digital-release-certified-silver-by-british-phonographic-industry.html (accessed January 1, 2021).

Goldman, V. (1978), "Althia & Donna: Nah Pop No Style, A Strictly Roots. . .," *Sounds*. Available online: http://www.rocksbackpages.com.ezproxy.lib.monash.edu.au/Library/Article/althia--donna-nah-pop-no-style- a-strictly-roots (accessed March 8, 2020)

Goodyer, I. (2003), "Rock Against Racism: Multiculturalism and Political Mobilization, 1976–81," *Immigrants & Minorities*, 22 (1): 44–62.

Hebdige, D. (2003), *Cut 'n' Mix: Culture, Identity and Caribbean Music*, London: Routledge.

Katz, R. (1978), "Althea And Donna: Why It's a Hit Beyond Words," *Daily Mail*, January 2. Available online: http://www.rocksbackpages.com.ezproxy.lib.monash.edu.au/Library/Article/althea- and-donna-why-its-a-hit-beyond-words (accessed March 8, 2020).

Katz, D. (2012), *Solid Foundation: An Oral History of Reggae*, London: Bloomsbury.

McGraw, J. (2018), "Sonic Settlements: Jamaican Music, Dancing, and Black Migrant Communities in Postwar Britain," *Journal of Social History*, 52 (2): 353–82.

Muschette, K., N. Francis, D. Smith, T. Johnson, K. Taylor and S. Badchkam (2020), "Sexual Agency in Contemporary Jamaica: The Case of the Nyhabinghi Empress," *Educational Research (IJMCER)*, 2 (6): 21–4.

Melville, C. (2019), *It's a London Thing: How Rare Groove, Acid House and Jungle Remapped the City*, Manchester: Manchester University Press.

Newton, D. M. (2013), *Paving the Empire Road: BBC Television and Black Britons*, Manchester: Manchester University Press.

Palmer, L. A. (2011), "'LADIES A YOUR TIME NOW!' Erotic Politics, Lovers' Rock and Resistance in the UK," *African and Black Diaspora: An International Journal*, 4 (2): 177–92.

Peel, J. and S. Ravenscroft (2005), *Margrave of the Marshes*, London: Bantam.

Schaffer, G. (2014), *The Vision of a Nation*, Houndmills Basingstoke: Palgrave Macmillan UK.

Spencer, Neil (2011), "Reggae: The Sound that Revolutionised Britain," *Guardian*, January 30. Available online: https://www.theguardian.com/music/2011/jan/30/reggae-revolutionary-bob-marley-britain (accessed January 1, 2021).

Taylor, A. (2020), "Interview with Trinity—Natural Chanter," *Reggaeville*, October 2. Available online: https://www.reggaeville.com/artist-details/trinity/news/view/interview-with-trinity-natural-chanter/ (accessed January 1, 2021).

Walker, K. (2005), *Dubwise: Reasoning from the Reggae Underground*, Toronto: Insomniac Press.

Wardle, H. and L. Obermuller (2019), "'Windrush Generation' and 'Hostile Environment': Symbols and Lived Experiences in Caribbean Migration to the UK," *Migration and Society*, 2 (1): 81–9.

11

Plastic Bertrand, "Ça plane pour moi" (1977)

Patrick McGuinness

As a nine-year-old Belgian in an English boarding school in 1978, I was often called upon to explain my country's flash-in-the-pan one-hit-wonder of a musical export: "Ça plane pour moi," by Plastic Bertrand. Forty-three years later, I'm doing it again, but in the august company of critics and scholars.

That's a trajectory that tells me more about myself than it does about Plastic Bertrand, but my aim, in this contribution to the annals of ephemera that is a book on one-hit wonders, will be threefold. First, I will trace the song's origins, along with its contested history, in the context of Belgian punk and punk's love-hate relationship with pop culture. Second, I will explore the questions it raises about voice, language, and originality. Third, I will comment on its *belgitude*, and how it fits into a specific set of cultural and linguistic matrices characteristic of Belgian literary, artistic, and musical production. I will not do these three things in chronological order, but as I go along.

The first point to make is that, while "Ça plane pour moi" conforms to the "one-hit-wonder" format—singularly successful, briefly ubiquitous, and scoring high on the earworm scale—Plastic Bertrand himself was—is—a musical artist of some range and longevity. Roger Jouret, to give him his real name, was a member of the short-lived but influential Belgian punk band Hubble Bubble, whose two albums *Hubble Bubble* and *Faking* are still in circulation. Notable bands from that era include Raxola and The Kids, who are still going strong and represent a Belgian punk scene that was international in influence and in reach, and existed on a Brussels-London axis that involved cross-channel collaborations that produced songs in French, English, and Dutch.[1] Since "Ça plane pour moi," Jouret/Bertrand has been involved in a range of ventures, from singing and producing to acting, guesting on reality shows, and appearing in film cameos (*Wolf of Wall Street* and *Three Kings*, among others). Other activities include cofounding a contemporary art gallery in Brussels, working with ABBA on a children's musical, competing in international Scrabble competitions, and collaborating with Belgian anarchist and filmmaker Noël Godin.

---

[1] *Bloody Belgium: A Compilation of Early Belgian Punkrock '77-'81* (no label, 1997). https://www.discogs.com/Various-Bloody-Belgium/release/405645; and *Bloodstains Across Belgium* (Atomium Records, 1997). https://www.discogs.com/Various-Bloodstains-Across-Belgium/release/405126.

A feature of the one-hit wonder as a phenomenon is that it both consumes its maker and casts them aside. The one-hit-wonder label is at once a ball-and-chain and a hot-air balloon: your hit holds you back and drags you down, while also soaring away without you. In fact that is what "planer" means in French: to soar, to glide, to hover, to roam vertiginously in the skies. While "Ça plane pour moi" "soared" away like so many other one-hit wonders, the part of Roger Jouret that is not Plastic Bertrand has amassed a sizable portfolio of different activities. Enough, at any rate, to keep this particular balloon sufficiently ballasted and the artist behind it sufficiently grounded.

Back in my Bristol boarding school in 1977/8, I wasn't to know this. But, in what I supposed was an ambassadorial role for my country, I felt obliged to make sense of the song's lyrics for my contemporaries. As I tell my own children today *ad nauseam*, listening to music was different in those days. We huddled around the "wireless" (as the teachers called it) and listened to the Top 40 on Sundays, and around the TV on Thursdays to watch *Top of the Pops*. Some of my schoolfriends went home for weekends and recorded the charts on their parents' "music centers" so we could listen to the cassettes. Learning the words was another whole drama, and we all sang imperfectly heard lyrics with gusto. Another thing I didn't know back then was that there's a word for this: *mondegreen*, a term coined by Sylvia Wright in 1954 to define mishearing lyrics in a way that makes sense, and is often evocative and poetic, but bears no relation to the words themselves. We've all done it—the *mondegreen* is integral to hearing, and especially to our attempts to make sense of song lyrics in a world where it was impossible to look them up. Schools were mondegreen-factories, full of the kind of productive and often inspiring misunderstandings that a quick check on the internet or the smartphone kills stone dead today. Just as the productive misinterpretation has its place in the history of ideas, so the mondegreen has its own place in the history of listening.

As for the tune—three chords, four notes, the words delivered in a staccato monotone that sounds more spoken at speed than sung—it was so dangerously easy to remember that just seeing the word "planer" in a Baudelaire poem today is enough to trigger days of Bertrandian parody-punk earworm. The disproportion between the straightforwardness of the melody and the surreal incoherence of the words was a challenge when it came to parsing the lyrics of "Ça plane pour moi," but I was at an advantage among people for whom the whole song was a mondegreen: no one else spoke French. The lyrics themselves are random without being totally nonsensical, and I am impressed at how much of them I caught back in 1977. They do not bear translating (though people have debated the various *nuances*[2]), but they constitute the monologue of a young man having the classic all-round good time: there's drink, a hangover, possible drugs, strongly implied sex, and a compliment, delivered in English, in which a girl calls him "King of the Divan." The song ends with a fight, where the girl trashes his pad and walks out. The title phrase, which is also the refrain, means, in colloquial French: things are going well for me; they glide; they soar; they hover.

---

[2] See https://www.david.gibbs.co.uk/plastic/plastic_lyrics.htm.

Despite its incoherence, the French is clipped, hip, *argotique*, streetwise, punky, snarly, and ironic, while the accent—and this will become important later—was, to my ears, much more like the French I heard at home, in Wallonia, than the French I heard in Plastic Bertrand's native Brussels.

"Ça plane..." was released in late 1977 as the B-side to "Pogo Pogo," Plastic Bertrand's inaugural single. It immediately became the song-*vedette* and the songs were swapped on subsequent pressings—the first of many reversals and inversions in this hit's history. Both songs were composed by Lou Deprijck (music) and Yves Lacomblez (words), stalwarts of the Belgian punk scene, and recorded at Studio Morgan in Brussels. Hubble Bubble had disbanded following the accidental death of their bass player, and the band's manager introduced Jouret to Deprijck, who saw him as the right performer to front his punk-parodic product. Jouret, in his Hubble Bubble days, had sported traditional punk looks, including the safety-pin-through-cheek motif which adorns the first cover of "Ça plane.../Pogo Pogo." For the performances and the video, the look changes: more obviously New Wave, Bertrand's demeanor is more androgynous, the make-up more glamorous, the clothes silky and shiny. According to Deprijck, Jouret was sent to London to buy his Plastic Bertrand clothes at Vivienne Westwood and Malcolm McLaren's Kings Road shop—a detail that tells us something about punk's readiness to traffic in designer wear and commercialism (Figure 11.1).

An album, *Plastic Bertrand—An 1* [*Plastic Bertrand—Year 1*], was put together in a week to capitalize on the phenomenal success of the song, which peaked in the UK charts at Number 8, and at 47 in the US *Billboard* charts. Bertrand featured three times on *Top of the Pops* in a year, quite an achievement for a foreign-language song

Figure 11.1 "Ça plane pour moi" 7-inch (RKM, 1977).

that even French speakers were at pains to elucidate. The second appearance was a UK consecration, because Bertrand was accompanied by Legs and Co, *Top of the Pops*' resident dance troupe. Bertrand became a celebrity in the French-speaking world and remains today a frequent tourer not just in France and Belgium but in Québec. In the UK, appearances in the 1990s and 2000s on *Eurotrash*, *Clarkson*, and other variety shows, along with their equivalents in Holland, Germany, Spain, and as far afield as Japan and Korea, ensure that a song, a look, and an act that began as parody keeps coming back as meta-parody.

When I encountered "Ça plane . . ." in England, it was a cultural/national out-of-body experience. I had heard the song on RTL and various French and Belgian radio stations at home, and I knew it from the way, on Wednesdays, Fridays, and Saturdays, it thumped out of "La Travure," the little nightclub behind my grandmother's house in Bouillon. The club, where my parents had had their wedding party in the early 1960s, had no soundproofing and broke every rule about noise, underage drinking, and opening hours in the book. My bedroom was at the back of the house, so I heard not just the music but the arguments and the fights outside. I knew it as a Belgian song because Plastic himself was all over the TV shows, and when I arrived in England, here he was again: his Belgitude foregrounded rather than submerged beneath a one-size-fits-all cliché of Frenchness. He joined Magritte, Maeterlinck, Hergé, and Brel in the category of Belgians who could never have been other than Belgian and never sought to be, who took what Paris offered but didn't conform to it. As Simenon replied, when asked why he didn't change his nationality: "There was no reason for me to be born Belgian, so there's no reason for me to stop being Belgian." Patriotism through indifference to patriotism is very Belgian, but there was another context to Plastic Bertrand's emergence. "Ça plane . . ." was released in late 1977, around the same time as Jacques Brel released his final, valedictory album, *Les Marquises*, and Plastic was still pogo-ing around the international charts a year later, when Brel died. There's a kind of irony, not lost on us Belgians, that one of the greatest singer-songwriters in any language was taking his leave at exactly the same time as a manufactured parody act that described itself as "sheer nonsense" was making its entrance.[3]

According to Deprijck (interviewed in *Le Soir* in 2017), the "planer" of the title is a mocking wink ("un clin d'oeil") at Michel Delpech's 1975 hit "Tu me fais planer" ("You make me fly"), a schmoozy, soft-focus, sentimental piece of Gallic schmaltz, for which the video ("le tube" in French) was Delpech on a crowded dancefloor of slow-dancing couples, singing the song we're hearing over his partner's shoulder. The refrain, "wouoouhouhou . . ." was a tribute to the Beach Boys, and the voice an attempt to mimic what Deprijck called the "eructations of Johnny Rotten." "Ça plane . . ." felt in ironic dialogue with the prevailing anthems of coupledom as represented not just by Delpech but by the likes of Johnny Halliday and Claude François, who merged the French *chanson* tradition with rock and disco in ways that proved hugely successful in

---

[3] Plastic Bertrand, quoted in *Plastic Bertrand—An 1*, CD liner notes.

the French-speaking world but never made it across the channel. That this jumped-up lip-synching Belgian ex-punk with a three-chord song, daft lyrics, and a one-trick dance routine was suddenly all over our screens and airwaves seemed a classic piece of belgitudinous *autodérision*, as well as one in the eye to the French.

The song was Number 1 in thirty-one countries and had sold 20 million copies by 2010, when an article appeared in the Belgian daily, *Le Soir*, about a legal dispute between the composer, Lou Deprijck, and Bertrand/Jouret. The article became, in turn, an international hit, picked up by newspapers and websites, talk shows, and social media across the globe. The ownership of "Ça plane . . ." was now in question: in 2006, the Belgian record label AMC, owners of the original tapes, took Lou De Pryck (Deprijck's trading name) to court for using the original recordings in his own version of the song. But Deprijck claimed that it had been his voice from the start. More: it was his voice on Plastic Bertrand's first album and on the three subsequent albums. His story was that he had always planned to perform the song, but didn't have the right look, and Jouret/Bertrand was chosen. When Bertrand's voice was deemed unsuitable, Deprijck recorded it himself and Bertrand merely mimed it. What we had been hearing all these years was not Plastic Bertrand's voice but Deprijck's own, "lippée" by Jouret.

Accusations and counteraccusations followed: in 2006, a Brussels court deemed Plastic Bertrand "the only person, juridically, to have the status of artist performer of the song"—a fatal piece of legalese designed precisely to avoid answering the question of who *actually* sang the song. In 2010, a court-appointed linguistic analyst concluded that the voice on the original hit single was indeed Deprijck's and not Jouret/Bertrand's. On what basis? Not just on the basis of voice analysis but on the basis that the accent was a Walloon accent, from the south of Belgium (Deprijck is from Lessines in the Hainaut), and not the Brussels accent of Plastic Bertrand. It had for decades been an open secret that Bertrand had indeed recorded the song, but that his recording had been discarded and replaced with Deprijck's. Bertrand admitted the song was not his, but that he had been bribed with a share of the rights and the promise—never honored—that he could record his own version.[4] When Atomium Records brought out, in 1997, the album of Belgian punk classics *Bloodstains across Belgium*, the sleeve notes call Plastic Bertrand "Mr Fake himself." It's hard not to think that the "secret de polichinelle," as it was called—the "open secret"—of who sang "Ça plane pour moi . . ." was not being referenced.

The whole saga—whose voice, whose song, what constitutes "performing," how is "singing" a song different from "performing" it, what is it to "own" a musical work, what is the difference between the legal right and the moral right to a work, what does it mean to mime, to lip-synch, to dub or be dubbed, and what is the relation of the performer to the performed?—seems to go to the heart of the one-hit wonder as a pop product. It also, however, plays an interesting and very Belgian variation on accent and language, and on the cultural politics of Belgium's linguistic communities.

---

[4] *Le Soir*, November 30, 2017: https://plus.lesoir.be/127090/article/2017-11-30/ca-plane-pour-moi-lhistoire-dun-tube-vieux-de-quarante-ans. Accessed July 9, 2021.

"Ça plane . . ." is not a great song, and it may not even be a good song, but it is very Belgian in one respect above all: people are still arguing about who owns it, and where, in Belgium, it comes from. Belgium is a country of micro-distances: Lessines is 56 kilometers, or 34 miles, from Brussels, yet Deprijck and Jouret speak sufficiently different French for a forensic linguistician to come to a definitive conclusion about the accent on a punk single. Of all the people involved in the ongoing dispute, Yves Lacomblez is the least affected. In an interview for *La Dernière heure* in 2012, he laughs off the Deprijck-Bertrand tussle and notes that they at least agree on one thing: that he wrote the lyrics.

Listening to Plastic Bertrand with my English ear, it would indeed be what it eventually became: a piece of Eurotrash, a daft, cheap, catchy, and disposable musical *curio* unable to decide whether it wants to take the money and run, or take the money and run while also ironizing the whole business of taking the money and running. The modern excuse for so many acts of self-ignorance has been self-knowledge, and it's a question that punk asked itself in various ways, from The Sex Pistols to The Clash. Commercialism was the song's future, regardless of its origins, and Plastic Bertrand milked it (and was milked by it) in the coming decades in ways that financially benefited Deprijck, regardless of who sang it, and arguably thanks to the fact that Plastic Bertrand lip-synched it. It was the falsity that authenticated its energy.

From the Belgian point of view, and listening with my Belgian ear, the song is a rather different artifact: the country that made Jacques Brel has nothing to apologize for anyway, but "Ça plane . . ." was also the product of a very Belgian set of influences and relationships to the dominant culture of France and French music. As I noted earlier, while the song's style was firmly based on English punk, and was also the product of a relationship between English and Belgian musicians, the aural ecosystem in which it flourished was the French-language *chanson*, the world of French and francophone radio, as well as the biculturalism of the Brussels music scene, which was not only *sui generis* but functioned as a meeting point between London, Paris, and Amsterdam. From that perspective, a different set of coordinates prevails. In a soundscape saturated with the self-importance of the French *chanson* and the sentimental cheesiness of French pop, Plastic Bertrand's ironic one-hit wonder took on the role of a great deal of Belgian art and literature, which was to deride and mock and undercut the *suffisance* and entitlement of France. Not for nothing do the sleeve notes for *Plastic Bertrand—An 1* contain the line: "Thanks to Moliére [sic], Coneille [sic], Racine . . . and the others." Like its poets and novelists, Belgium's musicians, composers, and singers exist in the margins of the dominant culture while also occupying its spaces with a different and denationalized sense of who the French language belongs to. This was and remains a feature of Belgian francophone art, from the Symbolist poets of the 1880s and 1890s, via the Belgian surrealists, up to poets such as Jean-Pierre Verheggen (author of *Le Degré Zorro de l'écriture*) and musicians such as Stromae. I recognized the song's *belgitude* then, and I recognize it now, and it has defined a great deal of my academic and creative writing.

*

Coda: The Double

As a child, the discovery that *Top of the Pops* was mimed was hard enough to bear. But I'm glad I was an adult when I heard that not only did Plastic Bertrand not write the music or the words but he didn't sing them either. Truly, Belgium had found its anti-Brel.

The song has a further dimension, which tells us something about the relationship between Belgian and British punk. When Deprijck composed the tune, he also offered it to Alan Ward, who was working with him in the studio after moving to Brussels. Ward's band, Bastard, included The Damned guitarist Brian James (a long-standing belgophile musician) and the Raxola frontman Yves Kengen, and Ward is credited on the LP *Plastic Bertrand—An 1* as the album's sound engineer. Ward, who had suggested to Deprijck speeding up the recording of "Ça plane . . ." to achieve its trademark manic tempo, took on the song for his own new band, Elton Motello, and recorded it with the same musicians as Plastic Bertrand's version. In Ward's hands, however, Deprijck's melody became the single "Jet Boy Jet Girl." With Ward's lyrics, it too was a monologue, but this time spoken by a fifteen-year-old boy in a sexual relationship with an older man. The sound is dirtier, more authentic, the guitar (by Mike Butcher, another English musician in the Brussels outpost of Morgan studios) more obviously punk-driven, and the voice raw and seething with anger and pain. The refrain was more down to earth, alternating between "Jet Boy Jet Girl" and "He gives me head," while references to murder, penetration, and glue-sniffing complete the look. Roger Jouret had himself played drums for Elton Motello, and appears in old band photographs and on the cover of the single "Jet Boy Jet Girl," which is also B-sided by "Pogo Pogo." Just as the same stock can produce distinct but related dishes, so Deprijck's tune produced two distinct but related singles (Figure 11.2).

Figure 11.2 "Pogo Pogo" 7-inch (Pinball Records, 1977).

To search out Elton Motello's performance is to behold the Mr Hyde to Plastic Bertrand's Dr Jekyll: Ward, dressed in a torn T-shirt, dances jerkily and flings his arms out, made up like a cross between Pierrot lunaire and Frankenstein's monster. He smacks his own head to the words "He gives me head" and dislodges an explosion of powder. At one point in the performance, Plastic Bertrand comes onstage and pogoes up close to him, dressed in an immaculately neat pair of white trousers and a striped Jean-Paul Gaultier-style sailor top. Bertrand points knowingly, "Elton" feigns horror and surprise. It is a recognition scene between twins with very different fortunes: one is an antiseptic pop hit; one is a reviled, taboo-breaking flop, now a cult classic. One is punk as parody and as product; the other is, well, punk. Each band's first album also tells us something about time and duration, about the hubris, the chanciness and the fatalism of the music industry, and about their different fates: Plastic Bertrand's album was titled *Year 1*, Elton Motello's *Victim of Time*. For two songs that began in the same place at the same time, the titles evince a very different conception of how Time would treat them: the One-hit wonder and Non-hit wonder.

12

Nick Gilder, "Hot Child in the City" (1978)

Richard John Parfitt

Among the rough trade of the metropolis stands like a fawn in the forest a child. In that dark wood she is the green fruit on a rotten tree. Innocence is about to meet Experience. A lazy drum fill falls into a pattern not unlike the Rolling Stones' "Honky Tonk Woman" (1969). It slopes and slides as the bass arrives. The guitar harmonic mirrors the fluorescent lights of the city. We hear a three-chord turnaround. There is danger. We will never know her name or what her game is, but the songster tells us she is a Hot Child in the City. We've seen the videos and read the books so we imagine a strawberry blonde under a wide-brimmed hat wearing a cheap summer frock and red plastic sandals revealing painted toes. Barefaced and freckly with fat lips sucking on a Ring Pop. Waiting for the man. And when the man arrives and the car stops she leans in and you can just about see—in the demimonde—the driver: lean and leathered elbow resting on the doorframe, and we are reminded of the scene from *Pinocchio* (1939) when our runaway hero is lured away to Pleasure Island—that amusement park where "being bad is a lotta fun" and children are turned into donkeys. And the songster groans. Discreetly implores. Perhaps a touch too much: come on down to my place baby (1978), and the Hot Child is led away by a John in a black jacket and a cream silk shirt exposing his swanlike neck, while in gold floating capitals we read off the record sleeve:

> HOT *adjective:* sexually attractive or sexually desirable
> CHILD *noun:* schoolgirl, juvenile, minor, junior; stripling
> They are the Nick Gilder Band and their 45rpm is Number 1 on the *Billboard* Chart.
> The song is sung from the POV of the customer.
> JOHN *noun:* a prostitute's client.

Hot Child in the City produced by Mike Chapman, best known for writing glam rock smashes such as The Sweet's "Teenage Rampage" (1973), a pop record which so infuriated Queen of Clean and mother of three Mary Whitehouse that she wrote, "This record, thanks to the publicity given to it is now No 1. in the charts."[1] BAN THIS FILTH!

---

[1] Ben Thompson, *Ban This Filth! Letters From the Mary Whitehouse Archive* (London: Faber & Faber, 2012), Kindle Edition, 105.

It's a sign of the times. You can't stop the rock. This is power-pop. This is paedo-pop. For someone with a social conscience Nick Gilder seems unconcerned, if not a little lascivious, and possibly overexcited when he sings to the Hot Child, Come on down to my place—and we'll make LOVE, hitting a high note reminiscent of sexual rapture. It's Angelic. Diabolic. Musicologically speaking, it's a slow dance balls to the wall verse chorus verse chorus [tasteful guitar solo] middle eight chorus × 2 sort of affair. You know the score. You've heard it before. Production-wise it's as close to sonic perfection as you'd expect from a pop alchemist like Mike Chapman. A *smash hit* then. Both these words calculated in their muscularity. The violence implicit. The old one-two. The track has, if I may use the scholarly term, razzamatazz. It is heavy with production tricks and hookworms, feeding upon blood, causing malnutrition, fatigue, and, in extreme cases, death. As the song ends the vocal whispers seductively in our collective ear, *Hot Child*, and the whole thing, is over in a Wham Bam Thank You Ma'am three minutes and twenty seconds.

In an interview with *Rolling Stone* magazine Nick Gilder said, "I'm intrigued by sex. I write stories around it. I've seen a lot of young girls, 15 and 16, walking down Hollywood Boulevard with their pimps. It hurts to see so I tried writing from the perspective of a lecher."[2] This interview earned Gilder the nickname "Nabokov of the Jukebox," but if Gilder's libertine is Nabokovian, we have a narrator who does not display the manipulations usually associated with sexual intimidators. Unlike, for instance, Professor Humbert, we have no access to an interior monolog that might betray the inclinations of a lecher, and instead are seduced by an upbeat vocal delivery that is engaging and instantly commercial, perplexing the listener with its congenial charm. If this is social comment, then it is lost in the mix and I am inclined to think retrospective. It was, after all, a time of the Burt Reynolds mustache, Virginia Slims, a time when young girls were routinely and without remark objectified and hypersexualized in advertising.

In a 1975 advert for Love's Baby Soft a young woman dressed as a child licks her lips and sucks on a lollipop as the voiceover tries to seduce us with the line "There's one person nobody can resist, and that's a baby," while the slogan "Because innocence is sexier than you think" scrolls across the screen.[3] Maybe Gilder is simply reflecting the times and even riffing off the history of popular music where the fantasy of the Hot Child is so ubiquitous and well referenced I am reluctant to list any. Whether it be the Rosetta Stone of debauchery that is Sonny Boy Williamson's "Good Morning Lil' School Girl" (1937) or Sting's "Don't Stand So Close to Me" (1980), the message is clear: that girl is half his age (Figure 12.1).

We shouldn't be surprised. Teenage prostitution has long been subject to exploitation by big entertainment. One of the seminal films of the 1970s, *Taxi Driver* (1976) stars a twelve-year-old Jodie Foster as a child prostitute. In that movie, the director, Martin Scorsese, seemed to encapsulate the raw power of a decade so noxious with machismo that it could only explode in sexual violence across the screen. In *Pretty Baby* (1978), the director Louis Malle has a twelve-year-old Brooke

---

[2] Cited in Fred Bronson, *The Billboard Book of Number One Hits* (New York: Billboard Books, 1988).
[3] Available at www.youtube.com/watch?v=l7IP5SV6GqQ. Accessed May 29, 2021.

Figure 12.1 Love cosmetics.

Shields living in a house in New Orleans as a child prostitute who is "auctioned off to a man who will deflower her." Or perhaps you'd prefer to stay at home and watch the made-for-television drama *Little Ladies of the Night* (1977), the highest-rated TV movie of all time. There's more. A whole lot more. Back in the day rock 'n' roll crossover movies such as *Permissive* (1970) used the tagline "She is the Child of Today. She is Permissive" and arguably gave rockers license to behave badly and sing about it with perhaps more impunity than they might have. At any rate, by 1984 it was estimated that in the United States the porn industry was worth $7 billion, more than the film and the record industries put together. As Bobby Flekman, A&R for Spinal Tap once said: "Money talks and bullshit walks." This mockumentary on one of England's loudest bands is well known as a satire so close to the bone that on release, "everybody thought it was a real band."[4]

> You're sweet, but you're just four feet
> And you still got your baby teeth
> You're too young and I'm too well hung
> But tonight I'm gonna rock ya

---

[4] According to Rob Reiner, director of *This Is Spinal Tap* (1984). "Tonight I'm Gonna Rock Ya Tonight" is the opening song of the film.

Writing about the Lolita Syndrome, Simone de Beauvoir singles out these cinematic dream merchants for creating the child woman. De Beauvoir writes that the adult woman might inhabit the world of the man, but the child woman moves in a universe in which the man cannot enter. The child woman is neither perverse nor immoral, unlike real women, whom men regard as "antagonistic, something like a praying mantis."[5] Writing a paper on child abuse entitled "In the Street They're Real, in a Picture They're Not," Joseph R. Rimer stresses the detail that sexualized constructions of children are conceived differently: Rimer calls this "associated distancing, detachment, anonymity, and cultural othering,"[6] however. The passive taking-part in an entertainment experience of a dubious nature is something we all do simply by having the radio or television switched on.

Vladimir Nabokov first coined the term "nymphet" in his novel *Lolita* (1955), which he initially defined as a being "between the age limits of nine and fourteen,"[7] while Edda Margeson writes that "Nymphets do not exist in their own right. Nymphets are the product of a male that projects his own image onto particular individuals and the individual engaging in the male's fantasy."[8] Lana Del Rey, capitalizing on the aesthetic of the nymphet, even has a song called "Lolita" (2012), while Bertram and Leving write of an explosion of Lolitamania in pop music, identifying Lana Del Rey as the most commercially successful of the current Lolita-inflected artists.[9] Some say Del Rey "glamorises abuse," while others say she empowers. In an essay in the *London Review of Books*, Patricia Lockwood writes that "*Lolita* is the greatest novel ever written not about love, but about advertising. Nubile red-lipsticked America—revealed at the crucial moment to be already corrupt."[10] This is the Lolita myth. Art turned upside down.

Google "songs about teenage prostitutes" and you'll find over 100 well-known tunes with lyrics of varying value and meaning, from Iron Maiden to Christine and the Queens. Frank Zappa even has one called "Teenage Prostitute," while Black Sabbath go straight for "Dirty Women." The Beatles, The Kinks, The Andrews Sisters, 50 Cent, and Slick Rick: it seems that everyone's got a song about being in the life. Writer and historian Rhian E. Jones told me that this type of song revolves around agency and power.[11] Songs

---

[5] See de Beauvoir, *Brigitte Bardot and the Lolita Syndrome* (London: New English Library, 1962).
[6] Rimer, "'In the Street They're Real, in a Picture They're Not': Constructions of Children and Childhood Among Users of Online Child Sexual Exploitation Material," *Child Abuse & Neglect* 90 (April 2019): 160–73.
[7] Alfred Appel, ed., *The Annotated* Lolita, *Revised and Updated* (New York: Vintage, 1991).
[8] Edda Margeson, "Tracing Lolita: Defining the Archetype of the Nymphet in 20th and 21st Century Literature and Culture," *Emergence: A Journal of Undergraduate Literary Criticism and Creative Research* 3 (2012). Available online: http://emergencejournal.english.ucsb.edu/wp-content/uploads/2018/05/Tracing-Lolita.pdf (accessed September 09, 2021).
[9] Cited in Rachel E. Davis, *"Tell Me You Own Me, Gimme Them Coins": Postfeminist Fascination with* Lolita, *Lana Del Rey, and Sugar Culture on Tumblr*, unpublished thesis (University of Tennessee at Chattanooga, 2017).
[10] See Tom Breihan, "Lana Del Rey Hits Back at Critics Who Say She 'Glamorises Abuse,'" *The Guardian* [online]. Available online: https://www.theguardian.com/music/2020/may/21/lana-del-rey-hits-back-at-critics-who-say-she-glamorises-abuse; and Patricia Lockwood, "Eat butterflies with me?" *London Review of Books* 42, no. 21 (November 5, 2020).
[11] Interview via Twitter, June 12, 2021.

about teenage prostitutes by male lyricists tend to fall into two groups. Either the girl is fetishized (as in "Hot Child") or vulnerable and to be rescued ("Roxanne"). In both cases she is objectified. Jones reasons that the uncomplicated nature of pop and rock songs means that the power dynamics around gender and class are rarely examined, but points out that the lyrics for "Yes" (1994), written by Richey Edwards of the Manic Street Preachers from the POV of a sex worker, address the exploitation and alienation inherent in her world, and in doing so reflect some feminist critiques of capitalism, even if the song ultimately fails to offer a way out. Perhaps a lot to ask of a pop song. But as my favorite Dutch philosopher once said: "Prevention is Better Than Cure."[12] And so, we have the cautionary tale. The parable. The prime mover being the "House of the Rising Sun," described by critic Dave Marsh as "the first folk rock hit" and known to many as a story about what happens when a good girl goes bad.[13]

In 1937 Alan Lomax was driving around America in a Studebaker, collecting folk songs from housewives, preachers, and laborers when he met a coal miner's daughter who sang the blues. Georgia Bell Turner was her name and it was her sixteenth birthday. The neighborhood had no electricity and no radio and so it was uncertain how she had learned the song that was her favorite. Georgia sat and watched as "her mother sang a few songs into Lomax's Presto disc recorder machine," and when her turn came, Lomax pointed the microphone toward her. He always loved this part: "Every time I took one of those big, black, glass-based platters out of its box, I felt that a magical moment was opening up in time."[14] Unaccompanied but complemented by the spooky white noise of the decaying wax cylinder, Georgia Bell Turner's vocal is mature and rich in tone and has a woozy swing in 3/4 time signature that takes you there. Anthony described it as sad and strong. "For ninety-eight seconds, I travel through time back to 1937."

Popular music scholars tend to obsess over the notion of authenticity without being able to define it. The idea of an ideal. An unfound original. Every song the fruit of the seed planted long ago. Although not the first recording of the song, Alan Lomax included Georgia Bell Turner's version of "Rising Sun Blues" on his *Popular Songbook* record and by the early 1960s the song was a folk standard known as "House of the Rising Sun." But as is usually the case, we can go back further. Some say "House of the Rising Sun" may have its roots in a sixteenth-century broadside ballad called "The Unfortunate Rake," but there is a dissimilarity with these and "Hot Child," not just in the POV but in premise. What differs is that "The Unfortunate Rake" and "Rising Sun Blues" are allegories warning of the dangers and perils of cavorting with handsome young sailors while seeking pleasure through drinking ale in an age when syphilis was a death sentence and antibiotics were yet to be invented. In this way the Hot Child perverts (no pun intended) the narrative and has the storyteller as voyeur gradually closing in from the margins. Circling the target before taking aim. The narrator as

---

[12] See www.rcn.org.uk/get-involved/campaign-with-us/prevention-is-better-than-cure.
[13] *The Number Ones: The Animals' "The House Of The Rising Sun"* [online]. Available online: https://www.stereogum.com/2003744/the-number-ones-the-animals-the-house-of-the-rising-sun/columns/the-number-ones/ (accessed June 15, 2021).
[14] Cited in Ted Anthony, *Chasing the Rising Sun: The Journey of an American Song* (New York: Simon & Schuster, 2007).

hunter and the titular character as prey. Dead Meat. And I am reminded of the novel *The Hunger Games*, where teenagers are selected to compete in a televised event. A city forced to sacrifice its own children for the sake of public entertainment. And what is the popular music industry if not a spectator sport where people stop and stare and then move on to the next one. Although "Hot Child in the City" claims to have a moral agenda, it is difficult to find one, and perhaps like the murder ballad, it just simply is. Then again, maybe there is something latent in the formalities of popular music songwriting that has made us immune to the worn-out, hackneyed phrases that are the currency of the pop lyricist. In the context of the glam 1970s this certainly seems to be the way of things. Thirty-six years after the record was Number 1 on the *Billboard* Charts, celebrity interviewer Gary James asks a seemingly reluctant Nick Gilder about the writing process of "Hot Child in the City":[15]

> James: How long did it take you guys to write that song?
> Gilder: Not very long.
> James: Like how long?
> Gilder: It's hard to say exactly. I just sat down and wrote the lyrics one day.
> James: Nick, what you really have to do is find this Hot Child in the City and make her part of your act.

This reminded me that the Hot Child existed. That Nick Gilder was inspired to write the song after watching teenagers soliciting on Hollywood Boulevard. It's a song about a runaway. About a sexual fantasy. About somebody's daughter. Walking the streets for money. A hustle here and a hustle there. As I play the track one last time, the singer warbles his curiously childlike castrato vocal and we imagine a smooth operator in a windowless room. A loveless motel on the edge of town. In the summer. In the city. In the dark of an alley. A piece of scrubland. The back of a car. Up against the wall. The place could be anywhere and everywhere but, in our hearts, we know it to be that proverbial house in New Orleans.

References

Anthony, Ted (2007), *Chasing the Rising Sun: The Journey of an American Song*, New York: Simon & Schuster
Collins, Suzanne (2009), *The Hunger Games*, New York: Scholastic, Incorporated
Beauvoir, Simone de (1962), *Brigitte Bardot and the Lolita Syndrome*, London: New English Library
Bronson, Fred (1988), *The* Billboard *Book of Number One Hits*, New York: Billboard Books
Davis, Rachel E. (2017), *"Tell Me You Own Me, Gimme Them Coins": Postfeminist Fascination with* Lolita, *Lana Del Rey, and Sugar Culture on Tumblr*, unpublished Honours Theses, University of Tennessee at Chattanooga
The Guardian (2021), "Lana Del Rey Hits Back at Critics Who Say She 'Glamorises Abuse.'" Available online: www.theguardian.com/music/2020/may/21/lana-del-rey-hits-back-at-critics-who-say-she-glamorises-abuse (accessed June 14, 2021).

---

[15] Available online: http://www.classicbands.com/NickGilderInterview.html (accessed June 15, 2021).

James, Gary, Interview With Nick Gilder, *Classic Bands*. Available online: www.classicbands.com/NickGilderInterview.html (accessed June 15, 2021).

Lockwood, Patricia (November 5, 2020), "Eat Butterflies with Me?" *London Review of Books*, 42 (21). Available online: https://www.lrb.co.uk/the-paper/v42/n21/patricia-lockwood/eat-butterflies-with-me (accessed September 9 2021).

Margeson, Edda (2012), "Tracing Lolita: Defining the Archetype of the Nymphet in 20th and 21st Century Literature and Culture," *Emergence: A Journal of Undergraduate Literary Criticism and Creative Research*, 3. Available online: http://emergencejournal.english.ucsb.edu/wp-content/uploads/2018/05/Tracing-Lolita.pdf (accessed September 09, 2021).

Nabokov, V. (1997 [1955]), *Lolita*, New York: Vintage International.

Nabokov, V., ed., (1991), *Alfred Appel, the Annotated* Lolita *Revised and Updated*, New York: Vintage

Rimer, Joseph R. (April 2019), "'In the Street They're Real, in a Picture They're Not': Constructions of Children and Childhood among Users of Online Child Sexual Exploitation Material," *Child Abuse & Neglect*, 90: 160–73

Rolling Stone Magazine (1978), "Nick Gilder Interview," *Rolling Stone* 280 (December 14, 1978)

Royal College of Nursing, Prevention is better than cure. Available online: www.rcn.org.uk/get-involved/campaign-with-us/prevention-is-better-than-cure (accessed June 14, 2021).

Thompson, Ben (2012), *Ban This Filth! Letters from the Mary Whitehouse Archive*, Kindle Edition, London: Faber & Faber.

Discography

Del Rey, Lana (2012), "Lolita" (Howe & Robinson), on *Born to Die* [CD]. Interscope Records.

Dylan, Bob (1965), "Can You Please Crawl Out Your Window," (Dylan). Columbia

Gilder, Nick (1978), "Hot Child in the City," (Gilder/McCulloch). [Vinyl 7"] Chrysalis

Manic Street Preachers (1992), "Little Baby Nothing" (Edwards, Bradfield, Jones, Moore). Columbia

Manic Street Preachers (1994), "Yes" (Edwards, Bradfield, Jones, Moore), on *The Holy Bible*. Columbia

The Police (1980), "Don't Stand So Close to Me" (Sting). A&M

The Rolling Stones (1969), "Honky Tonk Women" (Jagger/Richards) [Vinyl 7"]. Decca Records

Spinal Tap (1984), "Tonight I'm Gonna Rock Ya Tonight" (Guest, Shearer, McKean, Reiner). Polydor

The Sweet (1974), "Teenage Rampage" (Chapman and Chinn) [Vinyl 7"]. RCA Victor

Williamson, Sonny Boy (1937), "Good Morning, Schoolgirl" (Williamson). Bluebird

Filmography

Little Ladies of the Night (1977), [Film] Dir. Martin J. Chomsky, Spelling Goldberg Productions.

Permissive (1970), [Film] Dir. Lindsay Shonteff, BFI Flipside

Pretty Baby (1978), [Film] Dir. Louis Malle, Paramount Pictures.
Taxi Driver (1976), [Film] Dir. Martin Scorsese, Sony Pictures Home Entertainment
This is Spinal Tap (1984), [Film] Dir. Rob Reiner, Embassy Pictures
Pinocchio (1939), [Film] Dir. Norman Ferguson, T. Hee, Wilfred Jackson, Jack Kinney, Bill Roberts, Walt Disney Productions

13

The Vapors, "Turning Japanese" (1980)

Abigail Gardner

Five white men dressed in Panda suits rampage around Tokyo's Shibuya district at night time. They skateboard down streets, crash into bins, tear through shops. It's *Jackass— The Movie* (2002). As they rip through central Tokyo, "Turning Japanese" by the British band The Vapors soundtracks their antics. Released in 1980 on United Artists, it reached Number 3 in the UK charts, 36 in the US, and 1 in Australia. "Vapors" is the American spelling of "vapours"; the band are not from the United States. And pandas are not Japanese.

The song perpetuates what Anthony Sheppard has termed "extreme exoticism,"[1] that is, where sonic stereotypes act as a quick indication of "Otherness." In the early 1980s, the Vapors were one of a number of UK new wave, punk and pop bands flirting with this form of exoticism, and this chapter places their one hit into a broader popular cultural imaginary. For the past thirty-eight years, The Vapors' version of "Japanese-ness" that appears in the song and its surrounding metatext has dominated their marketing and remains prevalent in their social media. Looking at these posts and images along with the original video and artwork for the single, I consider the song's "exotic" signature and argue that "Turning Japanese" mines a seam of audiovisual "extreme exoticism" that fetishizes the very idea of "Japan" while confusing it and denying it any agency. In short, "Turning Japanese" is an Orientalist track.

The Vapors are from Guildford, Surrey, in the UK. Formed in 1978, they were spotted by The Jam's bass player, Bruce Foxton, who offered them a support slot on the 1979 "Setting Suns" tour and went on to jointly manage them with John Weller. With just the change of one vowel, the band were due to go out on a fortieth-year anniversary revival of that tour, now titled "Setting Sons." The original line-up was Dave Fenton (vocals and Rhythm guitar), Edward Bazalgette (lead guitar), Howard Smith (Drums), and Steve Smith (bass). They had started off with a "u" in their name but dropped it to appeal to the American market. They released two albums, *New Clear Days* (1980) and then *Magnets* (1981), following which they disbanded. Fenton pursued a legal career, Bazalgette went into television (and has produced episodes of

---

[1] Anthony Sheppard, *Extreme Exoticism: Japan in the American Musical Imagination* (Oxford: Oxford University Press, 2019).

the British series *Dr Who* in 2015 and 2016, and *The Last Kingdom* in 2019), Howard Smith ran a record shop in Guildford, and Steve Smith carried on playing in bands. After an informal get-together in 2016, the band reformed with a different drummer and have since released a new album called *Together* (2020). Their recent music, the single "Wonderland" from that album, has got to Number1 in United DJs Top 30 charts, a "global station with world-class DJs" and the "That Was Then, This is Now" Heritage Charts and online television show.[2]

They have an active Facebook site with just over 6,000 followers, which hosts "behind the scenes" YouTube links about life on the road, life under the Covid lockdown, and news about current releases and chart successes. Commemoration practices are in evidence too on their own official website, with references to the fortieth-year anniversary of their hit single and tour:

> 40 years ago, this week, in mid-August 1980, the band headed to the Antipodes to play a 13 gig tour of Australia. They were their first shows outside the UK and followed on from the chart success of Turning Japanese in the territory. With a packed itinerary, the band also appeared on various TV shows which helped to propel TJ to number 1 in. . . . They were even presented with gold discs on the trip! With input from the band & crew, we will be commemorating the trip, and their subsequent trip to another Vapor-hungry territory, the USA, with an in-depth article soon.[3]

It is this 1980 single whose aesthetic continues to dominate the site and much of their contemporary marketing material. The red-and-white profile image for the Facebook site is the band's name against a Japanese setting sun/fan logo, with "Turning Japanese" written on top of the sun. This logo and the single anchor the page, act as an identifier, an assurance if you like.

When asked on email via a contact at the official Facebook site why he chose to sing about "Turning Japanese," Fenton replied that he was looking for a rhyme: "It could have been Portuguese or Lebanese or anything that fitted with that phrase, it's nothing to do with the Japanese. It's actually a love song about someone who had lost their girlfriend and was going crazy over it."[4] Even though it might have had "nothing to do" with Japan, the song and its role as a career-defining "wonder" owe much to the deployment of Japan as a cipher for exoticism. The song tells of lost (or spurned) love. Fenton sings of having only a picture of his lover left and that not seeing her means he is "Turning Japanese." Lyrics about wanting doctors to take photos of her insides so he can look at her "from inside" suggest obsession. He can't have her and so he feels alone and lives in a world with no sex or drugs or fun or wine. No one understands him. Adrift in a world he is alienated and in mourning.

Underpinning the title and its repeated chorus, "Turning Japanese" starts with an "Oriental (or 'Asian') Riff" of nine notes, four on the G, two on the F, two a third down

---

[2] See www.uniteddj.com and www.thisisnow.tv.
[3] Comment posted August 19, 2020 on www.thevapors.co.uk/2020/08/19/down-under-40-years-ago/.
[4] Query posted to www.facebook.com/TheVaporsOfficial, September 28, 2020.

on D, and back to the F. Sheppard's work on the relationship between Japanese music and the American imagination offers a rich source of information on the history and function of this motif, a "melodic cliché" consisting of a standard rhythmic pattern with parallel fourth harmony.[5] He notes that it is a "fool's errand" to find its origin, yet traces out a series of compositions from the late nineteenth to early twentieth century that use it. Crucial to his argument is that the motif makes sense as part of a broader cultural mapping of the "exotic," and this recognizable musical motif acted as a sonic shorthand to signify the "exotic" "Far East" or Asia. He writes how

> Musical exoticism has most often been achieved through the reuse of sonic stereotypes that work efficiently to signify otherness to the audience. Musical details such as parallel fourths or pentatonicism do not function in isolation in exoticism but instead are dependent on the immediate context and on previous representational usage.[6]

The sonic stereotype we hear in "Turning Japanese," twice at the beginning before the vocals come in, and then twice to introduce the second and third verses, works to signify this otherness that Shepherd refers to. The parallel fourths are echoed in the lead guitar later in the song and further stereotypes that herald "the Far East," such as gong-like chimes, feature in the latter half of the song. And as Shepherd remarks, this signifier only makes sense to an audience through context and use. Surfacing in American popular song and musicals from 1880 onward, the riff was used in songs about geisha, Tokyo, mulberries, and Chinatown. From early on in its history, Japan and China were conflated within this riff.[7] In his work on nineteenth-century British music and Orientalism, Scott argues that "Musical Orientalism has never been overly concerned with establishing distinctions between Eastern cultures and that interchangeability of exotic signifiers proved to be commonplace rather than astonishing."[8] The ability to continue to blur distinctions relies on a lack of knowledge of differences and the continuing existence within a cultural landscape of "Oriental" and "Asian" as markers of unspecified Otherness.

Mid-twentieth-century examples of this interchangeable use of the exotic sonic signature can be found in Helmut Zacharid's "Tokyo Melody," penned for the 1964 Olympics, and Bobby Goldsboro's "Me Japanese Boy" (Bert Bacharach and Hal David, 1964), which both include short musical phrases based on the Oriental riff, as does Carl Douglas's "Kung Fu Fighting" (1974), all used to herald an idea of "The Orient." The "Orient" is, of course, somewhere that only exists from the point of view of "the West," based on a Western consciousness which includes a "battery of desires, repressions, investments and projections."[9]

---

[5] Sheppard, *Extreme Exoticism*, 70.
[6] Ibid., 10.
[7] Ibid., 76.
[8] Derek Scott, *From the Erotic to the Demonic: On Critical Musicology* (Oxford: Oxford University Press, 2019), 76.
[9] Edward Said, *Orientalism. Western Conceptions of the Orient* (London: Penguin, 1993), 90.

The Orient is contingent, contextual, and historical, as well as a "familiar trope in the Western imagination."[10] It is a colonial concoction, housing a diverse range of countries, cultures, and histories. It is both present and absent. The Orient for Said was both real, "adjacent to Europe," "an integral part of European material civilization and culture," and "imaginative."[11] The Orient was a place that made sense in relation to where "the Occident" might be and what colonial relationships were at stake between them. Minear notes that where Europe's Orient was the Middle East, America's was the Far East.[12] Its place was in opposition to the known, part of a colonial matrix.

I should know how persuasive it is as a place. In 1986, largely on the back of having watched David Bowie and Ryuichi Sakamoto's performances in *Merry Christmas Mr Lawrence* (dir. Oshima, 1983), I took a degree in "Oriental Studies" and then went to an institution of "African and Oriental Studies." This information doesn't tell you that I studied Japanese, because Japan is erased within the term "Orient." Under that umbrella term, you could study Chinese, Japanese, and Arabic. The defining line was everywhere east of Istanbul. And this is clearly in line with Said's views on Orientalism. In his piece on Japanese cinema, Gary Needham refers to this control whereby Orientalism involved

> the exercise of power operating through a body of knowledge (everyday, common sense and academic) that results to the legitimacy of "the West" to govern, speak for and to shape the meaning of the "Orient." The Orient refers both to a geographical entity, most often Asia, and an imaginary construction, which has historically enabled the justification of colonial conquest and imperial mentalities to foster imagined spaces, representations and identities of the other.[13]

Turning Japanese is one of those "imagined spaces" and its emergence was part of a broader consumption of Japan.

Post-Punk Orientalism

With Japan's newly prominent economic presence came cultural visibility. This was in part due to the expansion of a Japanese domestic film and anime industry, whereby Studio Ghibli was set up in 1985 and films such as *Akira* (1988) were released into UK and US cinemas, along with films such as *Ran* (dir. Kurosawa,1985) and *The Ballad of Narayama* (dir. Imamura, 1983). As in 1858, when Japan emerged from a 200-year self-imposed period of isolation known as "Sakkoku," this wave of Japanese

---

[10] Ken McLeod, "Afro-Samurai: Techno-Orientalism and Contemporary Hip Hop," *Popular Music* 32, no. 2 (2003): 259–75.

[11] Said, *Orientalism*, 1.

[12] See Richard H. Minear, "Orientalism and the Study of Japan," *The Journal of Asian Studies* 39, no. 3 (1980): 507–17 (p. 508).

[13] Gary Needham, "Japanese Cinema and Orientalism," in *Asian Cinemas: A Reader and Guide*, ed. Dimitris Eleftheriotis and Gary Needham (Edinburgh: Edinburgh University Press, 2006), 8.

cultural artifacts appearing in the UK might be considered as a more recent instance of the French 19th *Japonisme*, whereby Japanese motifs, styles, and trends appeared in European art works and Japanese culture was fashionably collectible.

This collectability was apparent in UK punk and post-punk bands' embrace of the audiovisual fantasies of the Orient. Japan, the UK four-piece led by David Sylvian, released *Quiet Life* in 1979, collaborating with Giorgio Moroder on the track "Life in Tokyo." In 1981 they released *Tin Drum*, whose album cover had Sylvian eating rice from a bowl with chopsticks in front of a picture of Chairman Mao. The year 1978 had seen the release of Siouxsie and The Banshees' "Hong Kong Garden," with lyrics that referred to "slanted eyes" and "small bodies." In 1983 David Bowie appeared alongside Ryuchi Sakamoto from The Yellow Magic Orchestra in *Merry Xmas Mr Lawrence*. That same year Bowie released "China Girl" from *Let's Dance*. Bowie, of course, had long experimented with Japanese art forms, having explored Kabuki via his work in the 1970s with choreographer Lindsey Kemp, and worked with fashion designer Kansai Yamamoto. Part of the allure of the prevalence of Japan appearing as sonic and visual tropes was a punk aesthetic determined by bricolage,[14] whereby images and sounds were decontextualized, ripping apart any agreed meaning. Hebdige's work in this area has been much critiqued, not least for its methodology, but this part of his observations on the stylistic plundering that punk was involved in remains a useful lens through which to view the aesthetic practices that were part of this "ripping up and starting again."[15] The Vapors were plundering a musical library of sounds of Asia by using the Oriental riff, which itself was a simulacrum used by Western musicians to conjure up their idea of the Orient. To this they added the use of (written) characters and symbols that suggested Japan, but either were factually incorrect or historically problematic.

Throughout the band's working life, in the early 1980s and more recently, one image dominates their merchandise. It is the Rising Sun Flag, a red circle with sixteen red rays on a white background. It is associated with the Japanese military, who used it between 1870 and the end of the Second World War in 1945, and has more recently been used by the Japan Self Defence Force (with eight rays as opposed to sixteen). Different from the flag of Japan, which is a red circle on a white background, it signifies, to some, Japan's imperial past in China, Taiwan, and especially South Korea, where as recently as 2018 diplomatic arguments ensued over its use.[16] The Vapors' Facebook site's icon is a Rising Sun Flag, with "Turning Japanese" in the circle (sun) and the band name below. A post on December 7, 2020, advertises "Turning Japanese bandanas/Scarves as modeled here by Dave Fenton and Ziggy Fenton. Use them as face coverings, head coverings, neckerchiefs, belt ties. Tie them to your bags, guitar cases, wear them on

---

[14] See Dick Hebdige, *Subculture: The Meaning of Style* (London: Methuen & Co., 1979).
[15] Orange Juice, "Rip It Up" (Polydor, 1983), also leant its name to Simon Reynolds' history of post-punk, *Rip It Up and Start Again* (London: Faber and Faber, 2006).
[16] See Alexis Dudden, "Japan's Rising Sun Flag Has a History of Horror. It Must Be Banned at the Tokyo Olympics," *The Guardian*, November 1, 2019 and Ohtaka Masato, "Japan's Rising Sun Flag Is Not a Symbol of Militarism," *The Guardian*, November 12, 2019. Available online: https://www.theguardian.com/commentisfree/2019/nov/01/japan-rising-sun-flag-history-olympic-ban-south-korea (accessed December 14, 2020).

Figure 13.1 © Benjamin Wardle 2020.

your motorbike/scooters etc."[17] Dave wears his over his mouth and nose as a Covid-19 mask; Ziggy (a dog) sports his as a neckerchief. The Vapors are not alone in having used this image. Vivienne Westwood used it as part of her Seditionaries' collection, and it surfaced in The Clash's merchandise in the form of a "kamikaze t-shirt." Siouxsie and The Banshees used it in 1984 in a poster for their June 24th gig at Hammersmith Palais in London.

The "Turning Japanese" official video uses settings and props to underpin the "Japanese-ness" of the song. The band perform in what looks to be a Japanese house, clearly a set. There are tatami mats and shoji screens, the Japanese traditional straw mat flooring, and paper sliding doors. A geisha appears to serve them, and toward the end, we see a man practicing kendo. As a supportive promotional video, it works well to establish the Orientalism of the song, which continues in the UK single cover art (Figure 13.1).

The title of the song is written vertically, as is Japanese, and there is a "Japanese" woman on the right. Although she is not Japanese. This garment is a Chinese one, as is her hairstyle. The traditional Japanese dress, the kimono, would be more patterned, have an "obi" belt tight under the breasts and the feet would be shod in "geta," platformed wooden sandals.

---

[17] See www.facebook.com/TheVaporsOfficial.

Figure 13.2 © Benjamin Wardle 2020.

On the back of the single is an image of a Japanese samurai wielding a "katana," his sword. They are "stock" images of a Japan that reside in a Western Orientalist vision: inaccurate, extinct, and yet with continuing mythic currency (Figure 13.2).

The common interchangeability of Japan with China continues in a monochromatic marketing poster for the band's 1980 Australian tour, posted on their Facebook site on August 19, 2020, in commemoration of its fortieth anniversary.[18] "Ace presents The Vapors Turning Japanese" is the headline, above a bamboo slatted mat on which there is a bamboo leaf fan and a meat pie in a bowl on which a pair of chopsticks rest. Two Chinese characters (known as *kanji* in Japanese) are placed above and below the fan. The top character is 議 (gi), which means discussion, deliberation, thought, or opinion, and the bottom one appears to be an old version of 会 (kai), which means meeting or coming together. Together (議 会) they mean "parliament" in both Chinese ("Yi Hui") and in Japanese ("gikai"). Read the other way around (会議 kaigi), it would mean meeting. On the poster, this second character is the wrong way around. Similar to the Japanese trend of using random Anglo-American words on T-shirts, a consumption of "the West" that historically signified "coolness" or "delinquency,"[19] this image relies on an idea of "the East." The chopsticks are Chinese because they are blunt at the end, not tapered.

[18] www.thevapors.co.uk/2020/08/19/down-under-40-years-ago/.
[19] See Lois Barnett, "The Modern Boy and the Screen: Media Representation of Young Urban Men Wearing Western Style Clothing in 1920s and 1930s Japan," in *Japan Beyond Its Borders: Transnational Approaches to Film and Media*, ed. Martin Centeno, Marcos Pablo and N. Morita (Seibunsha: Birkbeck Institutional Research Online, 2020). Available online: https://eprints.bbk.ac.uk/id/eprint/40885.

On the Discogs audio recording database, The Vapors are described as "relatively short-lived,"[20] but their "infamous and cartoonish one hit wonder" has enjoyed longevity and given them the ability to reform and tap into an Anglo-American heritage market.[21] And even though "The Japanese music scene still welcomes a lot of heritage English Punk and New Wave bands, [the band] were unable to make any progress with any of the promoters out there, mainly due to the language barrier."[22] "Turning Japanese," it seems was, and is, unlikely to be "big in Japan." However, if you want to learn how to play the "Turning Japanese" intro, you can turn to "ultimate guitar tab" and learn the "teriyaki flavoured riff."[23] Teriyaki is a sugary, soy-glazed dish more popular outside of Japan than within it. It is part of the Japan of the Occidental contemporary popular imagination, which, far from being outdated, is an "integral part of modern consciousness."[24] The Asian Riff, the wrong chopsticks, the upside-down kanji. The geisha, samurai, and shoji are all ingredients in that consciousness, and listening to "Turning Japanese" is an encounter with 1980s' pop-punk's Orientalism.

References

Adams, F. G., L. Klein, K. Yuzo, and A. Shinozaki (2008), *Accelerating Japan's Economic Growth Resolving Japan's Growth Controversy*, London: Routledge.

Anon (no date), *Yorkshire Magazine*. Available online: https://www.on-magazine.co.uk/news/arts-news/that-was-then-this-is-now/ (accessed December 14, 2020).

Barnett, L. (2020), "The Modern Boy and the Screen: Media Representation of Young Urban Men Wearing Western Style Clothing in 1920s and 1930s Japan," in M. Centeno, M. Pablo and N. Morita (eds.), *Japan Beyond Its Borders: Transnational Approaches to Film and Media*, London: Seibunsha (Birkbeck Institutional Research Online). Available online: https://eprints.bbk.ac.uk/id/eprint/40885.

Barthes, R. (1982), *Empire of Signs*, New York: Hill and Wang.

Cooper, L. (2019), "Alley Oop: 30 One-Hit Wonders –U.S. Pop," *Popular Music and Society*, 113–16. doi: 10.1080/03007766.2019.1678332.

Corbett, J. (2000), "Experimental Oriental: New Music and Other Others," in Georgina Born and David Hesmondhalgh (eds.), *Western Music and Its Others: Difference, Representation and Appropriation in Music*, Berkeley: University of California Press, 163–83.

Dudden, A. (2019), "Japan's Rising Sun Flag Has a History of Horror. It Must Be Banned at the Tokyo Olympics," *The Guardian*, November 1. Available online: https://www.theguardian.com/commentisfree/2019/nov/01/japan-rising-sun-flag-history-olympic-ban-south-korea (accessed December 14, 2020).

---

[20] www.discogs.com/artist/227256-The-Vapors.
[21] McLeod, "Afro-Samurai," 263.
[22] www.facebook.com/TheVaporsOfficial, September 28, 2020.
[23] See tabs.ultimate-guitar.com/tab/the-vapors/turning-japanese-tabs-87848.
[24] Steven L. Rosen, "Japan as Other: Orientalism and Cultural Conflict," *Intercultural Communication* 4 (November 2000): http://www.immi.se/intercultural/nr4/rosen.htm.

Fenton, D. (2020), "The Vapors UK," *The Vapors Official*. Available online: https://www.facebook.com/TheVaporsOfficial/posts/3686325304765533 (accessed December 14, 2020).

Hebdige, D. (1979), *Subculture: The Meaning of Style*, London: Methuen & Co.

Keister, J. (2005), "Seeking Authentic Experience: Spirituality in the Western Appropriation of Asian Music," *The World of Music*, 473: 35–53.

Kheshti, R. (2015), *Modernity's Ear: Listening to Race and Gender in World Music*, New York: New York University Press.

Laclau, E. (1996), *Emancipations*, London: Verso.

Marshall, C. (2016), "Barthes's Tokyo, 50 Years on," *Los Angeles Review of Books*, December 13. Available online: https://lareviewofbooks.org/article/ways-seeing-japan- roland (accessed December 13, 2016).

Masato, O. (2019), "Japan's Rising Sun Flag Is Not a Symbol of Militarism." Available online: https://www.theguardian.com/world/2019/nov/12/japans-rising-sun-flag-is-not-a-symbol-of-militarism (accessed December 14, 2020).

McLeod, K. (2013), "Afro-Samurai: Techno-Orientalism and Contemporary Hip Hop," *Popular Music*, 32 (2): 259–75.

Minear, R. H. (1980), "Orientalism and the Study of Japan," *The Journal of Asian Studies*, 39 (3): 507–17.

Napier, S. (2009), "Differing Destinations: Cultural Identification, Orientalism, and 'Soft Power' in Twenty-First-Century Anime Fandom," in *From Impressionism to Anime: Japan as Fantasy and Fan Cult in the Mind of the West*, Hong Kong: Hong Kong University Press.

Needham, G. (2006), "Japanese Cinema and Orientalism," in Dimitris Eleftheriotis and Gary Needham (eds.), *Asian Cinemas: A Reader and Guide*, 8–16, Edinburgh: Edinburgh University Press.

Ohtaka, Masato (2019), "Japan's Rising Sun Flag Is Not a Symbol of Militarism." Available online: https://www.theguardian.com/world/2019/nov/12/japans-rising-sun-flag-is-not-a-symbol-of-militarism (accessed December 14, 2020).

Rosen, S. L. (2000), "Japan as Other: Orientalism and Cultural Conflict," *Intercultural Communication* 4 (November, 1404-1634). Available online: http://www.immi.se/intercultural/nr4/rosen.htm.

Said, E. (1978), *Orientalism. Western Conceptions of the Orient*, London: Penguin.

Sano-Franchini, J. (2018), "Sounding Asian/America? Asian/American Sonic Rhetorics, Multimodal Orientalism and Digital Composition," *Enculturation, A Journal of Rhetoric, Writing and Culture*. Available online: http://www.enculturation.net/sounding-Asian-America.

Scott, D. B. (2003), *From the Erotic to the Demonic: On Critical Musicology*, Oxford: Oxford University Press.

Sheppard, W. A. (2019), *Extreme Exoticism: Japan in the American Musical Imagination*, Oxford: Oxford University Press.

Stevens, C. (2008), *Japanese Popular Music: Culture, Authenticity and Power*, London: Routledge.

"This is Now TV" (2020), MPG Ltd. Available online: https://www.thisisnow.tv.

Worley, M. (2017), *No Future: Punk, Politics and British Youth Culture, 1976—1984*, Cambridge: Cambridge University Press.

Yeğenoğlu, M. (2008), *Colonial Fantasies: Towards a Feminist Reading of Orientalism*, Cambridge: Cambridge University Press.

Zon, B. (2017), *Music and Orientalism in the British Empire, 1780s-1940s Portrayal of the East*, Oxford, New York: Routledge.

Discography

Bowie, D. (1983), "China Girl," *Let's Dance*, EMI America.
Japan (1981), *Tin Drum*, Virgin.
The Vapors (2020), *Together*, Manmade Soul Ltd and The Vapors Own Records.
The Vapors (1980), *Turning Japanese*, United Artists Records.
The Vapors (1981), *Magnets*, Liberty.
The Vapors, T. (1980), *New Clear Days*. United Artists Records.

Filmography

Imamura, S. (dir.) (1983), *The Ballad of Narayama*, Toei Company.
Katsuhiro, O. (dir.) (1988), *Akira*, Akira Committee Company Ltd., Bandai Co, Kodansha, Mainichi Broadcasting System, Sumitomo Corporation, Toho Company, Tokyo Movie Shinsha Co. Ltd.
Kurosawa, A. (dir.) (1985), *Ran*, Herald Ace Inc. and Greenwich Film Production S.A, Nippon Herald Films, Orion Classics.
Oshima, N. (dir.) (1983), *Merry Christmas Mr Lawrence*. Recorded Picture Company.

14

Aneka, "Japanese Boy" (1981)

Richard Elliott

"Japanese Boy" entered the UK chart during the first week of August 1981 at Number 60, rising the following week to Number 19 and earning its singer Aneka an appearance on the weekly television show *Top of the Pops*. As was customary for the program, Aneka mimed to the recorded version of the song while a studio audience danced along. Unlike some of the other artists on the show—such as rock 'n' roll revivalist Shakin' Stevens, whose "Green Door" was enjoying its third of four weeks at the Number 1 position—Aneka appeared without accompanying dancers. Instead, she performed alone, dressed in a kimono and sporting a wig of straight black hair fringed with red and featuring a knot through which two hair sticks had been arranged in the shape of an X. Her appearance was clearly designed to complement the Japanese theme of her hit song, even as it seemed to flaunt its inauthenticity. As the song's outro faded, host Simon Bates quipped that Aneka was "the tallest Japanese person I've ever seen—she's also got a Scottish accent." A fortnight later, Aneka was back on the show, having accelerated through the charts to knock Stevens from the top spot. This second appearance was more spectacular, with Aneka flanked by five bewigged dancers twirling oil-paper umbrellas. Audience members waved umbrellas, ribbons, and banners throughout the performance.

"Japanese Boy" spent one week at the top of the UK chart, before making way for Soft Cell's synthpop update of the Northern Soul classic "Tainted Love." It logged a total of nine weeks in the Top 40, becoming one of the defining sounds of the British summer. It also enjoyed an international career that would see it reach Number 1 in Belgium, Finland, Ireland, Sweden, and Switzerland (where it spent seven weeks at the top), and make the Top 10 in Austria, France, Israel, the Netherlands, Norway, and West Germany. Chart performance outside of Europe was more modest, but the song reached Number 42 in the Canadian RPM chart, Number 19 in the South African chart, and Number 15 in the US *Billboard* Disco chart. The song's widespread popularity led to Aneka appearing on a variety of international pop shows, including Italy's *Discoring*, Spain's *Aplauso*, and the Dutch *TopPop*. Her visual style on these programs was modeled on the *Top of the Pops* performances: kimono, wig, hair sticks, and a gestural repertoire that included bowing, clasping her hands together, and using one hand to perform a wave-like dance motif during the chorus. By the singer's own account, the song went on to sell over 5 million copies.[1]

Aneka's pop career was brief. Her follow-up single, "Little Lady," found success in Austria, Belgium, Finland, Germany, the Netherlands, and Sweden, but peaked at Number 50 in the UK. A third single, "Ooh Shooby Doo Doo Lang," stayed in the West-German charts for an impressive fifteen weeks and gained a number eight position in Austria's Ö3 chart, but sales elsewhere were lacking. The sense of fleeting success was evident in this song's lyrics, which asked the listener to recall the singer's recent big hit. Subsequent singles failed to chart in any of the territories where Aneka had found success. A self-titled album was released in 1981, briefly entering the album charts in Finland and Sweden, but making little impact elsewhere.

As defined by the scope of this book, Aneka can be considered a one-hit wonder. At the same time, her subsequent (albeit brief) success in non-Anglophone countries offers a pertinent reminder that the term "one-hit wonder" relies on an Anglophone (particularly a UK- and US-dominated) conception of popular music. This might usefully be interrogated through greater awareness of pop scenes that remain less well documented in Anglophone music journalism, scholarship, and fan discourse. In this chapter, I suggest that a "song itinerary" or "song biography" approach might be a useful step in widening the horizon of pop song studies.[2] "Japanese Boy" provides a good case study for considering the biography or itinerary of a song, in that it has reappeared and been reinvented in many ways since its 1981 debut. While we may confer the title of "one-hit wonder" onto Aneka, we can consider "Japanese Boy" as an object with an ongoing, viral existence. To set the ground for such an undertaking, I will first disentangle the Aneka persona from its creators, then note how both the persona and the song engage in Orientalist imaginations of Japan before concluding with some brief observations on the journey that "Japanese Boy" has taken since 1981.

---

[1] The chart positions listed in this paragraph use data from the Hung Medien database. Accessing the entry for "Japanese Boy" via the Hitparade.ch website provides data for the Swiss charts and links to Hung Medien data for Germany, Austria, the Netherlands, Belgium, Sweden, and Norway; see https://hitparade.ch/song/Aneka/Japanese-Boy-776 (accessed January 20, 2021). Sales figures are provided in the television programme *Bring Back . . . One Hit Wonders*, Channel 4 (UK, broadcast June 9, 2006) and in the newspaper feature "Global Popstar Turned Tour Guide Gran, Aneka Relives Her Days of Stardom," *Daily Record* (August 18, 2011). Available online: https://www.dailyrecord.co.uk/entertainment/music/music-news/global-popstar-turned-tour-guide-1109722 (accessed January 20, 2021).

[2] My use of the phrase "widening the horizon" is influenced by Philip Hayward's book of the same title, which urges popular music scholars to both "broaden the horizons of Popular Music Studies" and take "a broader consideration of the nature and horizons of post-War musical imagination and its association with issues of cultural identity and pluralism" (Philip Hayward, "The Cocktail Shift: Aligning Musical Exotica," in *Widening the Horizon: Exoticism in Post-War Popular Music*, ed. Philip Hayward (Sydney: John Libbey, 1999), 15). "Japanese Boy," as an example of pop exotica and a song with a long international career, would seem to map well onto both these points.

Aneka

Aneka was the joint creation of the singer Mary Sandeman, her musical collaborators Bob Heatlie and Neil Ross, and the German record company Hansa. Sandeman, born in 1947 in Scotland, had started her musical career early, taking part in Scottish Gaelic festivals, or mòds, from the age of twelve. At nineteen, she won the gold medal at the Royal National Mòd of 1966 in Inverness. Her earliest recordings date from this era, a series of three EPs on the Glasgow-based Thistle label: *Memories of the Mod*, *The Dark Island*, and *Mary Sandeman*. The latter contains "Gach Taobh a-Nis," a Gaelic version of Joni Mitchell's "Both Sides, Now," which provides an early insight into Sandeman's taste for cross-cultural translations. Sandeman's involvement in Scottish traditional and Gaelic language songs continued into the 1970s and, in 1976, she took first place at the Pan Celtic Festival in Killarney for her rendition of "Thoir Dhomh Do Làmh." This song was released the same year as a single on Dara, a record label owned by Scottish folk duo The Corries, with an English-language version ("Give Me Your Hand") on the B-side. "Give Me Your Hand" featured again on the album *Introducing Mary Sandeman*, released in 1979 by REL (Radio Edinburgh Limited), a company established by Neil Ross. Ross mixed and produced Sandeman's album, and musical arrangements were handled by Bob Heatlie, who would go on to write "Japanese Boy" for Sandeman, as well as several hits for Shakin' Stevens (including "Merry Christmas Everyone" in 1985). The liner notes to the 1979 album described Sandeman as "the foremost exponent of Gaelic songs in Scotland today" and referred to the singer's "enormous versatility" and desire to surprise and delight listeners with the selection of pieces included.

The desire to take the leap from the steady, if unspectacular, world of traditional song to that of commercial pop seems to have emerged from conversations between Sandeman, Heatlie, and Ross. Having composed the synth-based pop song "Japanese Boy" and arranged release via Hansa (the home to German disco outfit Boney M and the owners of the Berlin studio where David Bowie recorded his *Low* and *Heroes* albums), the team looked around for a suitable alias for Sandeman and settled on "Aneka." One version of the persona's origin story involves a search through a phone directory for a name that might be passed off as Japanese. The result was that Sandeman found herself living a dual role as a singer of Gaelic songs and an international pop star. In a 2011 interview she recalled, "I did several concerts as Aneka but I continued with my normal singing. The night 'Japanese Boy' went to No.1, I was doing a show at the Edinburgh Festival." The incongruities only increased as the song took off abroad: "I once found myself, as a Scot, making a television appearance in Belgium being made-up to look Japanese by a Spaniard and then doing an interview in French. After performing 'Japanese Boy,' I took off the wig, sang a Gaelic song, and later wondered 'What is going on?'"[3] This mixing of repertoires also featured on the Aneka records; most versions of the "Japanese Boy" single came backed with a piano-based version of Robert Burns's "Ae Fond Kiss" (compositionally credited as 'Trad. Arr. Neil Ross'),

---

[3] Mary Sandeman, quoted in "Global Popstar."

while the *Aneka* album mixed new pop songs with material closer to Sandeman's 1979 album.

Following the rise and fading away of her Aneka persona, Sandeman continued performing her folk-based material, with occasional recordings appearing on REL. In 2006, the television show *Bring Back . . . One Hit Wonders* tracked her down to her home in rural Scotland and found her willing to discuss the Aneka era but unwilling to take up the host's invitation to join other one-hit wonders for a show in London. By the time of the 2011 *Daily Record* interview, Sandeman had retired from the music business and was working as a tour guide in Stirling; she also acted as Chair of the Gaelic Language Promotion Trust for twenty-five years before stepping down in 2017.[4]

Exoticism

Sandeman's Aneka persona, especially when deployed to perform "Japanese Boy," depended for its effect on a range of visual and sonic tropes identified by Anthony Sheppard as "Pop Orientalism."[5] In his book *Extreme Exoticism*, Sheppard traces the American fascination with Japan as it is manifested in music from the nineteenth through to the twenty-first centuries. Writing about Katy Perry's controversial performance of her song "Unconditionally" at the AMA show, in which the singer appeared dressed as a geisha, Sheppard notes:

> Perry's performance paid homage (consciously or not) to the full history of Orientalist representations of Japan going back through Madonna, 1950s Hollywood films, to silent film Madame Butterflies, and to all of the Tin Pan Alley sheet music covers that depicted white female performers dressed up as Japanese. The AMA production of "Unconditionally" was a simulacrum of a simulacrum. It was not modelled so much on any specific aspects of Japanese culture and performance traditions as it was a faithful reflection and, indeed, even celebration of white European and American *japonisme*. [6]

Aneka's performances of "Japanese Boy" can be described similarly: a deployment of tropes and motifs common to Pop Orientalism that melds them with the emerging tropes and motifs of 1980s synthpop and music video performance. In addition to the visual tropes already mentioned (kimonos, wigs, hair sticks, umbrellas), it is worth noting the eight dancers enacting kung-fu-inspired choreography on the *Aplauso* program and the rather awkward mise-en-scène used on *TopPop*, which featured a

---

[4] "New Chair and Vice-Chair," Website of Urras Brosnachaidh na Gàidhlig / The Gaelic Language Promotion Trust. Available online: https://glpt.org.uk/new-chair-and-vice-chair/ (accessed January 22, 2021).

[5] W. Anthony Sheppard, "Pop Orientalism," TED Talk Posted on Musicology Now (February 12, 2014). Available online: http://www.musicologynow.org/2014/02/pop-orientalism.html (accessed January 20, 2021).

[6] W. Anthony Sheppard, *Extreme Exoticism: Japan in the American Musical Imagination* (New York: Oxford University Press, 2019), 397.

fencing duel in the background and a group of Japanese tourists in the foreground to whom Aneka enquires as to the whereabouts of her lost Japanese Boy. But, while the disparity of the song's lyrics with the person(a) singing them merits further discussion (and has been fuel for extended commentary when these performances have been shared on YouTube), it is more pertinent here to note the song's sonic exoticism.

Musically, "Japanese Boy" sticks to a pentatonic scale throughout, following a common strategy for signaling "the East." The track opens with a statement of the main melodic figure on the treble keys of the synth, quickly answered by a two-second "Oriental" flute motif. This pattern is repeated and then a flurry of electronic tom-toms sets up the galloping bass figure that gives the song its disco feel. Very quickly, then, two sounds characteristic of Pop Orientalism are matched to two sounds that will become characteristic of 1980s synthpop. These are joined by Aneka's high-pitched, wordless vocals, further establishing the melody of the song's refrain and evoking the ethereal vocalizing common to exotica music of earlier eras. Aneka then sings the first verse in a way that accentuates single syllables, giving the sound of the lines a stilted feel as if being sung by a non-native speaker. Her voice is pitched high, and while this is Sandeman's usual register, it fits with cultural expectations of Asian vocal production. The song also features synthesized cymbal sounds at crucial punctuation points which stop just short of the stereotypical gong sounds often found in exotica and Orientalist music.

As if the cultural references were not clear from these elements, "Japanese Boy" repeatedly uses the "Oriental riff," a nine-note figure that has been used in hundreds of pieces of music as musical shorthand for "Asia" or "Asianness." Its origins have been traced back to a piece of musical theatre from 1847, *The Grand Chinese Spectacle of Aladdin, or The Wonderful Lamp*, which featured a piece called "Aladdin Quick Step." Martin Nilsson has detailed, via several musical examples from the nineteenth and twentieth centuries, how the riff moved from a general to a more focused Orientalism (albeit one that still blurs distinctions between Chinese and Japanese music). It was a mainstay of songs used to mock Chinese immigrants in the United States and to reflect anti-Japanese sentiments during periods of perceived threat. It featured in ostensibly lighthearted material that relied on common stereotypes and essentializing gestures, such as George Formby's "Mr Wu's A Window Cleaner Now" (one of a series of "Mr Wu" songs recorded by Formby inaugurated by "Chinese Laundry Blues" in 1932). A variant appears in the 1970 Disney movie *The Aristocats*, where it is associated with the Siamese cat Shun Gon; the racism that many have detected in this depiction is exacerbated by vocalization of the riff (voiced by US ventriloquist Paul Winchell) as "Shanghai Hong Kong Egg Foo Yung." Prior to the riff's appearance in "Japanese Boy," two of the most recent uses had occurred in Carl Douglas's "Kung Fu Fighting" (1974) and The Vapors' "Turning Japanese" (1980)—both, incidentally, one-hit wonders. By this point the characteristic version of the riff was nine notes played in parallel fourths.[7]

---

[7] Martin Nilsson's research on the "Oriental riff" can be found in the archived version of his "Chinoiserie." Available online: https://web.archive.org/web/20120618021011/http://chinoiserie. atspace.com/index.html (accessed January 23, 2021). Nilsson's investigations were sparked by a discussion of the musical figure on the Straight Dope forum, which can be found at https://web. archive.org/web/20120825171332/ http://boards.straightdope.com/sdmb/showthread.php?s=788

As Anthony Sheppard has noted, "Musical details such as parallel fourths or pentatonicism do not function in isolation in exoticism but instead are dependent on the immediate context and on previous representational usage."[8] The deployment of the riff in "Japanese Boy," alongside other notable features of Pop Orientalism, relies on a cultural awareness of how musicians have been signaling East Asia for generations of listeners. The point is not so much whether Aneka's song deploys actual Japanese (or Chinese) scales, just as the point of Aneka's costume is not whether it is authentic Japanese dress. These are sonic and visual gestures that rely on long-standing tropes and motifs to signal what Charles Hiroshi Garrett refers to as "Asian difference."[9] Equally important is the catchy, or we might say beguiling, nature of the song, which itself is part and parcel of its Orientalism. One of the consistent features of exotica and Orientalism has been the idea of seduction, with the East (and other "far off" locales) portrayed as a place of seduction for the westerner. This works both in terms of place and space and at a human, gendered level in that the female figure is often used as the point of seduction and beguilement.[10]

Figure 14.1 Pop Orientalism.

73c3e3bb118b42ceb777e8e232733&t=300466&pp=50 (accessed January 23, 2021). The story is also told in a feature by Kat Chow for NPR, available online: https://www.npr.org/sections/codeswitch/2014/08/28/338622840/how-the-kung-fu-fighting-melody-came-to-represent-asia?t=1610607221902 (accessed January 20, 2021); thanks to Lawrence Davies for alerting me to this last item.

[8] Sheppard, *Extreme Exoticism*, 10.
[9] Charles Hiroshi Garrett, "Chinatown, Whose Chinatown? Defining America's Borders with Musical Orientalism," *Journal of the American Musicological Society* 57, no. 1 (2004): 119–74. Available online: https://doi.org/10.1525/jams.2004.57.1.119.
[10] See Ellie M. Hisama, "Postcolonialism on the Make: The Music of John Mellencamp, David Bowie, and John Zorn," *Popular Music* 12, no. 2 (1993): 91–104; Frances A. Aparicio, "Ethnifying Rhythms, Feminizing Cultures," in *Music and the Racial Imagination*, ed. Ronald Radano and Philip V. Bohlman (Chicago: University of Chicago Press, 2000, 95–112); Hayward, *Widening the Horizon*; Timothy D. Taylor, *Strange Sounds: Music, Technology & Culture* (New York: Routledge, 2001),

Song Itineraries

If the Orientalist and exoticist tropes of "Japanese Boy" can be seen and heard as ways of taking listeners on imaginary journeys, it is also informative to trace the journeys that the song itself has taken since 1981. I have begun to tell this story in terms of the international trajectory of Aneka's hit recording between 1981 and 1982, but there is more to add to this in that the song has been covered by many artists and adapted to several languages. In November 1981 a German-language version was recorded by the fourteen-year-old Andrea Jürgens, at an early stage in her career as a Schlager artist. That same year, Armi (aka Armi Aavikko) released "Iltaloma," a Finnish version of the song, and French singer Marion released a version under the title "Sayonara Monsieur Kung-Fu." "Sayonara . . ." was also recorded by Atsuko (aka Atsuko Constant), with an instrumental version on the B-side played by Atsuko on the koto; further complicating the song itinerary, Atsuko released a Japanese language version, "Paris No Koïbito." The following year in Czechoslovakia, Hana Zagorová recorded a Czech rendition of the song as "Mimořádná linka (Praha-Tokio)," and, in Bulgaria, the group Кукери (aka Koukeri) included the song (as "Японско Момче") on their third album. In 1983, the Brazilian artist Martha Coração released "Um Garoto Japonês" as a single, the Portuguese lyrics recounting a different story to Aneka's but in a familiar musical setting. The same year found the J-Pop singer Yukano Yamaguchi releasing a Japanese-language cover version called "Chinese Boy." The covers and adaptations continued: Ádám És Éva's "Japán Fiú" (Hungarian, 1985); Kikka's "Japanese Boy Medley / Japanese Toy" (English-language Italodance, 1994); Marieband's "Japanese Boy" (English-language Danish rock, 1996); Hollywood Boulevard's "Japanese Boy" (English-language Italodance with rap, 1998); Hanaumi's "Japanese Boy" (English-language duet version featuring Korean-born, Norway-based singer Hanne Qvigstad, 1998); Sushi's "Japanese Boy" (English-language Eurodance, 1998); The Bates' "Japanese Girl" (German punk band singing in English, 2000); S.H.E.'s "對號入座 Take Seat by Number" (Taiwanese girl group singing in Mandarin, 2004); Shanadoo's "Japanese Boy" (English-language version by Japanese girl group based in Germany, 2007); Sahara Hotnights' "Japanese Boy" (Swedish rock band singing in English, 2009); and what is effectively a cover version of Andrea Jürgens's Schlager version by Luxembourgish singer Marisa Donato in 2019 (marketed as a tribute to Jürgens, who died in 2017).

Tracing the international trajectory of "Japanese Boy" and its variants, however briefly, offers a reminder of the ways in which songs have lives and afterlives. Following the versions of "Japanese Boy" allows us not only to question the idea of the "one-hit wonder" but also to consider the song as an object with its own career, an object that keeps a certain amount of stability even as it travels and shapeshifts. Lyrics change—translated into new languages and given new narratives—but riffs and melodies (and sometimes vocal styles) remain fixed enough to be recognizable. Furthermore, this mutating yet consistent object is, we have seen, made up of other objects with their

especially chapters 4 and 5; Roshanak Kheshti, *Modernity's Ear: Listening to Race and Gender in World Music* (New York: New York University Press, 2015).

own viral histories (the "Oriental riff," the "Eastern" pentatonic melodies). "Japanese Boy" is an object that keeps working, taking on (however problematically) the role of representing Japan for Western audiences one minute (most European versions), having its memes, musemes, and gestural appropriations arguably reappropriated the next (the Asian versions). Another aspect to note from the perspective of viruses, memes, and new emergences is that "Japanese Boy," like many such objects, now circulates in the digital space of online culture, most obviously as a series of YouTube videos. Accessing the comments to these yields the typical "who's here from X?" and "X brought me here" memes, in this case connected to Flash FM—a reference to the use of "Japanese Boy" as part of the soundtrack to the 1980s-set video game *Grand Theft Auto: Vice City* (2002)—or to or to the TV program *Our Man in Japan*, presented by James May (2020).

It could be argued that it is only worth tracking the itinerary of the song if we use each appearance to analyze its meaning in each new context. We might therefore want to ask, for example, where Shanadoo's 2007 version of "Japanese Boy" takes the twisting, turning story of cultural appropriation and reappropriation. Yet it is not only the new interpretative terrain opened by song itineraries that matters but also the sheer existence of such itineraries inasmuch as they tell us about the object- and virus-like nature of pop songs more generally. For the study of one-hit wonders, it is additionally interesting to reflect on a song that refused to be restricted to its initial incarnation, reinventing itself as it attached to new hosts. What further emerges from this particular itinerary is a sense of canonicity where none might have been expected, as "Japanese Boy" stakes its claim in various canons: of Orientalist pop, to be sure, but also of Schlager and Europop (worlds seldom taken seriously by popular music studies), of J-pop and Mandopop, of 1980s chart-toppers (endlessly compiled, recompiled, and re-televised), and, of course, canons of one-hit wonders.

References

Aparicio, Frances A. (2000), "Ethnifying Rhythms, Feminizing Cultures," in Ronald Radano and Philip V. Bohlman (eds.), *Music and the Racial Imagination*, 95–112, Chicago: University of Chicago Press.

Bring Back . . . One Hit Wonders (2006), [TV programme] Channel 4 (UK), broadcast June 9 .

"Global Popstar Turned Tour Guide Gran, Aneka Relives Her Days of Stardom," *Daily Record*, August 18, 2011. Available online: https://www.dailyrecord.co.uk/entertainment/music/music-news/global-popstar-turned-tour-guide-1109722.

Hayward, Philip, ed., (1999), *Widening the Horizon: Exoticism in Post-War Popular Music*, Sydney: John Libbey.

Hisama, Ellie M. (1993), "Postcolonialism on the Make: The Music of John Mellencamp, David Bowie, and John Zorn," *Popular Music*, 12 (2): 91–104.

Kheshti, Roshanak (2015), *Modernity's Ear: Listening to Race and Gender in World Music*, New York: New York University Press.

Sheppard, W. Anthony (2014), "Pop Orientalism," TED talk posted on *Musicology Now* (February 12, 2014). Available online: http://www.musicologynow.org/2014/02/pop-orientalism.html (accessed January 20, 2021).

Sheppard, W. Anthony (2019), *Extreme Exoticism: Japan in the American Musical Imagination*, New York: Oxford University Press.

Taylor, Timothy D. (2001), *Strange Sounds: Music, Technology & Culture*, New York: Routledge.

15

Toni Basil, "Mickey" (1981)

Tim J. Anderson

I was becoming a girl as instructed by girls but I knew I wasn't a real girl, at least not of this kind. I wanted to be a disco girl like Tina, who in every aspect conforms to some golden section of girldom: Her height relative to her shape, her prettiness relative to her smartness. Tina offered certainties. She issued instructions on how to dance, whom to like, and what to wear. . . . To me, she was wise and ruthless, a goddess of war. (Lavinia Greenlaw)

There's nothing better than being head cheerleader, let me tell you. (Toni Basil)[1]

In 1983 my junior high honor society took its annual trip to our state's only water park, Big Surf. My three-hour bus trip home from the Tempe, Arizona, chlorinated wave pool is marked by two things: my sunburn and how "Mickey" was seemingly played over and over as every young woman chanted the song's opening lines. As a fourteen-year-old boy who was then becoming familiar with hard rock, this tom-tom, chant-driven record felt like a one-hit wonder before I even knew what that meant. Yet even as annoyed as I may have been by the single then, the record was clearly undeniable. The chant of "Oh Mickey you're so fine, you're so fine you blow my mind! Hey Mickey! Hey Mickey!" bounced inside the long yellow tin tube with tires that we called a school bus somewhere in the Verde Valley, a more-than-halfway point between the Phoenix area and our home, Flagstaff. Even though I—and seemingly every other boy on the bus—disliked the song, I loved the chant and (although would never admit) its cheerleader-themed video. With every single young woman in the bus chanting together, it was clear that in the silence of young men was their moment.

I want to be clear: this loud, uniformed chant of young women was not the stuff of the fabled young, collective, and defiant acts of desire that composed part of

---

[1] Lavinia Greenlaw, *The Importance of Music to Girls* (New York: Picador, 2007), 85–6; Toni Basil quoted in Tom Nawrocki, "Toni Basil's Tenacious Tumble To 'Mickey,'" *Medium*, 2014. Available online: https://medium.com/cuepoint/toni-basils-tenacious-tumble-to-mickey-e0c5c6fd4eed (accessed September 8, 2021).

Figure 15.1 Toni Basil and the Carson High cheerleaders perform a formation for the cheer version of the "Mickey" video.

Beatlemania,[2] but more the shared, youthful camaraderie that Sheila Garratt describes of her teenage infatuation with the Bay City Rollers:

> Part of the appeal is desire for comradeship. With the Rollers at least, many became involved not because they particularly liked the music, but because they didn't want to miss out. We were a gang of girls having fun together, able to identify each other by tartan scarves and badges.[3]

Garratt notes that these concerts were the first time that she and the other, mostly female, fans "were experiencing mass power for the first and last time." What was exceptional for Garratt was that

> Looking back now, I hardly remember the gigs themselves. What I *do* remember are the bus rides, running home from school together to get to someone's house in time to watch *Shang-a-Lang* on TV, dancing in lines at the school disco.... Our real obsession was with ourselves.[4]

---

[2] See Barbara Ehrenreich, Elizabeth Hess, and Gloria Jacobs, "Beatlemania: Girls Just Want to Have Fun," in *The Adoring Audience: Fan Culture and Popular Media*, ed. Lisa A. Lewis (New York: Routledge), 84–106.

[3] See Sheila Garratt, "Teenage Dreams," in *On Record: Rock, Pop, and The Written Word*, ed. Simon Frith and Andrew Goodwin (New York: Routledge, 1990), 341–50 (343).

[4] Ibid.

What I had witnessed had little to do with a song. Instead, it was all about the joyful power of a unified chant. Quite a bit is wrapped up into "Mickey"'s chant. Like most hit singles, the chart success of Basil's "Mickey" rests in the exegetical: the record is a career peak of a multimedia artist with deep investments in popular dance, film, and video.

Released on Toni Basil's debut, *Word of Mouth* (Chrysalis, 1981), "Mickey" reached the Number 2 position in New Zealand and the UK, and the Number 1 position on the charts in Australia, Canada, and the United States. As a song, "Mickey" is derivative of Michael Chapman and Nicky Chinn's "Kitty," which was recorded and first appeared on 1979's *Smash and Grab*, the debut album of the UK pop group, Racey. While "Kitty" had no chart impact, Basil's update, which includes the opening chant, is from the start louder and includes a heavier bassline. "Kitty" is a fun single made by band familiar with pubs and live performance, but feels shaggy and diminutive when played against "Mickey." By comparison, "Mickey" is bombastic. Indeed, everything about "Mickey," *Word of Mouth*, and Basil in general is exceptional.

Word of Mouth began as an experiment in audiovisual accompaniments by a label devoted to that objective. Signed by the UK's Radialchoice along with four other artists including Betty Davis (née Mabry, Miles Davis's former wife), Basil's label aimed to be an early iteration of a kind of "360 firm". The company viewed itself as engaged in "management, publishing and record and film production." As *Cash Box* explained:

> the company's aims are not strictly limited to any one aspect of the entertainment industry, but rather, radiate out from production and management into broad media exploitation for its artists, which includes records, video and film works.[5]

The focus on film and video was particularly important. As the label's founder, Simon Lait, explained:

> There are a lot of great music artists around, but there are very few who can conceptualize what they do musically, into entertaining visuals. That's what cuts all our artists above many others. There are not too many people around who can make the transition to video mediums. . . . Above all we didn't want to be known as just another rock 'n' roll company. We made a very conscious effort to sign a particular type of artist.[6]

As *Cash Box* explained, *Word of Mouth* was not only being released in record format but as a "video album" as well: what distinguished the album from others before it, such as those by Blondie and ABBA,[7] was that "both Basil's platter and the video were

---

[5] Nick Underwood, "Radialchoice Bows Total Media Mgmt. Plan In U.K." *Cash Box* (March 22, 1980): 39–40 (39).
[6] Ibid., 40.
[7] Any claim that *Word of Mouth* is the first video album is up for dispute, as Chrysalis had released the first "video album" in 1979 with Blondie's *Eat to the Beat*. According to Ralph Heibutzki, *Eat To The Beat* "yielded a full-length filmed version (Warner Home Video, 1980), which Blondie called its 'video album,' the first such project in rock. While The Kinks' live *One For The Road* reached consumers first, Blondie's effort had been ready months earlier,

conceived concurrently, and the result is a multimedia product that's earned the singer/dancer platitudes like 'queen of the freeze-frames' and 'the First Lady of the videoage.'"[8] For Radialchoice, a label that wanted an artist who could produce "records you can watch," Basil was their choice.

Consisting of covers, unreleased compositions by others, and only two songs with Basil co-writing credits, *Word of Mouth* is a synth-driven pop pleasure. However, the Radialchoice release, which would be licensed and released by Chrysalis in the United States, was not Basil's first record label or signing. Having released a single in 1966 on A&M, titled "I'm 28" on the A-side and "Breakaway" on the B-side, Basil signed with Warner Brothers in 1976 along with twenty-six other artists such as George Benson, Funkadelic, and Ray Stevens, among others. Basil's signing came shortly after a heavily choreographed July performance at Los Angeles' Roxy Theatre in West Hollywood. According to one *Billboard* writer, Basil had a "great idea to incorporate the excitement of pro-level dance routines throughout a mainstream rock recording artist's act," and "with the disco movement at its peak, the time for a rock singer-dancer star couldn't be more right." Finally, combining this choreography with "a strong, flexible singing voice" Basil could "develop her own unique comedy personality."[9]

Indeed, dance and choreography had long been Basil's strong suit, and she was well known throughout both the film and music world. By 1976 Basil had helped choreograph numerous films, including the *T.A.M.I. Show* (Binder 1964), *American Graffiti* (Lucas 1973), *Head* (Rafelson 1968), the ABC music and dance variety program, *Shindig!* (Browning 1964–6), and tours by David Bowie and Bette Midler. At the same time, Basil had acted in *Easy Rider* (Hopper 1969) and *Five Easy Pieces* (Rafelson 1970), and danced in *Robin and The 7 Hoods* (Douglas 1964) and *Viva Las Vegas* (Sidney 1964) as the literal "Girl with the Red Dress On." In 1971 Basil, along with Don "Campbellock" Campbell, cofounded the important street dance troupe, The Lockers, that would go on to perform throughout the 1970s as ambassadors of the locking dance style that would inform so much of early hip hop (Figure 15.2).

All of which is to say that any writing about Toni Basil that both begins and ends by calling her a one-hit wonder is disappointing. Ms. Basil may, technically, have produced a single pop hit, but even the most cursory perusal of her biography makes it clear that there are few careers in entertainment, let alone popular music and art, quite as wide-ranging. As one reporter in 2013 noted, Ms. Basil was "a virtual Zelig of pop culture."[10] What has long made Ms. Basil unique has been her ability to connect with multiple arts communities. So clear was the case that the late dance critic and academic,

---

only to be stalled by union disputes." See "Blondie: Once More (Into The Bleach): Blondie Returns For Its Fifteenth Round," *Discoveries* (September 1999). See https://web.archive.org/web/20131203014556/http://rip-her-to-shreds.com/archive_press_magazines_discoveries_sept1999.php As I mention later, Chrysalis licensed and distributed *Word of Mouth* in the United States.

[8] See Anon, "New Faces to Watch: Toni Basil," *CashBox* (October 9, 1982), 10. Available online: https://web.archive.org/web/20131203014556/ http://rip-her-to-shreds.com/archive_press_magazines_discoveries_sept1999.php (accessed September 8, 2021).

[9] Nat Freedland, "Talent in Action: Toni Basil," *Billboard* (July 4, 1976), 35.

[10] Chris Willman, "Toni Basil at 70: Thirty Years Past Singing, But Still Cutting a Rug," *yahoo! Entertainment* (2013). Available online: https://www.yahoo.com/entertainment/blogs/stop-the-presses/toni-basil-70-thirty-years-past-singing-still-015312161.html (accessed September 8, 2021).

> Finally
> **DANCERS**
> That live up to the
> **POP MUSIC**
> of today
> **THE CAMPBELL–**
> **LOCKERS**
> Choreography!
> **TONI BASIL**
> The
> **ROBERTA FLACK**
> Special

Figure 15.2 Ad for Toni Basil's choreography of The Campbell Lockers, aka The Lockers, dance troupe for the ABC television special, *Roberta Flack: The First Time Ever*.

Sally Banes, placed Basil's work into the "age of postmodernism." Writing a preview for the *Village Voice* of Basil's 1981 performance at The Kitchen in New York City—a space devoted to innovative artists such as Laurie Anderson, Robert Longo, Cindy Sherman, Robert Mapplethorpe, and others—Banes called Basil a "kind of one-woman exemplar of two-tiered art, standing with one foot in the entertainment world and one foot in the avant-garde."[11]

Basil's affiliation with Dennis Hopper and Bob Rafelson positioned her firmly within a counterculture willing to engage in techniques, themes, and imagery left on the table by conventional narrative cinema, particularly those of a rapidly crumbling Hollywood studio system. Basil's connection with independent and experimental film is most pronounced in her work with the experimental American filmmaker Bruce Conner. The B-side to Basil's 1966 single, "Breakaway," was accompanied by a short black-and-white film of her dancing. Directed, shot, and edited by Conner, she is credited under her given name, Antonia Christina Basilotta. Johanna Gosse writes that

> Basil's dance in *Breakaway* was created specifically for Conner's camera lens. Her profilmic performance cannot be re-staged, since its existence is predicated on the presence of the camera, and especially, on Conner's kinetic cinematography and an array of in-camera and post-production visual effects—including

---

[11] Included in Sally Banes, *Writing Dancing in the Age of Postmodernism* (Middleton, CT: Wesleyan University Press, 1994), 134.

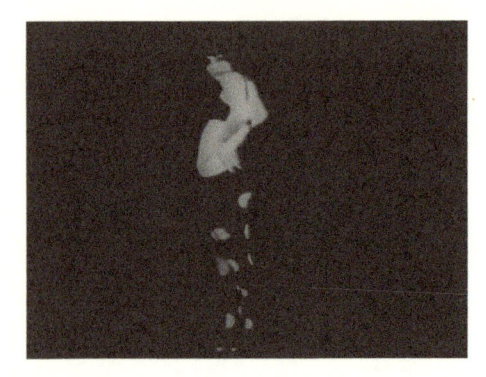

Figure 15.3 Toni Basil strikes a pose in Bruce Conner's experimental film, *Breakaway* (1966).

stroboscopic flicker, rapid zooms, smeared abstractions, and rhythmic audiovisual correspondences.[12]

Basil "appears on screen in a series of flickering long shots, wearing a black bra and polka-dot stockings and striking glamour poses against an empty black backdrop" that eventually results in frenetic gestures cut to film edits.[13] The effect is a film that "suggests strobe lights" and "colorful abstractions," accompanied by "multiple costume changes, including a white slip that gives her pale skin a delicate, almost ghostly appearance [as] Conner's camera dances with her."[14] Gosse explains that Conner and Basil "render her body into an ethereal streak of white light against black void, a spectral apparition that threatens to 'breakaway' from visibility entirely" (Figure 15.3).[15]

With video production becoming more and more affordable as the 1970s reached into the 1980s, the medium provided a more accessible palette to both play with and distribute mass gesture. By the beginning of the 1980s, Basil found herself creating music videos, two of which—Talking Heads' "Once in a Lifetime" and her own "Mickey"—would both become MTV staples and provide iconic imagery for the decade.[16] Codirecting and choreographing David Byrne's multiplied bent, jerking motions to accompany a composition that Robert Christgau of the *Village Voice* called "the greatest song Byrne will ever write," the duo produced magnified movements that have long accompanied Byrne's career.[17] Whereas Byrne's sinewy business-man-

---

[12] Johanna Gosse, "Pop, Collaboration, Utopia: Bruce Conner's BREAKAWAY in 1960s Los Angeles," *Camera Obscura* 30, no. 2 (2015):1–27 (8).
[13] Ibid., 4.
[14] Ibid.
[15] Ibid.
[16] Basil also codirected and choreographed the Talking Heads' "Crosseyed and Painless" video, which, like "Once in a Lifetime," emerged from the *Remain in Light* album (Sire, 1980).
[17] Robert Christgau, "Consumer Guide Reviews: Talking Heads, *Remain in Light*." Available online: https://www.robertchristgau.com/get_album.php?id=3402.

fixin-for-a-flood persona is clearly chromakeyed onto a background throughout the video, a fashion that compresses his gestures into two dimensions, Basil's "Mickey" video presents a three-dimensional depth that she exploits with choreographed cheer formations that offer multiple athletic arrangements of synchronized movements and symmetrical shows of strength.

Divorcing Basil and "Mickey" from this lineage of visual experimentation and choreography comes at a significant price, one that flattens the artist and the record into a novelty in the worst use of that term. What makes "Mickey" significant is the way Basil conceives of the song/record/video as a multisensory experience. For example, "Mickey" was accompanied not by one but two videos, the most famous of which includes six cheerleaders from Carson High School of Los Angeles. The less famous one involves a coterie of street dancers that she worked with, including Adolfo Quiñones, aka Shabba Doo, and Craig Rothwell, aka Spaz Attack, who act as if they are part of a band that is backing her while Basil interacts with them as they dance. While the video energetically combines numerous styles of street dance, it pales next to the thematic strength of Basil and her cheer squad.

In 1981 this emphasis on video accompaniment, while growing, was still unique. For a less-than-household name, video would provide a solution to a conundrum: how to effectively marry Basil's talents as a dancer and choreographer with her singing ability. Reporting in 1976, *Billboard* pointed out that while Basil's mix of dance and music at Roxy had appealing moments, "there are still problems of execution in making this concept work" and "Warner Bros. Management and Basil have not yet found the optimum format in blending all her talents within a mini-revue." Furthermore, the performance had "some intermittently mind-boggling moments . . . the reaction of celebrity-ridden audience was often not much more than polite."[18] Five years later the growth of the video would provide the solution to Basil's act that *Billboard* noted as necessary: "a tough-minded reorganization of the act to build and pace it better, so that Basil is able to move more smoothly between her dancing and singing efforts [as] Toni Basil has a stunning potential for major, and fast, stardom."[19] Music videos under Basil's experience and direction would be the format that helped solve this problem, and do so at a scale that would not demand constant touring with and supporting a large, expensive cast of dancers that few unproven acts could ever afford.

While the field of music video was rapidly growing, it was hardly the norm. Launched in summer 1981, MTV was nowhere close to becoming the US cable mainstay that would spur the field into overdrive. Yet the promise (and fear) that video could allow rock and pop acts to amplify the visual aspects of their acts was one that Basil, among others, began to embrace. Performing popular music through this medium would allow Basil to double down on both the impact of choreography and chant. Basil's timing could not have been better as "Mickey"'s release would be

[18] Freedland, "Talent in Action."
[19] Ibid.

Figure 15.4 From the less-famous group video for "Mickey." From left to right: Adolfo Gutierrez Quiñones, aka Shabba Doo, Toni Basil, and Craig Allen Rothwell, aka Spaz Attack.

assisted substantially by both the exciting rise of MTV and the video's focus on cheer. Throughout the summer of 1982, as Tom Nawrocki points out:

> By the time the kids went back to school, and football season was in full swing, a cheerleading video started to make sense, and "Mickey" finally reached the Top 40 in October 1982. MTV was in the business of serving kids just home from middle school, watching TV and eating Doritos while their mothers made excuses to be out of the house. A significant chunk of this audience wanted either to be a cheerleader, or to become the focus of a cheerleader's attention.[20]

The investment in the fantasy of cheerleading distinguishes "Mickey". Just as the record begins with a foot-stomping, hand-clapping chant, from the first frames of both "Mickey" videos, Basil is adorned in her dark-blue-and-red Las Vegas High cheer uniform. In the "band" video, her costume makes her look like one character among other individual "types", such as a "collegiate dancer" in a letter sweater and a "punk rocker" crowned with a spiked mohawk. In the cheer video the same uniform both aligns and pops Basil out from the Carson High squad (Figure 15.4).

Not only is the Carson High squad contrasted from Basil via their light blue uniforms, but Basil is relatively diminutive compared to these athletic young women who form moving pyramids, carry, and frame her as the lead, depicting one of the most common fantasies for young women in the United States: participating in the rhythmic teamwork, playful speech, and physical engagement that is the cheer squad. Drawing from Cornel West, Kyra Gaunt labels this emphasis of rhythmic, physical verbal ability as "kinetic orality," explaining that

> The expressive realm of "kinetic orality" is the social training ground upon which girls create a background of relatedness to one another; performances of

---

[20] Nawrocki, "Toni Basil's Tenacious Tumble."

race, ethnicity, and gender are embodied through song, chant, and percussive movement. By kinetic orality, I am referring to the transmission and appropriation of musical ideas and social memories passed on jointly by word of mouth and by embodied musical gestures and formulas. While the oral transmission of words and verbal language obviously sustains the inter-generational performance of hand clapping games, cheers, and double-dutch, all this is masterfully linked to the musical communication and expression enacted through patterns of hand clapping, foot-stopping, and other body-patting leading to a mastery over polyrhythmic expression and social interaction at a very young age.[21]

Basil's three-minute-and-forty-eight-second cheer video displays coordinated, synchronized clapping and stomping cheer routines and formations that arrange and exhibit both the potential shapes and power that cheerleading has to connect with this realm. Furthermore, it does so with no man in sight.

One of the most pronounced powers of kinetic orality—the ability to create a sense of powerful unification—is explored in William H. McNeill's book *Keeping Together in Time: Dance and Drill in Human History*. Dedicated to understanding the power of chants and marches that demand collective synchronization, McNeill reflects in the opening pages of the book the way he felt in basic training after being drafted in 1941:

> What I remember now, years afterwards, is that I rather liked strutting around, and so, I feel sure, did most of my fellows. Marching aimlessly about on the drill field, swaggering in conformity with prescribed military postures, conscious only of keeping in step so as to make the next move correctly and in time somehow felt so good. Words are inadequate to describe the emotion aroused by the prolonged movement in unison that drilling involved. A sense of pervasive well-being is what I recall; more specifically, a strange sense of personal enlargement, a sort of swelling out, becoming bigger than life, thanks to the participation in collective ritual.[22]

The US military (and possibly all standing militaries today) is, despite the long-time admission of women, a severely masculine space. In contrast, cheer provides a somewhat feminine analog as a space that places an emphasis on both strength and precision for rhythmic and physical unification. Just as the military openly recruits young men, cheer's space has long made its appeal to young women first. Cheer squads do more than simply provide vocal and physical "support" to athletes and teams. Most cheer squads in the United States exist at secondary and collegiate educational institutions alongside and interacting with drill teams, color squads, dance troupes, and marching bands, all of which are rarely divorced from an investment in generating and emphasizing musical rhythms. The importance of this educational alignment is that "cheerleading, an American invention with roots in the institutions of sports and

---

[21] Kyra Gaunt, *The Games Black Girls Play: Learning The Ropes from Double-Dutch To Hip-Hop* (New York: New York University Press, 2006), 3–4.
[22] William H. McNeill, *Keeping Together In Time: Dance and Drill in Human History* (Cambridge, MA: Harvard University Press, 1995), 2.

education, has become a staple in American culture. The cheerleader is a nationally recognized symbol invested with positive as well as negative cultural values." More importantly, as one cheer historian pointed out in the late 1990s, "although cheerleading began as a masculine activity, it is now perceived almost exclusively as a feminized role."[23] Although its beginnings in the late nineteenth and early twentieth centuries were established by young men, "by the 1950s women were established in two varieties of collegiate cheering, standard cheerleading squads and dance-oriented groups." The importance of this is that "[b]oth types of cheering represent a transition from the directly supportive role of the individual yell leader to an auxiliary entertainment role enhancing the pageantry of an athletic event."[24]

To this day, cheerleading is one of the few spaces in everyday American life that celebrates an athleticism that is most closely associated with feminine investments in rhythmic detail. While feats of strength are celebrated, so are the public performance of musical precision, flexibility, and emphatic wordplay the result of collective practice. The importance of the chant is not so much the words yelled but, as one late-1970s cheerleading handbook underscores, "[the] organization and coordination of words and motions, performed spontaneously throughout an athletic event, to generate crowd spirit and support."[25] The aim, "to generate crowd spirit and support," rests within collective wells designed to accommodate and support "snappy motions, sound and rhythmic effect, and easy learning."[26] The magic of the chants and yells is revealed as they electrify words that "have a tendency to seem childish at first reading."

> Take many of the traditional yells that we love so much, look at them, write them down, and then say the words over—they will probably sound silly, too. It is the manner in which the yell is presented and how it is yelled that makes it effective.[27]

Again, the effectiveness of the chant is not so much dependent on whether it affects the outcomes at an athletic event; instead, it is the generation of "crowd spirit and support" that is achieved only when the "*the sensation* of collective support" can be felt by the crowd so they may amplify it through their participation. To attain this effect, the emphases must be palpable. And while chants are closely related to cheers, as they both involve the world of language, cheers are performed during breaks in competition, and "chants are performed *during* games." As a result, chants do not need elaborate physical formations. Instead, a chant can be "simply accompanied by claps, stomps or snaps."[28] Chants are about rhythm and "the purpose of a chant is to help

---

[23] Mary Ellen Hanson, *Go! Fight! Win!: Cheerleading in American Culture* (Bowling Green, Ohio: Bowling Green State University Popular Press, 1995), 1.
[24] Ibid., 18.
[25] Randy L. Neil and The Staff of the International Cheerleading Foundation, *The Official Cheerleader's Handbook* (New York: Simon and Schuster, 1979), 85.
[26] L. R. Herkimer and Phyllis Hollander, *The Complete Book of Cheerleading* (New York: Doubleday & Company, 1975), 85.
[27] Ibid.
[28] Neil, *Cheerleader's Handbook*, 85.

you keep the spirit and energy level of your crowd up throughout a game."[29] Learning how to perform and execute an effective chant is a requirement for any cheer squad as it initiates and sustains audience participation. As another American cheerleading handbook from 1970 points out, "People who attend games like to get into the act. By participating in the cheering section, they feel that they are taking an active part in the game. Your job is to help them do it in an organized way."[30]

"Mickey"'s chant and video performance are almost synonymous with contemporary American cheerleading, a fact that is best illustrated by numerous cheerleading teams on YouTube performing their own versions.[31] But there is a structural point to make: the "Mickey" chant both opens the song and serves as a chorus. Offering the "catchiest" portion of the song at the beginning is a gamble that the listener will be hooked before they have time to ignore it, an option that sacrifices the revelatory powers of delay. The chorus of young women chanting about how Mickey is mindblowingly "fine" is made over the pronounced accompaniment of drums and handclaps. To get this performance,

> Basil went to cheerleading competitions to find girls who could back her up, and found two Los Angeles-based troupes: stomp-style cheerleaders from mostly black Dorsey High and stick cheerleaders, specializing in mounts, from largely Samoan Carson High.[32]

The Dorsey High cheerleaders performed the "Mickey" chant, while the Carson High cheer team appears in the video.[33] The combination of the two squads provides an example of deep, powerful syncopated punch of stomps, claps, and wordbursts that form an earworm the likes of which are rarely found in pop.

This sense of physical movement, particularly the sense of rhythm that is created by inventive word and hand play, is only matched by the likes of Shirley Ellis's records of "The Name Game" (1964) and "The Clapping Song" (1965). Both "Mickey" and the Ellis singles explore the realm of "kinetic orality," mastery of which is a deep part of African American practice, culture, and popular music. Kyra Gaunt explains this developed cultural sensibility in the opening words of her book:

> When we think of the music that drives the popular culture of African-Americans, our first thought is not a double-dutch: girls bouncing between two twirling ropes, keeping time to the tick-tat under their toes, stepping out with snatches of

---

[29] Ibid.
[30] Marylou Humphrey and Ron Humphrey, *Cheerleading and Song Leading* (Rutland: Charles E. Tuttle Company, 1970), 47.
[31] Perhaps predictably, the Irish girl group B*witched covered "Mickey" for the American teen comedy about cheerleading competitions, *Bring It On* (2000).
[32] Nawrocki, "Toni Basil's Tenacious Tumble."
[33] According to Nawrocki, "The Dorsey High girls were invited to appear, but they didn't bother to show up." Basil told him, "There was no MTV yet, so they didn't really see the point of a video. They thought, 'What in the hell is she doing now?' That's been the story of my life: 'What in the hell is she doing now?'" Ibid.

a song and dance that animate their torsos and release their tongues with laughter. Instead, what comes to mind is hip-hop, neo-soul, go-go, crunk, and R & B. The games black girls play—handclapping game-songs, cheers, and double-dutch jump rope—may not even register as a kind of popular music because the term is chiefly reserved for commercial production often dominated by men. Commercial popular music tends to exclude or simply incorporate the communal or everyday forms of popular music that cannot be assigned individual authorship or ownership: No royalties for the song-makers of double-dutch.[34]

Gaunt's work illustrates that the principles of Black popular music are filled with "musical games that are passed down by word of mouth and body," which partially explains the joy of "Mickey": the song's investment in both stomp and chant displays an achievable utopian moment of female-orchestrated unity and strength.

Indeed, one way to view "Mickey" is as an example of intergenerational and interracial female-oriented cooperation that highlights one of the many significant African American contributions to vernacular dance: its influence on American cheerleading. In this manner, "Mickey" is not so much a "new wave" record—a style and movement into which Basil is often lumped—but rather a concoction better connected to the disco movement of the 1970s. As Sally Banes explains, "The disco craze of the mid-seventies had instilled new values of unison and precision in social dancing," whereas street dance movements such as

> the Bugaloos have embellished all the smoothness and mechanization of dances like the "Hustle" and the "Bus Stop" with idiosyncratic gestures, pantomime, and special steps that have sources as diverse as cartoon characters, dada performance, African dancing and silent film comedy.[35]

By mining African American cheer vocabulary, Basil's employment of the chant and the video embraces and displays her long-term investment and celebration of American vernacular dance. As Basil explains, when handed the Chinn and Chapman song, she demanded that she include the chant over the protestations of the record company: "I was always a cheerleader and I remember the echoing in the basketball court of cheerleaders, of us, stomping, chanting. I said I would do it if I could put the cheerleader chant on it."[36] No doubt that every single young woman on my bus trip would be thrilled to know that Basil was willing to stand up for a chant that permitted them to collectively dream in one of the loudest, most affectionate, declarative, and public ways young women in the United States are allowed.

[34] Gaunt, *The Games Black Girls Play*, 1.
[35] Banes, *Writing Dancing*, 136.
[36] Quoted in Willman, "Toni Basil at 70."

References

Anon (1982), "New Faces to Watch: Toni Basil," *Cash Box*, October 9, 10. Available online: https://web.archive.org/web/20131203014556/ http://rip-her-to-shreds.com/archive_press_magazines_discoveries_sept1999.php (accessed September 8, 2021).

Banes, Sally (1994), *Writing Dancing in the Age of Postmodernism*, Middleton: Wesleyan University Press.

Browning, Phillip (1964–1966), *Shindig!*, Richard Dunlap, Selwyn Touber, Dean Whitmore and Jorn Winther (eds.)

Christgau, Robert (1980), "Consumer Guide Reviews: Talking Heads—Remain in Light." Available online: http://www.robertchristgau.com/get_artist.php?name=talking+heads (accessed September 8, 2021).

Ehrenreich, Barbara, Elizabeth Hess and Gloria Jacobs (1992), "Beatlemania: Girls Just Want to Have Fun," in Lisa A. Lewis (ed.), *The Adoring Audience: Fan Culture and Popular Media*, 84–106, New York: Routledge.

Fishel, Jim (1976), "200 Artists To 3 Labels Within Year," *Billboard*, August 28, 1, 18.

Freedland, Nat (1976), "Talent in Action: Toni Basil," *Billboard*, July 4, 35.

Garratt, Sheila (1990), "Teenage Dreams," in Simon Frith and Andrew Goodwin (eds), *On Record: Rock, Pop, and The Written Word*, 341–50, New York: Routledge.

Gaunt, Kyra (2006), *The Games Black Girls Play: Learning The Ropes From Double-Dutch To Hip-Hop*, New York: New York University Press.

Gosse, Johanna (2015), "Pop, Collaboration, Utopia: Bruce Conner's BREAKAWAY in 1960s Los Angeles," *Camera Obscura*, 30 (2): 1–27. doi: 10.1215/02705346-3078303.

Greenlaw, Lavinia (2007), *The Importance of Music to Girls*, New York: Picador.

Hanson, Mary Ellen (1995), *Go! Fight! Win!: Cheerleading in American Culture*, Bowling Green: Bowling Green State University Popular Press.

Heibutzki, Ralph (1999), "Blondie: Once More (Into The Bleach): Blondie Returns For Its Fifteenth Round." *Discoveries*, September. Available online: https://web.archive.org/web/20131203014556/ http://rip-her-to-shreds.com/archive_press_magazines_discoveries_sept1999.php (accessed September 08, 2021).

Herkimer, L. R. and Phyllis Hollander (1975), *The Complete Book of Cheerleading*, New York: Doubleday & Company.

Humphrey, Marylou and Ron Humphrey (1970), *Cheerleading and Song Leading*, Rutland: Charles E. Tuttle Company.

McNeill, William H. (1995), *Keeping Together in Time: Dance and Drill in Human History*, Cambridge, MA: Harvard University Press.

Nawrocki, Tom (2014), Toni Basil's Tenacious Tumble To "Mickey," *Medium*. Available online: https://medium.com/cuepoint/toni-basils-tenacious-tumble-to-mickey-e0c5c6fd4eed (accessed September 8, 2021).

Neil, Randy L. and The Staff of the International Cheerleading Foundation (1979), *The Official Cheerleader's Handbook*, New York: Simon and Schuster.

Underwood, Nick (1980), "Radialchoice Bows Total Media Mgmt. Plan In U.K." *Cash Box*, March 22, 39–40. https://www.yahoo.com/entertainment/blogs/stop-the-presses/toni-basil-70-thirty-years-past-singing-still-015312161.html (accessed September 08, 2021).

Willman, Chris (2013), Toni Basil at 70: Thirty Years Past Singing, But Still Cutting a Rug, *yahoo! Entertainment*. Available online: https://www.yahoo.com/entertainment/blogs/stop-the-presses/toni-basil-70-thirty-years-past-singing-still-015312161.html (accessed September 08, 2021).

Filmography/Videography

Binder, Steve (1964), *T.A.M.I. Show*, United States: AIP.
Hopper, Dennis (1969), *Easy Rider*, United States: Columbia Pictures.
Lucas, George (1973), *American Graffiti*, United States: MGM/Universal Pictures.
Rafelson, Bob (1968), *Head*, United States: Columbia Pictures.
Rafelson, Bob (1970), *Five Easy Pieces*, United States: Columbia Pictures.
Reed, Peyton (2000), *Bring It On*, United States: Universal Pictures.
Robin and the 7 Hoods (1964), [Film] Dir. Gordon Douglas, Warner Bros. United States
Sidney, George (1964), *Viva Las Vegas*, United States: Metro-Goldwyn-Mayer.

16

Trio, "Da Da Da" (1981)

Tim Quirk

The term "one-hit wonder" bears a patina of judgment, in that it emphasizes an artist's failure to capture a significant percentage of the world's attention more than once, rather than focusing on the fact that captivating the world with a song, however briefly, is a pretty amazing accomplishment.

The term "novelty song" is even sterner, as it suggests that the tune in question is somehow cheating, breaking important if undefined rules in a manner that more respectable compositions would never consider doing. So being a one-hit wonder who charted with a novelty song sounds pretty terrible. Better not to be remembered at all than remembered for *that*. At least you can die proud, rather than embarrassed.

Trio's "Da Da Da" laughs at such assumptions, just as it scoffs at the notion that a rock and roll song needs a bass guitar, or should sound like the people playing it have any idea what they're doing and aren't just making it up as they go along. It sounds funny, but it's not really a joke. It's as complete and perfect and bitter a work of art as "Like a Rolling Stone," but it's a more monumental achievement than that Dylan song, because it accomplishes everything it needs to with fewer than fifty words.

The song's official title, in the original German, is "Da Da Da ich lieb dich nicht du liebst mich nicht aha aha aha," which *is* a joke, because everything else about the song and the band singing it treat minimalism as the highest of virtues. The band's name is as efficient as it is descriptive: they had three members, so they named themselves Trio. The drum part can be played with one hand; the keyboard part can possibly be played with no hands, as it sounds like one of the pre-programmed melodies in a Casio. The recording gives each instrument equal weight, and adds almost no audio embellishments to any of them; the track is so clean, direct, and spare that when a female voice (Anete Humpe, from the German band Ideal) adds a harmony to the chorus just over a minute into the song, the lift she provides feels like a profound contribution, even though she, too, is simply repeating a single note over and over again via the syllable "da."

"Da Da Da"'s composition is genius, and its production is inspired, but so are most of Trio's sadly scant recordings. If they only had one hit, it's not because "Da Da Da" was an anomaly in their catalog but because it was the purest (and catchiest!) distillation of their vision—a vision so focused that any one of their songs encompasses everything they're attempting, yet listening to several in a row still feels revelatory. Two of the band's three members had played together previously when Trio formed in 1979. Stephan Remmler (vocals, keyboards) and Gert "Kralle" Krawinkel (guitar) had been in a group called Macbeats in the late 1960s. They got back together in the late 1970s, when both were teaching at the University of Oldenburg, then started looking for a drummer. Auditions required drinking aquavit with Stephan and Kralle as well as playing; apparently, Peter Behrens was such an amiable drinking companion they didn't bother making him drum before hiring him.

Once they did start jamming together, though, his drumming meshed well enough with their own playing that they decided to forego looking for a bassist. Their sound was complete and interesting as it was. Klaus Voorman, bassist for Manfred Mann as well as a session-man for luminaries including Lou Reed, Eric Clapton, and John Lennon, produced the band's debut LP. "Da Da Da" was written during the tour for that album.

The song has just two verses. In the first, Stephan Remmler explains that he loved the woman who has left him; he just never showed it. In the second, he says she was therefore right to leave him. Between and around those two verses, Remmler simply repeats the phrase "Da da da" and the words "I don't love you, you don't love me." Given such a small box of tools, the slow addition of individual elements is key to the song's power. It begins with just vocals, as Remmler intones "Aha aha aha aha," followed by a brief pause with no sounds whatsoever, and then we hear only Peter Behrens's percussion: a kick drum is hit once, a snare drum twice, kick drum once more, snare drum once more, while a beatbox sample ticks off metronome-like eighth notes. This pattern repeats three times before Remmler returns on the fourth to say "Aha" again; he then says "Aha" three more times (every other measure) before beginning the first verse.

But the only way we know it's the first verse is that Remmler has stopped just saying "Aha" and has started saying other things (in German) in between those Aha's. Musically, nothing has changed; it's still just kick, snare snare, kick, snare, that relentless metronome, and melody-less vocals. The song has taught us that new elements might be added as the song progresses but given us no reason to expect such additions to bring any kind of sonic relief.

So when the chorus comes in, even though it's just three more nonsense syllables ("Da, da, da"), we feel transported, because finally there's a melody to hang on to, provided by guitarist Kralle Krawinkel, who's playing every bit as simply as the drummer, but is at least playing distinct notes. As a bonus, we also get a female vocalist joining in on the "Da, da da" bit. Like Remmler, she's only singing one note, but at least it's a different note from his. Given the confusing monotony of the previous fifty-two seconds, the combination of their voices has the same effect as a gospel choir: we want to leap to our feet shouting "Hallelujah!"

We don't actually do that, but we can't help singing along every time the "Da, da, da" bit comes back around. But we're not just singing baby talk—we're experiencing the same giddy delight infants do when hearing noises they, too, can repeat. Perhaps this is why "Da Da Da" went to Number 2 on the German charts when it came out in 1982, and subsequently got released in thirty other countries. The song reached Number 1 in four of those (South Africa, Switzerland, New Zealand, and Austria) and made the Top 10 in ten others, eventually selling 13 million copies globally.

Trio weren't the only band charting internationally while singing in German in 1982/83—Nena, Peter Schilling, and Falco all did so as well. All four artists were considered part of the Neue Deutsche Welle (New German Wave), a term for any West-German musicians adding some Teutonic flair to the punk-inspired, synthesizer-driven music coming out of England and America at the time. However, Trio preferred the term "Neue Deutsche Fröhlichkeit" (New German Happiness) to describe their own sound. Though the absurdity of Trio's approach, and the childlike glee it can evoke, might make that moniker seem appropriate, their sound is not a particularly happy one. The keyboard suggests a lonely child of no genuine talent attempting to amuse himself, the drums only reinforce that feeling, and the guitar adds just enough melody to keep listeners from slitting their wrists. Meanwhile, the lyrics' repeated words and easy rhymes are as simplistic as a child's, but sung in an adult's jaded monotone, as though the horror and/or mundanity of life has stripped that adult of any ability to express himself more coherently. This is not music made by happy people; it is music made by people desperate to remember what happiness was, grasping at totems of joy.

Trio were not a novelty band. But they did have a novel sound, a deliberately cheesy sound, a sound relentlessly stripped of any unnecessary accoutrements until the existential dread it was attempting to combat could be seen clearly enough to be fought. This is the secret mission of all music, which is mankind's attempt to express an otherwise inarticulable desire to transcend our puny, mortal bodies and insignificant concerns in order to join with something eternal, even if that something doesn't really exist. Pop music is particularly good at this! It is unparalleled in its ability to fight existential dread, three minutes at a time. But existential dread can never be defeated, only fought to a temporary draw, and most pop songs are cheap weapons, prone to shatter if you rely on them one too many times. So we require an unending supply of *new* pop songs, unless or until somebody can make one out of less destructible material.

Though most listeners laughed when they first heard "Da Da Da," it was an international hit because some part of them recognized, if only subconsciously, that it was trying to be a different kind of weapon. You can get a sense of this dynamic in the promotional video Trio made for "Da Da Da." It's as simple as the band's music. The group members play their minimal instruments: Behrens stands behind a bare-bones drum kit (a kick, a snare, two cymbals), while Krawinkel spends much of the video in a folding chair with his hat pulled down over his eyes, waiting for those few moments he's called upon to play his guitar, and Remmler literally pulls a tiny Casio keyboard out of his pocket to play the five-note keyboard riff after the first chorus. Just three white walls surround them, each with three windows. Through the windows, via the magic of green screen technology that already felt ho-hum in 1982, we see panning aerial shots of a modern European city.

Like the band's playing, it's deliberately unimpressive—a testament to what can only be described as negative charisma. But just before the first chorus, at the fifty-two-second mark, Remmler gets a little smile on his face before he emphasizes the three syllables of the chorus by pointing and thrusting his right index finger in time with the words. As he finishes, with a triumphant flick of his shoulder, he has a look of supreme pride and satisfaction, as if he is David before Goliath has fallen, but after the shot that will slay him has been loosed.

It's not as flashy as a Pete Townshend windmill or a Chuck Berry duck-walk, but those finger points come from the same place—it's the move of a musician who's perfected this song before live audiences and knows not just how well this bit works but how necessary all the build-up was to making it achieve the desired effect. On the one hand, all that happens is the guitar comes in, new nonsense syllables get intoned, and a lady helps intone them in a slightly different register. On the other hand, that's all that *had* to happen. It's not much, but it's everything.

Remmler has every reason to be proud of himself: he and his bandmates are showing the world how little it takes to make walls crumble, even if those walls are just the icy ones around a listener's heart (those first, *then* Jericho). The chorus justifies the art-damaged German reserve that preceded it, by incorporating the same simple beat, and the same goofy words. But it throws all those into relief, letting us hear them from a new perspective, one in which they're no longer annoying but essential. We couldn't have gotten here without them, yet we're very glad to see them go.

And we're even happier at the end of the chorus, when Remmler adds the final two embellishments to the song: he plays five simple notes on the Casio keyboard he'd hidden in his pocket, then snaps his fingers to mimic the percussion instrument someone played in the studio (if they still had music classes when you were in elementary school, it sounds like it might be any one of the instruments the teacher kept in a milk crate and passed around to the rhythmically challenged—a cabasa, perhaps, that cylinder on a handle with loops of steel ball chain wound round it; then again, it could just be one of the band members running his finger across the comb he had in his pocket that day). Again, this is not a lot. But by Trio's standards, it's a Beethoven-level crescendo of sounds, an ecstatic orgy of sonic goodness. It doesn't last long, but neither do orgasms, and look how desperately we all chase after those.

When it's done, Krawinkel sits back down in his chair; that kick, snare snare, kick, snare loop keeps repeating; and Remmler gives us another monotone verse. Only now we know what's coming in the chorus, and we're impatient for it to happen again. Like any good lover, Trio knows this, and also knows the pleasure of the second chorus will be even greater if we're teased a bit, first. So instead of singing the chorus when we hope they will, they drop out the drums, leaving us with just the cymbals, that metronome, and Remmler repeating, "ich lieb dich nicht du liebst mich nicht" for four measures. This is uncanny: they've found a way to make the non-chorus parts of the song even *more* annoying and monotonous.

This just makes the second chorus even more glorious than the first, when it finally arrives. We get the guitar, we get the lady's voice, and we get those words anyone can sing, meaning anything we want them to: "Da da da!" You can imagine not just sold-out stadiums but entire cities rising up in triumph and adding their voices to that cry. We are all hungry babies who have finally had a spoonful of applesauce placed in our mouths, and we kick our little legs and squinch our little eyes with utter delight, and squeal for more, more, more. There is no more to come, though. This is a pop song, and two choruses are all we're allowed in this one. Yet those choruses echo in our brains, and anytime we hear the song in the future, that unalloyed glee will return in almost full force.

Volkswagen's ad agency recognized the reverberating power of that chorus fifteen years later, when they used the song for a 1997 commercial titled "Sunday Afternoon," in which two dudes, who may be friends or might be lovers, drive their Golf around a city, pick up an armchair by the side of the road, then ditch the armchair after realizing it has a disturbing odor. Since this was a commercial crafted to sell cars rather than a pop song designed to fill the void in our souls left by God's death, the VW spot flips the entire balance of the tune: it begins with the beautiful chorus, ends with the beautiful chorus, and plunks the beautiful chorus down in the middle, too. The commercial is only one-third as long as the actual song, but it somehow has more choruses!

Tellingly, the non-chorus bits are only used in the ad to signify moments of boredom or disgust: Remmler sings "ich lieb dich nicht du liebst mich nicht" when the duo are stopped at a traffic light, when they're driving through a particularly bleak part of the city, and when they first sense the sofa's awful stench. Every *other* moment of the commercial contains only the gorgeous "Da da da"'s. The lesson of the commercial is therefore the opposite one of the song itself: the ad acknowledges there will be brief lulls between periods of happiness but emphasizes how ephemeral those are. Mostly, life is composed of friends pleasurably singing, "Da da da!" because they're the right age and they bought the right automobile.

The song is wiser. It knows life is mostly composed of those lulls, and that the bursts of glee are rare things we must treasure. We don't get a lot of them; it's either dull or downright depressing in between, and just when we think one's due, the floor beneath us disappears. Even worse, if you look too closely at the good bits when they *do* arrive, you can see just how thin and unlikely they really are. But the song is magic because it makes a visceral case that none of that matters, so long as you get a couple of good bits. Just one or two hummable moments can erase the bleakness of everything else.

Da da da!

17

Nena, "99 Luftballons/99 Red Balloons" (1983)

Melanie Schiller

A few years ago, in the mailroom of the University of Groningen in the Netherlands, I unpacked my author's copy of a volume to which I contributed. A friendly Dutch colleague in a chatty mood walked by and asked what the book was about. "German popular music," I answered, only to have him break out in laughter. "German popular music?! That is a contradiction in terms!" he exclaimed before rushing off, laughing some more. Granted, Germans are not famous for their "grooviness" or general success in pop music. Perceived from the outside, when it comes to popular music, Germans might seem to either have terrible taste and seriously overappreciate the likes of David Hasselhoff or else adopt a kind of cold, robotic, or mechanical attitude. These stereotypes were at least partially challenged late one night a few months after the mailroom incident, when a staff outing ended in a karaoke bar. A German colleague and I passionately performed Nena's "99 Luftballons" and everyone could sing along—including the colleague who had laughed down the very idea of German popular music.

This may be just a personal anecdote, but our karaoke experience can be considered representative in a broader sense, as it points to the exceptional character of Nena's Number 1 worldwide hit. Few other German songs have met similar success on the international charts as "99 Luftballons" and its English version, "99 Red Balloons," which was released the following year. When the song first came out, in January 1983, it was a Number 1 hit in Germany. One year later, the English-language version made it to the top of the UK charts, where it stayed for three weeks.[1] In the United States, the German-language version "only" made it to second place on the *Billboard* Hot 100.[2] Given that "99 Luftballons" has remained their only worldwide hit, Nena is internationally perceived as a one-hit-wonder. That is not the case in Germany, however. With forty-two singles in the German Top 100 and thirty-two albums in the charts,[3] numerous live tours, industry prizes, collaborations, and television appearances

---

[1] *Official Single Chart Top 100*. Available online: https://www.officialcharts.com/charts/singles-chart/19840226/7501/ (accessed April 27, 2021).
[2] Billboard. *The Hot 100*. Available online: https://www.billboard.com/charts/hot-100/1984-03-03 (accessed April 27, 2021).
[3] Although it needs to be noted that many of these are re-recordings of old hits and best-of compilations. *Offizielle Charts*, "NENA: 99 LUFTBALLONS." Available online: https://www.offiziellecharts.de/titel-details-922 (accessed April 27, 2021).

over the course of a forty-year career, the group's singer and frontperson Nena (born Gabriele "Nena" Kerner) is still a very well-known celebrity in Germany.

This chapter describes how Nena's iconic 1980s anthem, in addition to being the *one* German song that everyone has danced to and can sing along with, is remarkable in a number of ways. At a general level, "99 Luftballons" illustrates how popular music is bound up with and articulates wider affective regimes in society, both transnationally and across time. Functioning as a kind of seismograph, popular music can be understood as indicating emergent, dominant or residual structures of feeling. That said, popular music is also constitutive of the cultural processes and society of which it is a part. In this sense, this chapter shows how "99 Luftballons" reflects a number of formative affects that were central to the highly politicized societies of the early 1980s. These include anxiety, paranoia, and melancholia, but also hedonism in the face of an anticipated nuclear apocalypse. These central affective tropes were prevalent in both West Germany as a pivotal site of Cold War tensions and more broadly, not least in the United States, where anti-Soviet propaganda fed a culture of fear. The chapter explains how Nena's danceable hit expressed such feelings in a lighthearted and accessible manner, while simultaneously also showcasing how popular music is always part of transnational cultural exchanges.

New cultural forms and genres often emerge as subcultural styles. When they enter mainstream culture, however, they often shed some of their characteristic stylistic and political features. Nena's music exemplifies this process: "99 Luftballons" is associated with the New German Wave ("Neue Deutsche Welle," NDW). This genre was politically motivated, critically reflecting on German history and national identity, among other things. Yet Nena explicitly rejects the idea that their apparently anti-war hit has any political messages; in fact, Nena's international success became a major source of national pride in Germany and international audiences often invoked well-established German stereotypes in trying to make sense of its popularity.

Ninety-Nine Anxieties: Cultural and Political Context

Before becoming world famous, Gabriele Kerner grew up in the midsized town of Hagen in Western Germany, where she joined a band called The Stripes in 1979. The band released one album and several singles with CBS Records and performed on a few German television shows, but never really managed to break through. After the group disbanded in 1981, Nena moved to West Berlin, where she started to socialize with the Nina Hagen Band. Under manager Jim Rakete's guidance, the band Nena (named after herself) eventually formed. Nena's first single "Alles nur geträumt" ("Just a dream," 1982) was also released with CBS and almost instantly became a hit after the band performed the song live on television. It reached Number 2 in the German charts. With the popular and youth media embracing Nena, the charming twenty-two-year-old small-town girl became a national superstar within a just few months.

The idea of "99 Luftballons" occurred to guitarist and lyricist Carlo Karges at a Rolling Stones concert in West Berlin in 1982. Thousands of balloons were dramatically released during the show, and Karges could not help but wonder what would happen if the wind blew them across the Berlin Wall, triggering the East German regime's paranoia and leading them to believe that something was afoot.[4] This apprehensive fantasy, as well as the song itself, can be seen as symptomatic of its time. Indeed, the sociopolitical climate was marked by anxiety brought on by an escalation of the Cold War, with Berlin as its central frontier. It was not only in Europe that the 1980s were characterized by the anxiety of living in the face of nuclear annihilation and the specter of mutually assured destruction. These fears were also negotiated in international popular culture, not least in post-apocalyptic action thrillers such as the popular *Mad Max* franchise; dystopian nuclear panic or WWIII films such as *Testament* (1983), *The Day After* (1983), and *Red Dawn* (1984); or narratives about the dangers of automated and computerized military technology such as *War Games* (1983) and *Terminator* (1984). Correspondingly, the English version of the track—"99 Red Balloons"—was only one of two songs about nuclear war to reach Number 1 in the UK single charts in 1984, the other being Frankie Goes to Hollywood's "Two Tribes" (1984), which topped the charts just a few months later.[5]

In the early 1980s, fears about a third world war were more than idle fantasies. By the beginning of the decade, the two main powers had at least 50,000 nuclear warheads between them, with a combined explosive capacity a million times that of the atomic bomb, which was dropped on Hiroshima.[6] Given that attempts at disarmament negotiations and the NATO Double-Track Decision remained inconclusive, in 1983 the German government agreed to allow the deployment of US atomic missiles, including the controversial Pershing II, on West-German territory. In reaction to the threat of an atomic holocaust, a massive peace movement mobilized hundreds of thousands of demonstrators. In June 1982, one of the movement's climactic moments, 400,000 people took to the streets to protest Ronald Reagan's visit to West Germany for a NATO summit,[7] which also fortuitously coincided with the Rolling Stones concert that inspired Karges to write the lyrics for "99 Luftballons" in Berlin.

"99 Luftballons" captured the zeitgeist of this highly politicized climate, which combined heightened East/West tensions, fear of nuclear world war, and surging protest and peace movements. On the one hand, the song articulates the fear of war. On the other, it channels a certain hedonism in the face of the potential for apocalypse. The lyrics tell a story of fatal misunderstandings, delusions of grandeur, and the desire to conquer unspecified (yet tacitly invoked) enemies: ninety-nine harmless balloons are released only to be mistaken for UFOs in a paranoid political climate. A general deploys a squadron of ninety-nine fighter jets to investigate the threat and the trigger-happy fighter pilots open fire. The "great firework" that results from shooting the balloons, in turn, provokes the neighbors and ninety-nine power-hungry "warministers." Metaphorical gasoline is poured and matches are lit, starting a catastrophic

---

[4] *Der Spiegel*, "99 Luftballons und das Chaos der Gefühle," March 26, 1984. Available online: https://www.spiegel.de/spiegel/print/d-13510424.html (accessed April 27, 2021).

[5] *Offizielle Charts*, "FRANKIE GOES TO HOLLYWOOD: TWO TRIBES." Available online: https://www.officialcharts.com/search/singles/two%20tribes/ (accessed April 27, 2021).

[6] Gasaway Hill and Mary Lynne, *The Language of Protest* (Cham: Palgrave McMillan, 2018).

[7] *Der Spiegel*, "Großdemo gegen Nato-Doppelbeschluss." June 10, 2008. Available online: https://www.spiegel.de/geschichte/kalenderblatt-10-6-1982-a-947064.html (accessed April 27, 2021).

war that lasts ninety-nine years. The song ends on a melancholic note. In the aftermath of the devastating nuclear war, the narrator walks through a post-apocalyptic world without winners. Amid the rubble, she finds a trace of the past: a balloon, which she lets fly.

Ninety-Nine Styles: From Subculture to Mainstream

In German public discourse, Nena is largely associated with the NDW music genre, which can be understood as emerging from punk and developing into post-punk and pop between 1979 and 1984. The genre started as a playful, stylistically diverse subculture. It was marked by political concerns, involving singing in German to distance itself from the dominant English pop of its time, an amateurish attitude, rejecting professionalism, and making critical and sometimes satirical comments on contemporary urban *tristesse*.[8] Lyrics were often descriptive, exhibiting a laconic or down-to-earth attitude. Indeed, NDW music did not put forward utopian worldviews or visions, rarely talked about love, and often sought a new, unadorned, and personal grasp of the present.[9]

Everyday problems and questions of German national identity were prevalent. Indeed, bands such as Middle Class Fantasies provoked listeners with song titles such as "Party in the Gas Chamber" (1981), whereas Deutsch Amerikanische Freundschaft (DAF) commanded its audience to "dance the Adolf Hitler" in the song "Der Mussolini" (1981). Although NDW was inspired by punk and new wave from Britain and the United States to a certain degree, it quickly developed into a distinct genre in its own right. Musically, it borrowed elements of reggae, funk, rockabilly, and ska. These were combined with synthetic sounds and musical as well as lyrical humor, reflexivity, ambiguity, wit, and ironic stylistic references to German Schlager in particular.[10]

The genre started as a small, DIY, and politically motivated subculture based on punk's "no-future" and hedonism. Yet NDW quickly developed a more poppy style and artistic ambitions. As its success grew, it was soon appropriated by the music industry and marketed as "fun pop" using artists that were no longer connected to the original subculture. Although Nena shared some common roots with important NDW bands such as Extrabreit, which also originated in Hagen, eventually the band had

---

[8] Barbara Hornberger, "*Neue Deutsche Welle*: Tactical Affirmation as Strategy of Subversion," in *Made in Germany*, ed. Oliver Seibt, Martin Ringsmut and David-Emil Wickström (London: Routledge, 2021), 135–44.

[9] Barbara Hornberger, "'NDW'/New German Wave: From Punk to Mainstream," in *Perspectives on German Popular Music*, ed. Michael Ahlers and Christoph Jacke (London: Routledge, 2017), 196.

[10] Schlager is a hugely popular music genre in Germany. It is typically associated with a highly standardized aesthetic and a traditional or reactionary worldview, including associations with conservatism and nationalism. Schlager songs primarily revolve around themes of romantic (heterosexual) love and homeland, and generally avoid potentially controversial or political topics. Historically it was also associated with Nazism during the period of the Third Reich. See my *Soundtracking Germany* (London, Rowman & Littlefield, 2020) and "Schlager," in *Music Around the World: A Global Encyclopedia*, ed. Andrew R. Martin and Matthew Mihalka (Santa Barbara: ABC-CLIO, 2020), 781–2.

few connections with the original new wave scene. Clearly, Nena belongs to the final, commercialized phase of NDW, in which it had shed its explicitly artistic and political ambitions.

Still, "99 Luftballons" shares some stylistic features with NDW. It is sung in German, which had become the main language of choice in pop and rock by then,[11] has a synthesizer sound, and incorporates different stylistic elements (funk and soul). There is also Nena's untrained voice and naive attitude, and the use of a (however, fictional) personal experience as a narrative starting point, which is combined with a danceable beat. All of this said, unlike much NDW music, the song does not describe a mundane situation but rather tells an epic science-fiction story with global reach. What is more, its critical message is not obviously undermined by irony or reflexivity—although the combination of an apocalyptic narrative with a lighthearted tune and danceable style can be seen as somewhat disjunctive. Accordingly, the song bridges the gap between the stylistic and political intentions of German post-punk, peace movement protest songs, German Schlager, and 1980s hedonism. Something of this can be seen in the fact that "99 Luftballons" stood in the charts besides Cindy Lauper's "Girls Just Wanna Have Fun." What is more, the German NDW-pop phenomenon Markus did have a major hit called "I will Spaß" ("I Wanna Have Fun," 1982) and the German singer Nicole had won the Eurovision Song Contest in Harrogate in the UK with a thematically comparable Schlager-song named "Ein bisschen Frieden" ("A Little Peace," 1981) the year before.

Although both "Ein bisschen Frieden" and "99 Luftballons" obviously tie in with Cold War affective regimes, neither Nicole nor Nena wanted their songs to be understood as political. Lyricist Carlo Karges, for instance, was vocal in pointing out that his text of "99 Luftballons" refers to a broader context—that is, not only to "the relationship between the nations, ["den Völkern"], but also all this paranoia in private life."[12] Karges's comment refers to the dominant cultural trope of anxiety in the early 1980s. For instance, in the *Billboard* Hot 100, "99 Luftballons" was listed next to Rockwell's song "Somebody's Watching Me" (1983), which is about the anxiety of being surveilled: "I always feel like somebody's watching me/and I have no privacy . . . can the people on TV see me or am I just paranoid?" According to Karges, the message of "99 Luftballons" is "that paranoia is dominating our lives. Mutual fear leads to treating each other more cruelly than is necessary. Because the one who strikes first has the advantage. That is dangerous."[13] Nena herself summarizes the song in similarly general and "apolitical" terms: "Something big suddenly erupts from a small occurrence. We're confronted with things that originally no one wanted."[14] Although explicitly unwilling to frame "99 Luftballons" as a political or protest song, Nena and Karges do suggest

---

[11] In 1982, almost half of all songs in the German charts were in German. Sebastian Peters, *Ein Lied Mehr zur Lage der Nation* (Berlin: Archiv der Jugendkulturen, 2010), 251.
[12] *Der Spiegel*, "99 Luftballons," my translation. The original German reads: "auf die Beziehungen zwischen den Völkern, sondern auch auf diese ganze Paranoia im privaten Bereich."
[13] *Der Spiegel*, "99 Luftballons."
[14] My translation of the original German, which reads as follows: "Aus'ner kleinen Geschichte wird plötzlich 'ne große. Man wird mit Sachen konfrontiert die ursprünglich niemand wollte." Quoted in Dörfner and Garms 1984: 64).

that the song articulates wider cultural and societal structures of feeling, including tropes of anxiety and paranoia, and a general feeling of having lost agency.

Ninety-Nine Stereotypes: International Success and Reception

Having become a Number 1 hit in Germany, the song traveled across the Atlantic thanks to a lucky coincidence. Christiane Felscherinow (known as Christiane F.) was in Los Angeles to promote her film *Christiane F.—Wir Kinder vom Bahnhof Zoo* ("We Children of Bahnhof Zoo," 1981), where she met with radio DJ Rodney Bingenheimer for an interview. Bingenheimer asked her about the latest trends in German music and Christiane wanted to play a song by her boyfriend's band: Einstürzende Neubauten. While cueing up a mixtape, however, she landed on "99 Luftballons" and played that song (in its original German version) instead.[15] Bingenheim started playing the song regularly on his show and other West-Coast radio stations started picking it up. Eventually, MTV took it into heavy rotation and *Rolling Stone* labeled Nena "Germany's hottest pop phenomenon."[16]

After the song entered the US charts, an English-language version was planned for release. The band tried translating the original but could not quite manage to get the sound right. Manager Jim Rakete therefore approached Kevin McAlea, who was then playing with Barclay James Harvest, and asked him to give it a try.[17] Having asked a German friend to translate the general gist of the song, McAlea focused on the "sound the lyrics were making" instead of the song's meaning.[18] In the translation process, the overall narrative remained relatively unchanged, though some details were amended. The now explicitly *red* balloons (in the original they are just balloons, no color specified) allude to the Soviet threat more clearly than the German version. Further, the lyrics tell the story of how, after the balloons' release, "back at base, bugs in the software flash the message, 'something's out there.'" More explicitly than the German original, this played into fears about automated and computerized war technology. The same year, on September 26, 1983, Soviet Army officer Stanislav Petrov unintentionally brought the song's narrative to life. An early warning system signaled that up to five US nuclear missiles had been launched and were approaching Soviet territory. In contrast to the fictional scenario presented in the song, Petrov decided not to retaliate. Even according to the logic of mutually assured destruction, this was a stroke of luck, for there were no US missiles: rather, the system had interpreted a reflection in the clouds as an enemy attack. In the song's narrative, however, the machinery of war roars into action, leading to "99 years of war." The English version also ends in post-apocalyptic rubble, with the narrator searching for a souvenir to prove that the

---

[15] Gavin Edwards, "Missed the '80s? Nena, and '99 Luftballons,' Alights Live in America," *The New York Times*, October 2, 2016. Available online: https://www.nytimes.com/2016/10/03/arts/music/nena-99-luftballons-interview.html (accessed April 27, 2021).
[16] Hollow Skai, *Alles Nur Geträumt* (Höfen: Hannibal, 2009), 181.
[17] Hill and Lynne, *Language of Protest*.
[18] Ibid.

contemporary world had once existed. In the end, she finds a red balloon and lets it fly. Although the song's general narrative does not differ significantly, the English version is more explicit in its references to the two superpowers and critique of technological developments and warfare. Resonating strongly with cultural anxieties and the climate of paranoia, it leaves less room for misunderstanding its political implications than its German forerunner. In later interviews, Nena has said that she dislikes the English version precisely because it is too "blatant."[19]

The success of "99 Luftballons" in the United States was preceded by a few early 1980s hits in German-language or German-inspired music. These include Peter Schilling's track "Major Tom (Coming Home)" (1982), the English-language version of which was a hit, and his album, *Error in System* (1983), which was on the American charts for more than twenty weeks. After the Fire's English-language cover of Falco's German song "Der Kommissar" (1982), which peaked at Number 5 in the *Billboard* charts; and Trio's "Da Da Da" (1982), which, combining English and German lyrics, was another international hit in 1982.[20] Similarly, Kraftwerk's earlier international successes, Iggy Pop's late 1970s Berlin albums, and David Bowie's Berlin trilogy put forward an image of Germany as an equally dangerous, gloomy, and enthralling place inhabited by man-machines, the latter two artists fostering a fascination with Berlin as the divided city. "Germany embodied the spirit of roboticism for American new wave kids," Rob Sheffield, a contributing editor at *Rolling Stone*, explained: "American kids fantasized about Berlin the way German kids fantasized about Detroit,"[21] while popular new wave artists such as Gary Numan, DEVO, and David Byrne of Talking Heads played with emotionlessness, robotic aesthetics. Against this cultural backdrop, a poppy and danceable new wave song about the end of the world from West Berlin made a lot of sense to American audiences.

Equally fascinated and bemused by Germany's musical successes, Tamara Jones wrote for the Associated Press in 1984 that "decades after most of the world began to rock, German artists are finally starting to roll as Teutonic tunes wend their way to the top of the revered American and British pop charts."[22] Jones associated the wider German musical landscape with "images of shrill Valkyries, apple-cheeked oompah bands and the smoky invitations of Marlene Dietrich rasping from the Victrola."[23] In this context, Jones saw the success of Nena's "99 Luftballons" as rather surprising, but also took the track to symbolize a broader respectable trend in German pop. While US fans and critics celebrated the "exotic" German phenomenon and its "fabulous '99 Luftballons,'" as *Billboard* had it,[24] the British music press was less amused. The rhetoric of the Second World War haunted British reviews, which featured military references and pervasive national stereotypes. The *New Musical Express*, for instance, sarcastically

---

[19] Andy Strike, "99 Red Herrings," *Record Mirror,* March 10, 1984, 14.
[20] For more on Trio, see Tim Quirk's chapter in this volume.
[21] Edwards, "Missed the '80s?"
[22] Tamara Jones, "Music Makers: German Music Gains International Success," *The Associated Press,* March 30, 1984. https://advance-lexis-com.proxy-ub.rug.nl/api/document?collection=news&id=urn:contentItem:3SJ4-JD20-0011-6470-00000-00&context=1516831 (accessed April 27, 2021).
[23] Ibid.
[24] *Der Spiegel*, "99 Luftballons."

remarked that "suddenly it really is Deutschland, Deutschland Über Alles. As the whole world turns Teuton."[25] It called Nena "the queen of German high street pop,"[26] while *The Guardian* described her "99 Red Balloons" as not only "unoriginal"[27] but a "weapon that could wreak more havoc than the zeppelin."[28]

Ninety-Nine Nationalisms: German Pride and Outlook

There are multiple tensions, then, between this song's danceable, lighthearted, earworm quality and its apparent (but disclaimed) political content and articulation of affective cultural tropes. These tensions play out differently in Germany, where the lyrics are easily understood, than among international audiences, who might neither know nor necessarily care about the song's narrative. Nena herself is always keen to emphasize the importance of the German lyrics, enthusiastically describing her experience of performing the song for an audience for whom "99 Luftballons" was their first contact with German language and culture. According to her, although they might not literally understand the content, they could "feel the message of the song."[29] Her emphasis on "emotional understanding" resonates with the idea of popular music being able to express structures of feeling—that is, the general organization of emotion in a given period. Structures of feeling might not be fully articulated; rather, they are formative processes that shape experience in particular contexts.

In that sense, Nena's emphasis of the importance of German lyrics also reflects broader discourses of German national identity and popular music in the early 1980s: whereas NDW initially aimed to distance itself from "imported" punk and post-punk by translating those genres into the German context on its own terms, it simultaneously took a reflexive, ironic distance from its own home country. Questions of German identity, at the levels of both mundane experience and national history, became imperative, yet NDW always addressed them with critical distance and often playful, sometimes provocative irony. In the later phase of NDW with which Nena is associated, however, the use of the German language had become strongly connected with notions of German (musical) pride, at least in public discourse. After decades of pop music dominated by the English language, at last Germans "dared" to sing in German again, as mainstream media discourse had it. Nena's international success catalyzed a newly emerging national pride, as German popular music moved beyond

---

[25] Biba Kopf, "Nena: The Girl From C&A," *New Musical Express*, May 5, 1984. Available online: https://www.rocksbackpages.com/Library/Article/nena-the-girl-from-ca (accessed April 27, 2021). "Deutschland, Deutschland Über Alles," here, refers to the first verse of the German national anthem sung during the Nazi period.

[26] Kopf, "Nena."

[27] *The Guardian*, quoted in *Der Spiegel*, "99 Luftballons."

[28] Ibid. My translation of the following German: "Nena kam mit '99 Red Balloons,' einer Waffe, die größere Verwüstungen anrichten kann als die Zeppeline."

[29] Patrick Garvin, "Cover Songs Uncovered: '99 Luftballons'/ '99 Red Balloons,'" *The Pop Culture Experiment*, March 26, 2018. Available online: https://popcultureexperiment.com/2018/03/26/cover-songs-uncovered-99-luftballons-99-red-balloons/ (accessed April 27, 2021).

imitating Anglo-American idols over and over again.[30] When in 1984 a journalist asked Frank Dietrich, the international manager for WEA Records, why music from Germany had not been internationally successful until this point, he gave the following answer: "The reason this didn't happen before is because the standard and quality of German music haven't been very good until now. . . . Before that, everybody was just copying the latest American and British trends; we lacked individuality."[31] Similarly, the Munich-based newspaper *Süddeutsche Zeitung* celebrated the German music success abroad: "It's pleasing, not to mention well-deserved, that the world (in particular that cultural superpower, the USA) is finally sitting up and taking notice of our German cultural achievements. . . . What if a whole new generation of Americans gets its picture of Germany from Nena? Worse things could happen."[32] Accordingly, Nena became a symbol for a reawakened sense of national achievement and an international cultural ambassador, a role that she largely embraced. Indeed, in an interview from 1984 she stressed that "when I go on tour in the United States, I want to perform in German as much as possible."[33]

Nena (the group) disbanded in 1987 and Nena Kerner pursued a solo career. She has continued to perform "99 Luftballons" (although never in English) and recorded other versions of the song (2002, 2009). Lyricist Carlo Karges died in 2002, but other members of the band remain influential figures in the German music industry.[34] In the international imagination, "99 Luftballons" is one of the most iconic songs of the 1980s. It is still firmly associated with the dire political climate in which it was produced, Berlin, and the Cold War in particular. The song has often been covered in diverse genres and different languages, becoming a classic at wedding parties worldwide. Its continuing international recognizability makes it a popular song to translate in German-language classrooms. The song's theme, style, and affective structure might well continue to resonate with contemporary audiences, proving popular music's potential for transhistorical affective appeal. Indeed, there is a wider trend of 1980s anxieties returning in international popular culture, with films such as *Mad Max: Fury Road* (2015) and TV series such as *Stranger Things* (2016–ongoing) recalling Cold War dystopian paranoia. Finally, as my colleagues and I know from personal experience, "99 Luftballons" has also taken on a second life as a staple in karaoke bars, as the *New York Times* points out.[35] For future karaoke nights, Nena's advice for singing her song is: "Take a deep breath before you start. And switch from the English to the German version."[36]

---

[30] Very similar arguments were made a decade earlier in connection with Krautrock, but NDW was commercially more successful in Germany (as well as internationally) and gained much wider media attention.
[31] Jones, "Music Makers."
[32] Ibid.
[33] Ibid.
[34] Uwe Fahrenkrog-Petersen, for instance, is an important music producer and composer.
[35] Edwards, "Missed the '80s?"
[36] Ibid.

References

Billboard. *The Hot 100*. Available online: https://www.billboard.com/charts/hot-100/1984-03-03 (accessed April 27, 2021).

Der Spiegel (2008), "Großdemo gegen Nato-Doppelbeschluss," June 10, 2008. Available online: https://www.spiegel.de/geschichte/kalenderblatt-10-6-1982-a-947064.html (accessed April 27, 2021).

Der Spiegel (1984), "99 Luftballons und das Chaos der Gefühle," March 26, 1984. Available online: https://www.spiegel.de/spiegel/print/d-13510424.html (accessed April 27, 2021).

Der Spiegel (1982), "Dreimal geweint," May 3, 1982. Available online: https://www.spiegel.de/spiegel/print/d-14349240.html (accessed April 27, 2021).

Edwards, Gavin (2016), "Missed the '80s? Nena, and '99 Luftballons,' Alights Live in America," *The New York Times*, October 2, 2016. Available online: https://www.nytimes.com/2016/10/03/arts/music/nena-99-luftballoons-interview.html (accessed April 27, 2021).

Hill, Gasaway and Mary Lynne (2018), *The Language of Protest*, Cham: Palgrave McMillan.

Garvin, Patrick (2018), "Cover Songs Uncovered: '99 Luftballons'/ '99 Red Balloons,'" *The Pop Culture Experiment*, March 26, 2018. Available online: https://popcultureexperiment.com/2018/03/26/cover-songs-uncovered-99-luftballons-99-red-balloons/ (accessed April 27, 2021).

Hornberger, Barbara (2017), "'NDW'/New German Wave: From Punk to Mainstream," in Michael Ahlers and Christoph Jacke (eds.), *Perspectives on German Popular Music*, 195–200, London: Routledge.

Hornberger, Barbara (2021), "Neue Deutsche Welle: Tactical Affirmation as Strategy of Subversion," in Oliver Seibt, Martin Ringsmut and David-Emil Wickström (eds.), *Made in Germany*, 135–44, London: Routledge.

Jones, Tamara (1984), "Music Makers: German Music Gains International Success," *Associated Press*, March 30, 1984. Available online: https://advance-lexis-com.proxy-ub.rug.nl/api/document?collection=news&id=urn:contentItem:3SJ4-JD20-0011-6470-00000-00&context=1516831 (accessed February 16, 2021).

Kopf, Biba (1984), "Nena: The Girl From C&A," *New Musical Express*, May 5, 1984. Available online: https://www.rocksbackpages.com/Library/Article/nena-the-girl-from-ca (accessed April 27, 2021).

Official Single Chart Top 100. Available online: https://www.officialcharts.com/charts/singles-chart/19840226/7501/ (accessed April 27, 2021).

Offizielle Charts, "NENA: 99 LUFTBALLONS." Available online: https://www.offiziellecharts.de/titel-details-922 (accessed February 17, 2021).

Offizielle Charts, "FRANKIE GOES TO HOLLYWOOD: TWO TRIBES." Available online: https://www.officialcharts.com/search/singles/two%20tribes/ (accessed April 27, 2021)

Peters, Sebastian (2010), *Ein Lied Mehr zur Lage der Nation*, Berlin: Archiv der Jugendkulturen.

Schiller, Melanie (2020a), *Soundtracking Germany*, London: Rowman & Littlefield.

Schiller, Melanie (2020b), "Schlager," in Andrew R. Martin and Matthew Mihalka (eds.), *Music Around the World: A Global Encyclopedia*, 781–782, Santa Barbara: ABC-CLIO.

Skai, Hollow (2009), *Alles Nur Geträumt*, Höfen: Hannibal.

Strike, Andy (1984), "99 Red Herrings," *Record Mirror*, March 10, 1984, 14.

Wagner, Peter (1999), *Pop 2000*, Hamburg: Ideal Verlag.

18

The Grateful Dead, "Touch of Grey" (1987)

Thomas Irvine

In Douglas Coupland's short prose collection *Polaroids from the Dead*, Dennis, a longtime Deadhead who "freedom dances" in the foyers and parking lots of 1980s Dead shows, encounters a younger fan, who asks him where he can score some acid. "If you have to buy it, then you won't be able to deal with it," Dennis answers, only to be told, "cry into your dime bag, you hippie weed." The snapshot then transfers to Dennis's inner monologue: "Really. These kids. Shows weren't always like that ... Dead shows were always the same as always until, *kablooey*, the MTV video happened and the kiddies began showing up, eager to party, not appreciating the true Dead spirit."[1] The MTV video was of the song "Touch of Grey," which drove the Dead's 1987 album *In the Dark* to the Top 10 of the *Billboard* charts. "Touch of Grey," recorded twenty-two years after the band came together in a more-or-less stable constellation, was their first and only chart hit of anything like this magnitude. They were a late one-hit wonder.

Like their California contemporary Ronald Reagan, who rose from B-Movie star to conservative governor of California and then president of the United States, the Grateful Dead were on a journey that traces a line of continuity between 1960s and 1980s America. Following their early successes in the late 1960s, the Dead just kept going while contemporaries such as the Jefferson Airplane or Big Brother and the Holding Company faded, and acts such as the Rolling Stones transitioned to global superstardom. Through the 1970s the Dead continued to make good money touring. By the mid-1980s unmistakable signs were mounting of growing popularity, driven by a younger generation's interest and commercial enthusiasm for the imagined Arcadian community of Haight Ashbury c. 1967. For the Dead's new followers, this era, which Sarah Hill calls San Francisco's "short 1960s," was their freaky alternative to the white-bread American "shining city on a hill" of Reagan's first inaugural address. The young protagonists of Hill's "long 1960s," a new generation of Grateful Dead fans, lived their nostalgia by joining the caravan of enthusiasts who had long followed the band from show to show.[2] These were the Deadheads, who, eschewing commercial

---

[1] Douglas Coupland, *Polaroids from the Dead* (New York: Harper Collins, 1996), 26–7.
[2] See Sarah Hill, *San Francisco and the Long 60s* (London: Bloomsbury, 2016), 301, for a discussion of tensions between "authentic and co-opted hippiedom." See also Rob Weir, "Tie-Dyes and Flannel

middlemen, wrote away for tickets to the band's own offices and communicated with each other through a media infrastructure that included numerous periodicals, some of which contained musical analysis and contextual explanations that prefigured pop musicologies of the future. There was even a printed directory intended "to facilitate communication between Heads [sic] and as a resource for people when they are on the road with the Dead."[3] Some fans (with the Dead's tacit understanding) taped the shows, so that every setlist, every variant version of a long-memorized song, every twenty-minute free improvisation ("Space") could be compared, discussed, dissected, and enjoyed obsessively as objects of collective veneration, like the relics of saints.[4]

As early as 1981 some critics smelled a rat. Richard Cook, reviewing a show at the Rainbow Theatre in London, wrote with frustration that the Dead had become "a rather efficient rock n' roll unit—and that's what slowly drains them of interest." Indeed, "the recovery of the Dead as a major live force Stateside has lent the old groaners an air of professionalism that . . . is hardly fitting for would-be brawny backwoodsmen."[5] Cook was a jazz critic with no particular brief for hippies. But his worries about the authentic Dead experience prefigure the dismay of Coupland's Dennis, dancing forlornly through the cavernous spaces of huge stadiums, looking for a "new generation of twirlers and spinners."[6]

In 1985 the Dead's reality lay somewhere between Cook's sniffy purism and Dennis's drug-addled feelings of loss. The origins of the album *In the Dark* lie in the band's decision to experiment with long-form video recording.[7] In April 1985 they booked (secretly) the Marin County Veterans Auditorium: material from these sessions would later form part of the film *So Far* directed by Jerry Garcia and Len Dell'Amico. At the time nothing much came of the recordings, perhaps due to the Dead's anarchic approach to life and business. In the early months of 1985, Garcia was busted for drug possession while driving to check himself into rehab, the band was embroiled in disputes with each other and CBS about a deal with the network they had made to produce the music for a revival of the TV series *The Twilight Zone*, and drummer Mickey Hart was negotiating with Buddhist academics in Massachusetts, inaugurating the group's long engagement as promoters of the Gyuto Monks from Tibet. In early

---

Shirts: The Grateful Dead and the Battle over the Long Sixties," *Journal of Popular Music Studies* 26, no. 1 (March 2014): 137–61.

[3] Alluding to the Dead song "The Wheel," the volume was aptly titled "The Deadhead's Directory: Bound to Cover Just a Little More Ground." See *Golden Road* 1 (1984): 31, Grateful Dead Archive Online, accessed June 30, 2021: https://www.gdao.org/items/show/825890.

[4] In a large literature on the Grateful Dead and their fans, including seven (!) PhD dissertations, see Andrew Flory, "Liveness and the Grateful Dead," *American Music* 37, no. 2 (June 2019): 123–45; Leora Lawton, "Jewish Deadheads: A Cultural Demographic Story," *Journal of Popular Music Studies* 27, no. 1 (March 2015): 69–89; John V. Ward, "Pilgrimage, Place, and Preservation: The Real and Imagined Geography of the Grateful Dead in Song, on Tour, and in Cyberspace," in *Sites of Popular Music Heritage: Memories, Histories, Places*, ed. Sara Cohen, Robert Knifton, Marion Leonard, and Les Roberts (New York: Routledge, 2015), 193–206.

[5] Richard Cook, "Grateful Dead: Rainbow Theatre, London," *New Musical Express* (October 10, 1981), Rock's Backpages. Available online: www.rocksbackpages.com/Library/Article/grateful-dead-rainbow-theatre-london (accessed July 1, 2021).

[6] Coupland, *Polaroids*, 27.

[7] The following paragraph draws on Dennis McNally, *A Long Strange Trip: The Inside History of the Grateful Dead and Making of Modern America* (London: Corgi Books, 2003), 736–45.

June the Dead canceled two shows in Sacramento for which tickets had already been sold so that members could attend performances of Wagner's *Ring* by the San Francisco Opera. By the end of the year the Dead, now routinely selling out their usual 8,000-seat venues, concluded that in the following summer they were going to need to move to stadiums. This they duly did, touring in summer 1986 with Bob Dylan and Tom Petty and Heartbreakers. In July 1986, soon after a concert in Washington, DC, Garcia collapsed and fell into a life-threatening diabetic coma.

After a slow recovery that included having to relearn some basic musical skills, Garcia returned to performing that October at a smaller Bay Area gig with the Jerry Garcia Band.[8] By November, word had reached the fanzine *Unbroken Chain* that the Dead had "rented an auditorium in Marin County and are planning to cut an album in the next few months."[9] On 15 December the Dead opened their return to concert performance, at the Oakland Coliseum, with "Touch of Grey," which Garcia had written with the Dead's long-time lyricist Robert Hunter in 1982.[10] Hunter's text might be read as a cynical statement about accepting bad circumstances ("I know the rent is in arrears / The dog has not been fed in years / It's even worse than it appears / But it's alright."), but in Garcia's setting, it comes across as more of a cheery reflection on cultivating a positive attitude.

Musically, the song is one of the more straightforward in the Dead's huge catalog. The verses unfold in a pleasant stepwise melody over vaguely honky-tonk guitars, the bridge is forgettably banal. The song's great strength is its repetitive chorus, powerfully aligned to Hunter's affirmative text "I will get by / I will survive." In the studio version, these lines are pleasantly interrupted by a memorable descending melodic hook from Brent Mydland on synthesizer.[11] The song sounded different after Garcia's recovery. As the band's biographer Dennis McNally writes, with its triumphant closing chorus "*we will* get by/we will survive"—greeted at the Coliseum show with a massive roar from the audience—"Touch of Grey" was to "assume anthemic associations to Garcia's resurrection, though it had been part of the repertoire for four years."[12] According to Garcia, at the Oakland concert "there wasn't a dry eye in the house."[13] Just after this concert, in early January 1987, the band returned to Marin County Veteran's auditorium, with the same sound engineers as the 1985 video recording but without cameras, to record their first album since *Go to Heaven*, released in early 1980.[14] "Touch of Grey" would turn out to be the album's crowning moment.

Much has been made of the Dead's ambivalent relationship with studio recording. Their albums tended not to sell well, to the frustration of the band and their record

---

[8] Ibid., 747.
[9] *Unbroken Chain* 1/7 (November/December 1986), n.p., Grateful Dead Archive Online. Available online: https://www.gdao.org/items/show/825881 (accessed June 30, 2021).
[10] On the song's early performances see McNally, *Long Strange Trip*, 730.
[11] My thanks to Christopher J. Smith for an exchange in a private communication about the song's structure.
[12] A version where the crowd's reaction is clearly audible is at https://archive.org/details/gd1986-12-15.nak300.damico.88884.flac16/disc101.flac (accessed July 1, 2021); see also McNally, *Long Strange Trip*, 749.
[13] Blair Jackson, "Touch of Grey," *Mix* 36, no. 9 (September 2012): 18.
[14] Ibid. provides a detailed technical account of the recording session.

labels. Most commercial recording studios were not well suited to the group's penchant for elaborate sound systems and the premium their performance style placed on live experience. But in early 1987 the band found themselves in a different place. They were boosted personally and financially by their popularity, clear from the easy move to larger venues. Changes in recording technology made a difference too. The album's producer, John Cutler, who had worked on the 1985 Marin sessions, used Dolby's latest noise reduction technology, which allowed recording on stage in the auditorium set up as if for a concert.[15] The result, in the view of Cutler and the band, was a more natural "live" sound.[16] As McNally relates (he would have been present as the band's publicist), the overall atmosphere was so relaxed that the Dead and the crew had time to experiment by playing with the lights off: "it was a fascinating, if not practical exercise, and gave them the name for the album—*In the Dark*."[17]

When the sessions were complete, the Dead family was optimistic.[18] Cutler even took to wearing a T-shirt embossed with the words "think platinum." In late winter, tapes from the sessions reached Arista Records in New York. The label's vice president for operations, Ray Lott, first heard them at home on a weekend. He called a meeting for first thing Monday to declare, "you're not gonna believe this, the Grateful Dead have written a fuckin' hit!" Mixing was finished in early May. A music video followed, recorded in early summer. The director, Gary Guttierez, replaced the band for most of the video with full-size skeleton puppets, who were filmed playing, singing, and dancing in front of a live audience in an atmospheric Pacific fog at Laguna Seca racetrack near Monterey. Managers at MTV loved it. As McNally explains, previously MTV's "taste . . . had run to Michael Jackson/Madonna flash dance, and then moved on to heavy-metal big-boob pieces." It was the Dead's "peculiar luck," he continues, that the network's bosses now "decreed that some old guys would be nice."

The Dead's summer of success followed. By the end of the Dylan tour, one critic, Derk Richardson, wrote that "it was easy to suspect that the agin' folk hero was actually capitalising on the popularity of the Grateful Dead."[19] In September, "Touch of Grey" reached Number 9 in the *Billboard* charts; *In the Dark* soon went platinum. Huge press coverage followed. The Band posed for the cover of *Forbes*. The "Grateful Dead Radio Hour," a local radio staple in the Bay Area, found syndication nationally.[20] Soon after *In the Dark* topped out on the charts, Arista released Garcia and Dell'Amico's visually adventurous film *So Far*, recorded at the original 1985 sessions at the Marin County Veteran's auditorium. Despite its extensive use of computer editing and incongruously superimposed images, it went to the top of the video charts, earning plenty of money for the band and the label.[21] Perhaps the most potent index of the Dead's triumph was the announcement early in the summer that the popular Vermont ice-cream producer

---

[15] Ibid., 17; McNally, *Long Strange Trip*, 749.
[16] Jackson, "Touch of Grey," 17.
[17] Ibid., 750.
[18] This paragraph draws on Ibid., 750–4.
[19] Ibid., 756.
[20] Ibid., 757.
[21] Ibid., 757–8.

Ben and Jerry's was naming a new flavor "Cherry Garcia."[22] Initially the band was nonplussed about this infringement of their brand, but the two sides soon reached a licensing agreement.[23] The Dead's victory lap ended with a new three-album contract with Arista, under the terms of which the Dead were promised an astronomical $3.50 per sold CD.[24]

"Touch of Grey" was a surprise hit with more than financial consequences. In hindsight, the summer of 1987 marks the inauguration of a new era for the Dead in the popular and even academic imagination. From then on, the Dead—despite the end of the band as a touring group when Garcia died in 1995—never left the popular heights they climbed in the mid-1980s. Their transformation from hippie sideshow to living incarnation of the "long 1960s" was complete and lasting. Like the neighborhoods of San Francisco where the band got its start, the Dead phenomenon was becoming gentrified—that is to say, wealthy and exclusive in ways it never had been before. As the vignettes in Coupland's *Polaroids from Dead* illustrate so vividly, in the late 1980s Deadheads were just as likely to arrive at shows in their (or their parents') luxury cars as they were to roll up in a rickety school bus. They crossed the carnival of the stadium parking lot armed with tickets purchased with a credit card over the phone from Ticketmaster and not by mail from the band's own office. Indeed, it was not long before a new generation of writers such as Coupland reclaimed the Dead phenomenon as an object of serious literary contemplation, bestowing upon it yet more social and cultural capital. Academic musicology followed. At first "Dead scholarship" faced skepticism, but today Dead musicology boasts an admirable scholarly infrastructure including edited collections, monographs, regular slots on conference programs, and most of all a dedicated archive at the University of California Santa Cruz, supported by the band's surviving members.[25] It is ironic that none of this would have happened without "Touch of Grey" and the explosive commercial success it brought.

With the move to a more scholarly habitus, discussions about the place and meaning of the Dead in the history of popular music and culture occasionally acquire exalted tones. For example, Ulf Olsson, in his 2017 monograph *Listening for the Secret: The Grateful Dead and the Politics of Improvisation*, brings the Dead into conversation with the most prestigious of twentieth-century thinkers on music and popular culture, Theodor W. Adorno. Seemingly uninterested in the reaction the snobby Adorno himself would likely have had to the Dead's easygoing American vernacular, Olsson argues that the band articulated a form of musical knowledge that could only have come to outsiders who had been, as the Dead were, at first (in the "short 1960s") embraced by

---

[22] James Hirsch, "What Fun, Rock 'n' Roll Ice Cream," James Hirsch, "What Fun, Rock 'n' Roll Ice Cream," *The New York Times*, June 28, 1987. Available online: https://www.nytimes.com/1987/06/28/business/whats-new-on-the-supermarket-shelf-what-fun-rock-n-roll-ice-cream.html?searchResultPosition=1 (accessed September 6, 2021).

[23] Special to the *New York Times*, "Company News: Ben & Jerry's," *The New York Times*, July 30, 1987. Available online: https://nyti.ms/3n53Xf (accessed September 6, 2021).

[24] McNally, *Long Strange Trip*, 758.

[25] Nicholas Meriwether, "'The Thousand Stories Have Come 'Round to One': Studying the Grateful Dead Phenomenon," in *Reading the Grateful Dead: A Critical Survey*, ed. Nicholas Meriwether (Lanham: Scarecrow Press, 2012), 24–48. See also the "Grateful Dead Research Guide" on the UCSD website: https://guides.library.ucsc.edu/grateful-dead (accessed July 1, 2021).

the culture industry and then cast out "as pathetic left-overs" and "waste products."[26] Gesturing toward an aphorism from Adorno's *Minima Moralia* about the "rectilinear" dialectic of winners and losers in history ("knowledge . . . should also address itself to those things [that] might be called the waste products and blind spots that have escaped the dialectic"), Olsson suggests that the "band's position outside of or on the margin" of a dialectic of historical "victory and defeat" makes them "a promising object for any analysis of the culture industry."[27] In the world of high critical theory, "escaping the dialectic" is as good as it gets.

What one thinks of this line of argument depends on what one thinks of both Adorno and the Dead. But the success of "Touch of Grey" does not exactly rhyme with a historical role as "pathetic leftovers." Olsson is clearly troubled by this, and concludes, drawing on Garcia's description of the band as "the town whore who's suddenly become respectable," that their new popularity "probably was quite provisional and conditional."[28] The short material history of the band's one and only hit I have sketched here suggests other interpretations. Around 1985, I would suggest, the Dead found themselves far from "blind spots" in popular or critical consciousness. Instead, chaotic as they may have been, they saw the future more clearly than many others in the music industry. It was an article of faith for them that economic and artistic success depended on some sort of relationship with their audiences. Long before social media, the Dead understood that their audience wanted a relationship with the band, which they pursued using interactive tools, as slow and analog as these may have been. When Garcia and Weir sang "we will get by" in Garcia's first post-coma "Touch of Grey," the roar of approval from the crowd indicated more than recognition of a catchy tune or some other transaction under the negative sign of the culture industry. Adornian critique is not designed to capture such moments.

Indeed it is this relational aspect that deserves more sustained attention than I can offer here. The Dead's attitude to their audience unknowingly prefigured the business model of streaming services, who purport to connect artists more organically to fans. The band would no doubt have resisted, in their own way, the financial exploitation of talent that blights today's online music economy. Their prescience extended to the technological as well. Others have noted the significant overlap between members of the wider Dead "family" and protagonists of early social computing in the Bay Area.[29] Notable among these was Stewart Brand, a long-time fellow-traveller of the Dead, who, in the mid-1980s, turned his book form *Whole Earth Catalog* into the WELL ("Whole Earth 'Lectronic Link"), a proto World Wide Web with a significant Deadhead presence, transferring the ethos of Deadhead fan periodicals to the more immediate electronic bulletin board. Closer still to the Dead was the writer John Perry Barlow, who, alongside Hunter, wrote many of the band's lyrics. Barlow worked with Brand on

---

[26] Ulf Olsson, *Listening for the Secret: The Grateful Dead and the Politics of Improvisation* (Oakland: University of California Press, 2017), 6.
[27] Ibid., 5–6.
[28] Ibid., 6.
[29] Fred Turner, *From Counterculture to Cyberculture: Stewart Brand, the Whole Earth Network, and the Rise of Digital Utopianism* (Chicago: University of Chicago Press, 2010).

the WELL and went on to become an influential, if usually controversial, contributor to debates about how the Web should work. Today's discussions about "internet freedom" would be impossible to imagine without either of them. Is it a coincidence that the summer of "Touch of Grey" coincided with the birth of a new relationship between people, music, and technology? I am not so sure.

19

A View from the Ground
Latin Quarter, "Radio Africa" (1986)

Michael Jones

I am a one-hit wonder (OHW). This sounds like the introductory statement made by a newcomer to an addicts' self-help group. It shares with that milieu a similar toxic inner cocktail of guilt, despair, and shame. Why? Because there are so many negative subtexts that give the term its dismissive and controlling power. Essentially to be an OHW says, "You are a novelty and as such are insubstantial and to be disdained." "You are conceited, your talent (such as it was) was limited and the single hit exposes its lack of substance and staying power." This is a lot to deal with, and "dealing with it" has given me insight into music industry as a practice.

In my experience, being an OHW was, in fact, a ten-year life arc—beginning in May 1981 and ending a decade later. That is, if it can be identified as having ended *at all*. The point is, I still "feel" like a songwriter, still write songs; if I was a guitarist, I could still play guitar. What has not happened since that "end-time" is that a specific type of investor in symbolic products (better understood as a major record company) has never since believed that I could be a market success for them. In this way, what ended in 1991 was the "status" of being a "signed act." Nothing else changed, and everything else changed.

Along with my band, I was "dropped" by RCA Records in 1991. Traumatic though this event was, I cannot give this a specific date, and that is an odd sensation to report. The "hit" (in the UK at least) had come several years before, in March 1986. It is worth noting that the album this was taken from was a significant seller in some European and Scandinavian countries, and thereby hangs much, but not all, of the tale. Many subsequent records were released, but all for independent record companies—to the point that releases since 2000 have been made by a "micro-indie" and lie far beyond the parameters of this discussion.

'Achieving' the Status of OHW

My consistent fall-back position over the several intervening decades is that, given the condition of the record market in "pre-Napster" times, it is quite remarkable to have had a hit record of any kind. These were the years of market dominance by the "major" record companies. It is pointless to attempt to condense here the factors that led, in the UK, to the rise to industrial prominence of those companies, but "The Beatles" is a useful shorthand for that process. Once the Beatles had shown that not only was there a market for "home-grown" "stars" but that such musicians could also generate the "raw materials" for the symbolic products invested in and configured by record companies, the formerly predominant Live Performance and Music Publishing industries began to adjust to the release cycles of the majors and to take a comparative, music-industrial "back seat" in the "star-making" process (where the overarching point is that the Music Industry needs consistent, large-scale market success to sustain itself).

What we need to consider here is that, in those pre-internet times, the process that secured large-scale market success for some recordings had been evolved by major record companies in entirely appropriate terms. The primary market challenge was that routes to potential customers were restricted to a rigidly fixed and limited set of channels for "exposure" of new products. These channels consisted of an extremely limited number of television companies that offered, between them, a tiny number of spaces in which new record releases could be promoted. Alongside these, there was an equally limited number of national and local radio stations with an equally fixed number of shows and spaces within shows that new releases might be played. Similarly, where print publications were concerned—the only other media route to potential buyers and obviously non-sonic ones—there was an equally fixed number of weekly and monthly publications dedicated to popular music with limited opportunities in the daily press for promoting new acts or records. Given these constraints, the challenge was to enter the appropriate conduits with the correctly attuned marketing and promotional materials that would stimulate specific subsets of radio listeners, TV watchers, and magazine readers to become aware of, and then to go out and buy, a specific, new record.

The aim in all this was to prompt very high "first day" (and "first week") sales. A sufficiently high volume of sales would then propel the release into the weekly record sales charts. Three effects were then likely (but not guaranteed) to follow: first, radio stations would incorporate "emerging hits" into their lists of frequently played tracks and so increase the exposure (and implied attractive worth of the recording). Second, "emerging hits" prompted more prominent and widespread coverage of the acts featured on those tracks, and this additional approval also stimulated sales through exposure and endorsement. The third effect was, then, that the bulk of record buyers tended to buy records that were already popular.

What dramatized all of this was that dedicated magazines, radio programs, and, crucially, television programs "charted" the rise and fall of the sales of recordings. Rather like Premiership football has become (and its marketing owes a lot to the example set by the Recording Industry), the focus on "the Charts" became a national, cultural phenomenon. We have only to consider viewing figures for the BBC's "flagship" program *Top of the Pops* as evidence for this claim. An appearance on the program became a badge of honor for a track and for the musicians appearing on that track (which also worked to obscure the marketing and promotional "push" behind its sales). What came with high visibility and its implicitly *undiscriminating* popularity was (for those same musicians) the sting in the tail that "hits" were not approved in all quarters, or by all cultural arbiters.

The sensation that to be an OHW is a source of shame derives, in part, from this recognition: my band was never "cool." Unfortunately, it is a sensation reinforced from within the Recording Industry itself: in a period in which it was album rather than singles sales that counted for company profit, the OHW was also disdained by the investor in a symbolic product. What this meant was that, for the cultural arbiters who repudiated "chart successes," the OHW was a thing to be derided because the act demonstrated deficit cultural significance, but for the major record company, the OHW was money wasted and their recourse was simply to exercise their contractual option *not* to release further records by the act. To be dropped is a kind of semi-public shaming (evidently you are not "good enough"). This is to be trapped in the faces of a vise, a severe and severely negative double-whammy; it is impossible to push hard in both directions at once, and to push against either is only to meet intractable resistance *from both sides*. The energy wasted in pushing is a zero-sum game; the status of "OHW" can never be recovered from, and this is why it is particularly difficult to deal with or, really, to live with.

What I hope to do here is not to exorcise a ghost, because the status of OHW is not just a lived reality but a *living* one. It is not something that can be exorcised because it cannot be erased from the historical record. Even so, to become an OHW is not, or not entirely, to be a victim either of corporate misdealing or cultural virtue signaling: the musicians need to take some responsibility for their contribution to the failed enterprise (because, implicitly, this is an attribute no musician desires). On this basis, I want to deal with each contributory element, in turn.

Just Victims of the Corporate Drive-By

To return to the 1980s and 1990s, in the face of the simultaneously easily identified but extremely constricted channels of access to record buyers, for an industry in which "Nobody Knows" what records will sell and which will not, the prevailing and generalized strategy was to sign more new acts than any company could effectively support (which gives the lie to the idea that somehow record companies "nurture" their signings). Essentially, releasing a record resembled entering a runner and rider into a horse race, with the crucial (and, from the musicians' perspective, "cruel") difference that "betting" continued once the race has begun. This meant that, as the company accrued early market information, the odds on any "rider" could lengthen or shorten. Consequently, "long shots" were abandoned by being starved of promotional resources while those resources would be switched to records that looked like they would not only enter the charts but enter at the higher rungs and so stimulate media attention. The challenge then was to ensure that sales momentum increased rather than decreased.

So it is that not just inside the record company but inside the "team" of people most centrally involved (including the musicians and their manager), the build-up to and initial experience of "release" are very much those of the release of an arrow from a long-bow: much muscle power exerted to draw back the bowstring; much focus on and discussion of prevailing winds and the quality of the air; the initial surge of energy as the actual "release" fuels the flight of the arrow, and then all this anticipation manifesting as a distracting mixture of passivity ("it's out of our hands") and anxiety ("what can we do to get it there?!"). "The public," of course, never experiences this collective "backstage" tension. That it exists, though, should convey that what makes a "hit" is something more than the "genius" of the act or the "hook," or the "production values" of an individual song and recording (though, of course, these are important, as well).

In all of this, and from the songwriter's perspective, the fate of the record is, first, far removed from the initial circumstances of writing the song. It is also far removed from the control of the musicians involved. What enters or fails to enter the charts, and what happens once in the charts, happens to a *product*, not to a record. In this, what counts is how well or how badly the configuration of the product and the preparation for its market entry have been conducted. Ultimately, because they not only contribute to product-making but are integral to it, musicians bear responsibility for their part in this configuration and preparation. Even so and often beginning far earlier in their industrial lives than might be appreciated, musicians develop the reflex of being reactive to decisions taken about them, and so are always "on the back foot" and often entirely ignorant of decisions taken in their name. Yet it is the musician and songwriter who must live with the outcome of all the decisions made and actions taken. To make this observation is not to imply that the songwriter and musicians are divorced entirely from the promotional and marketing effort, they are not; it is just that how they are included fundamentally exceeds their will and self-determination.

Songwriters and musicians are not divorced from the promotional and marketing dimensions of record release, because it is their images and, effectively, their psyches that are mobilized (though never fully with their understanding or approval) in and by those practices. To clarify, it is my contention that *all* musicians who look for market success share three inescapable identicalities: they each make a sound, they all look a certain way, and they can all tell stories about why they sound and look as they do. In turn, *all* these elements are drawn into the symbolic product that has a recording at its core. This is not accidental. Khalil has discussed the utility offered by symbolic products: while symbolic products are diverse, they are valuable generally because, as he puts it, they enhance the sense of self-regard.[1] Considered in these terms, a symbolic product, because of its intangible nature, is one that relies for its effect on how adroitly a musical "act" connects with and animates equally intangible social values held by a significant proportion of those who are most likely to respond to it positively. This "positive response" is argued in a number of ways by a range of influential theorists— as acts of "Subjectivity" or toward the construction of "Identity," as "Affect" or as an experience of "Agency." It would be reckless here to try to evaluate all of these complex theorizations of how music is used. My own take on this is that it is not music, alone, that promises utility for the end user.

Where the music industry is concerned, a symbolic product is constructed as a confection of the "Sound, Look and Story" of the originating musicians. From both

---

[1] See Elias L. Khalil, "Symbolic Products: Prestige, Pride and Identity Goods," *Theory and Decision*, 49 (2000): 53.

the music company and musicians' perspectives, it is how utility can be brought to advertise and manifest itself to an individual end user that is the goal of their joint activity. Cultural and market success occurs when an individual product helps to conjure or to animate a particular "structure of feeling" within an individual and across the groups with which such individuals identify (wherein we may hold "values" but how we experience "the World" draws them into play as shifting mosaics of feeling).[2] Understood in this way, what counts for sales success is how effectively a symbolic product suggests to an end user (under specific social and cultural conditions) that some aspect or aspects of themselves will be affirmed in their use of the product. The difficulty then is that such is the imprecision in configuring the product, such is the need on the part of investors to generate profit and reduce risk, such is the massive and intense competition between products and between musicians, and such the inchoate drive of musicians to generate appreciation and acclaim that the outcome is always more likely to be market failure than market success.

Taking Responsibility

Considered against this kind of background, being an OHW should not intrinsically be a badge of shame, it should be the reverse—it is indeed a "wonder" to have a hit, at all. Even so, an OHW I am and, while it should be obvious from remarks thus far that I lay the responsibility for this at the feet of the "product-making process," it is still the case that I initiated the product and that needs to be added to the account; some, but not all, of the production missteps follow that initiation.

"Radio Africa" came out of my head. Sometime in 1982 I had watched a documentary on the Brandt Report. I was an active member of the Anti-Apartheid movement at the time (as, too, every other then-contemporary left-wing cause) and the idea that African countries (mostly formed artificially by nineteenth-century imperialism) could, by being somehow more economically savvy, join the world capitalist system seemed risible to me. My only memory of forming the lyric is that I was on the 12C bus in Liverpool heading into the city center, and I connected "bad news" to "Radio" and "sad news" to "Africa." This, though, was not simply a lexical connection. I am not a singer and not a player of instruments, but I always connected words to a pulse of some kind. So it was, I would have tapped out these words using hands or feet (while attempting not to draw attention to myself on a crowded bus) to build a momentum to which emergent thoughts and phrases could be fitted. The challenge would then be to remember the patterns so that I could sing (in my flat, tuneless fashion) the growing song into a cassette recorder at the earliest opportunity.

By a "pulse" I mean something more than a beat, but less than a melody. My memory of this "pulse" is that it came from Joni Mitchell's "Jungle Line" from the album *The Hissing of Summer Lawns* (1975), and specifically the use of a recording of The Royal Drummers of Burundi. This gave my own rendering and reading of the putative song

---

[2] See Raymond Williams, *The Long Revolution* (London: Chatto & Windus, 1961).

an energy and an urgency that led to its completion. From records I kept, this is the thirty-first song I wrote, of approximately 270. At least seventy others were recorded and released on a series of ever less successful albums—essentially one hit in this case meant, "one hit single in the UK"—but this is a digression; the discussion needs to be picked up back at "Joni Mitchell," because herein lies the nub of the problem.

Not Cool

It is difficult to convey to anyone who did not live through it how seismic was the impact of Punk Rock in Britain. Oddly, Liverpool had almost no Punk Rock and did not spawn a Punk Band of national significance. What Liverpool *did* have was Eric's. This was a club, ironically in the same street as the by-then-demolished Cavern, that was not intended or envisaged as a Punk venue, but which quickly became synonymous with Punk. I refused to attend Eric's because so left wing was I by that time that I had decided that *all* pop music was "Bourgeois Ideology." This misguided judgment meant I missed everyone who was anyone in UK and US Punk. It also meant that I made no connection with a scene that spawned an avalanche of post-Punk bands, among them Echo and the Bunnymen, Wah Heat, the Teardrop Explodes, Orchestral Manoeuvres in the Dark, Dead or Alive, and Frankie Goes to Hollywood. So it was that I was a "Liverpool songwriter" (because I wrote songs in Liverpool) with not an iota of cultural capital. Worse still, as the impulse for my thirty-first song indicates, my creative spark derived from *pre*-Punk, "wordy" singer-songwriter music, notably but not solely Joni Mitchell. If it was possible to have *deficit* cultural capital, I was that man. As, too, was my co-songwriter, someone who battened on to a friend who had won a publishing contract with Chappell and Company.

That particular back story is too lengthy to detail but battening on to the battener meant that I became someone without cultural capital drawn into a world of commercial music-making. His windfall from the Chappells deal (he became his friend's lyricist) was a Tascam portastudio. I then became his lyricist! Having four-track recording "in a box" was remarkable. To us, and to our immediate circle, our songs sounded like records. Galvanized by this, another friend who had enjoyed a brief but successful spell as a student union promoter and was determined to break into "the Music Industry" began to take our first "demo tape" to record companies, where he represented us as a "band"; we weren't (Mistake One).

By the time a band had been formed to meet quite a significant record company interest (I paid a hefty amount for a guest list at a "showcase" gig at London's Marquee club for representatives—in threes and fours—from nine record companies; see fig. 19.1), the band did not meet the expectations conjured by the demo tape; it had not gelled, and it had no identity (Mistake Two). Even so, the demo tape found its way into the hands of a DJ from Radio Caroline (which was still broadcasting) and he played it consistently. This allowed for a tiny amount of leverage which materialized as a second showcase gig, this time at London's Mean Fiddler club. Here, a newly formed independent record company saw us, and its equally new managing director offered us a "deal"—a recording contract—on the basis that we were "the new Fleetwood Mac" (Mistake Three).

A View from the Ground

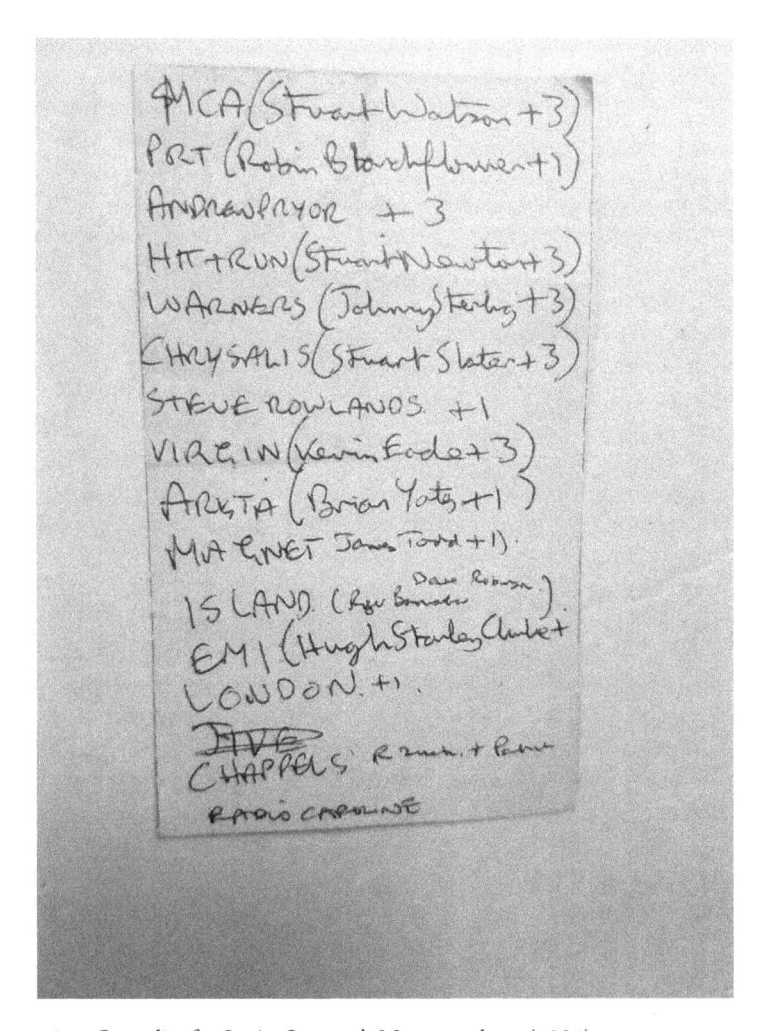

Figure 19.1 Guest list for Latin Quarter's Marquee show (1984).

Here the mistake was not so much to sign the deal (because rather like Brian Epstein at Parlophone this was the "Last Chance Saloon") but Mistake Four was to fail to contest the idea that we could and wanted to emulate the band with which, erroneously, we were compared. Viewed from a distance, we were now an indie band on an indie label. That company's release of the record put us into the Top 10 of the Indie Singles chart (just below the Cocteau Twins and New Order), but this particular "indie" label had none of the necessary trappings of a Factory, a 4AD, or a Creation Records. This lack of an attempt to parlay indie credibility then became Mistake Five.

There was no time to reflect on, and attempt to correct, any of this—the main backer of the new company quickly sold his controlling interest to Arista Records, who, themselves, were caught up in the sale, by the US corporation General Electric, of RCA Records to Bertellsman's, a major German (print) publisher who had acquired

Arista from US Columbia Pictures some years before this and had merged it with the German label, Ariola. The indie release was re-released but this time with BMG's "backing." This was sufficient to "chart it" (via the counterproductive strategy of a tie-in with the later disgraced TV presenter and record producer Jonathan King—Mistake Six). So it was that we came into a company in turmoil that had destroyed any indie credibility we might have been able to muster. Inside that company, save for the two employees re-employed from the indie label, no one was "invested" in us as a band— notably and especially the Marketing department who simply could not square how the band looked and sounded with a story that devolved on to two songwriters who still thought "the Revolution" was at hand.

All of this amounts to Mistake Seven, our inability to recognize our "product" status, the inability to re-group and to try to make it clear to the record company to whom we thought we appealed, how they could be reached, what we thought it would take to reach them, and what our contribution would be in and to all this. Essentially, we, or at least the two songwriters at the heart of affairs, were introspectively arrogant—"we write great songs, give us the money to record them, you sell them, we hate you!" We were dumb as paint.

Latin Quarter was the best of times and the worst of times. As an "arc," the experience has never truly ended. I understood the process I had been through, retrospectively. Accidentally I came to teach music industry out of theorizing that experience. Being an OHW, and one without any kudos, has dogged that teaching from day one, because I teach from the position of being a loser rather than a winner. Even so, I am acutely aware of the composition of symbolic products, and equally acutely aware of my own negative implication in one particular symbolic product. What academia has shown me is that any amount of teaching does not make up a deficit in cultural capital. For example, at a job interview at one UK Russell Group university, a panel member, a film studies lecturer, commented that the others should "look in the bargain bins" if they wanted to know what records I had made. I still scour Netflix for his movies.

So it is that, rather like Nathaniel Hawthorne's Hester Prynne, I have tried variously to hide, minimize, embrace, or ironize my "scarlet letter(s)," but they always bleed through. Spare a thought, then, for someone at the heart of a "One-Hit Wonder." A song becomes a record because a force for making profit from the production of symbolic products invests money, resources, and time into that configuration process. Inside this, musicians are as much the victims of their own naivety as they are the bad (or even good) faith of the small army of people who work over and around, rather than with, them on their conversion into commodities. No commodity can decide its own fate in a market, but the human commodity lives where the tide of market forces lands them. "Be prepared" is my watchword to students, to this day.

References

Khalil, E. L. (2000), "Symbolic Products: Prestige, Pride and Identity Goods," *Theory and Decision*, 49: 53–77.
Williams, R. (1961), *The Long Revolution*, London: Chatto & Windus, 48–71.

20

A View from the Desk

Product Management

Sarah Hill

This chapter should be read as the b-side to Mike Jones's chapter on "Radio Africa." Whereas Mike offered a songwriter's firsthand view of the journey into the charts and out of them, here I offer an alternative perspective, from a guy in a suit. My interlocutor in the conversation is someone whom I knew growing up in Oakland, who went on to work in artist marketing in the San Francisco Bay Area. He agreed to talk to me on the condition of anonymity. So let's call him Eric Lyles.

Sarah Hill: I'd like to ask you about the "old days" of the music industry. When a band got signed, how much time were they given to break before they would be dropped?

Eric Lyles: It could happen in the most organic way. Every artist is different, and if you're looking at the radio market in the United States, it's very different to how it is in Europe. In the US, radio is divided into formats, which coincide with advertising demographics. So Top 40, you get a lot of advertising for adults aged eighteen to thirty-four. If you look at Adult Top 40, the target is geared toward the soccer mom: the woman who's in her car, driving her kids to soccer practice or to school. Usually, those artists have been played to death on Top 40, and then they make their way to Adult Top 40; they are proven and familiar hits. Obviously that's changed over time, where now Top 40 and Adult Top 40 share a lot of artists, but back in the 1990s and 2000s they were two separate and distinct formats. In fact, the Lilith Fair phenomenon broke out of Adult Top 40. Alternative goes after young men, young teens; Classic Rock obviously goes after adult males.

SH: So if you're thinking about classic Top 40 singles that we all know from the 1970s, 1980s, whatever, are you assuming AM radio?

EL: I'm not sure about delineation, but when I think about AM radio, I think about my youth in the mid-70s. I think about KFRC 610. I remember listening to Top 40 on the AM dial, but when I wanted to listen to rock, I'd be on FM: KSAN, KSJO, KOME, all those.

SH: KITS.

EL: Yes: Live 105, The Quake. I know Top 40 graduated to FM at some point, but when I thought of rock radio, I always thought of FM, and when I thought of Top 40, I always thought of AM.

SH: There's a thing in popular music studies, where Top 40 AM radio equals "commercial," and FM equals "authentic." The distinction between "commercial" and "authentic," "pop" and "rock," is a whole can of worms. But thinking about the stuff that you and I would have grown up listening to on our transistor radios, we wouldn't necessarily have thought of any of those songs as being attached to an album. So we would have bought the single of Amii Stewart's "Knock On Wood," whatever it was, and left it at that.

EL: I totally agree with that. So when you heard the Sylvers' "Boogie Fever," you didn't think, "Oh my God, I cannot wait to buy the Sylvers' entire album." However, I would have bought the 45. But when I was listening to rock radio, I remember they would go deep into the albums. So I remember hearing several cuts from Blondie's *Parallel Lines*, which inspired me to go buy that release. That was one of my first LPs. I had heard "One Way or Another," I heard "Sunday Girl" on the radio, I heard "Heart of Glass"—obviously "Heart of Glass" was also on KFRC—but "One Way or Another" and "Hanging on the Telephone" were all being played on rock radio.

SH: Absolutely. So if you're working for a label in the late-1970s, and you have Blondie on your books, and they haven't really broken through because they're sort of alternative, punk, edgy, whatever, do you try to bring them over to mainstream radio? Or do you say, you know, they made "Dreaming," and they made "Atomic," and they made these other songs that are great and they stand alone, but they're not really getting us the younger, AM demographic, and that's fine?

EL: The way the exposure is now, obviously, with streaming there are algorithms that say, "If you like this artist then you'll probably like this artist." I remember asking a friend of mine who worked in the industry, "Do you think there could be another music revolution, like what happened with Nirvana?" Basically Nirvana came on the scene and wiped out everything that came before it. All the hair bands were gone when Nirvana started breaking. There was this sound that was emerging that spoke to a segment of the population that hadn't been served before. The music was basically reflecting what was happening in society and at the same time shaping it—think: the grunge look. I remember hearing "Smells Like Teen Spirit" on KMEL, which was an urban station in San Francisco, and knowing, this is the *zeitgeist*. I remember exactly where I was when I heard them play "Smells Like Teen Spirit" on KMEL. It was like, "this is crazy. This is a music revolution." Hearkening back to that conversation with my friend: he was arguing to the point that the way music is consumed nowadays, with the advent of the internet, and how people talk about music and post about music, his argument was that there will probably never be another music revolution in that way.

SH: But that doesn't mean that the fans of the hair bands also moved over to Nirvana.

EL: I think it tapped the possibility of such an audience that was undeniable. It was just so crazy. The fact that it was on urban radio, it was bigger than just "here's a great song on the radio"; it was a reflection of society. It was what was happening in society at the time.

SH: And it was not intentional on the part of the record label.

EL: No. As a record executive, one wishes for something to just happen where all the stars align. I mean, how was THAT song going to get on the radio? It sounds *nothing* like *anything* on the radio. Nothing! At the same time, that's what made it so genius.

SH: So would you have said at the time, "Ok, this is a great single, but it's the last thing I'm going to hear from Nirvana," or would you think, "What are they going to do next?"

EL: It was hit after hit from *Nevermind*. People were buying into the brand of Nirvana. It was as if what they were saying was something that had never been voiced before. Obviously it hit a nerve.

SH: Thinking back to Blondie, Debbie Harry is an example of a woman who has had longevity, a great career. But there were plenty of women around at the same time who were probably marketed for immediate impact and not for lasting power. So, say you were on a label in the 1970s and somebody came up to you and said, "You've got to hear this song by Andrea True Connection"—

EL: Yeah. I don't know how Andrea True came about, but I knew the story, you knew the story, that she used to be a porn star, so somewhere down the line they probably needed something to make it more titillating, and just said, "Play this catchy song by a porn star." Because we all knew the story.

SH: But really, there would be no reason for Andrea True to have had a record contract. She recorded "More More More," and there was probably some crafty label exec who said, "Ok, I know how to sell this, because 'Love to Love You, Baby' is on the radio, and we can soft-porn it."[1] Is it as cynical as that? That somebody would just say, "Here's a song and we can just make a bomb off of it"? Like, this is going to be a hit just on the back of who she is and what she does for a living?

---

[1] Donna Summer's single, "Love to Love You Baby" (Giorgio Moroder, Pete Bellotte, Donna Summer), was released in 1975, and hit a peak *Billboard* position of No. 11 in February 1976. Andrea True Connection's single, "More More More" (Gregg Diamond) was released in February 1976, and reached a peak chart position of No. 4 in the United States. Although Eric and I mention these two songs in relation to mid-1970s music industry marketing strategies, there is another way of hearing the Donna Summer single—along with Serge Gainsbourg and Jane Birkin's "Je t'aime moi non plus"—as a clear link between popular music and the 1960s/70s sexual revolution. See Jon Stratton, "Coming to the Fore: the Audibility of Women's Sexual Pleasure in Popular Music and the Sexual Revolution," *Popular Music* 33, no. 1 (January 2014): 109–28.

EL: What was a selling point back in the 1970s, in light of how far the women's movement has come, wouldn't be a selling point today. The way they marketed artists back then is very different to how they market artists now. You can't go for the lowest common denominator anymore.

SH: No. But you could then.

EL: Again, look at what they said about Heart when they were launching that record, and someone in marketing was giving an interview about the Wilson sisters. That's well documented.[2]

SH: But that just suggests that they didn't believe in the Wilson sisters as musicians.

EL: Or they wanted to be more titillating for rock programmers, who were all men. In *Between A Heart and a Rock Place*,[3] Pat Benatar's memoir, she talks about how the progam directors, who were all men at the time, would just tap their lap and say, "Why don't you come sit on my lap and see how we can get your record on the radio?" And she'd say, "I'm gonna kick your ass." I mean, here's a classically trained operatic singer, singing rock 'n' roll, who's already done so well in her career, and she's still being treated like a piece of meat. Remember, back then a lot of the labels' heads and radio programmers were like a boys' club.

SH: That reminds me of the book *Signed Sealed and Delivered*, which is full of interviews with women, all of whom stress how few women were visible in the music industry in Britain back in the 1960s, 1970s, and 1980s.[4] So it's really no surprise that nobody knew how to market a woman. Or that they reached for the lowest common denominator. But the thing that interests me, particularly in terms of the one-hit wonder, is what would make a record label say, we don't have to invest long-term in this person, but this song is going to get us a Top 10 hit and a whole lot of money?

EL: That's basically a singles deal. Artists were signed to a deal where they were given a set amount of money for one single. That's why you have something like Aqua and "Barbie Girl." What comes after "Barbie Girl"? Or the Vengaboys: "we like to party. We like, we like to party." It's basically a song with one big hook. It probably went up the chart, then went down the chart. You would probably never hear from the artist again, but it was fast money for a record label. But you can't really sustain a record label on singles deal; you have to have artist development. And that involves really investing in an artist financially, and a belief behind the talent of the artist.

SH: But as a promoter, if you're on that label, you have to be enthusiastic.

---

[2] He is talking about Heart's debut album, *Dreamboat Annie* (Mushroom, 1975). In an effort to drum up publicity for the album, the label ran—without the band's approval—a full-page ad in *Rolling Stone*, designed as a tabloid cover, with a headline suggesting that the two Wilson sisters were in fact lovers. That experience was the inspiration for their hit, "Barracuda," from Heart's third album, *Little Queen* (Portrait, 1977).

[3] Pat Benatar, *Between A Heart and a Rock Place* (New York: Harper Collins, 2010).

[4] Sue Steward and Sheryl Garrett, *Signed Sealed and Delivered: True Life Stories of Women in Pop* (London: Pluto Press, 1987).

EL: If the record promoter/label person is going to radio and saying, "Play this song, buddy," he or she might as well not go to the station. Nowadays, a promotion department has to have a story behind the song before they walk into a station. The song has to have metrics: it's breaking in 400 countries; it's streaming on all these platforms; people are talking about it. Radio is almost the last place you go to see if you have a hit. It's an investment, like you're taking time out, you're committing man/woman power to get this played on the radio, so you've got to look at all the metrics—people are talking about it; people are downloading it; people are spinning it; people are doing whatever they're doing with it—and then you go to radio and say, "Look at all this consumption." For example, if a promotion person is trying to get a song played, he or she may make the case for the artist by referencing that a noted, mega artist just mentioned this song in casual conversation. Or it's got a sync—say a television show used it as a theme song, or in a montage. You saw this with *Grey's Anatomy*: there would be a montage of someone getting shot, then them on the gurney, and being rushed to the hospital, and they're playing Snow Patrol's "Chasing Cars" or The Fray's "How to Save a Life." I remember Josh Groban was in an *Ally McBeal* episode, where he sang a song at a funeral, and it resonated with people and became a huge hit on Adult Contemporary radio.

SH: But that would also show a really good awareness of what demographic was aligned with *Ally McBeal*.

EL: Also the type of song. You're not going to put Josh Groban on Modern Rock radio.

SH: No. And you're also not going to take that song to KFRC and say it was on *Ally McBeal*.

EL: Right. It wouldn't be a Top 40 song; it would have an Adult Contemporary feel to it.

SH: So one thing is that I don't remember a delineation between charts in my youth. In my memory, there was the singles chart, and there was the albums chart. Did I really think about radio formats? I mean, I knew that if I went to Live 105 I would hear New Order and the Smiths and Depeche Mode, and if I went to KFOG I would hear Crosby, Stills and Nash and the Doobie Brothers. So you would know on the dial where to go for your taste. But that's not to say that I wouldn't have been aware of what the Top 10 was. I think actually it was around the time that I went off to college that I became so aware of my own little niche to the point that I didn't really understand what people were hearing on KFRC anymore. Like when "Borderline" was a big hit for Madonna, I thought, "Yeah, but she's not going to last." Like, really not understanding that that was the beginning of a long career. Because it could have been the only hit for her, and we would be here today saying, "That was a great hit in 1984, and whoever heard from Madonna again? Do you remember that song by that woman who wore all the crucifixes?" It would be easy for me then to have placed her in a one-hit-wonder category, because she was so unlike anything I was listening to on my own radio stations. So it's interesting to me to think about when a single can turn into something bigger, and when it's enough just to be a sole hit.

EL: Think about how artists can seamlessly make it to other formats. Like Duran Duran, with "Planet Earth"—when they first came out on the scene, they looked like part of the New Romantic movement, but I think they also realized, "This is limiting. We can expand our audience more, we can have a crossover, from this new niche format of Modern Rock to Top 40 radio," which would give them wider exposure. I'm sure there was a concerted effort from that first album, the *Duran Duran* album, to *Rio*, where they were like, "We're going to go for the world now." You know. They're not going to be just this New Romantic act that is going to be limited solely to Modern Rock radio. They're going to be—

SH: —all over MTV.

EL: Right. I mean, "Hungry Like the Wolf" was very different from "Planet Earth." You can see that the budget changed. And even the look. There was a concerted look—the cover of that album is a Nagel. They're going for mass mainstream taste.

SH: But that's based on groundswell opinion. You're tracking sales and radio play and all the rest of it in order to be sure that your investment is going to be worth it. So theoretically could someone have turned around and said, "'Planet Earth' is enough"?

EL: It depends on how it was performing on the radio.

SH: It seems like there are a lot more examples of bands that could have just been one-hit wonders, but that by some miracle of God somebody actually listened to the B-side, or somebody flipped the record over and listened to the fourth track on side two, and thought, "Yeah, this might actually pick up." My question is really about how that happens, but I realize I'm assuming that one of these bands that became a one-hit wonder had actually been contracted to record and release a whole album.

EL: Right. I think there are two things. There's one where they've been signed to an album deal, and another where the record company is trying to make fast money, saying, "We want a singles deal with this song. We're going to buy the rights to this single, distribute it, make the money"—basically hit it and quit it. Or: "We'll go for single to single. We'll invest in a singles deal from this artist. Ok, this song was explosive; let's see what the next single is." And then they'll have an option of picking up that singles deal or not.

SH: So in the meantime, this is a band or a musician who is desperate for a contract.

EL: It depends on what they want. I mean, not all artists want contracts. Maybe they have a one-off hit; it's hard to generalize. Sometimes all a band will have is one song in them. They may have recorded a whole album, but because of different factors—and it's not just the artists, it could be some other things. Like maybe the cycle in radio is changing, maybe the music tastes are changing. It can't be just, "well, they just weren't prolific." They *could* be; it *could* be that they only had one hit in them, never to be heard from again.

SH: That's a really good point. The example I could think of would be Jesus Jones, "Right Here, Right Now."
EL: But they also had "International Bright Young Thing." A better example would be EMF.
SH: "Unbelievable."
EL: That Jesus Jones album was really good, by the way. But they had two hit songs off it on Alternative radio.
SH: But that one song, "Right Here, Right Now," just *spoke*. Because the video was like, "I'm watching the Berlin Wall fall down; I'm watching the end of the Cold War," all the rest of it. And it's just a great little pop song, you know.
EL: But to your point, EMF and Jesus Jones came out around the same time. With EMF's "Unbelievable," I thought, "This song is amazing." So I'm waiting for the next single—and there was no next single. Like, is that it? And I'm still waiting. But there was nothing next for EMF. At least not in the States.[5]
SH: That leads to a couple of big questions about one-hit wonders: why do we know those hits? And who was behind the momentum that got us to know them?
EL: One-hit wonders may be only known for one song, but if that song is so meaningful it takes on a life of its own, and almost eclipses the band itself.
SH: That happens especially with movies. Like with *Guardians of the Galaxy*: the whole plot schtick is that the main character is human, and his mother, before she died, made him a bunch of mixtapes of her favorite songs from 1973/74/75. So the soundtrack is "Fooled around and Fell in Love" and "Hooked on a Feeling," all these really great songs from that time. You hear them and think, that's it: feathered hair and bell-bottoms, the whole bit. The soundtrack revived some great old songs, because they mean something authentically to the characters in the movie, but they also stand alone as these weird little time capsules.
EL: Look at the advent of K-Tel, Ronco, the compilation albums. Yes, they did have artists that had longevity—you'd see Pure Prairie League, or Little River Band; I had one called *Starbust* that had James Taylor on it—but you also had these one-hit wonders, like Jigsaw, with "Sky High." Those compilations were where you could find one-hit wonders in one package.
SH: But would the musicians have actually made any money off those compilation albums, or would the money just have gone to the record company?

---

[5] EMF's "Unbelievable" (EMI, 1990) went to No. 3 in the UK and No. 1 on the *Billboard* Hot 100. Jesus Jones's "Right Here, Right Now" (Food, 1990) reached No. 2 on the *Billboard* Hot 100 and 31 on the UK singles chart. Their album *Doubt* (Food, 1991) also included the singles "Real Real Real" (No. 4 *Billboard* Hot 100; No. 19 UK singles chart) and "International Bright Young Thing" (No. 6 *Billboard* Hot 100; No. 7 UK singles chart). Although Jesus Jones cannot therefore be called a "one-hit wonder," it is true that "Right Here, Right Now" has had the most fruitful afterlife of all of their singles. Jesus Jones songwriter and frontman Mike Edwards has written convincingly about the financial benefits of capturing the *zeitgeist*. See his "Still Here, Right Now," *The Guardian* (August 9, 2003): https://www.theguardian.com/music/2003/aug/09/popandrock.

EL: I've never worked on royalties or the publishing side, so I don't know the breakdown of that section of the industry. *Music Business Worldwide* just did this article on royalties.[6] The argument was that the artists should be credited with a lot more than what they're getting through streaming services, because the record companies take so much of it. It's really worth a read, and I think it will shed light on how things are broken down for artists, especially one-hit wonders. Is it still that all you need is one hit and you're set for life? In this model, what's happening now, I don't think that's the case.

SH: That used to be the myth, though. That you could have the one big hit single—

EL: —and you'd be set for the rest of your life.

SH: But I'm betting somebody like Andrea True would not have made a whole lot of money off "More More More." I think she was a cautionary tale. Or take your pick. The Vapors' "Turning Japanese": would they have made a living off that single?

EL: That's a good one. First of all, it's a good song, it's a catchy song. There are lyrics that are misinterpreted in that song. There's a lore to that song, which is that it's about masturbation. So there's been a lot of things going for that song, because there's a grassroots whisper—like, "Do you know what that song's about . . . ?" Plus, it's a fun pop song. So I think there are a lot of factors that made that song a hit: what does it mean to be turning Japanese? And then the whispers start, "Well, it's really about jerking off," or whatever. So that contributes to the lore of the song itself. And what is a cyclone ranger?

SH: Apparently it's "a psyched Lone Ranger," but somehow "cyclone ranger" made more sense to everybody. And now, post-traditional record contracts and stuff, somebody like Psy and "Gangnam Style"—huge, huge, biggest song ever, out of nowhere, and in Korean –

EL: And again, there was—I don't want to say "a lore" about that song, but there was this interesting curiosity about "what is a Gangnam Style?" Also that dance was part of it, another tie-in that made it a huge hit. Maybe it could not have existed without the other assets. And that's a really important thing that I think you need to bring up: where stars align. Maybe it wouldn't have succeeded based on the song itself, but think about the visuals: this person who by no means looks like a conventional pop star, he's in a suit, he looks like he should be in *Men in Black*, he's very short—just not a conventional pop star, doing this synchronized dance, and what does "Gangnam Style" even mean? There's a mystery and an allure to it.[7] So what are the assets and the elements that go into being a one-hit wonder? Is it just the song itself? In

---

[6] He's referring to Tim Ingham, "The Harsh Reality About the Music Business, and a Pantomime Led by Clueless Self-Regarders," *Music Business Worldwide* (January 19, 2021). Available online: https://www.musicbusinessworldwide.com/the-harsh-reality-about-the-music-business-and-an-awkward-pantomime-led-by-clueless-self-regarders/ (accessed September 7, 2021).

[7] For five years Psy's "Gangnam Style" (2012) was the most-played clip on YouTube, and was the first video on the platform to reach 1 billion views. The single topped the charts in thirty countries, and the dance found its way into almost every corner of public life.

this new world that we live in, that's multimedia, you need to do something to grab onto. There's so much stimulus and choice and distraction, sometimes a gimmick will raise its hand. Like "Macarena." Or the song is tied to a catchphrase, like OMC's "How Bizarre," or Right Said Fred's "I'm Too Sexy."[8]

SH: We talked a little bit about how a song can capture the *zeitgeist*, or just be dropped at exactly the right time: the Berlin Wall's falling, so here I am watching television, singing "there's no other place that I'd rather be." So you can play into historical events, if you're lucky. Or you can just do something that's purposefully catchy. You mentioned "Barbie Girl" earlier. I bet the songwriters behind that single would probably say, "We knew what the formula was that was going to get us a song that was catchy to the nth degree, and irritating to the nth degree, and all of these levels we had to hit, and so we knew by an algorithm how this song was going to break." Those are undeniable, maybe unavoidable hits. But what happens when a song gets played a lot on radio, but that doesn't translate to actual sales?

EL: That's a "turntable record"—a song that gets a lot of radio play but makes very little money for the record company. There are songs that have an amazing life on radio, that research well. I think now it would be strange if something researched well but didn't have the metrics behind it, which means it wasn't getting streamed, it wasn't selling. The metrics are a lot more specific now than, say, back in the 1990s or early 2000s. But back then a turntable record got a lot of airplay, but consumers didn't feel the need to lay down their money and actually purchase the song.

SH: So is a turntable record a song that wouldn't be worth anthologizing on *Now That's What I Call Music*?

EL: I think that's a song you *would* find on that kind of compilation. The record company would want to make money off of it, because probably no one is buying the album of that one artist. But if the song is on a compilation, it's another revenue stream for the label.

In this conversation Eric and I focused on radio formats and metrics, a label's strategy for optimizing its investment in an artist, and the changing landscape of music marketing and promotion in the post-internet era. From Eric's perspective, the label "one-hit wonder" could be seen as a marker of financial success, not just a derogatory term for cultural failure. The distinctions between the type of artist management that Eric mentioned and Mike Jones's experience with Latin Quarter are vast; but they both illustrate a business model that no longer exists.

---

[8] For "How Bizarre," see Geoff Stahl's chapter in this volume. "I'm Too Sexy" (Tug, 1991), reached No. 2 on the UK charts, and the Top 10 in ten countries, including the No. 1 spot on the *Billboard* Hot 100.

21

Shakespear's Sister, "Stay" (1992)

Áine Mangaoang

If you listen to any greatest hits pop compilations for long enough, you'll hear songs from all eras and singers across the world uttering the delightful word "stay" in their choruses. From the doo wop, R&B vocalizations of Maurice Williams and the Zodiac's crooning "Stay" in 1960, U2's understated rock single "Stay (Faraway, So Close)" in 1993, to Rihanna's more recent starkly pleading piano ballad "Stay" (2012), the feel-good, tropical house beats of DJ Kygo's "Stay" (2015), or the rapper Post Malone's "Stay" (2018), to sing a chorus of "stay" is to achieve that sweet spot of intimate yearning while simultaneously remaining wonderfully vague enough to be applicable to a multitude of situations, and appeal to millions of people the world over.[1] Even more specifically, to cry or belt out the three lyrics "stay with me" in the chorus seems to be a key to pop music triumph, at least checked against the likes of Lorraine Ellison's "Stay with me (Baby)" (1966), Faces' "Stay with me" (1971), Erasure's "Stay with me" (1995), or Sam Smiths mega-hit "Stay with me" (2014). For pop listeners, hearing the lyrics "stay with me" appears to connote feelings of love, loss, and longing—and often all at once.

Perhaps it is of little surprise then that in the rather chaotic musical landscape of the early 1990s, dominated by gangsta rap, grunge, and the onset of Britpop, a relatively unknown band called Shakespear's Sister released the only Number 1 single of the band's career in January 1992. This single, "Stay," has become an ever-enduring power ballad based around the immortally catchy refrain "stay with me," sung eight times throughout the song's nearly four minutes. Taken together with its iconic music video, the song has continued to live on as a gothic-pop anthem that defies expectation, and to draw in new fans despite the duo disbanding less than a year after the song was at the top of the charts.

Founded in 1988, Shakespear's Sister was created by Irish-born, UK-based singer-songwriter Siobhan Fahey, with American singer-songwriter Marcella Detroit joining soon after. Fahey was a member of the 1980s pop group Bananarama (who had themselves enjoyed considerable chart success with hits such as "Venus" and "Cruel

---

[1] There are, in fact, far too many songs titled "Stay" to mention here, and that does not include well-known variations on this theme such as The Drifters "Please Stay" (1961), Marvin Gaye's "Please Stay (Once You Go Away)" (1973), East 17's "Stay Another Day" (1994), or K-pop singers Chanyeol and Punch's "Stay with Me" (2016).

Summer"), before leaving the group in 1988 to pursue her own musical projects. Between 1988 and late 1991, the duo released several singles and one album to modest acclaim; it took the band three years to have the bestselling song of their career. Released in January 1992, "Stay" reached Number 1 in the UK Singles Chart and remained at the top for eight consecutive weeks—a record that stands today for the longest held number 1 by a "girl group" in the UK Singles Chart.[2]

The band's name is in itself quite telling of their underlying feminist goals, with human error playing a notable role just because. In *A Room of One's Own* (1928), Virginia Woolf tells us a story about a fictitious sister of William Shakespeare, whom she names Judith. What if, she asks us to imagine, Shakespeare had had a sister, who was equally gifted? While the course of William Shakespeare's life included education, theater, writing, and working at a theater in London, what were Judith Shakespeare's prospects in the Elizabethan era? What would have become of her? For Woolf, it would have been impossible for any woman to have written the plays of Shakespeare in the age of Shakespeare because this hypothetical Judith would have been uneducated, abused, exploited, and ridiculed to the point of being driven to suicide, all for trying to follow her dream. She would die unknown and forgotten, while her brother lives on in fame and fortune. Without "a room of one's own," there was no possibility for women to be creative artists or to build their own legacies.

Manchester band The Smiths took up this tale of a suicidal teenager in their 1985 song "Shakespeare's Sister," written by Johnny Marr and Morrissey. The track opens with the stereotypically morbid-yet-playful Smiths lyrics against a jaunty guitar riff and Morrissey's miserable monotonous voice singing, "young bones groan, and the rocks below say 'throw your skinny body down.'" It was precisely this cheerless Smith's song, that itself was centered on Woolf's egalitarianist manifesto, that provided the inspiration for Fahey's new musical project. Nevertheless, it was the cover of the band's first single that started out with a woodcut sign announcing "Shakespear's Sister," an accidental misspelling that Fahey and Detroit decided to keep as their own. And so Shakespear's Sister was born.

The Song, the Sound

If this world is wearing thin and you're thinking of escape
I'll go anywhere with you, just wrap me up in chains
But if you try to go alone don't think I'll understand
Stay with me, stay with me[3]

"Stay" was the second single released from the band's second and final album as a duo, *Hormonally Yours*. Recorded between August 1990 and May 1991, when both Fahey

---

[2] Jack White, "The Longest-reigning Official UK Number 1 Singles by Female Acts," *Official Charts* (website). Available online: https://www.officialcharts.com/chart-news/the-longest-reigning-official-uk-number-1-singles-by-female-acts__32517/ (accessed September 07, 2021).

[3] "Stay" (Detroit, Fahey, and Stewart), from the album *Hormonally Yours* (London, 1992).

and Detroit were pregnant, the album's title is a reference to this intensely emotional time both women experienced together. They described it as a "self-deprecating" album, "yet it's very female without being militant or apologetic. It's just . . . what we are."[4] Fahey and Detroit cowrote the album's twelve tracks, with additional cowriters invited to join for some of the songs, including David A. Stewart, best known as half of the British pop duo Eurythmics (and at that time, husband of Fahey). He is credited with the original idea of writing a song that would contrast with the band's other material, a song that would really showcase Detroit's voice and wide vocal range. Stewart brought the outline of the song to Fahey and Detroit, who then together added the melody and lyrics. Simultaneously, Fahey and Detroit have said they were heavily influenced by a vintage sci-fi movie, *Cat-Woman of the Moon* (dir. Arthur Hilton, 1953), which they watched repeatedly while writing and recording the album. *Hormonally Yours*, then, is a concept album of sorts, where different songs narrate the movie's plot of astronauts travelling to the dark side of the moon and discovering it is inhabited by beautiful cat-women. The peculiar lyrics to "Stay" and the even more bizarre music video that followed were directly inspired by this unlikely B-Movie.

Musically, the song is almost a microgenre in and of itself. It plays with pop convention and subverts genre expectations in a way that keeps the listener absorbed and surprised. In a way, "Stay" begins much like a conventional pop ballad from the era, scattered with sonic spillovers from 1980s pop precursors like Jennifer Rush's "The Power of Love" (1984) and Madonna's "Like a Prayer" (1989). Starting in common time and in A-flat major, Detroit's soprano voice tenderly sings the first verse solo, accompanied by sparse synthesized chords. It builds to a dramatic climax at the end of verse one with the line "But if you try to go alone, don't think I'll understand," where the word "understand" leads into Detroit singing an intense, yet brief wordless vocable. This sound captures and suspends the word "understand" for even longer, almost as if she is unwilling to let go of it completely. Curiously, her voice is put through a type of phaser-effect, a digital-delay with variable echo almost at micro-second level, perceptible on some transients in the vocals. These studio effects serve to set the vocal apart from the longer, dark-sounding reverb in the accompanying synths. So while the beginnings of the song may bear some resemblance to a standard pop ballad, or even a church hymn, the additional studio techniques lead to a slightly destabilized, unnerving feeling overall. This juxtaposition of the earthly chorale tones with the otherworldly effects is skillfully taken even further in the song's accompanying music video.

Detroit's vocals then move into a high, yet somewhat understated chorus, returning to the tonic and climbing up the scale singing the words "stay with me" as her voice moves from A-flat, to B-flat, to C, and then repeats itself over chords I-V-VI. All of this is sung above a gospel-inflected chorale, where a choir of solemn voices reinforces the hymn-like qualities of the chorus by singing "stay with me" in three-part harmony below Detroit's simple melody. Each word is sung as its own whole note, with "me" (C) sustained across two bars, holding on for eight measures over what starts as a common chord progression but, frustratingly, fails to resolve in its first iteration. This ambiguous

---

[4] "Shakespear's Sister," in Colin Larkin, ed. *Encyclopedia of Popular Music*, 4th ed. (Oxford: Oxford University Press, 2006).

ending of the chorus only adds to the feeling of Detroit's voice evoking a state of limbo, as the listener waits and waits for a resolution to the chorus only for it instead to return to verse two. The sequence is repeated with verse two and then we hear the chorus for a second time. However, after the second iteration of the chorus, complete with the same harmonious choir accompaniment as before, the song takes a sudden swerve into a distinctly different bridge section. Here Fahey takes over as lead vocalist with noticeably darker lyrics: "You'd better hope and pray / That you make it safe / Back to your own world," she sings, tauntingly.

In contrast to Detroit's soprano range, Fahey's contralto voice drops to the octave below where Detroit left off. The song shifts into the darker-sounding relative F-minor, and Fahey's vocals appear sharp without phaser-effects applied. Her voice seems more proximate, sounding closer to a low speaking voice, and with a more general reverb applied. This abrupt sonic shift or "drop" is reinforced with the addition of percussion for the first time, the drums and drum machines with gated reverb, some distorted electric guitars, and a gnarly synth bass that amps up the rock-centric sound for the first time in the song. Musically "Stay's" drop is not unlike Phil Collins's "In the Air Tonight" (1981), both in terms of the song's two-part structure and the subsequent groove that ensues after the drumkit enters. The steady, repetitive sound of the percussion remains throughout the second half of the song, though the song really starts to groove during the synth's striking countermelody that acts as a conduit between the bridge and the return of the chorus for a third time at exactly 3:00. The slightly unorthodox shift between the song's two distinct sections and the two very distinct vocalists end up emphasizing the acousmatic intimacy of Detroit's part of the song and becomes a form of "hyperintimacy by contrast," to borrow Emil Kraugerud's term.[5] Despite the unconventional shift from the chorus to the bridge sections, the way that these wholly contrasting sections are woven together by the end is quite remarkable, even if the song ends with a rather anti-climactic fade out. The successful merging of the song's two distinct sections was, nevertheless, aided in no small part by the affecting narrative exhibited in the song's official music video.

"I'm not entirely confident he's getting the medical treatment he needs"

For many, the name Shakespear's Sister immediately evokes their iconic image: dressed head to toe in black, the two women's jet-black hair, pale make-up with mountains of black eyeliner, cemented their status as gothic queens. While the sound of Shakespear's Sister was the work of Fahey and Detroit, Shakespear's Sister's *look* was the result of a further collaboration. The song's chart longevity and, ultimately, the band's legacy were reinforced by their utterly memorable music video for "Stay," directed by

---

[5] See *Come Closer: Acousmatic Intimacy in Popular Music Sound.* PhD Dissertation, University of Oslo, 2020, p. 132.

Figure 21.1(a) and (b) Stills from Shakespear's Sister "Stay" (dir. Muller, 1992). Above: In the first part of the video Detroit unconvincingly tends to the unconscious, unnamed man; "I'm not entirely confident he's getting the medical treatment he needs," one YouTuber commented under the video (2020).[6] Below: Fahey, as the Angel of Death, enters the scene from the song's bridge, dressed in a crown and black, sparkly catsuit.

Grammy-award-winning music video director Sophie Muller.[7] With input from Fahey and Detroit, Muller constructed a melodramatic plot for the music video based on

---

[6] This comment left under the music video for Shakespear's Sister "Stay" (Official Video) received over 39,000 "thumbs up" and 217 replies. I have removed the YouTube username from this comment to maintain anonymity. This version of the music video was uploaded by the band's record label London Records on October 10, 2017, and has received over 21 million views and 7.9k comments at the time of writing. Available online: https://youtu.be/YCYaALgW80c.
[7] Up until then, Muller was primarily known for her work with the Eurythmics/Annie Lennox, Sinéad O'Connor and Sade. Muller won several awards for her video for "Stay" and would go on to direct videos for many of the most famous names in pop music, including, in particular, a host of women artists and female-leading bands such as Alicia Keys, Björk, Beyoncé, Dixie Chicks, Garbage, Hole, No Doubt/Gwen Stefani, Pink, PJ Harvey, and Sophie Ellis Bexter.

the power ballad's brooding and dramatic lyrics to create the narrative of a woman realizing her lover is about to die, her pleading with him to stay alive, and fighting with the Angel of Death over his unconscious body.

Detroit plays the role of the lover, an unnamed man plays the part of an unconscious love interest, Fahey embodies the role of death—even though she performs it with the seriousness of pantomime devil—and the two women appear in their signature gothic make-up and black costumes (see Figures 21.1(a) and (b)). Indeed, the song's original inspiration from *Cat-Woman* is notable from the outset: the video is set in a spaceship on a lunar landscape, in a time period that could be past or future. Absurd, apparently ancient medical equipment flanks the man's motionless body, although as is perhaps typical in music video creative license, he appears not to be hooked up to a single one of the medieval-looking machines. Instead, Detroit's character gently serenades him with her repeated mantra "stay with me," while tenderly holding his hand and tending to him with a cold flannel for the song's first half (Figures 21.1a and b).

As the song moves to the bridge section and Fahey's vocals take over, Fahey's exaggerated character appears on screen bathed in light, dancing wildly down a white staircase as rays of light bounce off her black sparkly catsuit in quite a chaotic fashion. Fahey's Angel of Death character saunters over to Detroit to take her lover away with her, but instead a tug-of-war ensues between the two characters—between life and death itself—as they each pull at one of the man's arms as he lays between them. All of a sudden (probably from all the tussling), the man wakes up and goes straight into Detroit's open arms—a declaration of his choosing life over death, and light over darkness. In response, Fahey's character shrugs her shoulders, rolls her eyes, and leaves the pair of star-crossed lovers to continue their reunion in peace. She struts back up the white staircase, exits the spaceship, and the video ends on this image as the song fades out. Although Fahey brings a darker timbre vocally, and plays the antagonistic character to Detroit's heroine, Fahey does in fact bring a real lightness to the video in terms of her brighter color palette on screen married with her overall wacky appearance. The duo's theatrical performance is excessive and extravagant, artificial and flamboyant in every sense—high camp at its finest.[8]

In the early 1990s heyday of MTV and VH1 music channels, the song's (and album's) chart domination for multiple weeks was undoubtedly sustained by this striking video's heavy rotation on television sets around the world. One exception to this was Germany, where the censorship board took particular offence to the women's witch-like performance and banned the video from being broadcast on the grounds of blasphemy.[9] Of course such controversy had the reverse effect of creating even more hype around the video, and once word got out about the ban, people were suddenly really interested not only in the video but also the album and the band. In addition to dominating the UK singles charts for eight consecutive weeks, the song also found

---

[8] For more on camp's musical possibilities see Freya Jarman, "Notes on Musical Camp," in *The Ashgate Research Companion to Popular Musicology*, ed. Derek Scott (London: Routledge, 2016), 189–204.

[9] It seems the Germans' interpretation of the video concluded that the duo raised the man from the dead, and as such, this kind of sorcery was deemed inappropriate viewing material for a German audience. See Detroit and Fahey quoted in Emma Elizabeth Davidson, "How Iconic Goth-pop Duo Shakespears Sister Put a 26-Year Feud to Bed," *Dazed* (online magazine, 2019). Available online: https://www.dazeddigital.com/music/article/44380/1/shakespears-sister-reunion-new-single-interview (accessed September 07, 2021).

success further afield, reaching Number 1 in international charts including Ireland and Sweden, and placing in the Top 5 in Australia, Austria, Germany (in spite of the video ban!), Switzerland, and the US *Billboard* Hot 100. The music video was also lauded with prizes for the band and for Muller, including a Brit Award for British Video of the Year. Reaching—and staying at—the top of the charts for long as they did had a colossal impact on Detroit and Fahey, then women in their thirties and both mothers with young children at home (including the two babies born in 1991). As Fahey remarked, "when you're number one, the whole world sort of reaches its arms out and hugs you, and it's brilliant!"[10] Their 1992 calendar was quickly filled with repeated appearances on *Top of the Pops*, invitations to headline major festivals such as Glastonbury, and being summoned by Prince to support him at Celtic Park in Glasgow. On the back of all this, it seemed as though they had the whole world at their feet.

All's Well That Ends Well?

By 1993, however, it was all over for the duo. Despite the accolades, awards, and their feminist ideals, rumors of disharmony between the two women were rife by late 1992, and they parted ways in a fairly acrimonious fashion at the 1993 Ivor Novello Awards. Fahey, purportedly in hospital awaiting back surgery at the time, sent her publicist to accept the award on her behalf—Best Contemporary Collection of Songs for *Hormonally Yours*—an album that by that time had spent fifty-five weeks in the UK charts and achieved double platinum status. Fahey wrote a note for her publicist to read out loud, in which Fahey publicly announced Detroit's dismissal from the band: "I wish Marcy all the best for the future, all's well that ends well," while Detroit stood at the side of the stage, aghast that such a statement was made, and in such a public manner.[11] Much like the tantalizingly unresolved fade-out in their biggest hit, the duo stopped speaking to each other after this.

Yet the song continued to *stay* in popular culture in the years and decades that followed, popping up in the most unlikely of places. It appeared as a cover on the English extreme metal band Cradle of Filth's 2006 album *Thornography*, where the vocals were shared between soprano Sarah Jezebel Deva and growled by the band's lead singer Dani Filth. A few years later the original song re-entered the UK charts for a second time in history after *The X-Factor* contestant Cher Lloyd covered the song in 2010. More recently, the band's gothic-pop sound was cited as a major influence on the multidisciplinary artist FKA Twigs.[12] And in late 2020 a new wave of Gen Z Shakespear's Sister fans emerged, a possible consequence of 1990s popular culture nostalgia that proliferated on the internet during the coronavirus lockdown. These new, young fans largely found the band through the subgenre of YouTube reaction videos known as "first time hearing" videos, where

---

[10] Fahey in the *Hormonally Yours* documentary (1992). Available online: https://youtu.be/yByFmosZT3k.
[11] As quoted by Marcella Detroit on the FAQ page of her website. Available online: https://www.marcella-detroit.com/info/faq.html.
[12] As quoted by Twigs in an interview with Louis Theroux on his podcast *Grounded* (2021), Available online: https://www.bbc.co.uk/programmes/p091pg54.

Figure 21.2 Nigerian YouTuber Empress Joy-Jean visibly reacts to the "plot-twist" of Fahey's audiovisual arrival in Shakespear's Sister's "Stay."[13]

established and novice YouTubers film and upload their reactions as they listen to (and watch) "Stay" for the first time (Figure 21.2).

Since we can only ever get to experience hearing something for the first time once, these "first time hearing" reaction videos enable us to rediscover some semblance of that feeling by witnessing complete strangers hearing our favorite songs for the very first time. By watching the reactions of random people around the world—tracing the contours of the melody in their furrowed brows, hands raised to the sky when a singer reaches a high note, or feeling the beat by mirroring their rhythmic head nods—we are invited to remember our initial multisensorial experience of that song. And a song like Shakespear's Sister "Stay," with its countless twists and turns, provides the perfect fodder for such first-time reactions. And they are countless: one can revel in someone else's initial reaction to Detroit's startling vocal range, the epic tonal shift from Detroit to Fahey, and the video's overall exaggerated and comparatively "vintage" MTV aesthetics (Figure 21.3).

In one final plot-twist, Fahey and Detroit's fractured relationship remained unsettled until unexpectedly, some twenty-six years later, Fahey reached out to Detroit for the very first time. The two patched up their differences to the extent that they started writing together again. In 2019, the tension within this dynamic duo was finally resolved with their first release as a pair since 1993—a track called "All the Queen's Horses." For this exceptional reunion they called upon Sophie Muller once again to direct this rare comeback

---

[13] Empress Joy-Jean's video "My First Shakespears Sister—Stay Reaction" (uploaded January 21, 2021) is representative of both the "First Time Hearing" subgenre of reaction videos on YouTube and of first-time reactions to Shakespear's Sister more generally. The video has received over 36,000 views, over 1,000 "thumbs up," and 141 comments at the time of writing. Available online: https://youtu.be/dXFMvOqpTZg.

Figure 21.3 Still from Shakespear's Sister's music video "All the Queen's Horses" (dir. Sophie Muller, 2019) featuring a cameo by RuPaul's Drag Race star Morgan McMichaels in a sparkly catsuit, referencing Fahey's character from the band's song "Stay" (1992).

music video. The autobiographical video contains flashes of the duo in the 1990s, making palpable reference to their ego clashes, the rivalry, jealousy, and misunderstandings that went on behind the scenes. Yet the song and video take a lighthearted approach to the melodrama that ensued between Fahey and Detroit by including comical intertextual references to "Stay." In one scene, a much older Detroit re-enacts her character from the video tending to a comatose man on a pub pool table, and in another scene, two drag queens give their take on Fahey and Detroit's "Stay" characters to maximum camp effect (Figure 21.3). Despite the decades of dramatics between the two that stemmed from their number one hit, the pair have come out smiling, and the music video for their comeback song culminates with the duo walking into the sunset, hand in hand. And so it seems that for Shakespear's Sister, the band have found a way to stay with each other in the face of everything. Perhaps, just sometimes, all's well that ends well after all.

References

Jarman, Freya (2009), "Notes on Musical Camp," in Derek Scott (ed.), *The Ashgate Research Companion to Popular Musicology*, 189–204, London: Routledge.
Kraugerud, Emil (2020), *Come Closer: Acousmatic Intimacy in Popular Music Sound*, PhD diss., University of Oslo.
Larkin, Colin, ed. (2006), "Shakespear's Sister," in *Encyclopedia of Popular Music*, 4th ed., Oxford: Oxford University Press, Available online: https://www.oxfordreference.com/view/10.1093/acref/9780195313734.001.0001/acref-9780195313734-e-39830
Woolf, Virginia (1929), *A Room of One's Own*, London: Hogarth Press.

22

OMC, "How Bizarre" (1996)

Geoff Stahl

Between 2017 and 2019, a number of news and social media platforms circulated stories and memes of world maps that failed to include Aotearoa/New Zealand. Images of the globe without the island nation took all shapes and sizes, from board games, to shower curtains, to even some airline maps.[1] Prime Minister Jacinda Ardern responded to this oversight with a humorous retort, and it peaked when it became a segment on *Last Week Tonight with John Oliver* (February 17, 2019).[2] This moment neatly distilled a certain kind of anxious national identity for a country at "the bottom of the world," a default self-deprecating sensibility that tends to put any overseas successes from the country into stark relief. When Aotearoa/New Zealand does appear on the map, it is usually through its sporting successes (most often through rugby and the iconic All Blacks or sailing's America's Cup) or its movie exports (*The Lord of the Ring* and *The Hobbit* series, for example).

Very occasionally, its musical artists enjoy international recognition (such as Split Enz, or, more recently, Lorde and Benee), although the country's pop successes tend to work in different, sometimes antithetical, registers. On the one hand, internationally NZ musicians take on an ambassadorial function, often a burdensome metonym of sorts where they come to stand in for a nation and/or a musical, and in some cases, ethnic/indigenous community, often cast as an exotic curiosity or fetish. On the other, domestically that success often tapers off precipitously into what is referred to regionally as "tall poppy syndrome." In a small nation, this means that with many other artists clamoring to be recognized the expectation is to give everyone a "fair go," in local parlance. Being too visible for too long converts into a form of cultural exhaustion and then a fickle disdain for anything which, having been deemed to have outworn its

---

[1] Hugh Morris, "New Zealand Keeps Getting Left Off World Maps—And Kiwis Aren't Happy," *The Telegraph* (November 13, 2017). Available online: https://www.telegraph.co.uk/travel/destinations/oceania/new-zealand/articles/new-zealand-missed-forgotten-left-off-maps/ (accessed January 12, 2021).

[2] See Eleanor Ainge Roy, "Jacinda Ardern Asks Why New Zealand is Left Off World Maps in New Tourism Campaign," *The Guardian* (May 2, 2018). Available online: https://www.theguardian.com/world/2018/may/02/jacinda-ardern-asks-why-new-zealand-is-left-off-world-maps-in-new-tourism-campaign (accessed January 12, 2021). The New Zealand segment from *Last Week Tonight* is available online: https://youtu.be/N0opzJL8BLk (accessed 26 June 2021).

welcome, might be construed as ostentatious, and thus contrary to discourses (and myths) of egalitarianism that otherwise dominate social and cultural life here.[3]

The international success of OMC's 1996/1997 pop hit, "How Bizarre," exemplifies many of these aspects of musical culture in Aotearoa/New Zealand. However, the song does so with a unique inflection due to its specific place of origin, South Auckland, and the nous of the key individuals behind the music, a combination of *Pākehā* (person of European descent) and Niuean/Māori pedigrees, the latter embodied in the cool, charismatic figure at the center of OMC, Pauly Fuemana. As is the case with so many one-hit wonders, there is a much richer, and tragic, story behind the single itself. With "How Bizarre," woven into the words and music is a tale about the urban Pasifika and Māori communities of South Auckland (Pauly is of Niuean and Māori parentage), local musical cultures and their complex relationships to local traditions and transnational connections, and the rise of indigenous and diasporic musical content on local and national radio and television and thus in the popular imagination more generally. One also hears in its hooks an allegory of the country's long association with DIY culture, tensions between Pākehā and Pasifika/Māori musical histories and experiences, as well as how the implementation of government and municipal cultural policy initiatives, aimed to cultivate local musical content domestically and to promote it internationally, made diasporic Island and indigenous musical cultures more viable and visible in not unproblematic ways (Figure 22.1).

The Making Of

"How Bizarre" was first released in Aotearoa/New Zealand in 1995, initially to a local radio station in South Auckland, Mai FM (owned by local Māori *iwi*/tribe Ngāti Whātua), where it started to gain traction. It made its way through the country's student and community radio networks, and was finally aired on commercial radio, at which point the song and video became ubiquitous. Notably, the local release was secured only by Polygram Australia first being convinced of its potential and fronting an advance.[4] They agreed to release it through Huh! Records, a local Polygram imprint set up by Simon Grigg (which gave him some local autonomy over releases). This is symptomatic of a long-standing music industry relationship between the two countries, where the Aotearoa/New Zealand market has often needed sign-off from overseas major labels for which music gets released in the country from international artists, with local artists, more so with Māori or Pasifika artists, subject to heightened scrutiny. Shortly thereafter, the single went to Number 1 in Australia, and in 1997 peaked at Number 1 on the *Billboard* Mainstream Top 40 chart, being the first song from Aotearoa/New Zealand to top any *Billboard* chart (notably, it was released only to

---

[3] See for example Suchitra Mouly and Jayaram Sankaran, "The Tall Poppy Syndrome in New Zealand: An Exploratory Investigation," *Transcending Boundaries: Integrating People, Processes and Systems* 285 (2000): 285–9.

[4] See Simon Grigg, *How Bizarre: Pauly Fuemana and the Song That Stormed the World* (Wellington: Awa Press, 2015).

Figure 22.1 *How Bizarre* (Huh Records, 1996).

media/radio as a single in the United States so was not available commercially, and as such did not reach the *Billboard* Top 100 Singles chart). Over the course of two years, it eventually reached Number 1 in Austria, Canada, and Ireland, among other countries. It was the country's first bona fide worldwide, Number 1 hit song, a title it held for nearly twenty years (Lorde's "Royals," from 2012, would come close, but never matched either the sales numbers or the number of national charts it topped). The significance of this was cemented by OMC's appearance on the UK's *Top of the Pops*, part of a whirlwind worldwide promotional tour that lasted many months, in recognition of the single reaching the Number 5 slot on the UK charts. It was one of the rare times an artist or band from Aotearoa/New Zealand, and certainly the first time someone of Niuean/Māori descent, appeared on the show.

The success of "How Bizarre" is in no small part due to its deft and infectious combination of lyrical and musical hooks, which elsewhere might seem incongruous but here imbue the song with its charming gestalt. The song is bright and upbeat, with melodic lines built around simple drum machine percussion, and an odd array of disparate sonic references that add to its warmth: flecked with mariachi horns, some Cajun-esque accordion fills, and flamenco, Spanish-style guitar flourishes (obliquely alluding to Phil Spector and Jerry Lieber's "Spanish Harlem," penned for Ben E. King in 1960, but sharing much more of its overall verve with Mink DeVille's 1977 cut, "Spanish Stroll") melded with the well-established "Maori strum" (a style of guitar playing associated with island song and popularized by Maori show bands from the 1930s onward).

The crux of "How Bizarre" hinges on its titular catchphrase, the song's sonic allusions anchored to the (seemingly) wry observations and elan of front man Pauly, whose droll delivery, done in a light rapping style and a distinctive Island accent, underlines the song's laconic vibe. Australian music critic Clinton Walker said at the time that he "sings and moves with the sharp easy grace of a young Marvin Gaye."[5] On its face, the song is a catalog of experiences, the outcome of which is contrary to what might otherwise be expected. The first, and most pointed, of these comes out of being pulled over by the police, an all-too-common experience for Māori and Pasifika peoples that often does not end well. The singer's passengers, Sister Sina (Sina Saiapaia, who sings the backing vocals) and Brother Pele (the group's DJ, Soane Filitonga), respond almost instinctively, by uttering comforting words or by averting their eyes. Assumed to be targets of racial profiling, the surprise comes when the cop reveals he pulled them over only to compliment Pauly on his vintage '69 Chevrolet. The accompanying video reinforces the laidback vibe of the song, with Pauly, Sister Sina, and an aspiring Filipino artist named Hill (standing in for Brother Pele) cruising in the classic Chevy through parts of Auckland, intercut with segments of dancers, writhing in front of circus posters, visual aids that help to make sense of the cryptic references to elephants, snakes, ringmasters, and acrobats (the circus references are a hangover from an earlier iteration of the song, when it went by the working title "Big Top").

Alongside Pauly, two other people are central to the success of "How Bizarre," each bringing their respective pedigrees to bear on its composition and promotion, forming an alchemical trio essential to its success: Alan Jansson and Simon Grigg. Jansson came out of the Wellington DIY punk and new wave scene of the late 1970s and early 1980s, from bands such as The Steroids and The Body Electric. He moved north to Auckland with some of the electronic gear used in the latter band and settled into songwriting, recording and production, and eventually setting up his own studio, Uptown Studios. Grigg has long been deeply immersed in the music industry as a label owner (he founded the indie label Propellor Records in the early 1980s, where Sina was one of his last signings), with a sojourn overseas in the industry. On his return to Aotearoa/New Zealand, he set up clubs and venues in and around Auckland and later South Auckland, where he first encountered Otara Millionaires Club (later OMC). Grigg would become Pauly's de facto manager, traveling companion, confidant and guide to the ins and outs of the global music industry, and in 2015 penned a book-length memoir of Pauly, mapping the arc of success of "How Bizarre" as well as his and Pauly's travails with the industry.

Toward the end of the 1980s, Grigg and Jansson, picking up on the diverse sounds coming out of South Auckland's Pasifika and Māori communities, felt there was a wealth of musical talent that was not being recognized. Some of this was straight derivations of African American genres, such as soul, funk, r'n'b, and hip-hop, but others also incorporated local musical traditions, animating a vibrant scene that by the end of the 1980s had coalesced into a Polynesian/Māori musical revival.[6] Recognizing

---

[5] Nick Bollinger, "OMC Profile," Audioculture (May 27, 2013). Available online: https://www.audioculture.co.nz/people/omc (accessed December 12, 2020).

[6] Sometimes referred to also as a "Pacific Renaissance." See Jared Mackley-Crump, *The Pacific Festivals of Aotearoa New Zealand: Negotiating Place and Identity in a New Homeland* (Honolulu: University of Hawaii Press, 2015).

these new sounds needed a wider audience, Grigg and Jansson gathered many of these artists together and released the compilation *Proud* (Second Nature, 1994). This was a landmark record and a snapshot of contemporary urban Polynesian and Māori music, one which had clear references to the sounds of American hip-hop artists. Significantly, the bands all sang in English, a point of contention between the producers and artists, the latter of which insisted on singing in English (Stephen Turner suggested of "How Bizarre" that "precisely because Polynesian culture has always been performed as authentic and indigenous for white settlers and tourists, Polynesians are happy to speak American. It defies a will to be authentic ... that is more white than brown").[7]

This was also the era of "Otara Sound," a not-so-veiled play on the DIY Pākehā indie bands associated with the South Island-based "Dunedin Sound."[8] Phil Fuemana, Pauly's older brother, was an integral part of the musical scene that spawned that sound, much of which was affiliated with the Otara Music Arts Centre, a community-based, local-government-funded institution that was renowned for its state-of-the-art recording studio. Pauly had made himself first known through Grigg's South Auckland club, Cause Célèbre. The Fuemana brothers' band, the Otara Millionaires Club, contributed the song "We R the OMC," a clear homage to Cypress Hill, but it showcased Pauly's distinctive rapping style and Jansson warmed to him. Not long after the compilation's release, Phil left the band to pursue other projects, running a label and producing other acts, leaving Pauly to carry on as what was now called OMC. Shortly thereafter, Pauly would begin working with Jansson, and over the course of 1995 the two began to compose together, penning "How Bizarre," among other tracks, with Grigg shepherding the single through the music industry hoops, overseeing the song's trajectory from demo to marketable product to international hit.

The fortuitous union of Jansson and Pauly should be set alongside other contextualizing factors, as they form part of the less visible machinations behind the success of OMC and "How Bizarre." The first of these is found in the recognition of government policy makers that after nearly a decade of cultural atrophy, stemming from neoliberal policies that cut across all aspects of social, cultural, and economic life in the country, music-making in a supposed free market needed a rethink. One ostensible upswing of the country's deregulated media market was the emergence of one of the largest radio markets per capita in the world, although this was a commercial radio space dominated by international artists; local artists still struggled to be heard on commercial radio.[9] The smaller student and community/iwi radio networks better supported local musical talent, which sometimes fed into the mainstream market, but this tended to be hit or miss. The establishment of New Zealand on Air (NZOA) in 1989 was an attempt on the part of the government to support local artists through

---

[7] Cited in Matthew Bannister, "Where's Morningside? Locating bro'Town in the Ethnic Genealogy of New Zealand/Aotearoa," *MEDIANZ: Media Studies Journal of Aotearoa New Zealand* 11, no. 1 (2008): 1–15. See also Tony Mitchell, *Popular Music and Local Identity: Rock, Pop and Rap in Europe and Oceania* (London: Leicester University Press, 1996).

[8] See Colin McLeay, "The 'Dunedin Sound': New Zealand Rock and Cultural Geography," *Perfect Beat* 2, no. 1 (1994): 38–50.

[9] See Michael Scott, "The Networked State: New Zealand on Air and New Zealand's Pop Renaissance," *Popular Music* 27, no. 2 (2008): 299–306.

"state-leveraged access to commercial broadcasting."[10] It also aimed to get NZ music heard in overseas markets, whereby "subsidies become a calculated state investment conditioned by the economic and cultural logics of the commercial broadcasting field,"[11] meaning that the defining evaluative criterion of this funding regime was the commercial viability of a song or album. A state-subsidized, contestable, workaround to the problems faced by local cultural production and musical labor exacerbated by neoliberalism, NZOA emerged at a moment in Aotearoa/New Zealand when the government was starting to recognize the value of supporting and promoting local talent, catalyzing a burgeoning cultural nationalism. The video for "How Bizarre," as well as its early radio play, was subsidized in part by funding granted through NZOA, which had deemed the single commercially viable and thus worthy of government support.[12]

While funding bodies such as NZOA shaped aspects of the song's local and international promotion, the industrial and institutional milieux are only a part of the context shaping the success of "How Bizarre," and while important, they should not be overstated. The song and Pauly himself are very much a product of South Auckland and its distinctive place in Aotearoa/New Zealand. The name Otara Millionaires Club, for example, is a sly reference to OMC's home suburb south of Auckland, Otara, an area that forms part of a unique and complex moral geography in the national imaginary (the 2014 documentary *How Bizarre* features numerous clips of Pauly patiently, but also proudly, explaining this to the hosts of the many international variety shows he performed on). South Auckland, which is used (often dismissively) as shorthand for the suburban cluster of Otara, Manurewa, Papatoetoe, and Mangere, is adjacent to the nation's most populous city and home to the largest Polynesian community in the country. An industrial and manufacturing hub, and where the Auckland airport also sits, it is home to generations of Samoans, Niueans, Cook Islanders, as well as Māori, many forced out of Auckland center due to rising costs of living, who have come to work, live, and mingle together in a rich Polynesian mosaic. These diasporic communities maintain strong cultural connections to their home islands as well as their kin networks in the United States and elsewhere, while also finding solidarity with its long-established Māori populace.

Made up of vibrant and diverse Island and indigenous cultures and communities, South Auckland is also an area that is marked by the ravages of long-term socio-economic deprivation. It is predominantly working-class, and a region where gangs and drug culture also have a foothold, part of the culture a younger Pauly was involved in but later rejected.[13] It is an area that many Pākehā New Zealanders come to know primarily through media-generated moral panics that spectacularize these latter aspects of Otara, with many of the positive aspects of life there downplayed or rarely represented in the national press. These latter characterizations of South Auckland obscure its diversity and cultural richness, as a place of working-class and Polynesian

---

[10] Ibid., 301.
[11] Ibid., 304.
[12] See Grigg, *How Bizarre*.
[13] See Graham Reid, "PolyGram's OMC Unearths Polynesia," *Billboard* (July 6, 1996): 1–2.

and Māori solidarity, that has roots extending back many decades. The area has long been home to many successful musicians and bands, artists who play across any number of genres, drawing on their own Pasifika and Māori musical heritages while absorbing influences from overseas, some of these coming from their diasporic kin in the United States, where a voice for the racially and socially marginalized has a well-entrenched musical outlet. That overseas struggle finds its analog locally, inflected most notably through the long history of Māori displacement from their land and their—as well as Pasifika peoples'—marginalization and stigmatization in state-subsidized welfare support structures and housing, much of which was aggravated by the neoliberal social policies of successive governments from the early 1980s onward. In spite of this, as Anne de Bruin suggested in 1996, there exists a strong sense of belonging in Otara, tied to its place as a "deliberate creation of the housing and industrial policies of the welfare state," a feeling of community "developed as part of the more widespread recent ethnic revival in New Zealand . . . strongly linked to religious ties within the community . . . and strengthened by the resistance to the negative stereotype so typically attached to Otara."[14] As a local musician said of South Auckland, it was Aotearoa/New Zealand's Bronx, with everything that implied: an area socioeconomically disadvantaged but musically and culturally rich.[15]

Afterlife

"How Bizarre" enjoys a half-life that continues to resonate within popular culture. In the current vogue for 1990s revivalism, the song often reappears in retrospectives revisiting that decade's musical hits. That half-life escalated to a second life through its recent remediation on social media platforms. Throughout 2020/2021 it resurfaced as a punchline response to the Covid pandemic, circulating as a meme on social media and a hashtag (#howbizarre) on Twitter. At the end of 2020, it was trending on TikTok, resurrected in the form of a series of skits in which people reveal their "big secrets" or coincidences to a friend or family member to lyrical snippets from the song.[16] In these latter examples, "How Bizarre" has swung back into view at a point where its pithy catchphrase has tapped into a particular structure of feeling.

Decontextualized as such, reduced to a trendy refrain, what is mainly silent between the notes, lyrics, hooks, and the Polynesian/Māori panache of Pauly Fuemana is the richness and paradoxes of the song's complexities. South Auckland's history and culture is the pulse driving "How Bizarre," animating an unassuming anthem for Otara that briefly took its place on the global stage, with Pauly serving as the region's unofficial ambassador. The arc of Pauly's career is indelibly marked by how he came to embody

---

[14] Cited in Anna de Bruin, "From Cultural to Economic Capital: Community Employment Creation in Otara," *Labour, Employment and Work in New Zealand* (1996), 88.
[15] Cited in Grigg, *How Bizarre*.
[16] Chris Marriner, "How Bizarre: Kiwi Classic Goes Viral on TikTok," *NZ Herald* (December 10, 2020). Available online: https://www.nzherald.co.nz/entertainment/how-bizarre-kiwi-classic-goes-viral-on-tiktok/B3IUW72VNAHZ6SOARLMFNZUW4M/ (accessed March 06, 2021).

these seeming disparities, often uncomfortably. As is the case with many "one-hit wonders," OMC continued to release singles, some of which met with modest success (1997's "Land of Plenty" for example), both locally and internationally, but they failed to match the global chart-topping glory of "How Bizarre." An inevitable parody version of the song almost shipped with the album, which aimed to further mine the song's success (this was nixed by Pauly), and songs were commissioned to appear on soundtracks (OMC was contractually obligated by Polygram to cover Randy Newman's "I Love L.A.," which showed up on Rowan Atkinson's 1997 film, *Bean: The Movie*). Alan and Pauly engaged in a legal stoush around songwriting royalties (ironizing the song's line exhorting the listener to "buy the rights"), had a falling out, a reconciliation, and then another falling out, in part over Pauly's increasingly erratic behavior. Thereafter followed media stories about the spending excesses Pauly indulged in (much of it on family and friends), a career that was faltering, and a follow-up album that never materialized. In 2006, ten years after the release of the single, he declared bankruptcy. Four years later, in 2010, Pauly passed away, at forty years old, due to a degenerative nerve disorder (his brother Phil, had died in 2005, at age forty-one). In some news stories, he seemed to fit an all-too-convenient media narrative of dissipation that also reproduced stereotypes about Pasifika and Māori peoples, a particularly racialized iteration of the "tall poppy" syndrome. What is often lost in that story, and something that only rarely made the mainstream media here and never internationally, was Pauly's deep commitment to his South Auckland *whānau* (family and friends) and the wider Pasifika and Māori communities. Some twenty-five years later, Pauly/OMC is not simply a musical footnote; he's left more of a footprint. Pauly had *mana* (status) and is still revered for helping put Otara and its "Sound," as well as Aotearoa/New Zealand, on the map.

References

How Bizarre: The Story of an Otara Millionaire (2014), [TV movie] Dir. Stuart Page, Māori TV, Aotearoa/New Zealand, August 25.
OMC: The Story of How Bizarre (2014), Radio New Zealand, August 23. Available online: https://www.rnz.co.nz/national/programmes/accessallareas/audio/20146848/omc-the-story-of-how-bizarre (accessed December 13, 2020).
Ainge Roy, E. (2018), "Jacinda Ardern Asks Why New Zealand Is Left Off World Maps in New Tourism Campaign," *The Guardian*, May 2. Available online: https://www.theguardian.com/world/2018/may/02/jacinda-ardern-asks-why-new-zealand-is-left-off-world-maps-in-new-tourism-campaign (accessed January 12, 2021).
Bannister, M. (2008), "Where's Morningside? Locating bro'Town in the Ethnic Genealogy of New Zealand/Aotearoa," *MEDIANZ: Media Studies Journal of Aotearoa New Zealand*, 11 (1): 1–15.
Bollinger, N. (2013), "OMC Profile," Audioculture, May 27. Available online: https://www.audioculture.co.nz/people/omc (accessed December 12, 2020).
de Bruin, A. (1996), "From Cultural to Economic Capital: Community Employment Creation in Otara," *Labour, Employment and Work in New Zealand*, 89–96. https://doi.org/10.26686/lew.v0i0.962.

Grigg, S. (2015), *How Bizarre: Pauly Fuemana and the Song That Stormed the World*, Wellington: Awa Press.

Mackley-Crump, J. (2015), *The Pacific Festivals of Aotearoa New Zealand: Negotiating Place and Identity in a New Homeland*, Honolulu: University of Hawai'i Press.

Marriner, C. (2020), "How Bizarre: Kiwi Classic Goes Viral on TikTok," *NZ Herald*, December 10, 2020. Available online: https://www.nzherald.co.nz/entertainment/how-bizarre-kiwi-classic-goes-viral-on-tiktok/B3IUW72VNAHZ6SOARLMFNZUW4M/ (accessed March 6, 2021).

McLeay, C. (1994), "The 'Dunedin Sound': New Zealand Rock and Cultural Geography," *Perfect Beat*, 2 (1): 38–50.

Mitchell, T. (1996), *Popular Music and Local Identity: Rock, Pop and Rap in Europe and Oceania*, London: Leicester University Press.

Mouly, V. S. and J. Sankaran (2000), "The Tall Poppy Syndrome in New Zealand: An Exploratory Investigation," *Transcending Boundaries: Integrating People, Processes and Systems*, 285: 285–9.

Morris, H. (2017), "New Zealand Keeps Getting Left Off World Maps—And Kiwis Aren't Happy," *The Telegraph*, November 13. Available online: https://www.telegraph.co.uk/travel/destinations/oceania/new-zealand/articles/new-zealand-missed-forgotten-left-off-maps/ (accessed January 12, 2021).

Reid, G. (1996), "PolyGram's OMC Unearths Polynesia," *Billboard*, 108 (27): 1–2. July 6. Available online.

Scott, M. (2008), "The Networked State: New Zealand on Air and New Zealand's Pop Renaissance," *Popular Music*, 27 (2): 299–306.

23

The Butthole Surfers, "Pepper" (1996)

Gina Arnold

If you've ever driven the 300-mile straight stretch down Highway Five, the interstate that links Northern with Southern California, you may be familiar with an exit called Buttonwillow. It is the last one before the road finally starts climbing up the Grapevine and into the San Gabriel mountains. Sometime late last century, my friends and I started calling that exit "Buttonhole Willow," after an advertisement we'd seen in the entertainment section of the San Francisco *Chronicle*—colloquially known as the "Pink Section" due to the color of the paper it was printed on—announcing a gig by a Texas band called the Buttonhole Surfers [*sic*]. Apparently, the band's real name was too salacious for a family newspaper.

I begin this chapter on the wonder of this band's one hit with this anecdote, in part as a reminder of the innocence of those times, but also to remind myself just how very different the past is from today—a different country, as L.P. Hartley once famously said. Just think how everything about that first paragraph is out of date, beginning with the fact that many fewer people drive from Northern to Southern California these days, so kids probably haven't memorized the names of the exits between Los Banos and Magic Mountain the way that children of my era did. Also, the Pink Section is no longer, nor is the wild sense of anticipation we got from flipping through its pages to the back every Sunday, eager to see what bands may be en route to our town. Nowadays if you want to know when a band you like is going to play in your town, the internet will gladly inform you the instant the show is booked.

Those are big changes but perhaps the biggest has to do with the connotations in the band's name. In 2020, a woman named Lisa Rieffel-Dunn posted a video on Twitter of her eight-year-old singing a self-penned song called "(I Wonder) What's Inside My Butthole?," which was shared 5 million times and written about with nary a worrisome thought about the direct object in the title. In 1996, as the Pink Section ad indicates, the Butthole Surfers name was considered scandalous—although unbeknown to the paper, the band could have called itself worse: sometimes it went by the moniker Fred Astaire's Asshole. Or, The Right to Eat Fred Astaire's Asshole. Or even, The Inalienable Right to Eat Fred Astaire's Asshole. Once, when I was talking to the band's lead singer Gibby Haynes, he told me that he had used the word "Butthole" to be endearing. "If I wanted to be shocking," he said, "I'd have called us the Shit Up Your Mother's Pussy

Surfers." Needless to say, I was shocked, as I was meant to be. But it was the high era of the PMRC—Parent's Music Resource Center—a quasi-political group of lawmakers' wives whose stated goal was to increase parental control over what music their children would have access to. The group wanted to censor any music that was "deemed to have violent, drug-related or sexual themes," which, as anyone who's ever listened to the radio knows, means the entirety of rock music. Anyone who flew in the face of that mandate was doing the Lord's work.

These are just some of the things you have to recall in order to understand why the ascension of a song by the Butthole Surfers to the Top 40 *Billboard* charts in the summer of 1996 was so astounding. Released in May, the song "Pepper," from their seventh studio album *Electric Larryland*, reached Number 1 on *Billboard*'s "Modern Rock" charts in July and 29 on the "Radio Airplay" Charts soon after. (Because it wasn't released as a single, it was ineligible to be on the Hot 100. Another sign of ye olde worlde: the sale of single songs as artifacts.) Prior to that moment the Buttholes were an underground sensation: this appearance above ground, in the mainstream, occurred in a very brief window of time when such things were possible, a window that had been opened a few years earlier by the band Nirvana. It's impossible to overstate the effect that band had on the music industry, the radio landscape, and on certain individual artists that Kurt Cobain had said he liked, but surely the charting of "Pepper" was its apex. Cobain once cited the Butthole Surfers on a list of the Top 50 artists that were influential to him, and the band had been signed to a major label, Capitol Records, on the strength of that statement.

So it was a strange time in the world of A & R, but even so there was really no precedent for a band like the Butthole Surfers to be on mainstream radio. Unlike other post-Nirvana faux grunge luminaries (Alice In Chains, Candlebox, Live, etc.), who had dirty hair and wore plaid but stuck to melodic rock and the loud-soft-loud rules, the Buttholes played a genre of music known as "pigfuck," a hideous term coined by critic Robert Christgau, who presumably thought it sounded like pigs fucking. Steven Slaybaugh of the AgitReader says that pigfuck "was embodied by elevated decibel levels, frayed sonics, and often salacious subject matter,"[1] and that's throwing roses at it: not for nothing did the cover of *Electric Larryland* depict blood gushing out of an eardrum being punctured by a pencil.[2] As that image implies, earlier Butthole work, and pigfuck in general, was full of tortured guitars, guttural shouts, and other sonic indignities. It had a surprising number of adherents. Even today you can find streaming playlists titled "pigfuck" on services like Last.Fm and Spotify and videos on Reddit.

Pigfuck is a very acquired taste, and the Butthole Surfers are both its progenitor and its highest priests. On albums like *Rembrandt Pussyhorse* (1986) and *Locust Abortion Technician* (1987), they melded punk rock and psychedelia, scatological lyrics and psychotic rhythms into performances that proved to be extremely popular, at least in a live setting. I wasn't a big fan of the pigfuck genre, but nevertheless I saw the

---

[1] See www.agitreader.com/news/pigfuck_top_10.html.
[2] In order to be able to be stocked in chain stores such as Walmart, it was later replaced by a 'clean' version, with the name of the band rendered in asterisks—B******* S******—and a photo of a gopher.

Buttholes perform numerous times and it was never less than heart-stopping. More than that: it was always a great day when the Buttholes came to town. My friends and I would fight to get a hold of tickets. Seeing them live could be brutal, though. Blinded by strobe lights. Deafened by a bullhorn. Mesmerized by dueling drummers ("Just like the Grateful Dead!" I screamed to my evening's companion, who stared at me uncomprehendingly before dropping to their knees, rolling in a ball and rocking back and forth 'til the set was over. As one does.). The whole experience could be quite nauseating, because behind the stage they'd be running these gory films about car crashes or sex change operations such that I, for one, would have to cover my eyes rather than look straight at the performers. Sweat would be pouring off all of us, people would tear off their clothes, fists would fly, something or someone would get set on fire . . . there was an edge of uncontained violence to every image, every guitar shriek, every beat. To go see the Buttholes was to cast yourself into a burning pit; your stomach would have butterflies all week in anticipation, but that was part of the point, I think. It was such a tame era, I now believe we were all looking for a way to make our goofy little lives of privilege seem heavier, more meaningful. We wanted to participate in history, and this was our only route. The Butthole Surfers, like many other bands of the time, were both extremely twisted and entirely apolitical, but around that time I also saw similarly intense performances by Einstürzende Neubauten and Mark Pauline, who shot flame throwers over our heads while we all cowered under a freeway overpass, and those were the only times I came close to understanding what my father must have experienced in living through the Blitz. In 1991, they toured with Lollapalooza, and seeing them in broad daylight was almost more disconcerting than seeing them at a nightclub, as Gibby often brought out a shotgun which he let off over the heads of the crowd. No joke.

Going to see the Buttholes was exhilarating, albeit much more like participating in an art installation than seeing a punk rock show, and that's odd, because I truly think the band had no interest in art. ("Art," Gibby once said, "is the last three letters in fart."[3]) In fact, he and the guitarist Paul Leary were both MBA students at Trinity University in San Antonio when they began the band. Haynes was considered a brilliant accountant (and fraternity boy), while Leary (né Walthall) was the son of the Dean of the Business School there. This circumstance perhaps explains why, despite the insanity they displayed in concert, they were nonetheless able to amass enough money on indie labels to build a recording studio and buy a ranch (which I visited once, for my sins), as well as how they wound up commanding the highest fee—$15,000 a night—for their live performances. It doesn't really explain "Pepper."

As could only be expected given that it comes from the band's major label debut, "Pepper" is tame by comparison to earlier Butthole compositions like "The Shah Sleeps on Lee Harvey's Grave" and "Sweat Loaf," but it does draw from the band's unusual bag of sonic studio tricks. The electric bass is bowed, at one point, the track slows down and speeds up, and one entire chorus is replayed backward, which adds a kind of sinister

---

[3] Quoted in Gina Arnold, "Gross National Product. Only in America: The Butthole Surfers," *Option Music Alternatives* 27 (July/August 1989). Available online: www.angelfire.com/ab/butthole/GNPOnlyinAMERICA.htm (accessed September 07, 2021).

frost to the mood of the music as well as alluding subtly to the Beatles, who first used the technique, known as "backmasking," on the track "Rain," in 1966. Later, of course, the sound of lyrics sung backward became associated with conspiracy theories and Satanism, when credulous Fundamentalist Christian parents decided that bands were sending subliminal messages about Satan to their kids, supposedly encoded in songs like "Stormbringer" by Deep Purple or "Dinner at Deviant's Palace" by Cradle of Filth. Such accusations were so ridiculous that they became fun to spoof—the otherwise innocuous band ELO, for example, embedded a message in one song ("The Secret Messages") which, when played forward, turned out to say, "Thank you for listening." That was in 1983, so by the time the Buttholes did it on "Pepper," the sound of a backmasked lyric was merely a sonic shorthand for "I am pretending to be scary for your parents." (Although by 1996 the PMRC had all but disbanded, they hadn't done so before they got the RIAA to ensure records have warning labels affixed to them—or that albums like this one had alternative covers—so any time that any outrageous band made a significant mark on the mainstream was still slightly celebratory.[4])

Backmasking notwithstanding, "Pepper" is far from an outrageous song. The lyrics seem inspired by Jim Carroll's song "People Who Died" (1980), in that it too runs through a list of people who have suffered various cruel fates. One character has lost his leg due to dancing with a train, for instance. Another dies in knife fight, a third dies of AIDS, and so on. The reason, the singer tells us, is that they are all in love with dying—much like the *denouement* of the song "Loser," by Beck, which was a hit two years previously and with which it shares many commonalities. "Loser" also uses backmasking (and for much the same purpose); both songs exhibit a dark, sardonic sense of humor; and both use a spoken word-cadence rather than singing and lyrics that, while not exactly poetic, are allusive, alluring, and imagistic, the furthest thing from pop. Like Jim Carroll (and Bruce Springsteen for that matter), "Pepper" names names—Marky, Sharon, Cherese, Mikey, Bobby, Tommy, "Another Mikey," Flipper, Paulie, and the "ever present football player rapist," whose existence in every corner of America is (rightly) taken for granted here. According to lore, these characters are all former friends of Gibby's from Texas who came to bad ends, but Gibby had a lot of other friends as well. In 1994 he shared space with Kurt Cobain at the Exodus Rehab Center the same week that Cobain escaped and shot himself, and he was playing in the house band at the Viper Room on the night that River Phoenix died. Clearly, at some point, the Butthole Surfers had slipped off their carefree perch atop what someone once described as a life of "fortuity and chaos," and into an evil place that just happened to be adjacent to some of the most tragic deaths of my generation. So whenever I hear "Pepper" I add an extra line or two under my breath and it spoils all my pleasure in it.

Otherwise, it would have been easy to celebrate their sudden appearance at the popular kid's table. But it wasn't like the success of "Pepper" was a happy ending for the Butthole Surfers; quite the contrary, and the band's story got darker, rather than lighter, after they hit the charts. I remember seeing them perform at the Greek Theater in

---

[4] Unlike almost every other act labeled fearsome by the PMRC (Sheena Easton, Madonna, Stryper, etc.), the Butthole Surfers were, in their heyday, genuinely frightening. And there's certainly an argument to be made that the *Electric Larryland* cover image was overly disturbing.

Berkeley around that time, opening for the Stone Temple Pilots, and they were a shell of their former selves—boring, even. What a comedown, given that for a great many people I know, seeing the Buttholes perform live provided them with one of the most unforgettable nights of their youth.

Although the band has appeared sporadically across the last quarter century, "Pepper" clearly put a period on the Butthole Surfers' career. In truth, they had fallen apart as a real touring entity even before the release of *Electric Larryland*: their follow-up record for Capitol, *After the Astronaut* (1998), was rejected by the label, and although it was released as *Weird Revolution* on an independent label in 2001, it is largely forgotten. The band attempted live comebacks in 2016 and 2018, but I for one don't relish the idea of seeing their particular brand of onstage debauchery performed by people who are, like myself, in our early old age.

On the flip side, maybe it's on brand. "The Butthole Surfers don't descend to the depths of squalor to make a point about the human condition," the *Trouser Press Record Guide* once wrote about them. "They just like it down there."[5] If that's so, then perhaps they are enjoying the indignities of old age better than the rest of us.

[5] https://trouserpress.com/reviews/butthole-surfers/.

24

Chumbawamba, "Tubthumping" (1997)

Matt Grimes

Who Invited the Anarchists to the Party?

It's May 1997 and Tony Blair's Labour government has secured a landslide victory in the UK general election. The youngest prime minister since 1812, Blair has already shown his hip credentials by soundtracking his election campaign with D:Ream's anthemic song "Things Can Only Get Better."[1] This is the era of Britpop. Oasis and Blur are locked in a battle over who is the greatest and coolest band in the world, no doubt helped along by some great public relations strategizing, and Oasis's Noel Gallagher has symbolized the Cool Britannia brand by sporting a Union Jack guitar. Even the Spice Girls have got on board with Geri Halliwell (aka Ginger Spice), wearing a Union Jack-style sequined dress at the 1997 Brit Awards,[2] and on any and every photo opportunity thereafter. It seems that "Brand Britain" is on the upturn and, reminiscent of the Swinging Sixties, is starting to find its global appeal again.

Blair, no doubt egged on by his overzealous spin doctors, decides to have a house party. Dubbed the "Cool Britannia" party, it reads like a who's who of the British media, cultural and sporting establishment, including global music superstars Sting, Elton John, Bono, David Bowie, Bob Geldof, and Mick Hucknall. However, Blair's real coup de grace that night is being filmed drinking champagne with Oasis' Noel Gallagher, a moment not lost on Chumbawamba,[3] and further cementing his "cool" credentials in the eyes of the British youth, already high on seeing the back of a repressive Conservative government.

---

[1] D:Ream, "Things Can Only Get Better" (Magnet Records, 1993).
[2] The Brit Awards are the British Phonographic Industry's (BPI) annual popular music awards.
[3] Chumbawamba's Dunstan Bruce told an audience at the Lucerne Bar, Prague, in the summer of 1997, "This song is dedicated to Noel Gallagher and Prime Minister Tony Blair. . . . They're great friends. They drink champagne together. . . . This song is called 'I Can't Hear You 'Cause Your Mouth's Full of Shit.'" Chris Mundy "Chumbawamba: Interview," *Rolling Stone*, February 5, 1998. Available online: https://www.rollingstone.com/music/music-features/interview-chumbawamba-184680/ (accessed May 25, 2021).

The idea of leading politicians and musicians forging mutually beneficial relationships is not new.[4] One year later and with New Labour still desperately trying to capitalize on the now worn-out Cool Britannia brand, it is the turn of Deputy Prime Minister John Prescott to turn up at the 1998 Brit Awards to try to maintain that link between New Labour and British youth culture. However, the night doesn't quite turn out how he expected. Someone has invited some anarchists to the party, and they have a serious point to make known.

Up to that point the Brit Awards already had a reputation for unruly behavior, with the likes of the KLF's Bill Drummond firing blanks from an automatic weapon over the heads of the crowd at the end of their 1992 performance. Later that evening KLF also dumped a dead sheep at the door of one of the ceremony's after-parties, with a message tied round the sheep's waist that read "I died for ewe, bon appétit." In 1996 Pulp's Jarvis Cocker emerged on stage during Michael Jackson's performance of his hit "Earth Song"[5] and "mooned" at both the audience and Jackson. However, whereas these instances of unruly behavior were generally aimed at musicians or the corporate music industries, being the clever political agitators that they were, Chumbawamba saw a great opportunity to make a far more poignant political point.

To a backdrop of video footage of British protest movements, and clad in jumpsuits emblazoned with phrases like "Sold Out" and "Label Whore," they open the ceremony with "Tubthumping," their Number 2 single and Brit-nominated best single of the year, the band changing a section of the lyrics to "New Labour sold out the dockers just like they sold out the rest of us," in reference to the Liverpool dockers who, up to that point, had been on strike for three years. Singer Dunstan Bruce recalls:

> We'd just done a huge benefit gig for them (the striking dockers) down in London. And then because we had this awards ceremony, we invited a couple of them along to the ceremony with us. So, if we did win the award . . . they were going to go up, collect the award and say something about their situation with the strike. . . . Somebody spotted John Prescott had turned up at this award . . . the dockers we were with said that Prescott had deliberately shunned them. He'd been a member of the union that they were involved in . . . and he refused to help them resolve this dispute.[6]

What follows their live performance gains the band some notoriety and lots of publicity:

> It was one of those occasions where . . . you know we'd all had a bit to drink, and we'd all cajoled Danbert and Alice [two members of Chumbawamba] into doing something about the fact that Prescott had turned up. And so they went and threw

---

[4] See for example J. Street, *Music and Politics* (Cambridge: Polity Press, 2012) and J. Garratt, *Music and Politics: A Critical Introduction* (Cambridge: Cambridge University Press, 2019).
[5] M. Jackson, "Earthsong" EPIC EAS7605, 1995, vinyl.
[6] Amy Goodman, "The Untold Story of Chumbawamba: Dunstan Bruce on '90's Anthem Song "Tubthumping" & What Came After It," *Democracy Now*, October 19, 2017. Available online: https://www.democracynow.org/2017/10/19/the_untold_story_of_chumbawamba_dunstan (accessed May 25, 2021).

some iced water (from a champagne ice bucket) over John Prescott and said, "This is for the Liverpool Dockers." [. . .] There was a massive backlash . . . we were vilified. But at the same time, we enjoyed the fact that we could again get into a position and say something about why we had soaked Prescott . . . bringing up the issue of why we'd done it was important to us.[7]

Sell Out 1?

To fully comprehend the political importance of what Chumbawamba did that night you have to go back sixteen years to 1982, when the band first formed. Emerging from the punk squatting scene of Leeds and the remains of two bands, Chimp Eats Banana and The Passion Killers,[8] their overtly political, but satirical take on politics and culture soon had them associated with the then-embryonic British anarcho-punk scene. In some ways inspired by seminal anarcho-punk band Crass, Chumbawamba also composed songs and produced multimedia texts and performances that stitched together ideologies such as anarchism, geo-politics, veganism, pacifism, animal rights and other ideologies and politics that were considered central to the anarcho-punk subculture.[9] Very much like Crass, Chumbawamba's musical attacks on politics were often subtle, using the very systems and corporate structures they were rallying against to make their point.

Indeed, their career as agit-prop pranksters began in 1982 under the guise of an Oi/skinhead band called Skin Disease. Championed by the music journalist Gary Bushell, the Oi! musical movement was very much aimed at working-class youth and seemed to attract a lot of fascists. Skin Disease submitted a self-produced and recorded song titled 'I'm Thick' (the only words in it being "I'm Thick" repeated sixty-four times) for an Oi/skinhead compilation EP called *Back on The Streets*.[10] As well as a string of cassette tape releases, as was very much fitting with the aesthetic and culture of the DIY/anarcho-punk movement of that time, soon to follow was an appearance for Chumbawamba on Crass Records' 1982 compilation album *Bullshit Detector 2*.[11]

With the disbanding of Crass and Crass Records in 1984, the British anarcho-punk scene began to lose momentum and fragmented, with many individuals and bands

---

[7] Ibid.
[8] I. Glasper, *The Day The Country Died* (London: Cherry Red Books, 2006), 375–9.
[9] See for example M. Grimes, *Life We Make: Identity, Memory and British Anarcho-Punk* (PhD diss., Birmingham City University, 2019) and R. Cross, "The Hippies Now Wear Black: Crass and Anarcho-punk, 1977–1984," *Socialist History* 26 (2004): 25–44.
[10] Whalley and Hartley, "I'm Thick," Skin Disease. *Back on the Streets*, Secret Records SHH138. 1982, vinyl.
[11] *Bullshit Detector* was a series of three albums released on Crass's own record label. The principle behind the *Bullshit Detector* series was for regional punk bands to submit a recording to Crass who then compiled them in three albums over a four-year period (1980, 1982 and 1984). The albums embraced the DIY spirit of punk, whilst providing an opportunity for those punk bands to be heard by wider national and international audiences. The final compilation, *Bullshit Detector 3*, was released the same year that Crass disbanded and along with them Crass Records.

going off in different political and sonic directions.[12] As noted by Aaron Lake Smith,[13] Chumbawamba began within their own working-class community by building coalitions and alliances with a number of left-wing organizations, openly supporting the national miners' strike by appearing at the picket lines and producing a benefit single for the miners and their families. Continuing with their DIY principles, they also set up their own record label, Agit-Prop, to self-release their first single, "Revolution."[14] With handwritten liner notes that suggested that revolution can only come by getting your message to a wider audience rather than residing in an echo-chamber, they experienced accusations, from their fans, of "selling out,"[15] by releasing "Revolution" on vinyl rather than cassette (an accusation they would face again fourteen years later).

Having their own label gave them the space to hone their politics and music without any interference, and in 1986 they released their first album, *Pictures of Starving Children Sell Records: Starvation, Charity And Rock & Roll—Lies & Traditions*,[16] as a direct response to and a critique of the 1985 Live Aid benefit concert and single "Do They Know Its Christmas,"[17] organized by Bob Geldof and Midge Ure to raise money for the victims of the Ethiopian famine. With songs such as "How to Get Your Band on Television" (also listed in two parts as "Prelude" and "Slag Aid"), Chumbawamba's critique was aimed at many of the artists for using Live Aid as an exercise in self-promotion rather than a political commitment to end famine. More records on their Agit-Prop label followed, seeing them develop a less abrasive approach to songwriting, including a foray into folk by reviving and recording old political folk songs for their album *English Rebel Songs 1381-1914*,[18] and a move toward a more pop sound with the album *Slap!*[19]

Using music as a vehicle for their politics, Chumbawamba always seemed in tune with, and supportive of, protest movements of the times.[20] They also embraced the technology of sampling and the acid-house rave/dance party culture, demonstrated in their infectious 1992 techno-inspired album *Shhh*,[21] their last release on their own Agit-Prop label. Their more contemporary and less punk-fueled approach to music-making brought them to wider audiences, and by placing more attention on their

---

[12] Grimes, *Life We Make*.
[13] Aaron Lake Smith, "Chumbawamba's Long Voyage," *Jacobin*, July 13, 2012. Available online: https://jacobinmag.com/2012/07/chumbawambas-long-voyage/ (accessed May 26, 2021).
[14] Chumbawamba, "Revolution," Agit Prop agit-one.1985 vinyl.
[15] Within popular music the term "selling out" refers to those bands or artists who sign to a major label thus compromising their independence from corporate structures, those bands or artists who licence their music for advertising, or those bands or artists who change or adapt their sound to make their music more appealing and profitable whilst compromising their musical integrity.
[16] Chumbawamba, *Pictures of Starving Children Sell Records: Starvation, Charity And Rock & Roll-Lies & Traditions*, Agit Prop Prop1, 1986, vinyl.
[17] M. Ure and R. Geldof, Band Aid "Do They Know Its Christmas," Mercury FEED1, 1984, vinyl.
[18] Chumbawamba, *English Rebel Songs 1381-1914*, Agit Prop Prop 3, 1988, vinyl.
[19] Chumbawamba, *Slap!* Agit Prop Prop 7, 1990, vinyl.
[20] Chumbawamba publicly aligned themselves with protest movements against the Poll Tax, Clause 28, The Criminal Justice and Public Order Act 1994, and road building.
[21] Chumbawamba, *Shhh*, Agit Prop Prop11, 1992, vinyl.

music and less on their label, they came full circle and signed a deal with independent record label One Little Indian.[22]

Anarcho-Punk Goes Pop

So how did a bunch of anarchists from the north of England come to write such an infectious and anthemic pop song, with a rowdy football chant of a chorus that, twenty-five years later, is instantly recognizable? For many, "Tubthumping" is a working-class anthem that rallies round the notion of the oppressed underdog, encouraging them to keep fighting on despite the setbacks life throws at them. It is a drinking song, unique and so simple in structure, with one verse and one chorus repeated over and over again, and so easy to remember, so easy to sing along to, that by its nature it was destined for chart success,[23] albeit as a single hit for a band already fourteen years and over thirty releases into their music career.

"Tubthumping" is an old English term dating back to the seventeenth century, when clergy would thump the Bible or pulpit to emphasize certain words. This practice was picked up by public speakers, often political, and it is now more commonly understood as meaning one who expresses their opinions in a loud or aggressive manner. Chumbawamba singer Danbert Nobacon recounted how the lyrics, mostly written by singer and guitarist Boff Whalley, came about:

> The actual origin of the story was that Boff was in bed at night with his wife and they heard the next-door neighbour coming home. He was super drunk, making a lot of noise. He's singing "Danny Boy," which became a lyric in the song. He goes up to the door, he puts his key in, he falls over, and he gets back up. It happened two or three times—he was just so drunk he kept falling over. Eventually he went in and went to bed, presumably, and fell asleep. It just clicked in Boff's brain when he woke up the next morning.[24]

The verse conjures up images of late-night drinking and nostalgia. Sometimes sandwiched between the melodic, female vocals of "pissing the night away" and a rendition of the ballad, "Danny Boy," Bruce delivers a recitative-style list of alcoholic drinks—"he drinks a whiskey drink, he drinks a vodka drink"—followed by images

---

[22] One Little Indian was an independent record label set up in 1985 by a number of 1980s anarcho-punk bands and managed by Derek Birkett, the former bass player of anarcho-punk band Flux of Pink Indians. In 2020 the label changed its name to One Little Independent after Birkett accepted that the label's brand was "perpetuating a harmful stereotyping and exploitation of indigenous peoples' culture." https://www.musicweek.com/labels/read/one-little-indian-changes-name-to-one-little-independent/080042.

[23] No.1 in *Billboard* magazine's Mainstream Top 40, Adult Top 40 and Alternative songs chart, No. 2 in the UK Charts, No. 6 in *Billboard's* Hot 100 and Top 10 in thirteen countries.

[24] Maria Sherman, "Chumbawamba on the Unlikely, Anarchic Legacy of "Tubthumping," 20 Years Later," August 2017. Available online: https://music.avclub.com/chumbawamba-on-the-unlikely-anarchic-legacy-of-tubthu-1798265072 (accessed May 30, 2021).

of alcohol-induced nostalgia: "He sings the songs that remind him of the good times," he notes, "He sings the songs that remind him of the best times." There is a familiarity of either being that drinker or at least witnessing that type of performance from a drinker, in a way that one could likely empathize with the cathartic spirit of singing away your troubles. But it's the repeated chorus – "I get knocked down, but I get up again, you're never gonna keep me down" – that is really infectious and underpins the track. Here, the Victorian-style music hall refrain—a memorable "hook"—is ambiguous in its ability to relate to anybody who has ever felt downtrodden, wronged or aggrieved, which points to the collective and communal spirit of the song and the sense of strength and determination of continuing against all odds. As Dunstan Bruce recounted in a 1998 interview:

> When we were recording this current album, we really didn't latch on to "Tubthumping" when we did it in the studio. The chorus we selected was one of 67 other choruses that we had for the song. Originally we didn't think much of the song, we weren't even going to play it live.[25]

As with all the songs Chumbawamba had written, they wrote "Tubthumping" as a collective, echoing their political ideologies that everyone has a place at the table. But it hadn't always been a particularly easy career, as noted by singer Alice Nutter:

> We made "Tubthumping" at a point when people had written us off. We made a really terrible record before it. We felt like our backs were against a wall, and if we were going to continue to exist as a band, we were going to have to pull together and be really tight. We wanted to prove ourselves to ourselves. It has a whole feel of "if you like it, fine. If you don't, fuck you." We all wanted to be there.[26]

After first penning the song in 1996, the band played a demo to One Little Indian manager Derek Burkitt. He wasn't interested in releasing the record and accompanying album *Tubthumper*,[27] unless they went back and re-recorded it to sound more punk than pop. With the possibility that the song may not get released, the band sent the album to record companies to see if anyone would release it. And, although EMI were not interested, EMI-Germany were, and offered a contract to the band, which they signed.

---

[25] "The Anarchists Are Taking over the Charts (and the World)," *Irish Times*, January 1998. Available online: https://www.irishtimes.com/news/the-anarchists-are-taking-over-the-charts-and-the-world-1.130759 (accessed May 30, 2021).
[26] Ibid.
[27] Chumbawamba, *Tubthumper*, EMI Electrola CDEMC 377, 1997, CD.

Sell Out 2?

Unsurprisingly to Chumbawamba, their decision to sign to EMI-Germany was immediately met with another round of accusations of "selling out" to the capitalist machine and thus betraying their anarchist, DIY punk ideologies. Indeed, these accusations were not unfounded or without some substance. For many years Chumbawamba had rallied and campaigned against multinational corporations, the arms trade, and apartheid in South Africa, of which EMI, previously Thorn EMI, were complicit through their electronics and defense arm. They had written and self-released a song in 1984 called "EMI/HMV" that critiqued the relationship between the two parent companies,[28] and they also recorded a version of Elvis' "Heartbreak Hotel" in 1989 for a compilation EP, *Fuck EMI*.[29] The backlash was the most virulent within the DIY/anarcho-punk scene, with long-time supporters and touring partners Oi Polloi and various other punk bands releasing a compilation EP entitled *Bare Faced Hypocrisy Sells Records: The Anti Chumbawamba EP* (1998),[30] an ironic play on Chumbawamba's 1986 album *Pictures of Starving Children Sell Records*.

Chumbawamba's response to the criticisms and accusations was bold and, in some ways, predictable. The band came out to defend their position by claiming that EMI, as a record label, had now severed its ties with the arms trade. Nutter said, "Being signed to EMI is a massive contradiction for a band like us and there's no avoiding that. I can understand people's disillusionment, but back in the 1980s, it did look like the indies could challenge the majors. Now there are no real independents because the majors have bought them all."[31] She claimed that by signing to EMI their music, and thus their politics and ideologies, would reach a wider, larger audience and have a greater impact, a reason often cited by many independent bands and artists who have signed deals with major record labels.[32] "We want to subvert popular culture, and to do that you need to be popular. We're very polite to EMI but that disguises a ruthlessness we have."[33]

The reasons for Chumbawamba signing to EMI were many. Guitarist and singer Boff Whalley recounts how they were stuck in a musical and political echo-chamber and that signing to EMI seemed the right thing to do:

> It was the culmination of several things. . . . But the biggest argument for signing was that we were in a rut, and we had this audience that expected us to do a certain thing; we played to the same people all the time and we weren't really going

---

[28] This appeared on the cassette album, *Another Year of the Same Old Shit* (1984), released on Chumbawamba's own independent label, Sky and Trees. The HMV trademark was acquired by the EMI record label in 1931.
[29] Various, *Fuck EMI* Rugger Bugger Discs SEEP2 Abbey Raid 1, 1989.
[30] Various, *Bare Faced Hypocrisy Sells Records-The Anti Chumbawamba EP*, Ruptured Ambitions Propa Git 5, 1998, vinyl.
[31] "The Anarchists Are Taking over the Charts (and the World)."
[32] Both The Clash and New Model Army signed to major record labels, claiming that they could spread their message of dissent and revolution among wider audiences. Even independent punk record labels, such One Little Indian, Crass Records, and Mortarhate, were approached by major record labels looking to "invest" in independent and DiY punk culture.
[33] "The Anarchists Are Taking over the Charts (and the World)."

anywhere fast.... I've got no regrets whatsoever; we got what we wanted out of the deal, ... we released some great records, we travelled all over the world, appeared on all these TV programmes and we made loads of money, a lot of which we gave away or ploughed into worthwhile causes.[34]

So, were Chumbawamba still able to remain true to their ideals after entering the belly of the corporate beast? Was their rationale just a distraction from the fiscal benefits of signing a £100,000 record deal with a major record label? Could Chumbawamba convincingly face down their critics? Closer inspection of the album *Tubthumper* begins to unravel the type of deal they perhaps managed to negotiate with EMI. Beyond the infectious music and lyrical working-class ideologies, the aesthetic of the inner booklet from the *Tubthumper* CD points towards revolution and subversion. It is littered with references to injustice, oppression, popular culture, politics, Situationism, McLibel, with quotes attributed to Malcolm McLaren, anti-road protestors, French graffiti, Plato, suffragettes, and many more.

Additionally, the sales of the single and subsequent album generated a lot of money and brought the band international media attention. When Alice Nutter appeared on US TV show *Politically Incorrect*,[35] she suggested that if fans couldn't afford to buy the record they should go and steal it, not from small independent record stores, but only from large chain stores. This led to Virgin Records removing *Tubthumper* from their shelves among claims that the band were being irresponsible and encouraging crime. Nutter responded, "We don't have a problem with Virgin's actions. They can feel singled out and outraged if they want. But if we are going to talk about shoplifting, let's widen the debate and talk about why people steal, as opposed to just talking about Chumbawamba."[36]

Similarly, they were invited to perform "Tubthumping" on *The Late Show with David Letterman*,[37] whereupon they chanted "Free Mumia Abu-Jamal" in the middle eight of the song.[38] They were never invited to go back on the show. Countless advertising agencies wanted to use the song, including Martini, who offered them £40,000 for thirty seconds of the song, to accompany an advert featuring Sharon Stone. The band's initial reaction was to decline but then they accepted and gave the money to a socialist community center in Madrid.[39] They did draw the line at some offers, however, including $1 million from Nike to use the song in a World Cup advert, and £500,000 from General Electric, who make engines for military aircraft, to advertise an x-ray machine. However, on the back of their success with "Tubthumping" they were later approached by General Motors and offered $70,000 to use one of their other

---

[34] Glasper, *The Day The Country Died*, 383.
[35] *Politically Incorrect*, 1998, Season 6, episode 21. Director unknown. Aired Jan 20, 1998, ABC Network.
[36] Smith, "Chumbawamba's Long Voyage."
[37] *The Late Show with David Letterman*, 1997, Season 5, episode 58, Director Jerry Foley. Aired Dec 9, 1997 CBS Network.
[38] Mumia Abu-Jamal is an American political activist and journalist who was convicted of murder and sentenced to death in 1982 for the murder of Philadelphia police officer Daniel Faulkner in 1981. Jamal's death sentence was overturned in 2001 after numerous campaigns and appeals.
[39] "The Anarchists Are Taking over the Charts (and the World)."

songs, "Pass It Along,"⁴⁰ in an advertisement. The band accepted and donated all the money to activist groups IndyMedia and CorpWatch.⁴¹

And the legacy of "Tubthumping" continued. When British right-wing political party Ukip used it at their 2011 annual conference, the band threatened legal action against them. Nutter stated, "we do not support either Nigel Farage or Ukip. In fact, we would go further and say that Nigel Farage is an arse, his party is made up of mainly bigots and its policies are racist."⁴² Similarly, in 2018 they forced controversial Australian mining magnate Clive Palmer to take down a YouTube video of him and a group of men singing along to the song. The band said they refused to let the political hopeful and "Donald Trump-lite egomaniac" Palmer from ever using the song, due to his "redundant views on climate change, immigration and abortion."⁴³

So perhaps Chumbawamba's strategy of courting the corporate music industries and corporate media really did pay off after all, despite their being labeled by many as sell-outs to independent culture and anarchist ideologies. As Boff Whalley stated on the band's website, "We pass the moral buck, let someone else justify the decision, and in turn know some people will vilify us for it. We'd discovered through all the years of having no money just how powerful it can be if it's in the right hands."⁴⁴ After thirty years of writing, recording, and performing, alongside declining commercial success and not being able to dedicate the time and enthusiasm to maintaining their relevancy, Chumbawamba had run its course and the band dissolved in 2012.

Their whole musical oeuvre is a testament to their absolute belief in bringing politics and culture to the public ear and their philosophy that music should be used to inform and educate. Despite many years of being out in the cold or being in a militant music echo-chamber, unlike many of their pop contemporaries and peers they took on the responsibility of using their unplanned fame as a platform to say something meaningful, to draw attention to the injustices of the world, and to try and effect change in it, no matter how large or small. Chumbawamba might have reached millions of people, and when those people are singing "Tubthumping" at their local pub karaoke night, or in sports stadia around the world, sadly how many of those people remember Chumbawamba as anything other than a pop one-hit wonder?

---

[40] "Pass It Along" is a single release from Chumbawamba's 2000 album *WYSIWYG*, the follow-on album from *Tubthumper*. Chumbawamba "Pass It Along," EMI Electrola 7243 8 89165 2 3, 2000, CD.

[41] IndyMedia is a network of activist journalist collectives that report on political and social issues. IndyMedia said they would use the money from Chumbawamba to publicise the flaws in work practices of companies such as General Motors. CorpWatch is a research group based in San Francisco who expose corporate illegal activities and wrongdoing. The money donated to them by Chumbawamba financed an internet campaign against General Motors by CorpWatch.

[42] Alexandra Topping, "Chumbawamba Go Tubthumping Crazy over Ukip's Use of No1 Hit," *the Guardian*, September 9, 2011. Available online: https://www.theguardian.com/politics/2011/sep/09/chumbawumba-tubthumping-crazy-ukip-song (accessed May 30, 2021).

[43] Naaman Zhou, "Chumbawamba Knock-down 'Trump-lite' Clive Palmer over Song Use," *the Guardian*, August 31, 2018. Available online: https://www.theguardian.com/australia-news/2018/aug/31/chumbawumba-knock-down-trump-lite-clive-palmer-over-song-use (accessed May 30, 2021).

[44] David Rowan, "Chumbawamba's Tune Turns the Tables on US Car Giant," *the Observer*, January 27, 2002. Available online: https://www.theguardian.com/uk/2002/jan/27/davidrowan.theobserver (accessed May 30, 2021).

References

"The Anarchists Are Taking over the Charts (and the World)" (1998), *Irish Times*, Jan 1998. Available online: https://www.irishtimes.com/news/the-anarchists-are-taking-over-the-charts-and-the-world-1.130759 (accessed May 30, 2021).

Cross, R. (2004), "The Hippies Now Wear Black: Crass and Anarcho-punk, 1977–1984," *Socialist History*, 26: 25–44.

Garratt, J. (2019), *Music and Politics: A Critical Introduction*, Cambridge: Cambridge University Press.

Glasper, I. (2006), *The Day The Country Died*, London: Cherry Red Books.

Grimes, M. (2019), *Life We Make: Identity, Memory and British Anarcho-Punk*, PhD diss., Birmingham City University.

Goodman, A. (2017), "The Untold Story of Chumbawamba: Dunstan Bruce on '90's Anthem Song 'Tubthumping' & What Came After It," *Democracy Now*, October 19, 2017. Available online: https://www.democracynow.org/2017/10/19/the_untold_story_of_chumbawamba_dunstan (accessed May 25, 2021).

Mundy, C. (1998), "Chumbawamba: Interview," *Rolling Stone*, February 5, 1998. Available online: https://www.rollingstone.com/music/music-features/interview-chumbawamba-184680/ (accessed May 25, 2021).

Politically Incorrect (Jan 1998), Director unknown, 6, ep21, United States of America.

Rowan, D. (2002), "Chumbawamba's Tune Turns the Tables on US Car Giant." *the Observer*, January 27, 2002. Available online: https://www.theguardian.com/uk/2002/jan/27/davidrowan.theobserver (accessed May 30, 2021).

Sherman, M. (2017), "Chumbawamba on the Unlikely, Anarchic Legacy of 'Tubthumping,' 20 Years Later," August 2017. Available online: https://music.avclub.com/chumbawamba-on-the-unlikely-anarchic-legacy-of-tubthu-1798265072 (accessed May 30, 2021).

Smith, A. L. (2012), "Chumbawamba's Long Voyage," *Jacobin*, July 13, 2012. Available online: https://jacobinmag.com/2012/07/chumbawambas-long-voyage/ (accessed May 26, 2021).

Street, J. (2012), *Music and Politics*, Cambridge: Polity Press.

The Late Show with David Letterman (Dec 1997), [Film] Dir. Jerry Foley, 5, ep58.

Topping, A. (2011), "Chumbawamba Go Tubthumping Crazy over Ukip's Use of No1 Hit," *the Guardian*, September 9, 2011. Available online: https://www.theguardian.com/politics/2011/sep/09/chumbawumba-tubthumping-crazy-ukip-song (accessed May 30, 2021).

Zhou, N. (2018), "Chumbawamba Knock-down 'Trump-lite' Clive Palmer over Song Use," *the Guardian*, August 31, 2018. Available online: https://www.theguardian.com/australia-news/2018/aug/31/chumbawumba-knock-down-trump-lite-clive-palmer-over-song-use (accessed May 30, 2021).

Recordings

Chumbawamba (1985), *Revolution*, Agit Prop agit-one.

Chumbawamba (1986), *Pictures Of Starving Children Sell Records: Starvation, Charity And Rock & Roll-Lies & Traditions*, Agit Prop Prop1.

Chumbawamba (1988), *English Rebel Songs 1381–1914*, Agit Prop Prop 3.

Chumbawamba (1990), *Slap!* Agit Prop Prop 7.
Chumbawamba (1992), *Shhh*, Agit Prop Prop11.
Chumbawamba (1997), *Tubthumper*, EMI Electrola CDEMC 377.
Chumbawamba (2000), *Pass It Along*, EMI Electrola 7243 8 89165 2 3.
D:Ream (1993), *Things Can Only Get Better*, Magnet Records.
Jackson, M. (1995), *Earthsong*, EPIC EAS7605.
Ure, M. and R. Geldof (1984), *Do They Know Its Christmas*, Mercury FEED1.
Various (1982), *Back on the Streets*, Secret Records SHH138.
Various (1998), *Bare Faced Hypocrisy Sells Records-The Anti Chumbawamba EP*, Ruptured Ambitions Propa Git 5.
Various (1989), *Fuck EMI*, Rugger Bugger Discs SEEP2 Abbey Raid 1.

25

Meredith Brooks, "Bitch" (1997)

Asya Draganova

One-hit wonders are a bit like the teenage years we tend to romanticize: they seem to exist outside of a "predictable" continuum, they surprise with their boldness, they never repeat, but they leave a lasting memory . . . and maybe even challenge the conception that things need to make sense. So, I suggest that we should probably think of one-hit wonders not as an artist underaccomplishment but as extraordinary moments in music and memory,[1] the result of the special alignment of a range of cultural and social circumstances. Sometimes a single song leaves a more lasting, bright personal memory than many, many others, one that isn't even determined by the longevity of the career or the prominence of a music artist, but seems to be situationally determined by a range of personal and collective factors. For me, such is the song "Bitch" by Meredith Brooks: a feast of glaring contradictions that invite us to revel in the freedom to lose coherence for at least three minutes and fifty-eight seconds. The song earned significant chart success in key markets such as the US, UK, and Australia, maintaining a high position for many weeks and was nominated for a Grammy Award in two categories: Best Female Rock Vocal Performance and Best Rock Song.

Drawing upon a range of relevant sources, biographical reflections, auto/ethnographic elements, and textual analysis, this chapter focuses on the formulation of femininity as extreme fluidity in "Bitch." It seeks to contextualize and evaluate the contemporary significance of this one-hit wonder, seeking to identify how (and if) the song has "aged." The chapter tells some stories about me and a close friend of mine—Nadia—who grew up with "Bitch" as part of our teenage soundtrack. This chapter will try to locate "Bitch" in the time of its release but also to juxtapose it in relation to wider musical output of similar thematic content and/or commercial appeal . . . and at the center of that, it will tell some personal tales.

---

[1] B. L. Cooper, "Alley Oop: 30 One-Hit Wonders—US Pop!," *Popular Music and Society* 44, no. 1 (2021): 113–16.

"So, take me as I am": A One-Hit Wonder and a Post-Communist Bulgarian Friendship that Traveled to the UK

Since my teenage years, my signature contribution to parties and gatherings is to bring along my guitar. Foolishly blind to the masculine nature of the rock genres I was a fan of since an early age, I paid little attention to the fact that my repertoire consisted mostly of songs originally performed by male artists. It was at one of those teenage gatherings that my friend Nadia suggested I play "Bitch." I'd not considered it before, but this song had so much airplay when we were little that I quickly retrieved it from somewhere in the back of my mind to realize that it only contains like three chords, the lyrics are catchy, and we could easily turn this into a fun girl singalong. "I'm a bitch, I'm a tease, I'm a goddess on my knees . . . I am a sinner, I'm a saint, I do not feel ashamed": the lyrics must have captured a lot of the tensions and struggles of self-definition, the emblematic storms of puberty. They list some of the most prominent categories inhabited by women within the wider "social imaginary" and specifically within popular music culture:[2] the woman as a passionate lover, as a caring mother figure, as an innocent child, as a mysterious muse figure . . . the notion of a "bitch," for Westmorland, rejects these stereotyped roles,[3] but, for me, it simultaneously summarizes and embraces them in their contradictory positions on the perceived moral scale.

Still best friends until this day, Nadia and I traveled from our home country Bulgaria to study in the UK and eventually build our careers here. "Bitch" is part of the soundtrack of our journeys and of our friendship. So when the opportunity to write about a one-hit wonder came up, I had no doubt that this is the song and that I must involve Nadia in the writing. At the time, we had not seen each other for months due to the global Covid-19 pandemic, so once again "Bitch" was a chance for reminiscence and reflection, a long-distance reunion of sorts. Nadia said:

> My 14-year-old self thought this was the anthem of feminism, emancipation and general self-expression! What a title! The song literally reclaimed the meaning of a century old pejorative slang word for a person, more often than not a woman, who is belligerent, unreasonable or dominant. I thought "Bitch" felt like it wasn't about someone else's label of judgment but about accepting the multiplicity of meanings—just like accepting the multifaceted nature of any individual!

Indeed, Nadia and I both found the reclaiming of demeaning language used largely to address women was simultaneously naughty, funny, smart, and rebellious. "Bitch" is, to a great extent, a poppy and more commercially viable, yet not quite spineless, continuation of the feminist punk and riot grrrl traditions. Examples include names of

---

[2] See Arjun Appadurai, *Modernity at Large: Cultural Dimensions of Globalization* (London: University of Minnesota Press, 1996) and Kristin Lieb, *Gender, Branding, and the Modern Music Industry: The Social Construction of Female Popular Music Stars* (New York: Routledge, 2013).

[3] See Kalene Westmoreland, "'Bitch' and Lilith Fair: Resisting Anger, Celebrating Contradictions," *Popular Music and Society* 25, no. 1–2 (2001): 205–20.

bands such as The Slits and Hole, and on more contemporary punk, Pussy Riot and The Menstrual Cramps. Producing a hit like "Bitch" is indeed the product of both cultural production and cultural consumption practices that describe a particular moment in time,[4] and "Bitch" appears to be the middle-ground between the rawness of riot grrrl punk and the soft, commercial "girl power" phenomenon that gained popularity towards the late 1990s. For me, however, part of the interpretation of this song as successful—and of individual and collective significance—has to do with cultural translation, the ways in which the song acquired meaning in the specific context that it was listened to, interpreted, and—in our case—performed as a symbolic text.[5]

Growing up in post-communist Bulgaria, Nadia and I both built our identities upon our own perception of—or intuition for—what it is to be a "rebel girl" (nod, nod to Bikini Kill). Our preference for rock and metal music existed largely in opposition to the vanguard of Bulgarian popular music at the time—pop-folk: a style which, despite some of its cosmopolitan qualities—the mixing of local, multi-ethnic musical influences with "Western" or global song formulae and sound—was and continues to be problematic for women.[6] A child of newly available post-communist opportunities for profit, pop-folk utilized the "sex sells" formula very actively: hypersexual femininities were positioned at the very heart of the genre characteristics. The enlarged lips and breasts emanating Barbie proportions, the dependence on masculine male attention, and love were things that both Nadia and I saw as limiting, stereotypical expectations we wished to get away from. So, to identify as a "Bitch" was an attractive alternative for us:

> For a tomboy girl like me who wasn't enjoying the stereotypes of femininity, the song felt liberating and unapologetic. It was an affirmation for emancipation—"being me is cool and it is for the others to deal with it." At that age, you often take the lyrics literally, which makes Meredith's song particularly powerful and epic for any teenager growing up in the early 2000s.
>
> When I was growing up in Bulgaria, I felt like there was a clear split between the "girly" girls and those of us who were looking for our alternative self-expressions that defy stereotypes. The song felt like a confirmation of the fact that the one-dimensional image of an individual in the mainstream was something of the past, you/me/everyone is multifaceted, and the world is awaking to this fact!

---

[4] Jacob Derechin, "Hit Or Miss: What One Hit Wonders Show About the Production and Consumption of Cultural Products," *SocArXiv* (October 30, 2019), 12.
[5] I have written about this elsewhere. See, for example, "The 'New Flowers' of Bulgarian Punk: Cultural Translation, Local Subcultural Scenes, and Heritage," in *The Oxford Handbook of Punk Rock*, ed. George McKay and Gina Arnold (New York: Oxford University Press, 2021). 10.1093/oxfordhb/9780190859565.013.29 (accessed September 07, 2021).
[6] For more see Claire Levy, "Who Is the 'Other' in the Balkans? Local Ethnic Music as a Different Source of Identities in Bulgaria," in *Music, Space and Place: Popular Music and Cultural Identity*, ed. Sheila Whiteley, Andy Bennett and Stan Hawkins (Aldershot: Ashgate, 2004), 42–57 and my "Chalga as a Factor for Deformation of Cultural Identity in Post-communist Bulgaria," in *Language, Literature and Other Cultural Phenomena Communicational and Comparative Perspectives*, ed. Parpală and Popescu (Craiova: Editura Universitaria Craiova, 2019), 98–109.

For me, it was not just the lyrics: it was also the Meredith Brooks' electric guitar with a bit of distortion effect, even if in this specific song it was only used to perform a fairly nonpretentious chord sequence and a really short solo rather than to highlight instrumental proficiency. Things may have changed (a bit) now, but really, how often did my generation see a woman with an electric guitar—and messy hair, which is a bonus—on MTV? Liking rock and metal may have been the "go-to" alternative for girls like me and Nadia, but this genre category had its own gendered conventions and limitations—for example, a minimal number of women involved, and almost exclusively as singers rather than instrumentalists: something we may not have even considered at the time, but we do now, in an era of 50:50 initiatives and prominence for gender issues and inequalities.[7]

Today, many years on, we would still sing "Bitch"—a hymn of our friendship and shared memories—at parties on the occasions when a guitar is available for us to use. Our perception of "Bitch" has changed considerably over time and our singalong has now become a self-aware nod to nostalgia. In our early thirties, we have both become aware, too, that this song sends such complex messages around femininity and feminism, and that "Bitch" may be interpreted and critiqued as inconsistent with some contemporary tropes around equality and empowerment, because of its focus on embracing contradictions rather than any straightforward message.

"I don't want to be a pop-star": Embracing Contradictions, Complexity, and Feminism(s)

In Cooper's interpretation of one-hit wonders, the opportunity for some artists to produce a significant hit and their inability to repeat such commercial success are the result of both social and political factors. Meredith Brooks's "Bitch" is a continuation of the riot grrrl trajectory; yet, it lacks the raw anger of riot grrrl's punk rock and replaces that with a celebratory message around embracing contradictions. By resisting anger, Meredith Brooks participates in a much more accessible, positive, popular form of feminism which Westmorland describes as part of a wider "feminist carnival,"[8] represented by initiatives such as the Lilith Fair festival (1997–9) around the time of the chart success of "Bitch." Audibly, this song is separate from the riot grrrls and earlier feminist punk traditions represented by bands like The Slits, The Raincoats, and Huggy Bear. The song does not include the polyphony in the vocalizations—the moments where women sing together in symbolic sisterhood, the vocal techniques that allude to screaming or screeching and which articulate the urgency of discontent, and the atonal elements disturbing the expectations for melodic songs and therefore highlighting the sense of a lack of harmony in social and cultural realities. Instead "Bitch" sticks to a much more traditional pop-rock

---

[7] For more on this see Catherine Strong and Sarah Raine, eds., *Towards Gender Equality in the Music Industry: Education, Practice and Strategies for Change* (New York: Bloomsbury, 2019).
[8] Westmoreland, "'Bitch' and Lilith Fair," 205.

sound which, however, is still far enough from the "girl power" packaged by products such as Spice Girls prominent at the same time as Meredith Brooks's hit climbed the charts. In that sense, Brooks's "Bitch" offered a relevant alternative within the mainstream.

Elements that contribute to this alternative nature of the song, despite its mellowed-down feminist sentiment in comparison to other realms of rock, are the authorship, age, and the guitarist role of Brooks. She does not fit the "innocent but sexy" young adult formula exploited in the context of the Spice Girls, Britney Spears, or Christina Aguilera: when "Bitch" became a hit, Brooks was right at the end of her thirties. In popular music, women's aging is often associated with invisibility, stigma, and the restriction of career opportunities.[9] Brooks's hit, from this angle, can be inspiring in an entirely new way: breakthrough success is possible beyond the stereotype of young talent. Brooks, a skilful guitarist, also offers an alternative to the prominence of the singing and dancing female figure in pop. In many ways, therefore, we can interpret "Bitch" as a symbolic transitional space between feminist rebellion and "pop feminism"—a phenomenon that has become visible through the prolific commercial success of figures like Beyoncé, Taylor Swift, and Billie Eilish. Even though feminist traditions in popular music have been around for a long time, texts with a claim to feminist message continue to be much needed and are progressively central in popular music, responding to gender politics and ongoing inequalities. Householder has shown that as "feminism has filtered into mainstream consciousness, Millennials have come of age in a time when feminist theories have been absorbed by pop culture in a way that makes Beyonce's lyrics almost indistinguishable from the writings of Simone de Beauvoir."[10] So how can we locate "Bitch" on the contemporary feminist popular music landscape?

If we are to follow the "wave" approach to feminism, and the approximate time frames that it provides, we would conclude that "Bitch" can be representative of "third wave" feminism, which is (crudely summarized) associated with rejecting ideological rigidity and embracing different forms of femininity, and reaffirming the credibility of a variety of women's choices regarding career, family, appearance.[11] The contemporary "fourth wave," which has been seen as dominant over the last decade or so, builds on that by focusing on direct forms of campaigning, using the affordances of social media, to address key issues such as sexual harassment and underrepresentation across a range of industry sectors. By advocating for freedom—for the legitimacy and availability of a variety of different expressions and opportunities—both these "waves" become about choice and not about totality, which then creates, of course, an openness to perceiving

---

[9] This is an issue that Abigail Gardner covers with Ros Jennings in *Rock On: Women, Ageing and Popular Music* (Aldershot: Ashgate, 2012) and in *Ageing and Contemporary Female Musicians* (London: Routledge, 2019).

[10] "Girls, grrrls, *Girls*: Lena Dunham, Girls, and the Contradictions of Fourth Wave Feminism," in *Feminist Theory and Pop Culture*, ed. Adrienne Trier-Bieniek (Rotterdam: Sense Publishers, 2015), 19–33.

[11] See R. Claire Snyder, "What Is Third-Wave Feminism? A New Directions Essay," *Signs: Journal of Women in Culture and Society* 34 (1): 175–96.

feminism(s) as a set of contradictions and omissions criticized specifically within the field referred to as post-feminism.

In this context of *feminisms*, a multiplicity of approaches, "Bitch" is not obsolete but current in its description of a woman's roles/moods as a form of instability: "Rest assured that when I start to make you nervous, and I'm going to extremes, tomorrow I will change, and today won't mean a thing." Womanhood here is described by fluidity, not rigidity. However, the cheerful "Bitch" lacks the focused approach, the campaigning-like directness of more recent super hits, for example, "Run the World" (Beyoncé 2011, on women's economic prominence, career success, and racial equality), "Born This Way" (Lady Gaga 2011, embracing LGBT+ identities), "Don't Touch My Hair" (Solange 2016, gender and race intersectionality, reclaiming of personal space and addressing stigma), "The Man" (Taylor Swift 2019, criticizing masculine domination over the music and other industries), and "WAP" (Cardi B and Megan Thee Stallion 2020, a provocative, excessive pop celebration of sexual desire). In contrast to some of these twenty-first-century "anthems," "Bitch" is structured as a dialogue with a man, presumably a lover, for whom the female protagonist's contradictions are both "hell" and "dream," yet "nothing in between," as the male "wouldn't want it any other way": a suggestion that the contrasting emotional states and identifications of the protagonist are conceptualized as a form of (exoticized) appeal. Yet, for young singer-songwriter and activist Halsey, "Bitch" can still appeal beyond the realms of heterosexual identifications:

> I know this song isn't traditionally an LGBTQ anthem, but for me it is. The song was always a reminder to me that women can be multidimensional and that women are never just one thing. For me, growing up in the confines of heteronormativity, it encouraged me to be everything that I am. And that is loud and vibrant and proudly bisexual, no matter what anyone thinks.[12]

After all, Meredith Brooks's dialogue with a man in "Bitch" is metaphorical: it addresses everyone, and not just men, to consider the significance, contradictions, and fluidity of a multidimensional, contemporary womanhood. And it seems that Brooks might have been successful in her provocation: she was famously forced off stage twice by the aggressive crowds waiting to see the Rolling Stones during their 1998 tour in Argentina, attacked with booing and objects being thrown at her. Such incidents act as a confirmation that songs like "Bitch"—or rock music hits by female artists more generally—could trigger a response from a wider rock audience that was still unprepared to overthrow the masculine domination within the genre category.[13]

Two and a half decades on, we still see that rock and metal bands with female participation marketed this "unusual" feature, or were branded as "novelty" or "female fronted." Without explicitly addressing the potential sexist reading of the Argentina attacks, Brooks commented:

---

[12] Quoted in "The 25 Most Powerful LGBTQ Anthems Ever Made," *Nylon*. Available online: https://www.nylon.com/articles/best-lgbtq-songs.

[13] See also Rosemary Hill, *Gender, Metal and the Media: Women Fans and the Gendered Experience of Music* (London: Palgrave Macmillan, 2016).

I don't want to be a pop-star, I made an album that speaks about hope, resurrection, waking up, an album that has a very deep message. What is Rock and Roll? It's just an illusion, a moment. My life is worth more than a show.[14]

Brooks's words echo a disillusionment with the rock and roll industry, a possible critique toward the hit-focused, commercially oriented discourses of artistic achievement which open the gates to artist visibility but also to vulnerability—mental and physical challenges and even exploitation. The darker side of the global hit "Bitch" lies in its function to reduce Brooks's musical career and output to a single song that transcends her work into the ephemeral state of "rock and roll": while Brooks had been a musician all her life before and after having a hit, "Bitch" remains the prominent association with her artistic achievement.

I/We . . . "wouldn't have it any other way"

Now in our early thirties, my friend Nadia and I have become very aware of the complexities that inhibit the musical and cultural worlds that we participate in. We have gained the life experience and exposure to lose some of our spontaneity in our reactions to the world (and music), to be more critical, or sometimes even cynical. So, for us "Bitch" symbolizes a different era altogether: a song we enjoyed naturally, without too many questions. Indeed, "Bitch" is a naturally catchy tune that struck a chord in a particular moment in time but which, to a great extent, remains valid in its ability to capture and summarize the contradictions of pop feminism—a significant ideological, cultural, and commercial phenomenon in contemporary popular music. Here is what Nadia had to say about the song's contemporary relevance:

> I feel excited every time I hear it. It is packed with memories and emotions but also messages and statements that I would like to believe I don't have to tell any teenager today. I would like to believe they all know it is fine to change your moods every season. But then I remember how a 43-year-old male friend of mine was recently telling me how he always thought this is just another song by "angry young women" from the late 90s. . . . At work, at home, in the society at large, we still talk about ways to encourage diversity, the need for acceptance of yourself and others. Because 20 years later and we still see too much judgement via the criteria of stereotyped expectations. For me, therefore, "Bitch" remains as relevant as ever with its call for shameless liberty and assertiveness! . . . But I no longer see the song confined to feminism in its narrow sense of being only about women. It is way more universal than that—it is about all the different roles we play, take and create for ourselves and others.

[14] Quoted in "What Happened To Them?: Your Favorite Female Rock Stars From The '90s," *HelloGiggles* (2014). Available online: https://hellogiggles.com/reviews-coverage/happened-favorite-female-rock-stars-90s/.

Indeed, a reading of "Bitch" in relation to different "waves" of feminism and scrutinizing it on the basis of its relationship to pop, punk, and rebellion might lead us away from the essence of this one hit: that it is a *wonder*! The simple chords and melody, the memorable lyrics, the natural singalong, the relatability: this song contains universality and openness which are indeed next to impossible to repeat.

Acknowledgments

Special thanks to my dear friend Nadezhda Buhova (referred to as Nadia throughout the chapter) for providing the inspiration and motivation for this short piece. Thanks also for your sophisticated reflections on the personal significance of this song!

References

Appadurai, A. (1996), *Modernity at Large: Cultural Dimensions of Globalization*, London: University of Minnesota Press.

Bell, Emma (2008), "From Bad Girl to Mad Girl: British Female Celebrity, Reality Products, and the Pathologization of Pop-feminism," *Genders*, No. 48, Gale Academic OneFile. Available online: link.gale.com/apps/doc/A194279235/AONE?u=uce&sid=googleScholarFullText&xid=b416a7b9 (accessed June 2, 2021).

Blevins, K. (2018), "bell hooks and Consciousness-Raising: Argument for a Fourth Wave of Feminism," in J. R. Ryan and T. Everbach (eds.), *Mediating Misogyny*, 91–108, London: Palgrave Macmillan.

Brooks, M. (1998), quoted in Bellz, K. (2014), "What Happened To Them?: Your Favorite Female Rock Stars From The '90s," *HelloGiggles*. Available online: https://hellogiggles.com/reviews-coverage/happened-favorite-female-rock-stars-90s/ (accessed June 2, 2021).

Cooper, B. L. (2021), "Alley Oop: 30 One-Hit Wonders—US Pop!" *Popular Music and Society*, 44 (1): 113–16.

Currie, D., D. M. Kelly and S. Pomerantz (2009), *'Girl Power': Girls Reinventing Girlhood*, Oxford: Peter Lang.

Derechin, J. (2019), "*Hit Or Miss: What One Hit Wonders Show About the Production and Consumption of Cultural Products*," doi: https://osf.io/preprints/socarxiv/97n3p/

Dimova, Z. (2019), "Chalga as a Factor for Deformation of Cultural Identity in Post-communist Bulgaria," in E. Parpală and C. Popescu (eds.), *Language, Literature and Other Cultural Phenomena Communicational and Comparative Perspectives*, 98–109, Halsey: Editura Universitaria Craiova.

Draganova, A. (2021), "The 'New Flowers' of Bulgarian Punk: Cultural Translation, Local Subcultural Scenes, and Heritage," in G. McKay and G. Arnold (eds.), *The Oxford Handbook of Punk Rock*, New York: Oxford University Press, doi: 10.1093/oxfordhb/9780190859565.001.0001

Draganova, A. (2019), *Popular Music in Contemporary Bulgaria: At the Crossroads*, Bingley: Emerald.

Gardner, A. (2019), *Ageing and Contemporary Female Musicians*, London: Routledge.

Gardner, A. and R. Jennings, eds. (2012), *Rock On: Women, Ageing and Popular Music*, Aldershot: Ashgate.

Grammy Awards (2021), "Grammy Winners 1998." Available online: https://www.grammy.com/ (accessed June 2, 2021).

Halsey (2021), quoted in "The 25 Most Powerful LGBTQ Anthems Ever Made" *Nylon*. Available online: https://www.nylon.com/articles/best-lgbtq-songs (accessed June 2, 2021).

Hill, R. L. (2016), *Gender, Metal and the Media: Women Fans and the Gendered Experience of Music*, London: Palgrave Macmillan.

Householder, A. K. (2015), "Girls, grrrls, *Girls*: Lena Dunham, Girls, and the Contradictions of Fourth Wave Feminism," in A. Trier-Bieniek (ed.), *Feminist Theory and Pop Culture*, 19–33, Rotterdam: Sense Publishers.

Levy, C. (2004), "Who Is the 'Other' in the Balkans? Local Ethnic Music as a Different Source of Identities in Bulgaria," in S. Whiteley, A. Bennett and S. Hawkins (eds.), *Music, Space and Place: Popular Music and Cultural Identity*, 42–57, Aldershot: Ashgate

Lieb, K. (2013), *Gender, Branding, and the Modern Music Industry: The Social Construction of Female Popular Music Stars*, New York: Routledge.

Maitland, S. (2017), *What Is Cultural Translation?* London: Bloomsbury.

Official Charts (2021), "Meredith Brooks." Available online: https://www.officialcharts.com/artist/3397/meredith-brooks/ (accessed June 2, 2021).

McKay, G. (2013), *Shakin' All Over: Popular Music and Disability*, Ann Arbor: University of Michigan.

Raine, S. (2019), "Keychanges at Cheltenham Jazz Festival: Issues of Gender in the UK Jazz Scene," in C. Strong and S. Raine (eds.), *Towards Gender Equality in the Music Industry: Education, Practice and Strategies for Change*, 187–200, New York: Bloomsbury.

Snyder, R. (2008), "What Is Third-Wave Feminism? A New Directions Essay," *Signs: Journal of Women in Culture and Society*, 34 (1): 175–96.

Statelova, R. (2008), "Chalga Girls and Chalga Boys: Poor Music and Lavish Physicality," in R. Statelova (ed.), *Through the Years: Rosemary Statelova at 70 (2011)*, Sofia: Institute for Art Studies Press, 124–34, Sofia: Institute for the Study of the Arts. [Стателова, Р. (2008) „Чалга момичета и чалга момчета: Слаба музика и пищна физика" в Стателова, Р. (ред.) През годините: Розмари Стателова на 70 (2011), София: Институт за изследване на изкуствата, 124—134]

Strong, C. and S. Raine, eds. (2019), *Towards Gender Equality in the Music Industry: Education, Practice and Strategies for Chang*, New York: Bloomsbury Publishing.

Westmoreland, K. (2001), "'Bitch' and Lilith Fair: Resisting Anger, Celebrating Contradictions," *Popular music and society*, 25 (1–2): 205–20.

Williams, J. (2017), *Women vs Feminism: Why We All Need Liberating from the Gender Wars*, Bingley: Emerald.

Zaslow, E., (2009), *Feminism, Inc.: Coming of Age in Girl Power Media Culture*, London: Palgrave Macmillan.

Songs

Cardi, B and Megan Thee Stallion (2020), "WAP" (single), Atlantic Records
Beyoncé (2011), "Run the World (Girls)," in 4, Columbia/Parkwood
Gaga, Lady (2011), "Born This Way," in *Born This Way*, Interscope
Brooks, Meredith (1997), "Bitch," in *Blurring the Edges*, Capitol
Solange (2016), "Don't Touch My Hair," in *A Seat at the Table*, Saint/Columbia
Swift, Taylor (2019), "The Man," in Lover, Republic

New Radicals, "You Get What You Give" (1998)

Jon Gower

It's one thing to have a one-off hit but quite another to see it resurrected for use in a US Presidential Inauguration. Yet that's precisely what happened to New Radicals' jaunty slice of power-pop. It was initially used as a sort of mini fanfare for Second Gentleman-elect Doug Emhoff's walk-ons during campaign rallies. Then came the total upgrade when the song closed the virtual "Parade Across America" for President Biden's inauguration.

The song had touched both men's lives, sufficiently so, in the case of the forty-sixth president of the United States, that he had written touchingly about it in his 2017 memoir *Promise Me Dad: A Year of Hope, Hardship and Purpose*. In it Biden recalled a morning with his son Beau, who died of brain cancer in 2015, at the age of forty-six:

> During breakfast, Beau would often make me listen to what I thought was his theme song, "You Get What You Give" by the New Radicals. Even though Beau never stopped fighting and his will to live was stronger than most—I think he knew that this day might come. The words to the song are: "This whole damn world can fall apart. You'll be ok, follow your heart."[1]

The cancer followed years of illness for a son Biden had had to raise singlehandedly after the death of his wife in a car crash. This was undoubtedly a very special father-son, son-father relationship, and indeed the president-to-be once described Beau as Biden 2.0, the very distillation of his father's spirit. Beau was a lawyer-turned-politician who became attorney general in Delaware. He also served in the US Army, where he took part in the Iraq war, for which he was awarded a Bronze Star and a posthumous Legion of Merit for his work in the Delaware National Guard.

---

[1] Quoted in relix.com/news/detail/after-22-years-new-radicals-will-reunite-to-perform-you-get-what-you-give-for-biden-inauguration/.

Gregg Alexander, frontman of the New Radicals, first heard of the Biden connection when a friend read in a Washington, DC, paper that the lyrics to "You Get What You Give" had been declaimed at Beau Biden's funeral:

> But I didn't understand why until I'd heard that Ashley Biden referred to the song during Beau's eulogy. And then later it was in Joe [Biden's] book. The song was also used in presidential and Georgia "get-out-the-vote" videos so perhaps between those two events, it catalyzed the invitation for us to perform.[2]

It was to be a one-day-only, one-off reunion performance—the band's first gig together since 1999; they broke up just months after the release of their only hit single—that would take place after the swearing-in ceremony on January 20th. It was the sort of invitation they could hardly refuse, especially as they'd already pledged their allegiance, so to speak.

In his introduction to the song on Inauguration Night Alexander underlined:

> It's such an unexpected honour, particularly after the tragic year of 2020 and the hope there's a little positivity in our song it can bring to the start of 2021 and the Biden/Harris administration. We pledged if Joe [Biden] won, we'd get together and play our little song both in memory and in honour of our new president's patriot son Beau. And also with the prayer of Joe being able to bring our country together again with compassion, honesty and justice for a change.[3]

It's one thing to perform the song, say, on a late-night chat show but quite another to celebrate a change at the helm of the most powerful country on earth. Alexander certainly felt the weight of responsibility:

> A presidential inauguration is vastly different from other potential reunions particularly when our democracy's at stake. Or when you learn that one in four Americans under 25 has thought of suicide in the last month. So you hope if someone hears you singing, "If you feel your tree is breaking . . . just bend" on TV, you might give them the tiniest reminder to hang on in the face of the negativity we unfortunately can't escape online or in the news every day.[4]

As Alexander also told *Rolling Stone*, the whole thing started as a bit of a joke:

> A friend whose team made the "get out the vote" videos asked me, "Gregg, the song has such personal meaning both to the Biden and Harris families. . . . If they asked, would you consider performing the song as New Radicals at the Inauguration?" It sounded so far-fetched I half-joked, "Only if you play guitar!" But a month later,

---

[2] www.rollingstone.com/music/music-news/new-radicals-you-get-what-you-give-inauguration-1116957/.
[3] The pre-recorded introduction is posted at Ibid.
[4] Ibid.

I received an official request, so I said, "Let's do it!" But seriously, my reaction was that I was deeply honoured, but subdued, as it's a sombre time in America.[5]

Four years of a Trump presidency had painted the landscape of America in very somber colors indeed, setting stark white against black, adding sudden sprays of teargas yellow, but with typical flourishes of Trump Inc gold as big money directed so many of the brushstrokes. And, of course, the polarized and polarizing colors of the country's political map, Democratic blue and Republican red, had been further deepened by the exaggerations and duplicities of Trumpism, which were anathema to so many bands and musicians, from elder statesmen such as Neil Young and Bruce Springsteen to Adele, who forbade Trump from using her songs at his rallies, as did Pharrell Williams and the estate of the late Leonard Cohen.

When it did happen, it all happened very quickly. Alexander and New Radicals' cofounder Danielle Brisebois received an invitation to take part in the parade less than a week before the inauguration event, instigating "a mad, fun scramble" to plan their performance from a soundstage in Philadelphia, Alexander's adopted hometown, where he recruited some session musicians, as original band members, by now living in California, were kept at home by Covid restrictions. Alexander avers that there have been "countless attempts to get the band to reform," which, of course, he finds flattering:

> Label heads have offered small fortunes for a second New Radicals album, but honestly, I'm relatively happy with my life. I do get a chuckle when I see us sometimes referred to as a "one-hit wonder" as some people may not realize that New Radicals ended by choice before our second single was released. But I view it as a cute pop term of endearment. I'm sure that if I had simply sung my song "Game of Love" with Santana when asked by the label, or my Euro hits I wrote for others, things would have been different. But, again, maybe then my life wouldn't be my own.[6]

"If there's one thing on Earth that would possibly make us get the band together, if only for a day, it is the hope that our song could be even the tiniest beacon of light in such a dark time," the front man said in a press statement, continuing that "America knows in its heart that things will get bright again with a new administration and a real plan for vaccines on the way. That's the message of the song . . . this world is gonna pull through."[7]

It was indeed a very dark time, as if someone had switched off the sun. The Inauguration on January 20 was held behind razor wire, checkpoints, and serried ranks of National Guardsmen following the insurrection at the Capitol two weeks previously on January 6: a full-on assault on American democracy which left five dead and a

---

[5] Ibid.
[6] Ibid.
[7] www.independent.co.uk/arts-entertainment/music/news/new-radicals-reunite-biden-inauguration-parade-b1788705.html.

nation stunned. A singularly dark day in US history. The Inauguration was meant to help banish the louring clouds, to let a new day in.

It had been so many years since the New Radicals had been in the public eye that Alexander felt obliged to explain who they were in his iPhone intro piece for the Inauguration performance: "I'm the guy on *Rolling Stone*'s Greatest One Album Wonder List . . . along with the Sex Pistols, Lauryn Hill and Jeff Buckley."[8] It is fitting that the New Radicals' song is musically energizing and shot through with optimism, with a title that sounds like one of those "what goes around comes around"-type aphorisms, something from a self-help manual for malcontents to help them get happy. The title of their first and only album, *Maybe You've Been Brainwashed Too*,[9] was a similar piece of bumper sticker philosophy. The stand-out single from the band's only album is politically charged, with untypically critical and censorious lyrics channeling youthful spleen, most of it saved up for the final verse, which is spoken as much as sung:

Health insurance, rip off
lying FDA, big bankers buying
Fake computer crashes dining
Cloning while they're multiplying

The New Radicals weren't alone, of course, in embedding or hiding social critique in amongst all that catchiness.[10] One need only recall Sinéad O'Connor's views on Irish unification in her songs, Rage Against the Machine literally shutting down the New York Stock exchange when they were shooting a video there, Michael Franti's commentaries on the failing world order, or even Pink Floyd railing against the education system. But none of them makes their trenchant points with quite the same pop breeziness as do the New Radicals. That final stanza, which gets so many things in its target sights all at once, goes on to reference other musical acts of the day. It invokes fashion shoots with "Beck and Hanson, Courtney Love and Marilyn Manson," suggesting they're all fakes and advocating that they should "run to their mansions." Some of that sentiment, Alexander has suggested, was born out of a need for names and words to rhyme with "mansion," although Manson doesn't really come that close. One is reminded of the Ramones' song "Teenage Lobotomy"—"Guess I'm gonna have to tell 'em/That I've got no cerebellum"—where they do manage to tease out a chime and rhyme from words in uneasy juxtaposition. So why the politics in catchy pop song format?

---

[8] www.rollingstone.com/music/music-news/new-radicals-you-get-what-you-give-inauguration-1116957/.
[9] New Radicals, *Maybe You've Been Brainwashed Too* (MCA, 1998). Although it reached No. 10 in the UK albums chart, and was certified Gold in the UK and Canada, and Platinum in the United States, it failed to trouble album charts in any other territory, and was firmly in the lower-half of the *Billboard* year-end charts.
[10] "You Get What You Give" was cowritten by Rick Nowels, the Grammy and Novello award-winning songwriter, who went on to pen ninety hit singles, including cowriting "White Flag" for Dido, three songs for Madonna's Grammy-award winning *Ray of Light* album, one of which, "The Power of Goodbye," reached No.1 right across Europe, and a string of singles for Lana Del Rey, with whom he has been a long-time collaborator.

Gregg Alexander told *Hollywood Reporter*:

> My favorite writers and artists had a human-politics aspect to their work, and that was something that drove me as well. I felt—perhaps too early on—that it was going to be a challenge to get even a portion of that sentiment across. As an experiment on the song "You Get What You Give," I had what at the time was one of the more political lyrics in a long, long, long time, to the point where some of the people I was working with were horrified. In a pop song, I was going after health insurance companies and corruption—"Health insurance rip off lying"; the FDA, the Food and Drug Administration, and the hypocrisy of the war on drugs, which was not real; "big bankers" and Wall Street. To allude to all that stuff in a pop song was, in retrospect, a naively crazy proposition.[11]

They were not the only 1990s popsters who paid attention to politics: Ben Folds of Ben Folds Five would go on to host the Arts Vote 2020 podcast, and Dan Wilson of Semisonic would write half a dozen songs on the Dixie Chicks album *Taking the Long Way* (Columbia, 2006), which criticized President George W. Bush and bemoaned the Iraq War. Fountains Of Wayne, on the other hand, created catchy power-pop which seemed to echo the positive sentiments of "You Get What You Give," similarly coupling dreams and difficult times in their song "Troubled Times":[12]

> Maybe one day soon it will all come out
> How you dream about each other sometimes
> With the memory of how you once gave up
> But you made it through the troubled times

Gregg Alexander was the pivot around which the rest of the band turned. He had already brought out two short and undistinguished albums, *Michigan Rain* (A&M, 1989) and *Intoxifornication* (Epic, 1992), to very little fanfare before forming the new outfit. *Michigan Rain* was a minor hit in Italy, while the second album reprised some of the songs on the first, but the ultimate fate of both albums was to be deleted from the catalog of A&M records and be consigned to the dollar bins in record stores. In this sense some of the New Radicals lyrics channel Alexander's discontent with the music industry and its vagaries.

The band name set out their stall without too much humility. Not only were they "radicals" who, according to the dictionary "advocate thorough or complete political or social change, or a member of a political party or section of a party pursuing such aims" but they were *new* radicals, suggesting that there was something wrong or insufficient about the old ones. By way of confirming their visionary status the song's opening declares them to be infected with the dreamers' disease—although

---

[11] See www.vice.com/en/article/xgz7a7/a-brief-history-of-new-radicals-you-get-what-you-give-why-did-they-play-at-joe-biden-inauguration.
[12] Fountains of Wayne, "Troubled Times," from the album *Utopia Parkway* (Atlantic, 1999).

in its recent iteration at Biden's inauguration the word "dreamers" could invoke another, destabilizing meaning. Biden's predecessor had made strenuous efforts to act against illegal child immigrants to the United States, known commonly as Dreamers. The Development, Relief, and Education for Alien Minors Act, known as the DREAM Act, is a US legislative proposal to grant temporary conditional residency, with the right to work, to unauthorized immigrants who entered the United States as minors—and, if they later satisfy further qualifications, they could attain permanent residency. It was to deter or deny such dreamers and their families access to the American Dream that Donald Trump tried to build his wall along the US-Mexican border.

The song itself is a solid, earworm-seeding contribution to the Great Alternative American songbook, with bright production, crashing corkscrewing guitar, and insistent, plangent piano chords. Over the top of it all, Gregg Alexander's helium balloon falsetto soars up like Prince, or perhaps Jimmy Somerville of The Communards, as he reaches for and attains higher registers. "You Get What You Give," which barely scraped into the charts at the time of release, is a veritable time capsule of 1990s optimism, which it captures in its uplift. You need only read the YouTube threads to the video to see how people feel an aching nostalgia for those times and for their own youth, a mélange of wistful missing-ness: "So miss the era"; "The world was a better place when this was released"; "Ahh, wrapping up 8th grade, chillin' at the mall, chasing girls, AOL instant messenger, late nights on the phone, sports, getting ready for high school"; "I remember waking up for elementary school turning on the tv early in the morning and getting ready to this song. . . .Man I miss those days."[13]

In the 1990s hip-hop was increasingly mixing it with pop; the spoken word section which overlays the song's bridge is a simple rap, which would be given an extra staccato beat in its very rare live rendition, while the chorus is similarly half-sung and half-spoken, as if Alexander is turning the words into slogans. The Inaugural Committee's video accidentally emphasized this aspect of the song with filmed clips of people all across the States holding up placards which proclaimed a variety of messages, a rash of sloganeering: "I'm excited that the country is united again." "Keep the faith." "Unity for all." "Let's write America's next chapter." "Black Lives Matter."

The video originally accompanying the song was filmed in Staten Island Mall and follows a goofball storyline of teenagers frightening dour-faced adults and chasing them around, on foot or the back of Lambretta scooters and shopping trolleys, in a sort of pubescent, barely choreographed, Busby Berkeley sequence. Dogs in cages are released to join the melee, only to be replaced behind the wire by some of the adults who have been caught in nets. There's a bun fight in the fast-food section while a burly mall cop is brought to ground by two teenagers. It's all heartily daft and therefore fittingly puerile in a song directly addressed to fourteen-year-olds, whom it name-checks or, rather, age-checks. Hyperactively, singer Alexander springs up all over the place like a Jack-in-the-box—on the elevator, going up in the lift wearing a trademark fisherman's hat, constantly adding to the kinetic craziness of what feels like a long video

---

[13] See the comments to the official video at https://youtu.be/DL7-CKirWZE (accessed June 26, 2021).

because the song is long—by Motown single standards at least—with a duration of close on five minutes. It's just a little short of anthemic length.

Unlike some bands who break up because of friction among its members or a label's failures to promote or otherwise support them, New Radicals came to an end all those years ago because its front man wanted to go into production and into songwriting for other artists. There was also the pressure of trying to conjure up a follow-up hit, and even a hint of early burnout. The band that re-presented the song in 2021 was different. Alexander now had jowls. Life had changed the members, quite naturally. But the communicable optimism had in no way diminished, and acted as a fitting torch song to open the Biden years, when hope needed to reach simply epidemic proportions.

27

Las Ketchup, "Asereje" (2002)

Eulàlia Febrer Coll

Some funny lyrics, memorable choreography, and an exotic appearance are three of the main components of Las Ketchup's worldwide hit that topped charts around the globe upon its release in 2002. Although it can be debated that they were not technically a one-hit wonder in Spain, since other tunes from the band's debut album made it onto radio, songs such as "Tengo un novio tántriko" (2002) never made it too far across the borders of the band's country of origin.

According to a summary provided by Guitérrez del Castillo and others,[1] "Asereje" reached the top of the charts in many countries: in Belgium, Italy, Portugal, Spain, and Switzerland, it was certified platinum, while it reached gold sales in Finland, France, Germany, and Sweden, as well as in Latin America. Other countries such as Canada, Greece, and the United Kingdom also included it in their Top 10 during the year of its release. The song's popularity impacted both the dance floors and the media in Europe and America for issues that ranged from its alleged attributions to satanic invocations, as the word *aserejé* was interpreted as "*a ser hereje*" ("to be heretic") by some,[2] to the quarrel raised by The Sugarhill Gang, who accused the Spanish trio of plagiarism. This last element may be one of the most commonly known "fun facts" regarding the history of the song and the band itself: several musicologists and music industry professionals were brought to the stand to testify in court, and to untangle what finally was punctuated as a misunderstanding by the prosecutors.[3]

Indeed, the lyrics in "Aserejé" represent a parodic mispronunciation of the first verses of the song "Rapper's Delight" (1979), by The Sugarhill Gang, which were phonetically interpreted to work as a Spanish adaptation, with no understanding of their meaning whatsoever. This effort is a significant attribute of the song's main character, Diego,

---

[1] See, for example, Jorge Pérez, "The Soundscapes of Resistance: Notes on the Postmodern Condition of Spanish Pop Music," *Journal of Spanish Cultural Studies* 7 no. 1 (2006): 75–9.
[2] See Cadena Ser, "La herejía del 'Aserejé,'" *Cadena Ser* (March 31, 2019). Available online: https://cadenaser.com/emisora/2019/03/29/radio_cartagena/1553848164_905824.html (accessed January 03, 2021).
[3] See Hector Fouce, *Rumbeando en los juzgados: dinámicas intertextuales y problemática legal en Aserejé*. In Congreso Espacios de comunicación. AE-IC., 21-24 enero 2014, Bilbao.

who is portrayed as a Spanish gypsy with a taste in foreign music, who is usually to be found enjoying night culture.

The correspondence of the original lyrics and their misshapen Spanish phonetic translation can be easily traced:

Rapper's Delight	*Aserejé*
I said a hip hop the hippie	*Aserejé ja de je*
the hippie to the hip hip hoppa ya don't stop	*de jebe tu de jébere sebiunouva*
the rockin' to the bang-bang boogie said	
up jump the boogie	—*majabi an de bugui*
to the rhythm of the boogie, the beat.	—*an de buididipí.*

The construction of these verses was, however, somewhat circumstantial, as the band's producer and songwriter Francisco Manuel Ruíz Gómez, better known as Queco, explains. In an interview taken a few years after the song's release, the producer described how his own bad English and need for a phonetic transcription of English words evolved toward a gibberish with no meaning at all:

> That was distorted towards not even using words, but the weirdest things that we could think of, such as the *sebiunouba*. . . . Then we picked up the page and when we had a sentence that could be well read, we left it there: "*Aserejé ja dejé tejebe tude jebere sibiunouba majabi an de bugui an de guididepi.*" I said "damn, this sounds fucking great" and got it a very simple melody just to remember it.[4]

The role of Queco in this scenario reflects the poor understanding of English by many Spaniards—of course, not all of them—despite their enjoyment of songs in this very language. In Spain, English is still to a great extent a point of reference for the composition of popular music: from the 1950s to today's hits, English continues to hold a high status as the original language for popular music, and as such has been frequently used by bands in Spain, with more-or-less success and accuracy.[5] One such hit, that Las Ketchup's producer well remembered, was none other than "Rapper's Delight," which had been popular in Spain during the 1980s—and poorly sung by fans in the country ever after, in a manner not different from "Rap God" (2013) by Eminem.

However, the content of the song suggested a different meaning in its American and Spanish versions, reflecting the realities of each country during the early 2000s, including different references tailored to fit each context. As Héctor Fouce points out, "it is not African Americans from New York's ghetto who are singing, but an Andalusian flamenco."[6] Even so, the main character of "Aserejé" is described as a "*rastafari afro-gitano*" (Afro-gypsy Rastafarian), which suggests the protagonist's

---

[4] Francisco Manuel Ruíz Gomez, interviewed for *El Mundo* (January 2, 2004), in *El buscavidas*. My translation. Available online: https://www.elmundo.es/laluna/2003/250/1072795130.html (accessed December 20, 2020).

[5] This is covered in detail by Eduardo Viñuela and Kiko Mora, *Rock around Spain: Historia, industria, escenas y medios de comunicación* (Edicions de la Universitat de Lleida, 2013).

[6] Fouce, *Rumbeando en los juzgados, 1221; my translation.*

taste for the hip-hop genre typified by The Sugarhill Gang, which is where Diego's most desired song ("*canción más deseada*") belongs.

For those for whom the Sugarhill Gang lawsuit and debates about the meaning of "Asereje" had passed unnoticed, there emerged an online debate—or rather theory—regarding the true plot in the song's lyrics,[7] which gained great traction in Spain: Diego was actually high ("Viene Diego rumbeando / con la luna en las pupillas y su traje aguamarina / van restos de contrabando"), and thus danced to his favourite tune. Unfortunately, the success of the song around Europe and later translation of its lyrics to English (in Spanglish, "Diego is coming rumbeando / With the moon in his pupils and his aquamarine suit / he brings remains of contraband"; in English, "Viene Diego rumbeando / With the magic in his eyes / Checking every girl in sight, grooving like he does the mambo") slightly disrupted this narrative. These first verses work as a scaffolding for the mis-sung chorus, making the intrinsic parody and intent behind the hit even more obvious. But the mistranslation of the original song's lyrics shows the need for an intertextual understanding of the process behind the transformation of "Rapper's Delight" to its later Spanish iteration.

Rubén López-Cano has shown how intertextuality can work in musical contexts, calling such rhetorical resources in popular music "true poetry which uses references to other genres or songs in a regulated and voluntary way to produce and sustain complex semiotic-expressive processes."[8] We can take this statement a step further than mere lyrical parody—which would represent only one type of intertextuality—and consider the sonic content of the track itself. There are many ways to interpret the "gypsy" protagonist of the song, as well as the singers' identity, that touch on Orientalist representations of the feminine and mysterious.[9] The descending chromatic scale that opens the *rumba*-inspired lyrics are reminiscent of the *Habanera* in Bizet's *Carmen* (1875), and allusions to the *rumba* or the expression "*ragatanga*"—a representation of the *rasgado* technique used in flamenco guitar playing—can also be linked to this very discourse. This recalls what López-Cano describes as *topics*—musical themes built in part or entirely from the characteristics of other musical and artistic practices, that "intertextually refer to other kinds of music different from the piece in which it appears and, from there, to other meanings."[10]

In this sense, the Orientalism in Las Ketchup's song finds itself at a crossroads between flamenco and pop where the language, style, and instrumentation remind the listener of what may be seen as a gypsy-flamenco *topic*. According to Ricardo Krauel, the gypsyness of Las Ketchup's sonic aesthetic has been profoundly rooted in the

---

[7] *El Mundo*, 2017.
[8] Rubén López-Cano, "Más allá de la intertextualidad. Tópicos musicales, esquemas narrativos, ironía y cinismo en la hibridación musical de la era global," *Revista Aragonesa de Musicología* 21, no. 1 (2005): 59–76 (p. 59); my translation.
[9] See Ricardo Krauel's, "Etnicidad, sexo, arte y mercado: *Asereje* y el flamenco-rock como encrucijada cultural entre la tradición y la modernidad," *Hispanic Research Journal* 7, no. 2 (2006): 99–112. See also the chapters on Aneka and the Vapours in this volume for more on Orientalist tropes in popular music.
[10] Rubén López-Cano, "Más allá de la intertextualidad. Tópicos musicales, esquemas narrativos, ironía y cinismo en la hibridación musical de la era global," *Revista Aragonesa de Musicología* 21, no. 1 (2005): 59–76 (p. 64); my translation.

subconscious of Western culture, by virtue of the fact that the gypsy representation (in many cases, of the Spanish gypsy) has been associated with an attraction practiced from the depths of an instinctive force, an irrationality and mystery charged with exoticism and sensuality.[11]

Krauel also sees the name of the band as proof of the patriarchal hierarchy with which the gypsy community has often been associated: the name of the (musical) father of Las Ketchup is that of the renowned guitar player and flamenco *cantaor* El Tomate (*The Tomato*). With such references, and further influences from Córdoba in particular and Andalucía in general, the imagery constructed around the band helped place the trio within a "Spanish stereotypical wrapping," that worked to *exoticize* them for non-Spaniards, and to offer an identity marker for their Spanish compatriots.

So here we find a gypsy figure who is singing an American rap, within the symbolic representation of a particular cultural environment, which complicates the song's parody, and "specific expectations and assumptions on race [and] cultural identification."[12] The song works to create a parodic space that shields the *flamencicity* of the singers, while also allowing a different reading for foreigners—one that does not include this paternalistic perspective, making it acceptable for the community that engendered the band.

There are problems with interpreting this strategy as a form of folklorism,[13] codified for the understanding of the Spanish audience but overlooked for the sake of the song's popularity beyond the country's borders. Flamenco is presented as a static tradition through a series of stereotypes, which are reproduced continuously even by more recent celebrities such as Rosalía. On the other hand, both Rosalía and Las Ketchup are proof of an ever-evolving tradition, which references Spanish gypsy culture while also transgressing its boundaries by intersecting it with pop, rock, and other genres.

In her work on Andalusian artists, Virginia Guarinos has noted the coexistence of two main characters in the flamenco genre: the gypsy and the poor person.[14] This latter character transforms the former in "an emblem of social marginalization, of the Andalusian 'lumpen proletariat'":[15] for "Aserejé"'s protagonist, a suboptimal understanding of English is understandable. If foreign languages are only accessible to "high" and "educated" classes, then Diego represents a familiar character in the community that surrounds Las Ketchup, and is also an icon of the values of gypsy Andalucía.[16]

Not all of the components of "Aserejé" are traceable to the graceful, anciently informed Flamenco tradition, but are rather strictly commercial, for the global

---

[11] Krauel, "Etnicidad, sexo, arte y mercado," 102; my translation.
[12] Ibid., 100; my translation.
[13] See Josep Martí, "La tradición evocada: folklore y folklorismo," *Tradición Oral* 1 (1999): 81–108.
[14] V. Guarinos, "Veite años, veinte canciones y veinte mujeres (o algunas más)," in *Las mujeres y los medios de comunicación*, coord. T. Núñez Domínguez and F. Loscertales Abril, 77–130.
[15] Rolf Bäker, "Lo decisivo fue la mezcla y esa mezcla sólo ocurrió en Andalucía. Algunas reflexiones acerca de la identidad andaluza en el discurso flamencológico," *Revista Aragonesa de Musicología* 21, no. 1 (2005): 109–20 (p. 112).
[16] For women singers this is complicated further by the objectification and sexualization of the singer's body, which make discussions of "pure flamenco" or "Andalusian sediments" secondary.

audience. This brings us back to the focus of the beginning of this chapter, and to the appeal of many other "summer hits" both in Spain and around the world: the song's choreography.

After the release of the single, Sony held a convention in Miami where they presented a videoclip of the song:

> They sang, but each one of them was doing something different with their hands. It was chaos. I convinced them so they did the same thing during the chorus, and curiously each one gave a different formula. We connected the three, and damn, it was very good. The next day they played the video four times, and all the executives were dancing to it.[17]

The success of the formula lies in the easily reproducible nature of the movements. Dance crazes or fad dances are certainly not new; from early expressions of choreographed movements, through swing, and ever since the 1960s, these novelty dances have followed, one after the other, to today.[18]

What made "Asereje" popular around the world, besides its funny lyrics and Orientalist tropes, was its participatory and easy-to-learn dance, much like the popularity of the "Macarena" (1996) some years before. "Asereje"'s choreography allowed people to "practice the dance before truly committing to it,"[19] and to get in or out of the dance thanks to its short, highly predictable cycles. This made it a starting point for many parody dances that followed, which helped increase the song's popularity in return.

Nowadays, a quick search on any music platform shows several versions and covers of the song, which have expanded and kept on resignifying it: from official club edits, such as Motown's, to punk rock alternatives, such as Audiosmog's cover, which shared the same pivotal moment on the market as the hit. The enduring popularity of "Rapper's Delight" has also made it suitable for advertisements such as Paco Rabanne's recent spot for a new cologne.[20]

Las Ketchup reappeared at a gig in Norway in 2018 after some time out of the spotlight. After their initial success in 2002, they released one other recording, *Hijas del Tomate* (2006), which did not capitalize on their memorable first hit. The trio participated in Eurovision 2013 with a song titled "Bloody Mary," once again with a reference to their *tomato-centric* life, and with flavor infused with their Andalusian gypsy roots, but its popularity ended there. Although Las Ketchup singers Pilar, Lola, and Lucía did not produce any other works after this, their original hit has stayed in the memories of those who danced to it, and, more remarkably, it has prompted more profound debates than ever could have been imagined at the song's first hearing.

---

[17] Ruíz Gomez, *El buscavidas*. My translation.
[18] And the similarities between the "Asereje" choreography and the 1950s "hand jive" are easy to spot.
[19] Melinda Russell, "Give Your Body Joy, Macarena," in *From Tejano to Tango: Latin American Popular Music*, ed. Clark (London: Routledge, 2002), 172–90 (p. 176).
[20] See *#MillionNation—1 Million & Lady Million | PACO RABANNE*: Available online: https://www.YouTube.com/watch?v=COzVP0yQss8.

"Aserejé" fused the local, in its flamenco and gypsy-like influences, to the global, from old-school hip-hop to contemporary pop. It benefited from a story and a sonority that traveled between the exotic and the authentic, making it approachable by a wide public both within and outside Spain. Although its gibberish lyrics were the center of debates and legal proceedings, the portrait of a parodic Spanish gypsy man who dances to English tunes shows the song's depth of meaning and its role in the construction of ever-evolving processes of identity, which can be traced to other artists, to whom Las Ketchup have passed the torch.

References

Bäcker, R. (2005), "Lo decisivo fue la mezcla y esa mezcla sólo ocurrió en Andalucía. Algunas reflexiones acerca de la identidad andaluza en el discurso flamencológico," *Revista Aragonesa de Musicología*, 21 (1): 109–20.

Cadena Ser (2019, March 31), "La herejía del 'Aserejé,'" *Cadena Ser*. Available online: https://cadenaser.com/emisora/2019/03/29/radio_cartagena/1553848164_905824.html (accessed December 20, 2021).

El Mundo (2017, September 27), "Revelan el misterioso significado de la canción 'Aserejé,' 15 años después," *El Mundo*. Available online: https://www.elmundo.es/f5/escucha/2017/09/27/59cb7ad8468aeb04678b45dc.html (accessed January 05, 2021).

Eurovision Song Contest (2013, April 7), *Las Ketchup—Bloody Mary (Spain) 2006 Final* [video], YouTube. Available online: https://www.YouTube.com/watch?v=N8HnyH8PHVI (accessed January 05, 2021).

Fouce, H. (2014), *Rumbeando en los juzgados: dinámicas intertextuales y problemática legal en Aserejé*. In Congreso Espacios de comunicación. AE-IC., 21–24 enero 2014, Bilbao.

Guarinos, V. (2009), "Veite años, veinte canciones y veinte mujeres (o algunas más). Evolución de la imagen de la mujer andaluza a través de las cantantes y sus canciones," in T. Núñez Domínguez and F. Loscertales Abril (coord.), *Las mujeres y los medios de comunicación: una mirada de veinte años (1989–2009)*, 77–130, Sevilla: Instituto de la mujer.

Gutiérrez del Castillo, R. (2007), "La difusión de la música española en el extranjero," in José María Martínez (ed.), *Instituto Cervantes, Música y Artes Escénicas, Enciclopedia del español en el mundo*, 585–98, Barcelona: Plaza Janés.

Krauel, R. (2006), "Etnicidad, sexo, arte y mercado: *Aserejé* y el flamenco-rock como encrucijada cultural entre la tradición y la modernidad," *Hispanic Research Journal*, 7 (2): 99–112.

López-Cano, R. (2005), "Más allá de la intertextualidad. Tópicos musicales, esquemas narrativos, ironía y cinismo en la hibridación musical de la era global," *Revista Aragonesa de Musicología*, 21 (1): 59–76.

Manero, J. K. (2009), *Bust a Move: Dance Crazes Through the Ages*, San Diego: Punk Publishing Ltd.

Martí, J. (1999), "La tradición evocada: folklore y folklorismo," *Tradición Oral*, 1: 81–108.

Rabanne, Paco (2019, September 16), #MillionNation - 1 Million & Lady Million | *PACO RABANNE* [video], YouTube, Available online: https://www.YouTube.com/watch?v=COzVP0yQss8 (accessed January 05, 2020).

Pérez, J. (2006), "The Soundscapes of Resistance: Notes on the Postmodern Condition of Spanish Pop Music," *Journal of Spanish Cultural Studies*, 7 (1): 75–9.
Ruíz Gomez, F. M. (2004, January 2), *El buscavidas* (interviewed for El Mundo). Available online: https://www.elmundo.es/laluna/2003/250/1072795130.html (accessed December 20, 2020).
Russell, M. (2002), "Give Your Body Joy, Macarena," in W. A. Clark (ed.), *From Tejano to Tango: Latin American Popular Music*, 172–90, New York and London: Routledge.
SvenFreitag (2011, December 9), *Audiosmog—Ketchup Song Aserejé Rock* [video], YouTube. Available online: https://www.YouTube.com/watch?v=3n0Vg8okpzE (accessed December 27, 2020).
Viñuela, E. and K. Mora (2013), *Rock around Spain: Historia, industria, escenas y medios de comunicación*, Lleida: Edicions de la Universitat de Lleida.

28

Gotye ft. Kimbra, "Somebody That I Used To Know" (2011)

Ellis Jones

Gotye and the Gatekeepers

I had this strong feeling that I wouldn't have any other material that would, in such an unlikely way, worm its way through the various gatekeepers of the contemporary music world and find its way onto such a massive scale as this song did.[1]

Wally de Backer, the Belgium-born Australian musician better known as Gotye, seems to be under no illusions about his status as a one-hit wonder. He offered the pragmatic reflection in the epigraph in 2013, only two years after "Somebody That I Used To Know" met with such vast commercial and industry success that he became the Australian act with the second-most all-time Grammy wins, behind The Bee Gees. But de Backer has made no substantial effort to repeat his success; indeed, he has scarcely released any music under the Gotye name since *Making Mirrors*, the 2011 album on which his hit single featured.

De Backer's reference to "various gatekeepers" is unusual for a pop musician and is highly suggestive in the context of this book: perhaps one-hit wonders always indicate some similar victory over the standard functioning of cultural intermediaries, as audiences shrug off the guiding hand of tastemakers to coalesce behind an unlikely candidate. In which case, what curious taste the public displays when given the chance. One could argue that most one-hit wonders end up indirectly making a strong argument for the intermediated status quo: if the audience's "real" preference is for these silly, vulgar, or saccharine novelties, then long live the gatekeepers. Gotye's "Somebody That I Used to Know," though, is neither silly nor vulgar. Like some other songs featured in this book, its rise to the top of singles charts around the world seemed to indicate the brief victory of a certain middlebrow tastefulness. These middlebrow one-hit wonders support a different kind of claim about pop audiences: give the public a chance, and

---

[1] De Backer, quoted in Sophia Maalsen, "Somebodies as Multibiographical Sound," in *The Social Life of Sound* (Singapore: Springer, 2019), 233–46.

they might pleasantly surprise you. Whether tasteful or tacky, one-hit wonders cannot help but articulate to issues of cultural democratization, cultural gatekeeping, and public (dis)satisfaction with the normal operation of the cultural industries.

Gotye's record carries particular resonance in this regard, since it arrived during the peak years of the "demotic turn" in media—years in which "ordinary people" were feted as the saviors of the cultural industries in numerous, contradictory ways across media formats, from reality television to citizen journalism.[2] In short, this was a period in which debates over the trustworthiness of public taste intertwined with political concerns regarding the organization of culture and the distribution of social power more broadly. One particularly powerful formulation of this demotic turn was the optimistic (and borderline utopic) rhetoric that surrounded the internet in the late 2000s and early 2010s. The participatory emphasis of "Web 2.0" led many to believe that a radical reshaping (or wholesale dismantling) of the cultural industries was underway, and music was often positioned at the vanguard of such change. "When the major labels crumble," wrote one online advocacy group, "the diversity of mainstream music will blossom. It will be a revolution in pop culture. People will decide what's popular, not marketing."[3] Placed in this context, Gotye's unusual interest in gatekeepers begins to seem like an artifact of his time and place.

Looking back to that period, even from only a decade later, it is striking quite how much music was understood as connected to digital optimism in some form, and how even the most middlebrow and conventional music could be conceived of as a triumph of the people over the marketers. This is certainly true of "Somebody That I Used to Know," and of other middlebrow one-hit wonders in this period, such as Gnarls Barkley ("Crazy," 2006) and Feist ("1234," 2007), whose unexpected successes were linked to much-hyped "new" phenomena such as user-generated content and media convergence. These artists were making a case not only for their own worthiness but also (unwittingly) for the potential of new systems of musical discovery. The rest of this chapter is an attempt to be more precise about the connections between these songs, their shared aesthetic character, and their relation to the strong digital optimism of the time.

The Digital Handicraft

"Somebody That I Used to Know" epitomizes a particular aesthetic I will call *the digital handicraft*, which posits a frictionless integration of acoustic instruments, pop-rock songcraft, and digital production tools (especially tools made and sold by Apple Inc.). This aesthetic proved appropriate for a "Web 2.0" era in which the internet moved from being a "world apart," to an accessible, all-ages space of discovery. I will focus on

---

[2] See Graeme Turner, *Ordinary People and the Media: The Demotic Turn* (London: Sage, 2009).
[3] "Downhill Battle Presents the Reasons to Get Rid of the Major Record Labels," *Downhill Battle*. Available online: http://downhillbattle.org/reasons/ (accessed March 09, 2021).

a couple of aspects of that aesthetic here: the integration of sampling and songcraft, and a playful amateurism in audiovisual presentation.

Gotye's record is built around two alternating nylon-string guitar chords, sampled from "Seville" by Luiz Bonfá (1968), and looped throughout the song's verses and instrumental sections. The loop could just as easily be a pseudo-sample, and indeed de Backer considered re-recording the part himself. Although the loop opens the song, it functions in the mix as an ordinary rhythm guitar rather than an attention-seeking hook. Precursors to this kind of "integrated" sampling include the collage-style output of acts like The Avalanches (2000) and The Go! Team (2004), and the pastoral folktronica of the early 2000s, but Gotye's construction is distinct in its strict adherence to pop-rock formalism and a clear verse-chorus structure. This provides a familiarity that is aided by de Backer's vocal—the strained, throaty quality of which frequently lent comparison to Sting and Peter Gabriel, and which sits comfortably in a mid-Atlantic "organic" pop-rock tradition. The lyric is plain-spoken but again seems indebted to a retro-formalism, calling upon a distinctly unmodern vocabulary (such as the request to "have your friends collect your records"—this at the ultimate nadir of record sales, pre-vinyl revival).

Another surprise hit of the period, Gnarls Barkley's "Crazy," shares this combination of sampling and songcraft to similar effect (but in a different genre: neo-soul). It borrows heavily from the soundtrack of the Spaghetti Western movie *Preparati la bara!* (1968), but again in such a way as to fit with a certain formalism, and also has a lyric free of any novel or "youth" vocabulary. "Crazy" had a particularly strong connection to digital optimism: producer Brian Burton, one half of the Gnarls Barkley duo, was previously best known for his *The Grey Album*, a record of "mashups" combining Jay-Z and the Beatles, which became a cause célèbre for internet activists seeking copyright reform.[4]

This combination of sampling and songcraft proved a winning combination for both songs. In the UK, "Somebody That I Used to Know" and "Crazy" were playlisted on both BBC Radio 1 and BBC Radio 2—a clear indication that they were perceived (by gatekeepers) as capable of enthusing both younger and older listeners. Without wishing to descend into simplistic homology, there is a parallel between this hybrid aesthetic and the cultural politics of Web 2.0 in general: internet culture as novel but not off-putting, exciting but accessible to all ages.

A large part of Gotye's success with "Somebody" can be attributed to the accompanying music video, in which the digital handicraft aesthetic is strongly in evidence. In the video Gotye and featured vocalist Kimbra share their screen time with a large, Paul Klee-style painting of geometric, intersecting color blocks. Gotye and Kimbra perform their vocal parts, intercut with stop-motion sequences depicting the painting process, the singers' gradual melding with their now-painted backdrop through the application of corresponding body paint, and the removal of Kimbra's bodypaint—rendering her, as the departed former lover, literally out of the picture. While the music is earnest and sensitive, the video has a strong sense of playfulness.

---

[4] See Ellis Jones, "The Role of Mashup Music in Creating Web 2.0's Democratic Promise," *Convergence* 27, issue 4 (2021).

And although the viral success of the video was dependent on digital distribution via YouTube, its production seems markedly nondigital: indeed, it celebrates a rejection of the digital in favor of the artisanal and the handmade.

This combination of indie music and craft skills was a defining YouTube sensibility of the time. The US indie-rock band OK Go became masters of this particular media convergence, achieving virality with a series of music videos uploaded to YouTube, mostly either single-shot or stop-motion, and offering a characterful blend of high concept and low budget (at least in their earlier years, pre-corporate sponsorships). The most famous of these is the video for "Here It Goes Again," in which the band dance on treadmills in a winning combination of careful choreography and infectious, amateurish enthusiasm: these are not trained dancers. Feist's "1234" is another surprise hit of the same era which combines indie-folk sensitivity with a joyfully participatory video. The dancers are more professional here but, offset by everyday clothing, loosely exuberant choreography, and a warehouse backdrop, the overall effect invokes the "flashmob"—the internet-enabled mass gathering in public space that, during these years, transmogrified from low-cost direct-action tactic to low-cost promotional strategy. Feist's digital handicraft credentials were confirmed when the song and video featured in a 2007 Apple iPod Nano commercial.

The important aspect of these videos, for my analysis, is that they accommodate (and even celebrate) their low budgets by making a performance of their labor-intensive production. The videos by Gotye, Feist, and OK Go all "show their workings," building time-consuming and artisanal projects devoid of flashy digital effects. Collectively they offer a "crafty" response (in more than one sense) to a market increasingly flooded with competition for attention. As NPR radio host Ira Glass summarised, OK Go were "the polymath band who—with only five bucks and a camcorder—did what none of the giant record labels could, inventing a new way for a band to connect with fans and changing the way people think about music and the Internet."[5] The digital handicraft is self-consciously independent and yet is oddly free of an antagonist—something that is usually central to an indie sensibility;[6] also, such music expresses no real interest in locality (another key indie trait) and thus becomes a music made both on and for the internet. It is art-pop of a kind, but not aesthetically difficult so much as kooky and "random," and imbued with a certain entrepreneurial hustle. This kind of audiovisual presentation didn't *need* gatekeepers because it was coming to you under its own steam: independent music without snobbishness, independent music which wanted to be loved.

---

[5] "OK Go—About," YouTube, uploaded by OK Go, February 26 2009. Available online: https://www.youtube.com/channel/UC194cPvPaGJjhJBEGwG6vxg/about (accessed March 12, 2021).
[6] Holly Kruse, *Site and Sound: Understanding Independent Music Scenes* (Peter Lang, 2003), 149.

Earworm Democracy

So, Gotye's music suggested connections to an internet-enabled "demotic turn," not in the DIY production sense that "anyone can do it" but in the sense that, post-disintermediation, audiences might cultivate a new taste for middlebrow independent music. This optimism begs the question of how such "deserving" music might be expected to dismantle or dislodge the public's existing cultural affiliations. How was the public supposed to recognize good music when they heard it—especially if the intention was to operate without the conventional gatekeepers that might ordinarily support such taste-calibrating efforts? And what might this process of audience cultivation look, feel, and sound like?

Fortunately, this precise process of taste cultivation is observable in fictionalized form in the online comedy sketch "That Gotye Song" (2012), viewed over 7 million times on YouTube. In this five-minute video, two young men are in the front seats of a hatchback, traveling without urgency around suburban Los Angeles. They are chatting about nothing in particular, until "Somebody That I Used to Know" comes on the radio. Eurgh, they say. This one again. And yet, despite their protestations, they conspire to generate excuses to leave the song playing: "you want me to change it?"—"yeah, please"—"I actually don't know how your phone works." Through the song's opening two verses, they complain about the ubiquity of the song ("the amount this is played, it should be our national anthem"), their unfamiliarity with the lead artist ("I mean, who is this guy?"), and the unusual timbre of the recording ("it's like, the most annoying instruments"). In short, they question the song's validity based on its divergence from cultural, social, and musical norms. But then the chorus hits, and both characters break off from their protestations to sing along at full-pelt: "somebody that I USED to kno-ow!"

The humor in this sketch draws on the longer social history of guilty pleasures—songs that go against our "better judgement" and yet remain able to provide a powerful phenomenological encounter.[7] Such songs are often understood in dualistic terms as a triumph of the corporeal over the cerebral. But Gotye's song isn't cheesy nor particularly corporeal—I have claimed that it trades in a kind of middlebrow respectability, and a digital handicraft sensibility that blends songcraft with sampling. The joke here is clearly on the men's earlier willingness to waste their breath denying the undeniable, rather than on their subsequent enthusiastic engagement with the song. It hinges on music's capacity to upturn or suspend social norms, and to thereby reveal the shallowness of our fussy performances of discriminating taste. In keeping with the song's trade in sensitivity, masculinist constructions are also skewered: defensive bro-talk gives way to emotional expression with and through this record that, just a minute ago, consisted of "the most annoying instruments."

The online sketch also helps to highlight the song's unusual opening double-verse (which bores the men), and also that it is the chorus, belatedly arriving at

---

[7] See Christopher J. Washburne and Maiken Derno, *Bad Music: The Music We Love to Hate* (London: Routledge, 2004).

1.29, that actually pushes past their defensive acculturations. At this point they are helpless to resist participating. This is, of course, the standard pop song division of labor: unimposing verse for talking over, unshakeable chorus for singing along to. However, I think it is worth placing the catchiness of "Somebody That I Used to Know" in the context of a contemporaneous scientification of this musical effect, and an accompanying change in terminology. This was the age not of the "hook" but of the "earworm"; Google searches for this latter term spiked in 2009, and it was added to the *OED* in 2011. It is unsurprising, then, that Gotye's record was often written about using the term, including in a 2012 *Spin* article which takes the song's success as "proof that [. . .] De Backer knows his way around an earworm."[8] While the term may seem to offer a biological analogy, I think the earworm, in fact, finds its closest parallel in science-fiction—namely Douglas Adams's babelfish: the small creature which, when inserted into the ear, renders all foreign languages instantly comprehensible. The earworm is effectively an analogy drawn from the world of biotech, and as such it pertains to a twenty-first-century obsession with the "hacking" of human consciousness, either by digital or analog means.

This zeitgeist was epitomized in Richard Thaler and Cass Sunstein's 2008 book *Nudge: Improving Decisions about Health, Wealth, and Happiness*. A crossover bestseller from two behavioral economists, *Nudge* suggested that the best way to change human behavior was through small environmental adjustments that could be put in place without people realizing that any "nudging" was going on: an approach they labeled "liberal paternalism." As with the nudge, the promise of the earworm is that it might alter actors' behavior without them even realizing that it had done so—as is precisely evident in the comedy sketch presented earlier. It links to a tendency to see music as uniquely capable of "circumvent[ing] rationality"—a purported capability that the advertising industry is especially intrigued by.[9] In this age of TED Talks and Oliver Sacks bestsellers, music became a supposed shortcut to understanding and unlocking cognition, capable of revealing and exploiting the secrets of how our brains were "hardwired."

How does this relate back to digital optimism, and to cultural gatekeepers? The common thread is universalism, and an ideological attachment to the notion of the pre-social "base" human. The core promise of digital optimism was that access to information and global communication would lead to the resolution of conflict—in much the same way as was promised with the telegraph, the radio, and so on.[10] In this view gatekeepers—those who keep information from flowing freely—are the obstacle to progress; without them, the "universal language" of music would easily overpower our flimsy acculturations, with beneficial results. In the view of digital optimists,

---

[8] Kenny Herzog, "Still Can't Escape Gotye's 'Somebody'? Hear HIS 6 Biggest Earworms," *Spin*, 2012. https://www.spin.com/2012/07/still-cant-escape-gotyes-somebody-hear-his-6-biggest-earworms/ (accessed March 12, 2021).

[9] Devon Powers, "Strange Powers: The Branded Sensorium and the Intrigue of Musical Sound," in *Blowing Up the Brand: Critical Perspectives on Promotional Culture*, ed. Melissa Aronczyk and Devon Powers (New York: Peter Lang, 2010), 285–306.

[10] See Vincent Mosco, *The Digital Sublime: Myth, Power, and Cyberspace* (Cambridge, MA: MIT Press, 2005).

sociocultural boundaries and borders could only ever be an obstacle—an unfortunate remnant of "meatspace" that new media connectivity would simply extinguish, given time.

So, while conventional cultural populism holds a Panglossian faith in aggregate consumer taste as we find it, the short-lived cultural formation I have outlined in this chapter—a middlebrow populism, attached to Web 2.0, and encapsulated by Gotye's "Somebody That I Used to Know"—was different because it was distinctly teleological. It posited that consumers could and would learn to be better. In that sense it is in keeping with other historical projects to cultivate and "uplift" popular taste, such as the concerted efforts of English music publishing firms in the mid-nineteenth century.[11] Such efforts are always shot through with class politics. But the technological determinism pervading the Web 2.0 era made this a particularly laissez-faire attempt. It posited a kind of education without discipline, and taste-making without tastemakers, based on the frictionless logic of the digital mantra: "information wants to be free." Take away the gatekeepers, and let the earworms do the rest. The triumph of digital handicraft songs by Gotye, Gnarls Barkley, Feist, and others was taken as evidence that such processes had been set in motion. The intervening decade has given us plenty of cause to doubt the efficacy of such a hands-off faith in technology, both in popular music culture and in the wider world.

References

"Downhill Battle Presents the Reasons to Get Rid of the Major Record Labels," *Downhill Battle*. Available online: http://downhillbattle.org/reasons/ (accessed December 1, 2020).

Frith, Simon (1991), "The Good, the Bad, and the Indifferent: Defending Popular Culture from the Populists," *Diacritics*, 21 (4): 101–15.

Herzog, Kenny (2012), "Still Can't Escape Gotye's 'Somebody'? Hear HIS 6 Biggest Earworms." *Spin*. Available online: https://www.spin.com/2012/07/still-cant-escape-gotyes-somebody-hear-his-6-biggest-earworms/ (accessed December 29, 2020).

Jones, Ellis (2021), "The Role of Mashup Music in Creating Web 2.0's Democratic Promise," *Convergence* 27, issue 4, https://doi.org/10.1177%2F1354856520983758.

Kruse, Holly (2003), *Site and Sound: Understanding Independent Music Scenes*, Peter Lang.

Maalsen, Sophia (2019), "Somebodies as Multibiographical Sound," in *The Social Life of Sound*, 233–46, Singapore: Springer.

Mosco, Vincent (2005), *The Digital Sublime: Myth, Power, and Cyberspace*, Cambridge, MA: MIT Press.

Powers, Devon (2010), "Strange Powers: The Branded Sensorium and the Intrigue of Musical Sound," in Melissa Aronczyk, Devon Powers and Peter Lang (eds.), *Blowing Up the Brand: Critical Perspectives on Promotional Culture*, 285–306, New York: Peter Lang.

Preparati la bara! (1968), [Film] Dir. Ferdinando Baldi, Italy: BRC Produzione.

---

[11] See Derek B. Scott, *The Singing Bourgeois: Songs of the Victorian Drawing Room and Parlour* (Abingdon: Routledge, 2017).

Scott, Derek B. (2017), *The Singing Bourgeois: Songs of the Victorian Drawing Room and Parlour*, Abingdon: Routledge.
Thaler, Richard H. and Cass R. Sunstein (2008), *Nudge: Improving Decisions About Health, Wealth, and Happiness*, New Haven: Yale University Press.
Turner, Graeme (2009), *Ordinary People and the Media: The Demotic Turn*, London: Sage.
Washburne, Christopher J. and Maiken Derno (2004), *Bad Music: The Music We Love to Hate*, Abingdon: Routledge.

Recordings

Feist. "1234" (2007), *The Reminder*, Polydor.
Gotye, featuring Kimbra (2011), "Somebody That I Used to Know," *Making Mirrors*, Island Records.
Barkley, Gnarls (2006), "Crazy," *St. Elsewhere*, Warner Bros Records.
Bonfá, Luiz (1968), "Seville," *Plays Great Songs*, Dot Recordings.
"OK Go—About," *YouTube*, uploaded by OK Go, date unknown. Available online: https://www.youtube.com/channel/UC194cPvPaGJjhJBEGwG6vxg/about (accessed March 12, 2021).
"OK Go—Here It Goes Again (Official Music Video)," *YouTube*, uploaded by OK Go, February 26, 2009. Available online: https://www.youtube.com/watch?v=dTAAsCNK7RA&ab_channel=OKGoVEVO (accessed March 12, 2021).
"That Gotye Song" (2012), *YouTube*, uploaded by Phantoms, 11 July 2012. Available online: https://www.youtube.com/watch?v=NY4xE9rAY8k.
The Avalanches (2001), *Since I Left You*, XL Recordings.
The Go! Team (2004), *Thunder, Lightning, Strike,* Memphis Industries.

Contributors

Tim J. Anderson is Director of the Institute for the Humanities and Professor of Communication and Theatre Arts at Old Dominion University. Anderson studies the multiple cultural and material practices that make music popular, and has published numerous book chapters, refereed journal articles, and two monographs: *Making Easy Listening: Material Culture and Postwar American Recording* (University of Minnesota Press, 2006) and *Popular Music in a Digital Music Economy: Problems and Practices for an Emerging Service Industry* (Routledge, 2014). His latest research project focuses on records and the public sphere.

Gina Arnold, PhD, is a former freelance rock critic and the author of several books chronicling the origins of punk and grunge, including *Route 666: On the Road To Nirvana* (St. Martins's/Picador 1993) and *Punk In the Present Tense* (St. Martin's/Picador 1997). She teaches at the University of San Francisco and is the coeditor, with George McKay, of *The Oxford Handbook of Punk* (2021).

Philip Auslander is Professor of Performance Studies and Popular Musicology in the School of Literature, Media, and Communication of the Georgia Institute of Technology. He is the author of numerous scholarly articles and seven books, including *Presence and Resistance: Postmodernism and Cultural Politics in Contemporary American Performance* (University of Michigan Press, 1992), *From Acting to Performance: Essays in Modernism and Postmodernism* (Routledge, 1997), *Liveness: Performance in a Mediatized Culture* (Routledge, 1999; 2nd edition 2008), *Performing Glam Rock: Gender and Theatricality in Popular Music* (University of Michigan Press, 2006), *Reactivations: Essays on Performance and Its Documentation* (University of Michigan Press, 2018), and *In Concert: Performing Musical Persona* (University of Michigan Press, 2021). He received the prestigious Callaway Prize for the Best Book in Theatre or Drama for *Liveness*. He is also a screen actor and writer: *Dr. Blues*, a short film Auslander wrote, produced, and acted in, premiered at the Peachtree Village International Film Festival in Atlanta in October 2019.

Adam Behr is Senior Lecturer in Contemporary and Popular Music at Newcastle University and a codirector of the knowledge exchange body Live Music Exchange. His interests include the intersection of music and politics, cultural policy, and the creative industries. His research has included projects investigating the cultural value of live music, copyright and musical practice, the UK Live Music Census, music tourism, and Scotland's creative economy. As well as academic publications, he has written extensively for the web, including for Live Music Exchange and The Conversation.

Paul Carr is Professor in Popular Music Analysis at the University of South Wales. His research interests focus on the areas of musicology, the music industry, and pedagogical frameworks for music-related education. His most recent publications include an edited collection on Frank Zappa (2014), two chapters in *The Oxford Handbook of Music and Virtuality* (2016), a monograph on Sting (2017), a special edition of the journal *Popular Music History* (on Curating and Documenting Local Popular Music Histories, 2020), and *The Bloomsbury Handbook of Rock Music Research* (2020). He is also an experienced performing musician, having toured and recorded with artists as diverse as The James Taylor Quartet and ex-Miles Davis saxophonist Bob Berg. His report, *The Welsh Music Industries in a Post Covid World*, was released in November 2020.

Asya Draganova is Lecturer in Media and Communications at Birmingham City University and coleads the Popular Music Research Cluster at the Birmingham Centre for Media and Cultural Research. Her research interests include contemporary Bulgarian music, the Canterbury Sound, and heavy metal music heritage. Asya is also a guitarist and singer: this continuously inspires her to explore the cultural and social significance of popular music.

Richard Elliott is Senior Lecturer in Music at Newcastle University (UK). His research explores the intersections of popular music, media, and cultural studies. He is the author of the books *Fado and the Place of Longing* (2010), *Nina Simone* (2013), *The Late Voice* (2015), and *The Sound of Nonsense* (2018), as well as articles and chapters on pop music, literature, persona, memory, nostalgia, place and space, affect, language, and technology. His current research focuses on global popular musics and the materiality of song.

Eulalia Febrer Coll holds a PhD in popular music (Cardiff University, 2019) and is a lecturer in musicology at Conservatori Superior de Música de les Illes Balears (Balearic Islands, Spain), and Music Pedagogy at Universidad Internacional de La Rioja (La Rioja, Spain). Eulalia also collaborates with Centre de la Imatge i la Tecnologia Multimètida at Universitat Politècnica de Catalunya (Terrassa, Spain) and combines her teaching activities with her role as a COO at Electronic Dojo SL. Eulalia is the coordinator at Grup de Musicologia de les Illes Balears at Institut Menoquí d'Estudis (Balearic Islands, Spain), cofounder of Laboratori de Recerca Musical (Barcelona, Spain), and collaborator of Esport Talent Canarias (Canary Islands, Spain). Eulalia's research interests include music in ritual and spiritual practices, emotion and affectivity, and video-game studies.

Robert Fink is Associate Dean, Professor of Musicology, and Chair of Music Industry programs in the UCLA Herb Alpert School of Music, USA. He works on contemporary art and popular music, with special attention to rhythm, repetition, and sound. He is, most recently, coeditor of an Oxford University Press essay collection, *The Relentless Pursuit of Tone: Timbre in Popular Music* (2018), as well as the author of *Repeating Ourselves: American Minimal Music as Cultural Practice* (2005). He is a past president of IASPM-US and serves on the board of several academic journals. At UCLA, he led the successful push for a new hybrid BA in Music History and Industry, and in 2016, he won the university's Distinguished Teaching Award.

Dr Abigail Gardner is Professor of Cultural Studies at the University of Gloucestershire. She has written on music, gender, and aging and is currently researching for *Listening, Belonging and Memory* (Bloomsbury). Key publications include *Ageing and Contemporary Female Musicians* (2019), *Ageing and Popular Music in Europe* (2019), *PJ Harvey and Music Video Performance* (2015), and *Rock On: Women, Ageing and Popular Music* (2012, with Ros Jennings). She is the PI on an Erasmus + European project called "Mapping the Music of Migration" and produces community film and lo-fi media.

Philippe Gonin is Senior Lecturer at the University of Burgundy Franche-Comté. His research focuses on the creative process, analysis, and reception of rock, jazz, and film music. He has written books and papers on Magma, Robert Wyatt, The Cure, Pink Floyd, John Williams, Antoine Duhamel, and the Cartoon, among others. He published (with Jérôme Rossi) "Le cinéma populaire et ses musiciens en France" (EUD, 2020). He is also a guitarist and composer. His latest work, *A Floyd Chamber Concerto*, is available at https://philippegonin.bandcamp.com/releases

Jon Gower is a former BBC Wales arts and media correspondent and inaugural Hay Festival International Fellow. He has over thirty books to his name, including *The Story of Wales*, which accompanied the landmark TV series; *Y Storïwr*, which won the Wales Book of the Year; and *An Island Called Smith*, winner of the John Morgan Travel Writing Award.

Dai Griffiths is an independent scholar based in Oxford, UK, and the author of books on Radiohead and Elvis Costello.

Matt Grimes is a senior lecturer in music industries and radio at Birmingham City University. His research interests are British anarcho-punk and its ideological significance in the life courses of aging punks. He has published on the subjects of anarcho-punk, anarcho-punk 'zines, punk pedagogy, popular music, and spirituality, DIY/Underground music cultures/subcultures, countercultural movements, and radio for social change. He is the general secretary of the Punk Scholars Network and on the editorial board for the journals *Punk & Post-Punk* and *RIFFS*. Matt is also a lifelong supporter of Millwall FC.

Sarah Hill is Associate Professor of Popular Music and Fellow of St Peter's College, Oxford. She is Co-ordinating Editor of the journal *Popular Music*, and has published on issues of popular music historiography, popular music and politics, and popular music and cultural identity, particularly as it relates to the Welsh language. Her most recent book was *San Francisco and the Long 60s* (Bloomsbury, 2016).

Thomas Irvine is Associate Professor in Music at the University of Southampton. His book *Listening to China: Sound and the Sino-Western Encounter, 1770-1839* was published in 2020 by University of Chicago Press. He is currently an Alan Turing Fellow of the Alan Turing Institute in London, where he directs the project "Jazz as Social Machine." [He isn't quite sure, but may have been present at the 1987 Madison Square Garden Dead shows the week "Touch of Grey" topped the charts. Definitely was at one of the ones in 1988 . . .].

Ellis Jones is Lecturer in Music and Management at the School of Music, University of Leeds. His research analyses the impact of new media technologies on popular music cultures, and has been published in academic journals including *New Media & Society, Convergence,* and *Popular Music and Society.* His monograph *DIY Music and the Politics of Social Media* was published by Bloomsbury in 2021. He is also a composer and performer of popular music; his work in the band Trust Fund has received critical acclaim from publications including *Pitchfork, NPR, Rolling Stone* and *The Guardian.*

Mike Jones is Senior Lecturer in Music at the University of Liverpool. He established the MBA in Music Industries in 1999, which was replaced by the MA in Music Industry Studies in 2004 and joined by the MA in Classical Music Industry in 2017. He will contribute to the forthcoming MA, The Beatles: Music Industry and Heritage, launched in the Autumn of 2020.

Paul Long is Professor in Creative and Cultural Industries in the School of Media, Film and Journalism at Monash University, where he leads the postgraduate program in Cultural and Creative Industries. He has written widely on popular music heritage and issues of cultural history. He is currently writing a book on the economy of popular music heritage for Rowan and Littlefield for publication in 2022.

Patrick McGuinness is Professor of French and Comparative Literature at Oxford and a Fellow of St Anne's College. His most recent books are *Poetry and Radical Politics in fin de siècle France* (2015), a novel, *Throw me to the Wolves* (2019), and *Real Oxford* (2021), an exploration of the city behind the dreaming spires.

Áine Mangaoang is a musicologist at the University of Oslo. She is the author of *Dangerous Mediations: Pop Music in a Philippine Prison Video* (Bloomsbury, 2019), winner of IASPM-US Woody Guthrie Book Prize. Recent research on music, (dis) ability, place, and prison politics appears in *Musicæ Scientiæ* (2021), *Beyoncé: At Work, On Screen and Online* (University of Indiana Press, 2020), and the *Journal of World Popular Music* (2019). Her latest coedited book, *Made in Ireland: Studies in Popular Music* (Routledge, 2020), is a comprehensive introduction to the history, sociology, and musicology of Irish popular music in both local and global contexts.

Sam Murray is Lecturer in Music Business and Arts Management at Middlesex University. His PhD explored the independent music scene in Portland, Oregon, looking at the roots of the scene and the emergence of Portland as a prominent music city. He has also researched music policy in Portland, looking at the ways the city council has supported or hindered the local scene.

Richard John Parfitt is a musician, writer, and educator living in south Wales.

Tim Quirk is the singer and lyricist for the punk-pop band Too Much Joy and one half of an electro-pop outfit called Wonderlick. He's also been a regular contributor to *Raygun* and *The San Francisco Chronicle* and has overseen the music programming teams for Rhapsody and Google Play. His critical essays have been published in anthologies by Oxford University Press, *Best Music Writing 2010*, and *Popular Music*.

Melanie Schiller is Assistant Professor of Media Studies and Popular Music at the Department for Arts, Culture and Media at the University of Groningen (The Netherlands), and the author of *Soundtracking Germany—Popular Music and National Identity* (Rowman and Littlefield, 2018 and 2020). Schiller is on the executive board of the International Association for the Study of Popular Music (IASPM) Benelux branch, and was a member of the academic advisory committee of the German Society for Popular Music Studies (GfPM). Schiller has published widely on German popular music, including Kraftwerk, Rammstein, schlager, German beat music, and Berlin cabaret. Her current research focuses on popular music and populism in Europe and Sweden in particular, in the international research project "Popular Music and the Rise of Populism in Europe," funded by the Volkswagen Foundation, 2019–2022.

Geoff Stahl is Senior Lecturer in Media and Communication at Victoria University of Wellington, Aotearoa/New Zealand. His research areas include scenes and subcultures, urban studies, and semiotics. His publications include coauthoring *Understanding Media Studies* (Oxford University Press 2009), editing *Poor, But Sexy: Reflections on Berlin Scenes* (Peter Lang 2014), and coediting (with Shelley Brunt) *Made in Australia and Aotearoa/New Zealand: Studies in Popular Music* (Routledge 2018), as well as articles on urban musical culture in Berlin, Montreal, and Wellington.

Jon Stewart is Course Leader for the MA Popular Music Practice at BIMM Institute, Brighton. He has a wide range of research interests and has published work on Robert Johnson, Devo's work with Brian Eno, YouTube cultures, and his own experience as guitarist/songwriter for Sleeper and The Wedding Present. Jon's first monograph *Dylan, Lennon, Marx & God* will be published by Cambridge University Press in 2021.

Index

? and the Mysterians
   and migrant experience   23, 27
"96 Tears"
   and conjunto sound   23, 24
   and genre   21–2
   musical style   21–2, 24
   and Vietnam War   24
"99 Luftballons"
   and Cold War tensions   160–3
   English translation of   164–6
   lyrical meaning   161–4, 166
   and nuclear war   161–2

A&M Records   73, 142, 247
ABBA   73–5, 103, 141
Adele   245
Adult Contemporary (radio)   189
Alexander, Gregg   244–9
Alternative (radio)   185, 191
Althea and Donna
   vocal delivery   97–9
   youthful promise of   93–5, 99–100
Andalucía   254
Aneka
   Gaelic recordings   131–2
   visual style   129
anti-Apartheid movement   181, 227
Aotearoa/New Zealand   205–7, 210–12
appropriation (cultural, musical)   10, 80, 89–90, 136, 147
The Archies
   The Archie Show   52–3
   as artifice   52, 55
"Aserejé"
   and flamenco   252, 253–6
   and gypsy representation   254–5, 256
   intertextuality in   253
   plagiarism case   251, 256

   and "Rapper's Delight"   251–3
Australia   29–31, 67, 120, 125, 141, 206, 233, 259
authenticity   43, 52, 83, 85, 94, 98, 115, 129

Balderrama, Bobby   23–4, 26, 27
Bananarama   195
"Barbie Girl"   188, 193
Bardot, Brigitte   61–5
Basil, Toni
   as choreographer   142–5
   in experimental film   143–4
Baudelaire, Charles   104
Bay City, Michigan   25, 27
BBC radio   30, 67, 96–100, 178, 261
Beach Boys, The   25, 106
Beatles, The   23, 26, 32, 44, 51, 58, 71, 114, 178, 218, 261
Beck   218, 246
Belgitude, *see* "Ça plane pour moi"
Berlin   131, 160–1, 165, 167, 191, 193
Berry, Chuck   7, 22, 156
Berry, Richard   15, 16, 19, 21
Beyoncé   237, 238
Billboard   1–3, 5, 7, 8, 16, 24, 37, 39, 42, 46, 51, 69, 71, 74, 75, 80, 85, 105, 111, 116, 129, 142, 145, 159, 163, 165, 169, 172, 201, 206, 207, 216
Birkin, Jane   64–8
"Bitch"
   and feminism   234, 236–9
   and gender conventions   234, 236, 238
   and stereotypes   234, 235, 237, 239
Black Atlantic   94, 97
Blackburn, Tony   99
Blondie   141, 186, 187
blues   37–41, 81–3, 90, 115, 133
Blue Swede
   in international market   73–5
   as live band   73, 77

BMG   1, 184
Boston   37–8
Bowie, David   9, 32, 122, 123, 131, 142, 165, 221
Brel, Jacques   106, 108, 109
Brill Building   52, 54, 55
Brit Awards   201, 221, 222
British invasion   24, 71, 74
Britpop   195, 221
Brooks, Meredith
   breakthrough success   237
   as guitarist   237
   vocal performance   236
Bruce, Dunstan   222, 225, 226
Brussels   103, 105, 107–9
Bubblegum Pop   51, 54, 58
Buchanan and Goodman
   "Buchanan and Goodman on Trial"   9
   as innovators   6–7, 9, 10
Butthole Surfers
   and censorship   215–16
   in concert   216–17
   Electric Larryland   216, 219
   and unhappy endings   218
Byrne, David   144, 165

capitalism   51, 115
Capitol Records   73–4, 216, 219
"Ça plane pour moi"
   and *belgitude*   103, 106, 108
   legal dispute   107–8
   lyrical meaning   104–7
Carson High School   145, 146, 149
Casablanca Records   25, 73
Cashbox   37, 85, 141
catchphrases   79, 193, 207, 211
CBS Records   16, 73–4, 160, 170
charts
   Britain   1, 64, 67, 93, 97, 106, 119, 129, 159, 201, 207
   US   22, 44, 164
cheerleading/cheering squad   139, 145–50
choreography   2, 132, 142, 145, 251, 255, 262
Christgau, Robert   144, 165
Christian rock   44–5
Chrysalis   141 n.8, 142

Chumbawamba
   and anarcho-punk scene   223–4
   and New Labour   221–3
   and political agitation   222, 224
   and selling out   227–9
Clapton, Eric   99, 154
Clark, Petula   31, 62
Clash, The   124, 227 n.32
Cobain, Kurt   216, 218
Cohen, Leonard   80, 245
Cold War   160–1, 163, 167, 191
compilation albums   34, 46, 191, 193, 195, 209, 223, 227
Conner, Bruce   143–4
copyright   6–8, 11, 75, 261
counterculture   42–4, 84, 143
cover (versions)   9, 15, 16, 18, 22, 23, 26, 30–2, 34, 37, 45, 71, 73, 81, 84, 85, 89, 97, 135, 142, 165, 167, 201, 212, 255
Covid   120, 124, 211, 234, 245
Cradle of Filth   201, 218
crossover   44, 79–81, 84, 85, 90, 113, 190, 264

"Da Da Da"
   musical structure   154–5
   music video   155–6
"Danny Boy"   225
Deadheads   169, 173, 174
de Backer, Wally, *see* Gotye
de Beauvoir, Simone   114, 237
Deprijck, Lou   105–9
Detroit, Marcella   195–203
Detroit, Michigan   25, 81, 86, 165
disco   2, 25, 81–3, 89, 106, 129, 131, 133, 139, 142, 150
Disney   9, 76, 133
Domino, Fats   6–9, 30
double-dutch   147, 149–50
Douglas, Carl   121, 133
Dr West's Medicine Show   38–41, 46, 47
Dunbar, Sly   68, 100
Dylan, Bob   38, 70, 153, 171, 172

Easybeats
   career arc   29–30
Einstürzende Neubauten   164, 217
EMF   191

Emhoff, Doug 243
EMI 1, 73, 74, 76, 226–8
Europop 136
Eurovision Song Contest 74, 163, 255
exoticism 119–21, 132–4, 254

Fahey, John 83, 90
Fahey, Siobhan 195–203
Falco 155, 165
FBI 15–18
"The Flying Saucer"
    and copyright litigation 6–8
    as pastiche 5
    sampling in 6–7
FM radio 41 n.21, 54, 186, 206
Frankie Goes to Hollywood 161, 182
"Friday On My Mind"
    labor in 30–2
    production of 35
    song structure 31–4
Fuemana, Pauly 206–10, 212
funk 54, 81, 82, 84, 85, 87, 162, 163, 208
fuzz guitar 40–2, 46

Gainsbourg, Serge
    relationship with Brigitte Bardot 61–3
    relationship with Jane Birkin 64–7
    songwriting 62, 64–5
"Gangnam Style" 192
garage rock 16, 21, 24
Garcia, Jerry 170, 171, 173, 174
Geldof, Bob 221, 224
Gibbs, Joe 95, 96, 100
girl power 235, 237
Gnarls Barkley 260, 261, 265
Goldman, Vivien 93, 94, 96, 98
Gotye
    and digital optimism 260, 263–5
    and indie sensibility 262
Grateful Dead
    and Ben & Jerry's 172–3
    and fans 169–70
    and live experience 169–71
    and the music industry 172–4
    and recording 171–2
    and Theodor Adorno 173–4
Greenbaum, Norman
    musical roots 37–8

Grigg, Simon 206, 208, 209
grunge 19, 186, 195, 216
Guardians of the Galaxy 69, 75, 76, 191

Haight Ashbury 43, 169
Haynes, Gibby 215, 217
Hebdige, Dick 95, 123
"Hooked On a Feeling"
    BJ Thomas version 72
    Blue Swede recording 73
    Jonathan King version 72, 75, 76
    "ooga chucka" 72–3, 75
    Twinkle Brothers version 72
"Hot Child in the City"
    musical structure 112
    point of view in 112, 115–16
    and teenage prostitution 111–13, 114–16
"House of the Rising Sun" 115, 116
"How Bizarre" 193, 205–12
    and Māori/Pasifika representation 206–7, 208, 211–12
    musical style 207–9
    music video 207–8
    and state subsidy 209–10
Hunter, Robert 171, 174
"The Hustle" 2, 150

"I'm Gonna Be (500 Miles)" 3
Isley Brothers, The 82, 85

Jansson, Alan 208, 209
"Japanese Boy"
    cover versions of 135–6
    musical structure 133–4
    and Orientalism 130–2
jazz 6, 19, 38, 62, 79, 86, 170
Jesus Jones 191
"Je t'aime moi non plus"
    Brigitte Bardot recording of 62–3
    censorship of 65–7
    Jane Birkin recording of 64–5
Jet magazine 84, 86, 89

karaoke 159, 167, 229
Karges, Carlo 160–1, 163, 167
Kerner, Gabriele, *see* Nena
KFRC (610 AM) 185, 186, 189

King, Jonathan   69, 72, 75, 76, 184
Kingsmen, The
   vs. Paul Revere and the Raiders   16
   performance style   16
Kingston, Jamaica   93, 95
Kinks, The   21, 35, 114
Kirschner, Don   51, 52
"Kung Fu Fighting"   121, 133

labels, independent (indies)   19, 177, 183–4, 208, 209, 217, 227, 262
labels, major   26, 47, 177–9, 206, 216, 217, 227, 228, 260
Lacomblez, Yves   105, 108
Las Ketchup   253–6
Led Zeppelin   81, 87
Lilith Fair   185, 236
Little Richard   6, 7, 9, 58
Liverpool   62, 181, 182, 222, 223
Lolita   64, 114
Los Angeles   38, 40, 89, 142, 145, 149, 164, 263
"Louie Louie"
   FBI interest in   16–18
   recording of   17, 19
Lovin' Spoonful, The   38, 40

"Macarena"   1–2, 193, 255
McNally, Dennis   171, 172
mainstream   2, 6, 8, 22, 44, 55, 85, 94, 142, 160, 166, 186, 190, 206, 209, 212, 216, 218, 235, 237, 260
Marin County   170–2
marketing (music industry)   2, 18, 42, 98, 119, 120, 125, 178, 180, 184, 185, 188, 193, 260
Marsh, Dave   15, 21, 115
Martinez, Rudy   23, 24
Merry Christmas Mr Lawrence   122, 131
"Mickey"
   cheer squads in   139, 146–7, 149–50
   music video   139–42, 145–7
Modern Rock (radio)   189, 190, 216
The Monkees (tv show)   51, 52
Moody Blues, The   23, 46
Motown   54, 84, 87, 249
MTV   144–6, 164, 169, 172, 190, 200, 202, 236
Muller, Sophie   199, 201, 202

music industry/industries   2, 5, 7–9, 52, 84, 90, 110, 116, 162, 167, 174, 177, 178, 180, 182, 184, 185, 188, 206, 208, 209, 216, 222, 229, 247, 251

Nabokov, Vladimir   112, 114
Nena (Gabriele Kerner)
   and German national identity   159–60, 162–3, 166–7
Neue Deutsche Welle (New German Wave)   155, 160, 162, 163
New Radicals
   reunion of   244, 245
   and social critique   246–8
New Wave   37, 105, 119, 126, 150, 162, 163, 165, 208
Nirvana   186–7, 216
novelty song   2, 5, 6, 8–10, 38, 75, 94, 100, 145, 153, 238, 255
nuclear war, fear of   160–2, 164
Nutter, Alice   226–8

Oakland, California   40, 171, 185
Ohio Players, The   81, 82, 85
OMC
   Otara Millionaires Club   208–10
   and the Otara Sound   209, 212
   and South Auckland   206, 208–11
one-hit wonder (classification)   1, 16, 18, 19, 22, 24, 29, 47, 93–5, 97, 100, 107, 130, 132, 133, 136, 159, 169, 177, 184, 188, 190–3, 206, 212, 229, 233, 236, 240, 251, 259, 260
one-hit wonder (pejorative)   18, 103, 104, 139, 142, 153, 189, 245
organ, electric   22–4, 54, 64, 65
Orientalism   121, 122, 124, 126, 132–4, 253
Oriental riff   121, 123, 133, 134 n.7, 136
otherness   98, 119, 121

Palmers, Bengt
   as producer   72–4
   as songwriter   70–1
Parents Music Resource Center (PMRC)   9, 216, 218
Paris   64, 65, 106, 108
patois   98–9
Peel, John   96, 99

"Pepper"
  musical style   217–18
Philips (Recordings)   63–5, 67
Pittsburgh, Pennsylvania   80–2, 87, 89
Plastic Bertrand
  and miming   107–8
  and punk style   103, 105
"Play That Funky Music"
  musical structure   82–3, 88–9
  origin myth   81–2, 88
  as reverse crossover   79, 84–7, 89–91
PolyGram   1, 206, 212
Portland, Oregon   15, 16, 18, 19
Presley, Elvis   6, 7, 9, 22, 227
psychedelia   38–40, 72, 81, 216
punk   21, 22, 96, 103–5, 107–10, 119, 122, 123, 126, 135, 146, 155, 162, 163, 166, 182, 186, 208, 216, 217, 223–7, 234–6, 239, 255

race   86, 87, 90, 147, 238, 254
Radialchoice (label)   141–2
rap   135, 195, 248, 252, 254
Rastafarian(ism)   96, 98, 252
RCA Records   177, 183
Recording Industry Association of America (RIAA)   1, 3, 218
Reed, Lou   58, 154
reggae   68, 72, 79, 84, 94, 95, 97–9, 162
rhythm & blues (r&b)   8, 15, 85, 86, 150, 195
riff   19, 24, 40–2, 54, 81, 84, 88, 89, 120, 121, 123, 126, 133, 134, 136, 155, 196
"Right Here, Right Now"   191
riot grrrl   234–6
Rolling Stones, The   23, 51, 58, 111, 160, 161, 169, 238
Rolling Stone Magazine   84, 112, 164, 165, 244
A Room of One's Own   195–6
royalties   11, 75, 150, 192, 212

Saginaw, Michigan   23, 25
samples, sampling   2, 5–10, 100, 154, 224, 261, 263
San Francisco, California   40, 43, 46, 169, 171, 173, 185, 186, 215
Saturday Night Fever   2 n.2, 85
Schlager   135, 136, 162, 163

science fiction   9, 10, 23, 24, 163
Sex Pistols, The   108, 246
Shakespeare, Robbie   68, 100
"Shakespeare's Sister" (Smiths)   196
Shakespear's Sister
  Hormonally Yours   196–7, 201
  naming of   196
Siouxsie and the Banshees   123, 124
sitar   72, 75
ska   97, 162
Skifs, Björn   70, 72
Sly and the Family Stone   81, 89
"Smells Like Teen Spirit"   186
"Somebody That I Used to Know"
  digital production   260–1
  as earworm   264
  as guilty pleasure   263–4
  and middlebrow populism   265
  music video   261–2
  song structure   261
Sony   1, 73, 255
soul   45, 82, 86, 87, 94, 150, 163, 208, 261
Soul Train   84, 85
Spencer, Neil   63, 99
"Spirit in the Sky"
  and evolution of Christian rock   43–5
  fuzztone riff   41–2
  in popular culture   37, 46–7
Springsteen, Bruce   30, 32, 218, 245
"Stay"
  and B-movie plot   197, 199–200
  as camp   200, 203
  and censorship   200
  musical style   197–8
  music video   198–201
Stevens, Ray   54, 142
Stevens, Shakin'   129, 131
streaming, music   174, 186, 189, 192, 216
structure of feeling   83, 86, 88, 160, 164, 166, 181, 211
Sugarhill Gang, *see* "Aserejé"
"Sugar Sugar"
  song structure   53
  studio recording   54
  and unbroken chain of reproduction   56–8
Swedish Broadcasting Corporation   70–2

Swift, Taylor   237, 238
synthpop   129, 132–3

Talking Heads   144, 165
Talmy, Shel   29, 35
Tilbrook, Glen   34–5
Tokyo   119, 121, 123
Top 40   42, 44, 85, 104, 129, 146, 185–6, 189, 190, 206, 216
Top of the Pops   76, 97, 100, 104–6, 109, 129, 178, 201, 207
"Touch of Grey"
   live performances of   171, 173–4
   musical structure   171
Trio
   sonic characteristics of   153–5
True, Andrea (Andrea True Connection)   187, 192
"Tubthumping"
   as anthem   225
   and collective songwriting   226
   in corporate advertisements   228–9
   as historical term   225
   and nostalgia   225–6
   as subversive act   227–8
"Turning Japanese"
   and *Japonisme*   122–6

   marketing material   119, 120, 123–6
   musical style   123
   and "Oriental riff"   120–1, 126

"Unbelievable"   191
"Uptown Top Ranking"
   as "answer record"   95–6
   reception in UK   97–100

Virgin   97, 98, 228

Warner   1, 40, 42, 46, 142, 145
Westwood, Vivienne   105, 124
Who, The   21, 35
Wild Cherry
   and local scene   80–2, 85
   musical style   81, 84

"You Get What You Give"
   and Biden family   243–4
   and Biden inauguration   243, 245–6, 248
   and optimism   244–6, 248, 249
YouTube   77, 100, 120, 133, 136, 149, 201, 229, 248, 262, 263

Zappa, Frank   9, 39, 72, 114